HIGH AND LOW MODERNS

HIGH AND
LOW MODERNS

Literature and Culture, 1889–1939

EDITED BY

MARIA DiBATTISTA

AND LUCY McDIARMID

New York   Oxford
Oxford University Press
1996

Oxford University Press

Oxford   New York
Athens   Auckland   Bangkok   Bogota   Bombay   Buenos Aires
Calcutta   Cape Town   Dar es Salaam   Delhi   Florence   Hong Kong
Istanbul   Karachi   Kuala Lumpur   Madras   Madrid   Melbourne
Mexico City   Nairobi   Paris   Singapore   Taipei   Tokyo   Toronto

and associated companies in
Berlin   Ibadan

Library of Congress Cataloging-in-Publication Data
High and low moderns : literature and culture, 1889–1939 / edited by
Maria DiBattista, Lucy McDiarmid.
p.   cm.
Includes index.
ISBN 0-19-508266-4
1. English literature—20th century—History and criticism.
2. Modernism (Literature)—Great Britain.   3. Popular literature—
Great Britain—History and criticism.   4. English literature—19th
century—History and criticism.   5. Literature and anthropology—
Great Britain.   6. Popular culture—Great Britain—History.
I. DiBattista, Maria, 1947-   .   II. McDiarmid, Lucy.
PR478.M6H54   1996
820.9'00912—dc20   95-53155

1 3 5 7 9 8 6 4 2
Printed in the United States of America
on acid-free paper

for Sam Hynes

Acknowledgments

The editors are grateful to Elizabeth Maguire and Susan Chang for seeing this project through its initial phases and to Elda Roter for her expert advice all along the way. We particularly want to thank Henry Krawitz for his scrupulous attention to every detail of the volume in preparing it for publication. Thanks also go to Amanda Heller for her unobtrusive yet invariably helpful copyediting.

Contents

HIGH AND
LOW MODERNS

Introduction

⌗ ⌗ ⌗

MARIA DiBATTISTA

Hardy is Victorian," wrote Eliot in the autumn of 1921, "Shaw is Edwardian. Shaw is therefore more interesting to us, for by reflecting on his mind we may form some plausible conjecture about the mind of the next age—about what, in retrospect, the 'present' generation will be found to have been."[1] That Eliot once proposed to define his own generation in terms of Bernard Shaw's mind certainly stands as one of the less recollected facts of modernist literary history. And that Hardy, Shaw, and Eliot all enjoyed professional lives simultaneously remains a quirk of chronology not yet fully inscribed in our understanding of the early years of the modern era. In ways obscured by the traditional focus on *The Waste Land* and *Ulysses* as modernist touchstones and Bloomsbury as an insular coterie, the paths of the "high moderns" crossed those of older generations and of modern writers not quite so high. Virginia Woolf could go to a concert in 1915 and find herself seated opposite Shaw ("grown a white-haired benevolent old man," the thirty-three-year-old Woolf said of the fifty-nine-year-old Shaw),[2] and Leonard Woolf in 1919 attended meetings with H. G. Wells, whose books his wife reviewed. When Anita Loos, whose witty best-seller *Gentlemen Prefer Blondes* enraptured Joyce, visited London in 1926, she was regaled by Arnold Bennett, Wells, and Galsworthy, and entertained by Lady Ottoline Morrell, who showed her a note from Lytton Strachey touting her as "the divine A."[3]

Academic literary studies generally have preferred to discount the impact of these convergences, interminglings, and ecumenical tastes. They can prove distracting, even embarrassing, to literary historians intent on tracing unblurred genealogical lines or regularizing the erratic orbits of stellar literary "circles." It has been much more common to adhere to the protocol of separate spheres in determining the artistic value, social import, and historical impact of literary works in the days of early and "high" modernism. Thus the high moderns, as epitomized by Conrad, Eliot, Joyce, and Woolf, are generally characterized as self-conscious formalists wrestling with newly perceived instabilities of language and meaning; they are deemed writers whose imputed moral as well as aesthetic "difficulty" removed or elevated them from the prevailing low and middlebrow culture of their day. The more accessible (i.e., popular as well as easily readable), morally transparent, often socialist "low" modernists—Shaw, Wells, and Galsworthy, among others—are consequently treated as if they wrote to different audiences and moved through different worlds. The simple but telling evidence of dedications attests the contrary: Conrad dedicated *The Secret Agent* to Wells, and Galsworthy the second volume of *The Forsyte Saga*, *In Chancery*, his most sardonic vision of the making and unmaking of late Victorian marriage, to Joseph and Jessie Conrad.

The public dissensions of modernism in its ascendant phase only partly contradict this picture of conversant if not always amiable relations between high and low (or middling) writers. Wells's and James's debate over the "human interest" and social mission of the novel, for instance, and even Woolf's polemical distinction between the "materialist" Edwardians and the "spiritual" Georgians, seem less like a historically inevitable clash between senescent traditionalists and upstart modernists (since Woolf and James were on the same side) than an impending recognition that the division between the aestheticist high moderns and the materialist low moderns was not as marked, nor even as secure, as literary culture then (and has since) presumed. It is often overlooked that James's review of the "The Younger Generation" (1914), whose assessments provoked Wells to satirize James in *Boon*, proposed that Wells's "heartbreaking miscarriage" of literary effects derived "by multiplied if diluted transmissions" from Tolstoy, "the great illustrative master-hand . . . of disconnection of method from matter."[4] Nor is it often remembered that Arnold Bennett, the explicit target of Woolf's polemic on behalf of modernist experimentalism in "Mr. Bennett and Mrs. Brown," was an eloquent and purposeful voice for modern influences in *The New Age*, which had, as Samuel Hynes notes, the ear of the radical young. In its pages Bennett would join the battle again the purity crusades of the lending libraries (1909) and chastise the insularity of "the culture of London" when it guffawed at the Post-Impressionist Exhibition mounted by Roger Fry, whose biography Woolf would eventually write, at the Grafton Gallery in 1910.[5]

In the light of these neglected facts and forgotten associations, such disputes appear now more like family or intergenerational quarrels in which the contending parties seem to be putting up a spirited defense against the lurking threat of codependency. The high modernists in particular, while devoted to the pursuit of literature as a work of art and not as a casual entertainment or veiled political tract, had knowingly compromised the purity of art for art's sake by their canny appropriation of the naturalist's techniques of detailed inventory and frank sexual description; by their candid appeal to a general readership, as Woolf did in aligning her literary judgments with those of Johnson's "common reader"; and by their inventive and appreciative use of the profane, sexually explicit modern vernacular, at times incurring putative censorship as Joyce did in *Dubliners*, at times actual suppression as Lawrence did in *The Rainbow* and *Lady Chatterley's Lover* (but then a similar fate was awarded Wells's *Ann Veronica*). Most significant for the reconsideration of high and low moderns undertaken here, high moderns, even those who openly espoused the novel as an art form and who regarded poetry as a transhistorical utterance that linked individual poets in a continuing tradition, nevertheless regarded low cultural phenomena and entertainments unique to their times—the popular press, cinema, music hall, and the "art" of advertising—as an inalienable part of modern life, hence unavoidable subject matter whose forms as well as content might be assimilated or reworked, playfully imitated or seriously criticized, in their own art.

Yet until quite recently reading high and low modern works as coexisting, much less co-dependent, arts and letters has been a neglected if not thankless pursuit, given the prevailing view of literary critics, theoreticians, and historians that modernism was a cosmopolitan, international revolution that from its inception was split into oppositional or rival cultures. High and low have come to designate not only a vertical differential in aesthetic "positioning" vis-à-vis popular or mass culture but also to indicate a new historical dialectic unleashed by the advent of technological and economic modernization and all its stresses. Thus, in *The Political Unconscious*, Fredric Jameson remarks the dilapidations of various artistic realisms at the turn of the century, from which, he contends, emerged "not modernism alone, but rather two distinct literary cultural structures, dialectically interrelated and necessarily presupposing each other"—mass culture and high culture.[6] Andreas Huyssen elaborates on the necessary and mutual presuppositions of high and low cultures, contending that

> mass culture has always been the hidden subtext of the Modernist project. In the age
> of nascent socialism and the first major women's movement in Europe, the masses
> knocking at the gate were also women, knocking at the gate of a male-dominated
> culture. It is indeed striking to observe how the political, psychological, and aesthetic discourse around the turn of the century consistently and obsessively genders
> mass cultures and the masses as feminine, while high culture, whether traditional or
> modern, clearly remains the privileged realm of male activities.[7]

A historian who interestingly complicates this polarized view of the modernist divide between high and low culture is Eric Hobsbawm, whose *Age of Empire* chronicles the increasing separation of high and low culture as a "growing divergence between what was contemporary and what was 'modern.'"[8] This view has the advantage of preserving, with commendable wit, the historical irony that the "modern," which originally designated what was currently happening, the "modo" or "just now" of the present day, had by the early twentieth century parted company, perhaps irreconcilably, from whatever was currently in vogue in the popular culture. Hobsbawm attributes this widening rift to a variety of factors: the mass migration into metropolitan areas, which opened up a lucrative market for popular spectacles and mass entertainments; the increasing democratization of culture; and, most important in Hobsbawm's view, the technological revolution in the arts, culminating in and epitomized by the cinema.

Yet Hobsbawm makes the important observation that at the turn of the century, this incipient crisis in the arts was hardly discernible, given the bohemian avant-garde's fascination with the raffish show culture of popular milieus such as the music hall and cabaret. Moreover, radicalism in the arts was initially allied with radicalism in social causes. Hobsbawm himself notes the once hopeful fusion of artistic and social vanguards in the Arts and Crafts movement of William Morris, and in *The*

Edwardian Turn of Mind Samuel Hynes reminds us that the young Edwardians found in Dostoyevski "a link between literature and other liberating movements that engaged their interests—the new psychology, the revived interest in spiritual and mystical ideas, and the new experimental forms in the other arts."[9] "Indeed," as Hobsbawm remarks, "the fact that the same words were used to describe social, cultural and aesthetic innovation underlines the convergence. The New English Arts Club (1886), art nouveau, and the *Neue Zeit*, the major journal of international Marxism, used the same adjective as was supplied to the 'new woman'."[10] Rose Macaulay's multigenerational novel *Told By an Idiot*, which spans the age of Victoria to the 1920s, somewhat comically ascribes the "daring social, literary and intellectual cleavages" of the mid-nineties to a common enthrallment with novelty, whether in the arts or in social manners or domestic relations or modern gadgetry: "What with the New Humour, and the New Earnestness, and the New Writers, and the New Remorse, and the New Woman, and the New Drama, and the New Journalism, and the New Child, and the New Parent, and the New Conversation, and the telephone, and the gramophone, and the new enormous sleeves, there was a great deal of novelty about." Macaulay gives no thought—or quarter—to high/low discriminations in detailing how general was the "illusion of advance" in the mid-nineties, which appeared "to have struck both those who gloried in novelty, and those whom it shocked, as more than usually new."[11] She represents the new writing and the new morality and the new family and the new technology of communication (whether in the form of the new conversation or the telephone) and the new fashions as different expressions of a culture exhilarated by the audacity of its own emancipatory energies, whether productively or foolishly expended.

Still, the story Hobsbawm has to tell about the fate of the arts in *The Age of Empire* is how the modernist intent to "make it new" faltered in the face of radical social and economic transformations that challenged the hegemony of the high bourgeoisie as arbiters of culture and underwrote the growing visibility and commercial viability of what he calls "the plebeian arts." Hobsbawm's account of what he takes to be "a genuine cultural revolution" necessarily focuses on cinema as the most plebian as well as the most modern of arts. Hobsbawm proposes the arresting paradox that cinema was a new medium whose formal revolution in the visual presentation of movement and event appealed to a mass public since it transformed everything but content. This view of film is qualified by the reconsiderations offered in this volume of how close modern writers were in understanding the appeal of film as mental experience. For example, Louis Menand, in his revisionist essay on Kipling as a writer with unlikely but demonstrable affinities to Paterian aestheticism, links the florescence of the short story in the late 1890s with the emergence of cinema and asks us to consider cinema as "an invention in the history of narrative."

Hobsbawm's story of the triumphalism of popular culture is not exceptional, however, in the role it gives to the visual arts, especially film. More specialized studies of the relationship between high and low moderns share a similar disposition to analyze the visual over the literary arts. Indeed, art history and cultural studies have been more ready to engage this question than literary criticism. Kirk Varnedoe and Adam Gopnik's *High and Low Moderns* was an exemplary effort to document and analyze the way low subject matter was incorporated and transformed in the radical experiments of modern painting. Collections such as Patrick Brantlinger and James Naremore's *Modernity and Mass Culture*, responding to the growing academic prestige of work with declared or implicit postmodernist leanings, concern themselves with modern media—television and film in particular. Hugh Kenner's tracing of a "serviceable diagram of the England into which a new literature would attempt to insert itself" is somewhat anomalous among recent efforts to reconstruct the cultural landscape of early modernism. Rather than attempt to define and describe literary "cultures," Kenner confines himself to the evocation of "three publics," which he designates as the mass readership of the weekly papers such as *Tit Bits*, the audience for J. M. Dent's Everyman Library of affordable reprints just out of copyright (begun in 1906), and a "shifting and beleaguered 'highbrow' public apt to group itself into coteries or find itself being hectored from two sides, by C. S. Lewis for discriminating at all, by F. R. Leavis for not discriminating enough." Kenner, with latitudinarian sympathies, remarks that such a situation "was unhealthy, and still is."[12]

Kenner's attention to actual reading publics exempts him to a large degree from the difficulties besetting those critics who prefer to speak in more general and elastic terms of "cultures." The prevalent focus on visual media in particular has had the interesting and not altogether unforeseen consequence of further complicating the high/low distinction by conflating, often problematically, low culture with mass and/or popular culture. Varnedoe and Gopnik acknowledge that the dividing line between high and low culture has often detained cultural "pundits, both as a major fault line of anxiety and as a meeting point for otherwise opposite ideologies." Nevertheless, they acknowledge "the imperative need to have reliable, solid distinctions between high and low—whether as a challenge for future achievement or as a lost ideal." They thus propose a distinction between high art and low culture predicated on the differences between self-conscious and expert works that present "the primary material with which any history of art in this century must contend," and those "forms and styles associated with the rise of urban culture in industrialized nations that involve self-conscious, street-wise or commercial—as opposed to ostensibly 'naive'—creations." High moderns are both the inheritors and the transformers of a continuing "tradition of expanded freedom for the individual imagination." Low moderns are urban, cosmopolitan artisans producing more transient, epiphenomenal work of sociological and commercial, rather than intrinsically artistic, value.[13]

The merit of this distinction is that it permits a more relaxed movement back and forth over that "frontier dividing high from low culture." Varnedoe and Gopnik can thus relate how high modernist painters crossed over into the low cultural flatlands less to disport themselves than to traffic in the brisk urban trade in graffiti, caricature, comics, and advertising—that is, in those streetwise or commercial creations endemic to modern urban culture. To Gopnik and Varnedoe's discerning eye, these low cultural flatlands were stratified into an "overlord culture . . . directed by a few people toward a broad audience"—the culture whose most characteristic products are advertising and comics—and an "underbelly culture" whose more furtive temperament and iconoclastic imagination express themselves in graffiti and caricature. Despite such efforts to discriminate among audiences, media, forms, and social positions, the authors concede that "the theoretical literature in the division between high and low in modern life could appear to leave room for countless hybrid permutations among a set of terms such as elitist, populist, nostalgist, conservative, radical, optimist and skeptic."[14] To this list one might add Gramsci's concept, elaborated in the prison notebooks, of national–popular culture. Such terms describe the array of social and political *stances* that might legitimately compete with, even replace, more formalist, media-conscious criteria.

The felt necessity to provide such an alternate set of terms is itself symptomatic of a particularly obdurate problem in addressing the question of high/low. Critical attempts to draw firm boundaries soon collapse into loose taxonomies whose classificatory principles are admitted in advance to be insufficiently rigid when not patently inapplicable. Thus, for example, the room for other classificatory systems that Gopnik and Varnedoe allow is gingerly occupied by Naremore and Brantlinger in *Modernity and Mass Culture*. In introducing their volume, they propose a more expansive taxonomy that extends the familiar high/low opposition to encompass and identify, at the minimum, six "artistic cultures": high art, modernist art, avant-garde art, folk art, popular art, and mass art. Such categories, the authors admit, may not actually have existed, but they are employed for their heuristic value as "discursive fields" in which congregate the characteristic "ideologies, reading practices, and forms of subjectivity through which art can be received or understood." Brantlinger and Naremore are careful to stipulate that all of their categories defy evaluation in terms of any ideal or "correct" moral or social position one might posit, since "on the basis of the historical record, high culture is no more or less patriarchal and racist than mass culture." Cognizant of this intractable historical fact, they assign no instrinsic value to any of the "cultures" they identify nor to the place of any culture in the order they delineate. In moving from high art to mass culture, they do not suggest a descending order in aesthetic value, nor do they pretend to describe a "progressive" movement toward an expanded social consciousness or enlightened political agenda.[15]

Yet, however neutral their initial enumeration, the six separate cultures are defined primarily in terms of economic and social determinations that imply some ideological preferences. High art, modernist art and avant-garde art are said to encompass "the domain of those who have cultural capital," while folk, popular, and mass arts "are accessible to the general population."[16] Naremore and Brantlinger quickly agree that mass culture, whatever stipulations, even refinements, we might want to attach to its cultural character and function, is initially marked by two phenomenal qualities: its ubiquity and its visibility. They are equally quick to note the intriguing historical paradox that the very ubiquity of mass art rendered it either an invisible or an indistinct feature of the cultural lowlands until critics, in either an alarmist or a celebratory mood, took notice of what was always there to be seen. Mass culture, they imply, aspires not just to be everywhere but to be *seen* to be everywhere.

Interestingly, modernist culture, in the Naremore and Brantlinger schema, does not exemplify the high/low culture split so much as occupy a special position between the "great traditions" of high art, characterized as "pointing simultaneously toward the need to master a tradition and the need to develop free and autonomous individuals," and the avant-garde, which, unlike modernism, "welcomed machines and celebrated their utopian potential." Modernist art, "aggressively individualistic, contemptuous of bourgeois realism, and sometimes nostalgic for preindustrial society," is thus adjudged to be at once "reactionary and new." According to this now familiar, tendentious view, exemplary modernist works such as *Ulysses* and *The Waste Land* juxtapose or combine references to mass culture with fragments of classical literature to bruit their own social "autonomy," thus encouraging "the belief in the transcendent value of their own sophisticated craft."[17]

Given this relatively unqualified account of the relation obtaining between low cultural "artifacts" and high cultural "creations," it is not altogether unexpected that the most important thing Naremore and Brantlinger believe can be said about their six artistic cultures is that even if they exist in some "real fashion beyond intellectual and academic discourse, none of them is unchanging or complete unto itself." As they explain:

> Culture, like languages, is forever in a condition that Raymond Williams described as "emergent," and its various forms are constantly subject to transformation, combination, and dissolution. Nevertheless, most cultural theory and a great deal of artistic practice in the twentieth century could be described as an attempt to defend one of the first five categories we've named against the encroachments of a hypostatized mass art—or, conversely, as an attempt to wrest power from mass art on behalf of one of the other categories.[18]

Is the history of low and high moderns, then, a history of encroachments from below or from on high? Is it actually endemic to modernist art to incorporate the ephemera of low culture to dramatize the differing, transcendent value of their own creations? Although the essays in this volume do not directly engage in a polemical dialogue with such a relatively unchallenged, indeed common, view, they do present evidence that such adversarial models of high and low and the conflictual binarism on which they are based obfuscate the complicated, often surprisingly productive, relations—material and intellectual—between literary moderns of high and low persuasions. In recognition of the various ways in which "high" art "descends" to low or common company, this volume thus entertains "low modern" as a portmanteau term fashioned out of a near-oxymoron, since for some time to be modern in the literary and artistic sense meant essentially to be high-minded and high-toned about one's representations of the Real. Into this class is smuggled all the various guises in which the low moderns appeared: in the deliberate, relatively uninflected realism of their narratives; in their avoidance of literary experimentalism and its defamiliarizing techniques; in their embrace of the energies, themes, and techniques of the new entertainments and popular arts of film, jazz, and cabaret; in their readable politics and relatively untroubled morality; in their affinity for journalism as a mass medium that could convey information (if not prompt reflection).

Such a "new" cultural studies as we hope to inaugurate here, one enlivened by nondoctrinaire scrutiny of actual works during the historical period when the high/low division began to assert itself, takes its prompting from Raymond Williams's observation in *Keywords* that "hostility to the word *culture* in English appears to date from the controversy around [Matthew] Arnold's views." Williams further notes that this hostility "gathered force in [the late nineteenth and early twentieth centuries] in association with a comparable hostility to *aesthete* and AESTHETIC." He concludes his entry by commenting "that virtually all the hostility . . . has been connected with uses involving claims to superior knowledge . . . refinement (culchah) and distinctions between 'high' art (*culture*) and popular art and entertainment."[19] The aim of this collection is to rejoin the aesthetic and the social in a cultural studies that may note, while working to defuse, the hostility between high and low culture, especially over its differing terms of relation with the aesthetic. Like all that advertises or attempts, as Pound advised, to make itself new, there is much that may strike—and is meant to strike—readers as dimly familiar in the propositions and readings advanced in this collection. What may be most familiar to many readers is the rubric yoking literature and culture, a phrase we have appealed to precisely because it invokes a tradition of critical inquiry which recognizes literature as both an imaginative act and a historical fact of expression.

Such a recognition underlies the more radical and, as it transpires, invidious distinction between documentary and monumental art propounded by Renato Poggioli in his ground-breaking study of the avant-garde. Poggioli quite flatly asserts, "The wiser historians and critics know that unoriginal work, the mediocre or *manqué*, reveals the spirit of its own times in a sharp and direct way precisely because it remains a document and not a monument. . . . But this type of revelation brings to light not the *modernity* of this or that epoch, but its modernism." For Poggioli, a keen interpreter of the theory as well as the history of the avant-garde, the high/low distinction is not of primary consequence; the important, indeed critical, difference is between modernity and modernism. Poggioli detects modernism in art that "leads up to, and beyond the extreme limits," and associates it with "everything in the modern spirit which is most vain, frivolous, fleeting and ephemeral"—everything, that is, which is modish." Modernism is thus "the honest-to-goodness nemesis of modernity," cheapening and vulgarizing it. For Poggioli, the realm of low or popular culture, entailing "sports and the circus, the bar and jazz, the music hall and the film," appears in the guise of "an external and vulgar modernity, more of matter than of spirit, a modernity considered only as a snobbish variant of romantic 'local color.'"[20] Whatever the justice of Poggioli's sweeping disparagement of modish arts and popular entertainments, his distinction between modernity and modernism has the salutary effect of reminding us that the relation between high and low need not be sentimentalized, patronized, or exalted as one of sheer equivalence. What may be the more interesting approach now, however, is to examine the relation between high and low moderns *as* the vexed relation, never purely oppositional nor indulgent, between modernity and modernism in the literature of those years 1889–1939.

The findings of this collection dispose to the view that such relations were highly individualized, often contradictory, historically variable, and socially unpredictable. The reader will therefore find no pronouncement on the "character of the age," no general diagnosis of the modern condition, however useful such propositions might be in orienting discussion and debate. The imaginative and historical evidence pre-

sented here suggests that the broad but not incoherent range of social affects—apocalyptic and hopeful, anarchistic and demotic, guardedly utopian and defensively arcadian—that imbue modern works resist any such typifications. Moreover, as Edward
Mendelson remarks in his essay chronicling the argument Wells, Lawrence, and
Orwell conducted with and through one another on the future awaiting modern society, every imaginative writer, but particularly those directly engaging in social
prophecy, simultaneously holds official and unofficial positions, and these can often
be in secret contradiction or open conflict with one another. Mendelson, like many
of the contributors to this volume, looks to literary works as the most likely expression of "uncomfortable, subversive, and unofficial views" that rankle settled opinion
and necessarily complicate any general notion that might be entertained of a historically consistent, textually evident modern "ideology."

That no single, panoptic view of modern literary works and their cultural ideals
is allowed to direct this volume's critical assessment of high and low moderns has the
practical as well as the heuristic advantage of repairing the perceived breach between
culture, with aesthetics in dutiful attendance, and the raw energies and immediate
realities of common, everyday life. The essays in this collection reveal how modern
writers, whether of low or high persuasion, could, given the right occasion, cross over
the boundaries segregating them in self-sufficient domains with interesting and often
beneficial results. Thus, Eliot will appear here neither as an imagist Hamlet author-
ing a "piece of rhythmical grumbling" nor as ossified Anglican royalist, but as a living writer encountered and appropriated by younger American contemporaries to
promote a distinctly leftist politics. Conrad's morally opaque anarchist tale *The Secret
Agent* will be adjudged in its relation to the popular genre of detective thrillers or
"entertainments," to use Graham Greene's phrase for them. The socially privileged
figures of R. B. Cunninghame Graham and Lady Gregory will be seen confounding
convention and upending class feeling, Cunninghame Graham, the legendary Don
Roberto of South American adventures, by helping found the Scottish Labour party
and working assiduously as M.P., political journalist, and imaginative writer on behalf
of democratic socialism; and the titled, Anglo-Irish Lady Gregory by identifying with
the emergent Irish middle class that Yeats despised and sympathizing with what Lucy
McDiarmid calls the "rebel culture" of the Young Ireland movement of the 1840s and
the Fenian movement that followed.

The governing assumption of this collection, then, is that revisiting the moderns,
high and low, as they emerged, defined, and extended themselves during this formative period will yield little new understanding unless we reorient the terms and expectations of our inquiry. Such general reorientation profitably begins by jettisoning some
long-held attitudes toward literary modernity as a monolithic "project" intent on
securing artistic autonomy and accountable to no reality but that of its own high
imaginings. The attitudes, methods, and findings assembled here suggest certain critical inclinations that are helpful, if not absolutely requisite, toward fashioning a new
approach to what was new in modernity's way of thinking about itself in either high
or low culture. First, the contributors display no predisposition to think that reputations, high and low, were immediately consolidated and remained relatively stable,
invulnerable to the unsettlements of living writers and subsequent critics. Thus,

David Bromwich's essay begins by asking us to regard Eliot, against all the complacencies of settled opinion, as his contemporaries initially did—not as an imposing presence but as a somewhat elusive poet "averse to no stimulus, however morbid," and whose essays "were among other things deliberate curiosities, out-of-the-way solutions to problems the reader was meant to see as in no way impersonal." Eliot's individual talent might then have entered the tradition, Bromwich speculates, as one of "the unassimilable, the recessive geniuses of English poetry" and not, as Cynthia Ozick hailed him in her ambivalent tribute, "T. S. Eliot at 101," as the preeminent modernist who once seemed "fixed in the firmament like the sun and the moon," even if current sublunary politics have sent him, like modernism, into a state of eclipse.[21] Bromwich's account of the poetic relation between Eliot and Hart Crane takes its suspense as well as its provocation from reconstructing how Eliot might have appeared to a fellow modern haunted by the urban landscape of "Preludes," and whose sense of literary vocation extended to Chaplin as one of the "the poets of today."

Louis Menand, preparatory to his reassessment of Kipling's role in the history of modern British literature, revisits both early and recent attempts to promote—or justify—a "taste" for his work. Menand presents Kipling, then, as "one of the classic problems in taste criticism," which "begins when you like something a little bit more than your better judgment feels comfortable with—or, sometimes, a little bit more than everyone else's better judgment feels comfortable with."

If this collection is partially designed to make us reconsider our taste, it also works to uncover unsuspected, unduly neglected, but quite legitimate genealogies. Again, the case of Kipling, who inspired—or rather elicited—the ambivalent admiration of Henry James, Eliot, Orwell, and Edmund Wilson, is instructive. Menand's case for the historical importance of Kipling's genius as a writer of short stories depends on seeing him as a descendant of Paterian impressionism and a "contemporary" of the new art of film in rendering the "special effects" of certain kinds of experience. Or take the case of D. H. Lawrence, as Mendelson does. Lawrence's imaginative debt to Thomas Hardy has long been commented, but Mendelson uncovers a canny rewriting of Wells's *Tono Bungay* in *Women in Love*, and a still more exacting version in Orwell's *Nineteen Eight-four*. Lawrence's apocalyptic denunciations of the vitiation of instincts seems less eccentric once it is seen to echo, albeit at a more intense pitch, Wells's original interpretation of radium as a potent metaphor for the disintegrative energies of modern life.

In an ambitious effort of cultural and poetic reevaluation, Edna Longley proposes Edward Thomas as an unacknowledged founder of the Green movement, thus repositioning a peripheral and "parochial" Edwardian nature poet at the very inception of the change of consciousness that gave rise to ecocentrism and its global political agenda. Longley strikingly proposes that "modernism and Marxism fetishize the city, but in different ways," modernism by neglecting "nature poetry" and Marxism by criticizing pastoral for "repressing the exploitation not only of urban workers in the present but of rural workers in the past." Her reevaluation of Thomas's poetry, "whereby human actors and constructs share in a larger earthly drama," equally implies the aesthetic and political rehabilitation of "nature poetry" as the neglected or depreciated casualty of the modernist revolution. In analyzing Thomas's "inexpressible alienation" from modern life in the context of contemporary environmental theory, Longley uncovers an eco-sensitive poetry and a sense of history that is less bucolic and provincial than cosmic and prophetic in its vision of a natural world that contains, but is not exhausted by, the human species.

Finally, no paradoxical or contradictory feeling is ignored, derided, or smoothed out in order to project a seamless image of writers intransigently high or shamefully low. Perhaps the most complicated feelings shared by both high and low moderns were those aroused by the technological changes that permanently altered the material foundations of modern existence. The writers studied here are seen responding to technology not as an abstract "materialist" force but as actual objects in their physical and mental landscape—motor cars and airplanes, gramophones and film. Eliot's remark that in the *Sacre du printemps* Stravinsky transformed into music the "despairing noises" of modern life—"the scream of the motor horn, the rattle of machinery, the beating of iron and steel"[22]—is an elaboration of his more famous contention that the mythic method of *Ulysses* was "simply a way of controlling, of ordering, of giving a shape and a significance to the immense panorama of futility and anarchy which is contemporary history."[23] But if Stravinsky and Joyce were pioneers in modern methods, they were certainly not alone in appreciating how scientific discoveries and technological innovations provided artists not only with new subject matter but also with unpredecedented, often startling metaphors for reality. In this volume Shaw's treatment of automotive breakdowns and airplane crashes and Wells's prescient appropriation of the newly discovered phenomenon of radioactivity as a metaphor for social and moral dissolution are considered as significant expressions of what the modernist not only made but also *found* to be new in the modern experience and interpretation of the world.

In short, we propose with this volume to rethink the modernist canon and to free modernist scholarship from a restrictive focus on reactionary politics, the macaronic allusiveness of a single generation, or segregated cultural politics. Indeed, the gathering, centripetal force of the word *culture*, which, as Williams remarks, had the effect of partitioning public arts and entertainment, is one reason why we delimit our study to the years 1889–1939, years marked by the incipient formation and rapid crystallization of separate, if ever overlapping, cultural spheres. The rubrics, ordering, and grouping of the essays collected here are partly meant to correct for some needless distortion in the general view that this was a period in which deep rifts were beginning to striate the cultural landscape beyond the possibility of recovery or repair. We thus inaugurate the volume with Jay Dickson's essay on Queen Victoria, which contends that modern character, manners, and feelings irreversibly changed not as Virginia Woolf famously, if somewhat hazily, proposed in or about December 1910 but on a more precise and emblematic date—January 22, 1901, the day the queen died. Dickson remarks the enormous outpouring of popular sentiment for the dead monarch and the passing of the age she incarnated for over sixty years. To many modern writers, however, for whom Victoria was the maternal embodiment of the parent culture against which they were in active revolt, such mournful sentimentality was thought to perpetuate the melancholic attachment to bourgeois domestic values most characteristic of and baleful in the queen herself. Still, her passing left them, as Dickson amply documents, strangely bereft, haunted as they were by her cultural authority and her newly demonstrated power to arouse popular sentiment even or especially in death. Dickson thus diagnoses the psychological stalemate incurred by the queen's death: "As in Freud's model of melancholia, wherein the grieving person refuses to prove to himself that the mourned object has irrevocably vanished and thus retreats into his memories of it, the initial popular reaction to Victoria's death repudiated the finality of her loss." This melancholia, Dickson shows, was recorded in the works of Galsworthy, Woolf, and Joyce, and drew comment from Shaw, Edmund Gosse, and Thomas Hardy. These writers assumed the burden of confronting reality that "would involve a true admission of the passing of the queen and her era" and so attempt "to execute a *Trauerarbeit*—that is, a completed work of mourning— for the dead queen." Such a work of mourning found its most unlikely expression in Lytton Strachey, the iconoclastic biographer of *Eminent Victorians*. Dickson relates how Strachey, in writing his biography of the queen, eventually succumbed to the same overmastering feeling that had infused popular sentiment on her death, so that, as Gosse would remark, a work that had begun as "a satire has turned in his fingers into an appreciation."

From the death of a queen matriarch, an event that exposed the frayed threads of cultural unity, we thus proceed to the immediate question posed by our title: What *is* a high as opposed to a low modern? One answer can be derived by transposing this question into another key, differentiating high from low historically and canonically in terms of major or minor reputations. The study of reputation brings together history, aesthetics, and culture to assess the cultural and imaginative examplarity rather than the social typicality of a writer's work. As Gopnik and Varnedoe imply, one way to tell a high from a low modern is that the former endures longer as a fixture in the public mind as an indispensable figure in the renewing of artistic tradition. Moreover, reviewing major and minor reputations allows us to reencounter, in a way Hobsbawm does not allow, the moderns as contemporaries. We take T. S. Eliot to exemplify the vagaries of historical reputation, since his critical pronouncements are perhaps most responsible for authorizing and perpetuating the view that "elitist" difficulty was not simply an intransigent feature but the moral imperative of high modern art. Even though recent criticism has begun to modify this monochromatic picture of Eliot's own imaginative dispositions,[24] the perception that high and low moderns were permanently estranged is perpetuated by those who speak of and against high modernism as an elitist literature.

Two essays press for a more nuanced view of the making of Eliot's "high" reputation. David Bromwich recovers for us how Eliot appeared to his poetic contemporary Hart Crane—"as an elusive but not imposing presence" rather than an instantaneous modern icon, a poet whose "charm lay most of all in the relief he offered from importance." Bromwich portrays Crane as a poet who responded to Eliot's early poems, especially "Preludes," with its "saw-dust trampled street" and "early coffee stands." The same affinity for Eliot's haunted urban landscape led Crane to align himself with Chaplin as "poets of today." Reexamining the full range of Crane's work from *White Buildings* to *The Bridge* in light of these affinities, Bromwich relates how the city of Eliot was the dominant but never overwhelming note in poems where

Crane provided his own expression—and shelter—to the vagrant "social sympa-thies" and ambivalent erotic encounters endemic to life in the modern city. Harvey Teres's companion piece shows us how T. S. Eliot could also be put in the service of a leftist politics that argued the revolutionary potential of literature as "a new way of living and seeing." Teres recounts how William Phillips and Philip Rahv, the founders and chief editors of *Partisan Review*, a "little" magazine designed to promote proletarian literature, appropriated the high modern touchstones of poetic imper-sonality and sensibility as formulated in Eliot's early criticism to articulate broad cul-tural aims at a time when literary culture was not a high priority in revolutionary pol-itics. Teres assesses in what ways such an endeavor was salutary and in what ways Phillips and Rahv failed to reach the popular constituencies to whom a genuinely proletarian literature should have been addressed.

Dickson, Bromwich, and Teres, in studying the vicissitudes of historical reputa-tion, thus provide us with engrossing counterplots and important correctives to the received narratives that have tutored our common understandings of modern writ-ers. A. Walton Litz and Edna Longley write on literary figures accorded at best a minor repute, and in Florence Farr's case barely a passing nod, in the literary histo-ries of early modernism. Farr's involvement with Yeats and Shaw (she was "one of those women that men loved to shape," Litz acidly remarks) made her a figure in Irish bohemian circles at the turn of the century. Litz reminds us that she was also a liter-ary journalist of considerable interest, even power. Litz argues for her importance as a "transitional figure" between the drama of the 1890s and the newer generation of suffragettes. In works such as *The Modern Woman: Her Intentions*, Farr explored an impressive range of social issues and offered controversial solutions to the sex ques-tion. Farr's vision for the New Woman culminates in her series of essays on Ibsen's women for *The New Age*, four of which are reprinted here for the first time. In Farr's arresting journalistic portraits, the topical and the archetypal are mutually enhanced by each other's presence. High art and low journalism collaborate as Farr looks to the women imagined by a dramatist with the highest modern credentials to formulate her most original responses to pressing social and sexual issues of the day.

Edna Longley, as we have seen, presages a more urgent revival of Edward Thomas as a forerunner and prophet of contemporary environmental movements. In her provocative assertion that this Edwardian poet might be "a poet of the year 2000," Longley reminds us of the historic challenges of Thomas's poetic task—to develop a poetic structure that would express his love of nature while avoiding the literary arcadianism he openly repudiated. Thomas's solution, Longley advises, was to elab-orate an "eco-historical perspective" whose fundamental assumption "is that human endings matter, but they are not all that matters." Exploring that assumption in the dark forebodings of Thomas's criticism and poetry, Longley helps clear the ground for an eco-criticism that can perceive and perpetuate Thomas's own understanding of the organic, necessary relationship obtaining between poetic structure and the "cul-ture" of the Earth.

Farr and Thomas might have featured also in our next group, "Edwardian Mis-cellany," except that the accent thrown on them seemed to require a place apart as undervalued figures of the Edwardian transition. The Edwardian miscellany is our most direct and, we hope, exemplary attempt to resituate the high and low moderns in their historical moment, where they may be seen cohabiting, with all the tensions and guarded liking that ensue from such forced proximity, with the purveyors of more lowly arts. This group of essays gives a richly varied picture of the subtle, often eccentric loopings of what Samuel Hynes has characterized as the "Edwardian turn of mind." No mind was more argumentative and chimerical, more addicted to the excitements of the topical, than the mind of Shaw, which, we recall, Eliot took to be emblematic of his age. As Nicholas Grene convincingly shows, it is a mind so immersed in its own time that its visions and views proved, paradoxically but perhaps inevitably, to be quite resistant to subsequent modernization. Grene vividly recreates for us the enthusiasms and the opinions expressive of Shaw's mixed modernity: his avid interest in technological innovations, especially in modes of transport such as the motorcar and the airplane, which coexisted with a highly developed suspicion of scientific breakthroughs such as vaccination; his imaginative sympathy for and sponsorship of schemes to create garden cities and "model cities," even if financed, as such a scheme is in *Major Barbara*, by the profits of munitions manufacture. Moreover, as Grene soberly reminds us, "it was not the subfascist Yeats of the 1930s but the socialist Shaw in 1903 who called 'our political experiment of democracy the last refuge of cheap misgovernment.'" Such attitudes precluded Shaw from seeing the modern as anything but a stage in an inexorable advance toward an improved futurity. Given his creed of Creative Evolution, a late flowering of the Victorian faith in progressivism, Shaw was fated to remain estranged from the more radical expressions of the modernist revolution, in which apocalyptic thinking and experimentation in the forms of art and social life usually coincided.

Kipling, like Shaw, has been alternately excused or indulged as a writer very much of his own time, but Menand reminds us that Kipling's time was also that of Wilde and Pater, Conrad and Joyce and Eliot, and that he shared to a degree not yet appreciated a "common feeling for the nature of the aesthetic experience." Menand reasseses Kipling's art in the context of fin-de-siècle literature, especially the ghost story, which was often brilliantly adapted to communicate the felt interiority of all experience. Such a Paterian view of mind, the hallmark indeed of aestheticist psychology, was not confined to the art and literature commonly associated with the aesthetic movement, but influenced a far wider range of cultural expression. A vivid case in point is film, which Menand contends provided an allegory of modern psychology and was effectively dramatized as such in Kipling's enigmatic short story "Mrs. Bathhurst" (1904).

Edward Mendelson's essay provides yet another instance of how artificial was the border "between modernist experimental energy and conservative Edwardian safety." Mendelson is concerned to show how D. H. Lawrence's traffickings across the divide resulted in a surprisingly tense, productive argument about the meaning and course of modern apocalypticism. Lawrence's early enthusiasm for Wells's *Tono Bungay*, Mendelson relates, was founded on a particular understanding of how Wells, who might dream of social utopias in his nonfictional writings, imaginatively courted and foresaw disaster in his more pessimistic novels. Mendelson isolates those movements in Lawrence's own apocalyptic fiction, *Women in Love*, that seem to be conducting an argument with Wells's apocalyptic pessimism, an argument that was later to be taken up by Orwell in *his* apocalyptic fiction, *Nineteen Eighty-four*. Nowhere are the terribly mixed affects of modern literary politics more in evidence that in Orwell's siding with Wells against Lawrence in refusing to find a private escape from social disaster, even as he rebuked Wells for underestimating Hitler and for failing to grasp the scientific underpinnings of totalitarianism, a rebuke culminating in his claim that "much of what Wells has imagined and worked for is physically there in Nazi Germany."

Politics of a different order concern "The Lowly Art of Murder," an essay in which I survey popular detective fiction and find that its early reputation rested to a large degree on the antimodernism implied by its clever but morally unworried plots and by its confidence in portraying human character as objective, readable, and knowable, indeed reassuringly typical. Yet the lowly art of murder was from its inception concerned with the secretive, irrational work of instinct. The essay explores what happened when the high modernist Conrad appropriated the stock formulas and characterizations of popular narrative entertainments and not only transformed their function but also exploded their most volatile social theme—the social fate of the free woman.

The collection concludes with a series of essays that align themselves with—in fact exemplify—a new brand of cultural studies that is nondogmatic, scrupulous in its attention to historical particulars, and alert to the way artistic traditions can intersect with political enterprises but never fully coincide with them. R. F. Foster revisits a sexual and political scandal—the Parnell case—that held a strong fascination for both the literary and the popular imagination. It is to a unique document of the scandal that he returns, Kitty O'Shea's two-volume *Charles Stewart Parnell: His Love Story and Political Life*. Generally received as the confessions of a fallen woman, Mrs. O'Shea's "memoirs" delighted the Conservative press in Britain and shocked the Irish by portraying Parnell through his own letters, where he could be heard speaking dismissively of the "hollow" land movement and planning to run away with "My Own Wifie." In examining both the politics and psychology of a love story told from the interested perspective of one who lived it, Foster discovers how Mrs. O'Shea's "original" voice managed to emerge out of a ghosted, heavily editorialized memoir, and how the revelations proffered in this popular "confession" have been latterly confirmed by historiography oriented toward Parnell's public rather than private life.

In "The Demotic Lady Gregory" Lucy McDiarmid draws another connection between the transgressive activities of the Anglo-Irish gentry and Irish popular culture. She shows how Lady Gregory's early romantic entanglement with the dashing, Byronic anti-imperialist Wilfred Scawen Blunt combined with her youthful literary Fenianism to make the Irish felon, or political prisoner, an exemplary figure and muse for her cultural activities. Unlike the higher-cultured Yeats, who deplored the more mediocre examples of nineteenth-century Irish patriotic poetry, Lady Gregory cherished even the doggerel, especially the martyrologies, considering them "not without dignity if looked on as roughly hammered links in an unequally wrought chain." In Lady Gregory's eyes rebel culture constituted a type of indigenous popular culture inspired by male felons and disseminated by women writers.

Finally, Chris GoGwilt transports this collection to the antipodes of empire to analyze how "news from nowhere," the utopian politics of an anti-imperialist, democratic socialism, found an extremely supple vehicle in the sketch artistry of R. B. Cunninghame Graham. Journalism, a "low" form, given its servitude to the topical in disseminating information, becomes, as GoGwilt shows, an important cultural medium for a writer such as Cunninghame Graham, determined to expose the evils and human disasters of empire. GoGwilt traces how Cunninghame Graham's "news" on conditions overseas grafted "low" journalistic reportage to the impressionist narrative championed by his friend and correspondent Joseph Conrad to create a new, historically responsive form of sketch artistry that linked "the battlefront of socialist struggle with the frontier of colonial violence."

It is our hope that these essays may initiate a more subtle, adaptable, and traversable model of literary culture in which the richly textured life of the modern arts might be newly appraised in all its variegated, anomalous, disparate strands, some of which are elevated from, some lying closer to, the common weave. Neither of the cultural models currently available—the theory of contagion, which presumes the necessary, often predatory encroachments of high and low on each other's domain, and the theory of exclusion, which pictures high modernist males slamming the door in the face of low moderns variously characterized as "feminine," populist, commercially savvy, or sunk in a materialist bog—captures the suppleness, inventiveness, erotic ambivalence, misunderstandings, estrangements, and even the occasional tenderness of the relation. We hope to promote a more kaleidoscopic view of high/low modernity, in which zones of convergence and horizons of separation, though interspersed and always in flux, are accorded equal attention. Our aim is to observe and describe high modern writings in their contacts and commerce, their meetings and minglings, with low cultural forms of writing and entertainment. Judgment is neither reserved nor foreclosed on the outcome of individual encounters. In this there can be no prejudice to either camp.

Notes

1. T. S. Eliot, "London Letter," *The Dial*, 21, no. 4 (October 1921): 453.

2. Virginia Woolf, *The Diary of Virginia Woolf*, vol. 1, ed. Anne Olivier Bell (New York: Harcourt Brace Jovanovich, 1977), p. 33.

3. Anita Loos, *Kiss Hollywood Goodbye* (New York: Ballantine, 1975), p. 70.

4. Henry James, "The Younger Generation," revised and enlarged as "The New Novel" in *Henry James: Literary Criticism*, vol. 1 (New York: Library of America, 1984), p. 135.

5. See Samuel Hynes, *The Edwardian Turn of Mind* (Princeton, N.J.: Princeton University Press, 1968), pp. 331–32.

6. Fredric Jameson, *The Political Unconscious: Narrative as a Socially Symbolic Act* (Ithaca, N.Y.: Cornell University Press, 1981), p. 207.

7. Andreas Huyssen, *After the Great Divide: Modernism, Postmodernism, and Mass Culture* (Bloomington: Indiana University Press, 1986), p. 214.

8. Eric Hobsbawm, *The Age of Empire* (New York: Pantheon, 1987), p. 226.

9. Hynes, *The Edwardian Turn of Mind*, p. 337.

10. Hobsbawm, *The Age of Empire*, p. 227.

11. Rose Macaulay, *Told By an Idiot* (New York: Dial Press, 1983), pp. 114–15.

12. Hugh Kenner, *A Sinking Island* (New York: Knopf, 1988), p. 35.

13. Kirk Varnedoe and Adam Gopnik, *High and Low Moderns* (New York: Museum of Modern Art, 1991), p. 16.

14. Ibid., p. 18.

15. James Naremore and Patrick Brantlinger, eds., *Modernity and Mass Culture* (Bloomington: Indiana University Press, 1991), pp. 8, 14.

16. Ibid., p. 10.

17. Ibid., p. 10.

18. Ibid., p. 15.

19. Raymond Williams, *Keywords* (New York: Oxford University Press, 1975), pp. 81–82.

20. Renato Poggioli, *The Theory of the Avant-Garde* (Cambridge, Mass.: Harvard University Press, 1968), pp. 218, 220.

21. Cynthia Ozick, "T. S. Eliot at 101," *The New Yorker*, November 20, 1989, p. 119.

22. T. S. Eliot, "London Letter," *The Dial*, 23, no. 3 (September 1922): 454.

23. T. S. Eliot, "*Ulysses*, Order and Myth," in *Selected Prose of T. S. Eliot*, ed. Frank Kermode (New York: Harcourt Brace Jovanovich, 1975), p. 177.

24. See, for example, David Chintz, "T. S. Eliot and the Cultural Divide," *PMLA*, 110, no. 2 (March 1995): 236–47. Two other essays detect postmodernist inclinations in Eliot. See Michael Edward Kaufmann, "T. S. Eliot's New Critical Footnotes to Modernism," and Gregory S. Jay, "Postmodernism in *The Waste Land*: Women, Mass Culture, and Others," in *Rereading the New: A Backward Glance at Modernism*, ed. Kevin J. H. Dettmar (Ann Arbor: University of Michigan Press, 1992), pp. 73–85 and 221–246, respectively.

Historical
Soundings

Surviving Victoria

JAY DICKSON

History is hysterical: it is constituted only if we consider it, only if we look at it—
and in order to look at it, we must be excluded from it. As a living soul, I am the very
contrary of History, I am what belies it, destroys it for the sake of my own history. . . .
That is what the time when my mother was alive *before me* is—History (moreover,
it is the period which interests me most, historically).

—Roland Barthes,
Camera Lucida: Reflections on Photography

It seems to me still rather doubtful whether I shall kill Victoria or Victoria me.

—Lytton Strachey,
letter to John Maynard Keynes, November 11, 1920

I

If the British modern period must be given a starting date, we might do well to propose January 22, 1901, the day Queen Victoria died. The modernist imagination consistently seized upon the notion of a moment of historical rupture when human character and the old ways and mores of the nineteenth century irreversibly changed.[1]
Most of the dates proposed (such as Virginia Woolf's suggestion of December 1910,[2]
the month of the opening of the Post-Impressionist Show, and D. H. Lawrence's
selection of 1915[3]) acquired significance retrospectively. Yet even at the time of Victoria's death, almost all of her subjects were aware of its epochal importance, and they
remembered it long after. "In spite of all the excitements which have crowded upon
us since," Edmund Gosse wrote in 1923, "no one can forget the emotion of emerging
into the cold night of January 22, 1901, and seeing the newspaper boys, for once dis-

creetly silent, hurrying hither and thither with a huge announcement that the Queen was dead."[4]

Despite the queen's advanced age, her death came as a strong shock to her subjects. Indeed, the very length of her reign made the shock all the more jarring: Victoria had ruled for sixty-four years—longer than any other British monarch—and most of her subjects literally could not remember a time when any other sovereign had occupied the throne. So long had she reigned that in the hours immediately following her death at Osborne House, none of the palace staff had any idea of the procedures for keeping vigil over her body.[5] No one seemed to have prepared fully for the notion that this queen would one day follow the Prince Consort to the crypt she had built for him at Frogmore. As Gosse later noted, "[A]lthough [death] is the common lot of man, the world had ceased to be convinced that Victoria would undergo it. Logically, no one was foolish enough to conceive that she would live for ever, but sentimentally she had come to seem sempiternal, a portion of the order of things, a being without whose continuance future history must be impossible."[6]

Victoria's long reign had coincided almost exactly with the apogee of Britain's idea (if not the reality) of its own imperial might, as the jubilees of 1887 and 1897 had implicitly emphasized. She had become, in the minds of many of her people, the living example of the endurance of Empire. Arthur Balfour spoke for many when he declared in a speech before Parliament the week after the queen's death, "[W]e feel that the end of an epoch has come upon us—an epoch the beginning of which stretches beyond memory."[7] For Victoria's subjects, her passing emphasized the notion that they had somehow managed to outlive the Victorian era, especially in that her death coincided with the first month of the new century. Samuel Hynes has noted, "At the end of such a reign, and at the beginning of a century, men expected great changes—liberating, perhaps, but with unknown consequences and therefore disturbing."[8] For many of her subjects, Victoria's passing brought a sense of cultural insecurity, and accordingly her death became increasingly seen as an important moment of cultural transition, a flashpoint for the new age. In their eyes, it seemed that on or about January 22, 1901, human character had changed.

The modern period was thus not simply post-Victorian but also post-Victoria. During her lifetime the queen had often been referred to as the paragon of her age, an embodiment of its bourgeois domestic values. After her death this association only intensified for the writers of the early twentieth century, who mapped onto her life and person the very parent culture they wished both to repudiate and to outgrow. Yet, no matter how vehemently the moderns attempted to declare Victoria dead, they remained themselves subjugated to her continued imaginative authority. If they could not praise her, as had her contemporary mourners, neither could they declare her truly buried. By reenacting Victoria's own notorious obsessive melancholia for the dead, the moderns unconsciously affirmed the very affinity they tried to deny.

II

The immediate importance of Victoria's death to the vast majority of her subjects was perhaps best exemplified by the scope of their public mourning. Public offices throughout the empire were closed the day after her death, municipal squares were bedecked with dark crepe, and a good portion of the crown's subjects began to affect black clothing and armbands. In the succeeding months something like three thousand elegies were printed in memoriam.[9] Thousands of citizens from London to Windsor crowded the city streets to witness the passing of her bier, which was followed by the memorable spectacle of five kings walking or riding behind.[10] Few living could remember the state funerals for William IV or the Duke of Wellington, and Victoria's certainly outstripped both in terms of panoply in any case. Her funeral's sheer scope bespoke to her subjects that more than just the queen was being buried that day, suggesting that they were laying to rest the human symbol of their culture and mores.

John Galsworthy's account of Victoria's funeral in his three-part *Forsyte Saga* emphasizes the awareness of its overwhelming symbolism in the minds of the late queen's subjects. Galsworthy's trilogy recounts the transition between the nineteenth and twentieth centuries; Victoria's funeral comes almost midway through the three novels, as if to form the fulcrum of that transition. Indeed, in the mind of Galsworthy's protagonist Soames Forsyte, such a fulcrum is exactly what Victoria's death represents as he waits in the London streets for her funeral bier to pass:

> Well-nigh two generations had slipped by—of steamboats, railways, telegraphs, bicycles, electric light, telephones, and now these motor-cars—of such accumulated wealth, that eight per cent. had become three, and Forsytes were numbered by the thousand! Morals had changed, manners had changed, men had become monkeys twice removed, God had become Mammon—Mammon so respectable as to deceive himself. Sixty-four years that favoured property, and had made the upper middle-class; buttressed, chiselled, polished it, till it was almost indistinguishable in manners, morals, speech, appearance, habit and soul from the nobility. An epoch which had gilded individual liberty so that if a man had money he was free in law and not in fact. An era which had canonised hypocrisy, so that to seem to be respectable was to be. A great Age, whose transmuting influence nothing had escaped save the nature of man and the nature of the Universe. . . . Never again would a Queen reign so long, or people have a chance to see so much history buried for their money.[11]

Soames's musings mirror the general awareness throughout his middle-class milieu that Victoria's death meant exactly what Galsworthy titled this chapter: "The Passing of an Age." "Yes!" Soames reflects, "the Age was passing! What with this Trade-Unionism, and Labour fellows in the House of Commons, with continental fiction, and something in the general feel of everything, not to be expressed in words, things were very different. . . . Things would never be the same again as under good old Viccy!"[12] The cynicism in Soames's comments is readily apparent; Victoria's passing represents not only the obsolescence of middle-class security and prosperity but also the attendant hypocrisy and materialism. Nevertheless, the tone of his eulogy is primarily nostalgic and regretful; the age being buried with Victoria may be, in part, corrupt, but his sense of its importance and weight is undeniable.

Of course, Galsworthy's conflation of the monarch with her age has many precedents. With Victoria, the popular identification of a British monarch with her age was perhaps unmatched since at least the accession of the Hanovers; certainly it had not been so celebrated since then. Although she had endured her share of public crit-icism, particularly during the early years of her reign, by the time of her jubilees Queen Victoria had become "good old Viccy," the very darling of the collective heart of the middle class. Many perceived Victoria as one of them: her life had been pop-ularly understood as a testament to the dominant Victorian ideologies which espoused family, home, and piety, as was reflected in her garb (always defiantly out of fashion and homely) and in her published *Leaves from a Highland Journal.* Whereas Elizabeth I had been celebrated by her age for representing the best to which it could aspire, Victoria found favor in her time for embodying the pedestrian: the affecter of the most bourgeois of mores, she became seen as the living symbol of social and domestic stability.

This identification was particularly emphasized in the public imagination by her continual popular representation as mother to her country. She not only had given birth to nine children but had married most of them off to the great ruling houses of Europe; by the time of her death, she was the literal matriarch of most of the Conti-nental royal and imperial families. Moreover, even from the first years of her marriage to Albert, the popular press had stressed her roles as wife, mother, and keeper of the hearth: the veritable Angel of the House of Hanover. Consequently, many of the ele-gies written in her honor emphasized this maternal aspect, as if to suggest (as Hynes has pointed out) "that it was a commonplace of her reign; the queen-as-mother of her people is not treated poetically as an extravagant figure of speech but as an accepted truth."[13] Victoria's elegists repeatedly identified her maternal role as the source of her power and authority, as if her positions of queen and mother were wholly conflated. "Her hand could rock the cradle," one contemporary poet wrote, "and could guide / The doctrines of men."[14] This belief in her awe-inspiring mater-nal power ultimately resulted in her deception in many of these poems as no less than a heavenly mother, in what Hynes terms "a kind of Victoriolatry."[15]

So thoroughly was the queen perceived as the embodiment of the generative power behind her age that the prospect of her loss tremendously threatened the nation's sense of social security and continuity. The immediate reaction to her death manifested itself for many as a kind of separation anxiety, as if an entire culture were facing the prospect of forcible expulsion from the womb. Henry James, never one to take any change lightly, precisely captured this sentiment when he wrote to his friend Oliver Wendell Holmes, Jr., "I mourn the safe and motherly old middle-class queen who held the nation warm under the fold of her big, hideous Scotch-plaid shawl and whose duration had been so extraordinarily covenient and beneficent. I felt her death much more than I should have expected; she was a sustaining symbol—and the wild waters are upon us now."[16] Many of the elegies printed in Victoria's memory echoed this sense that the funeral for Britain's great mother meant the empire's as well. Even Victoria's most distant colonized subjects were imagined as participating in this com-munal mourning for her: "Our Queen is dead," Mrs. B. Hailes wrote in one such rep-resentative poem, "And dusky lips have said / 'Our Queen is dead' / 'We too are dead.'"[17]

This mutual identification of queen and country cut both ways, however. Because she was both symbol of and mother to her nation in the popular conscious-

ness, Victoria's death meant a threatened sense of social stability and cultural identity; yet by asserting this identification even more strongly, her subjects could feel
that she lived on in their own words and deeds. The shock of the passing of the
queen's mortal shell could be in part mitigated by the declaration of her public
immortality. If Victoria's body could not live forever, her immediate mourners suggested, her cultural legacy just might: *La reine est morte, vive la reine*. Her elegists frequently depicted Victoria as being enthroned in heaven after her death, watching
down upon her worshipful nation as if her guidance and cultural imprimatur were
immortal.[18]

Fittingly, the queen's posthumous stellification was itself strikingly replicative of
the cult of sentimental bereavement which she had promulgated during her lifetime
for her dead husband, Albert. Many of the elegies for Victoria depict her as actually
reuniting with her husband in heaven (in one memorable instance, he even awaits
her with open arms and a cry of "Weibchen mine!").[19] These suggest that the burden
of Victoria's lifelong melancholia had been in effect assumed by her entire nation:
how could she truly be gone if her work continued in the hearts of her people? The
ostentatious immediate mourning for the maternal arch-mourner thus asserted the
continuance of her legacy on this earth. Victoria's passing was to some degree paradoxically denied by the very acknowledgment of it. The immediate public mourning
for Victoria therefore served not to declare the finality of her loss, but to assert the
continuation of the national and domestic ideologies she was popularly understood
to espouse and represent.

Galsworthy himself seemed aware of this dynamic when dramatizing Victoria's
funeral in *The Forsyte Saga*. Soames Forsyte observes that as Victoria's bier passes, the
onlookers respond with

> a murmuring groan from all the long line of those who watched, a sound such as
> Soames had never heard, so unconscious, primitive, deep and wild, that neither he
> nor any knew whether they had joined in uttering it. Strange sound, indeed! Trib-
> ute of an Age to its own death. . . . Ah! Ah! . . . The hold on life had slipped. That
> which had seemed eternal was gone! The Queen—God bless her!
>
> It moved on with the bier, that travelling groan, as a fire moves on over grass
> in a thin line; it kept step, and marched alongside down the dense crowds mile after
> mile. It was a human sound, and yet inhuman, pushed out by animal subconscious-
> ness, by intimate knowledge of universal death and change. None of us—none of
> us can hold on for ever![20]

This collective expression of sentimental bereavement spectacularly illustrates the
paradox of the immediate public mourning for Victoria. On the face of it, Soames's
observation suggests that the queen's death threatens a breakdown of civil behavior
into atavism, as if Victoria had indeed been the last bulwark against the "wild waters"
(to use Henry James's phrase) of anarchy. At the same time, however, the very spectacle that Soames describes seems anything *but* anarchic or spontaneous: the groan
proceeds through the crowds in a systematic fashion, enforcing an impression of
cohesive national sympathy. Its neat restraint and rationalization by Soames's sentimental homilies suggests that Victoria's death signaled not so much the end of an era,

as he feared, but rather the reassertion of Victorian mores and precepts. Indeed, Galsworthy's Londoners respond after their cathartic release of their "animal subconsciousness" merely by returning sadly to their homes, suitably impressed by the display of imperial pride and unity. The drama of Victoria's loss for her nation becomes transformed into a containable melodrama, a ritual that minimizes—even denies—the finality of her loss while reaffirming national solidarity.

Queen Victoria had died, but her people were immediately afterwards unwilling to let her go entirely. As in Freud's model of melancholia, wherein the grieving person refuses to prove to himself that the mourned object has irrevocably vanished, and thus retreats into his memories of it, the initial popular reaction to Victoria's death repudiated the finality of her loss.[21] The popular cultural consciousness largely clung to hypostatized memories of the idealized queen, refusing to undertake the process of reality testing which would involve a true admission of the passing of the queen and her era. That task would be left to the Victorians' modern descendants, who would attempt to execute a *Trauerarbeit*—that is, a *completed* work of mourning—for the dead queen.

III

The voices that resisted the national inflation of the queen's memory at the time of her death were few, yet notable among them was that of Thomas Hardy, perhaps Britain's preeminent poet in 1901. Hardy was so esteemed at the time of Victoria's death that his elegy was given pride of place in the collection *The Passing of Victoria: The Poets' Tribute*. Unlike the other works in this anthology, however, Hardy's "V.R. (1819–1901): A Reverie" refused to treat the dead queen hagiographically. Rather, his elegy seems to criticize such attempts to stellify the queen, and thus represents an opening salvo in the battle to demythify Victoria.

As Hardy's elliptical title suggests, Victoria is never evident as an actual woman in Hardy's elegy. She is only a "purposed Life," given form through the divine "deedful word" of "the Absolute in Time," which declares, "Let one be born and throned whose mould shall constitute / The norm of every royal-rated attribute." These attributes are never fully enumerated: Victoria becomes for Hardy's speaker an inhuman and elided divine public presence that evades comparative description. Indeed, she ultimately evades the speaker altogether. No sooner is this presence created than it fulfills its public duties and vanishes: "Its fourscore cycles beamed with deeds well done, / And the world's heart was won. . . ." Hardy suggests that he and his contemporaries are perhaps too close to the queen to regard her as anything but a public paragon; he leaves the real work of evaluating her legacy not to his fellow writers but to succeeding generations: "Yet may the deed of hers most bright in eyes to be / Lie hid from ours—as in the All-One's thought lay she—Till ripening years have run."[22]

Hardy's words would prove prophetic. Since Victoria was beyond the ken of many of Hardy's contemporaries, later generations would set themselves the task of reassessing the meaning of the woman and her cultural legacy. A large part of that legacy, however, was the idealized and oversized persona created by her popular hagiographers; the moderns would have to confront not only Victoria the woman but

also Victoria "the purposed Life." Because Victoria had become, in the minds of contemporary subjects who mourned her, the idealized embodiment of all that they cherished about Victorian culture, they figured her as such in their eulogies. Gosse would
write in 1923, "[Her] phantom took divine proportions [immediately after her death];
she was clothed with the most extravagant and the most incongruous attributes.
. . ."[23] Gosse's arch tone makes clear, however, that the set of values one generation
celebrated in the person of Victoria would later be mocked, and even repudiated, by
their modern descendants.

George Bernard Shaw, who, like Hardy, bridged the transition from the Victorian to the modern era, noticed the conditions that were making this revision possible. In 1919 Shaw publicly denounced the many statues to Victoria that had been
worshipfully erected to her memory in the two decades since her death. Asking "what
crime Queen Victoria may have committed that she should be so horribly guyed as
she has been through the length and breadth of her dominions," Shaw noted:

> It was part of her personal quality that she was a tiny woman, and our national pas-
> sion for telling lies on every public subject has led to her being represented as an
> overgrown monster. Take Mrs. Caudle, Mrs. Gamp, Mrs. Prig, Mrs. Proudie, and
> make a composite statue of them, and you will have a typical memorial of Queen
> Victoria. Now if this were a bold republican realism which disdained courtly syco-
> phancy, it would be at least courageous, if unkind. But it is pure plastic calumny.
> Queen Victoria was a little woman with great decision of manner and a beautiful
> speaking voice which she used in public extremely well. She carried herself very
> well. All young people now believe that she was a huge heap of a woman. . . .[24]

In the interests of sycophancy and sentimentality, Victoria had become the avatar of
the very hypocrisies and human failings that writers of her era such as Jerrold, Dickens, and Trollope had attempted to satirize. For Shaw, the marmoreal refashioning of
the dead queen according to the exaggerated scale of her grandiose empire fatally
served to transform her into the embodiment of her era's greatest personal mon-
strosities.

Indeed, it became apparent to some that Victoria's death could mean not only
the end of all that was great in her empire but all that was morally questionable, or
just simply out of date. Even some of those who survived the queen well into the
twentieth century revised their attitudes toward the meaning of her death for the
nation. In her 1937 autobiography the novelist Elinor Glyn reflected that at the time
of Victoria's death, she had shared with many the apocalyptic sense that it meant
"the funeral procession of England's greatness and glory." In the intervening years,
however, Glyn had come to understand this longing for rigid social stability as "the
real sign of decadence in a race, . . . restraining the development of new ideas, and
the material standards and ideals of greatness which belong to the past."[25] Victoria's
passing did not mean the setting of the star of Britain, she believed, because the old
values the queen had represented had been effectively rethought and recast. Glyn
writes:

> It was generally felt that changes must follow the death of the Queen, and the inau-
> guration of a new century, and that new ideas, new standards and new hopes were

in the air. But I think that no one then dreamed how rapid, how complete, and in many ways, how terrible would be the transformation. The pace of the development of the whole world had, it seems, been slowed down for a decade by the failing strength of the little form in the black-draped coffin, and the leisureliness of the 'nineties was really that of a slow-motion picture. In deference to the views of the beloved Empress who symbolized England's nineteenth-century glory, inevitable economic and social changes had been unconsciously held back.[26]

In time this became the view of many early twentieth-century writers, who saw Victoria as the emblem of the Victorian resistance to modernity, the very figure of complacency and of moral and ideological self-satisfaction. Her famous mourning for Prince Albert seemed to them to typify what they saw as a Victorian flight toward nostalgia, preventing progress and hindering modernity. The playwright Laurence Housman (who himself reaped great dramatic capital from the dead queen's life in such works as *Victoria Regina*) would summarize the prevalent modern evaluation of Victoria by claiming that she was "the mourning widow, not only of a beloved and worthy Consort, but of a whole set of cherished notions, which in the 'Sixties and 'Seventies were already moribund, and are now finally dead and disposed of." Victoria's "mourning" for such notions, Housman suggests, served paradoxically to keep them alive during her lifetime. With her death, however, this melancholic mourning, which had sustained these attitudes, could be effectively completed, so that they could be considered "dead and disposed of." When Victoria perished, he suggests, so did Victorianism.[27] Leonard Woolf makes a similar argument in his 1970 autobiography, *Sowing*:

> When in the grim, grey, rainy January days of 1901 Queen Victoria lay dying, we [modern writers] already felt that we were living in an era of incipient revolt and that we ourselves were mortally involved in this revolt against a social system which, for convenience's sake, may be referred to as bourgeois Victorianism.[28]

Victoria's decline, then, could be read as coinciding with that of the social system to which she gave her name, while her death seems to adumbrate that system's necessary overthrow. British modernism thus became associated with a kind of cultural regicide.

More specifically, it also became implicated in a kind of cultural matricide. Whereas Victoria's mourning subjects would glorify her maternal solicitude, the moderns ridiculed her as a grossly outsized *magna mater* whom the twentieth century had to bury in order to survive. The dead queen seemed to embody everything the moderns detested about their parents' generation, and everything they would attempt to renounce or overthrow: slavish devotion to home and authority, bourgeois complacency, moral self-righteousness, intellectual limitedness, and—above all—the sentimental obsession with the past and the dead. Victoria became a composite not only, as Shaw suggested, of Mrs. Caudle, Mrs. Gamp, Mrs. Prig, and Mrs. Proudie, but also of Mrs. Pontifex, Mrs. Morel, and (in Joyce's most castigating moments) Mrs. Dedalus. By repudiating all that their cultural "mother" represented, the modern writers strove to achieve autonomy from her rule.

Mourning the mother would involve not only feelings of triumph and individuation but also tremendous guilt and nostalgia; having outlived her tyranny, the surviving children find themselves bereft of her care and example. Such feelings of ambivalence, I suggest, also became present in the modernists' mourning for their cultural mother. The dead queen could be mocked, or even repudiated, as the representative of Victorian bourgeois complacency, narrow-mindedness, and sentimental excess. Nevertheless, she also came to stand for much that the moderns missed about the preceding generation's era, including its personal and cultural fecundity and ethical and emotional self-confidence. The dead queen thus came to signify in modern fiction and letters the tremendous ambivalence toward the heritage of the nineteenth century. It thus became impossible to declare her (to use Housman's phrase) "dead and disposed of." In their inability to resolve their feelings for the dead queen, the moderns also remained in a state of melancholia for her, analogous in effect, if not in tone, to that of their forebears.

James Joyce's *Ulysses*, perhaps the quintessential modern novel, makes this ambivalence particularly clear. Victoria, recently dead at the time of the novel's action in 1904, figures as the reigning figure of the predatory past from which Stephen Dedalus attempts to emancipate himself. In his imagination Stephen often seems to conflate the dead queen with his own recently deceased mother, who herself requested that Stephen make an obeisance to the past in her name. Just as he dreams of his mother as an undead crone with "a faint odour of wetted ashes" on her breath, so too does he repeatedly imagine the dead queen as an "old hag with yellow teeth."[29] The attention to their hideous mouths implies that both women become jointly figured as vampires who threaten to devour the living; they become castrating nightmare visions of the maternal, fitted out with horrifying *vaginae dentatae*. Even Leopold Bloom, with his kind disposition toward the figures of the past, explicitly repudiates Victoria for her refusal to face the future. While musing at Paddy Dignam's funeral in the "Hades" chapter, Bloom reflects on the futility of Victoria's Frogmore memorial to Prince Albert: "Vain in her heart of hearts," he decides, "[a]ll for a shadow. Consort not even a king. Her son was the substance. Something new to hope for not like the past she wanted back, waiting. It never comes" (p. 84). Victoria becomes the Queen of the Underworld, reigning over a lethal realm of death and nostalgia which Bloom repudiates by chapter's end.

Nevertheless, despite the queen's metonymic antithesis to the modernity *Ulysses* so firmly embraces, Joyce suggests that Victoria cannot be so entirely repudiated. Although the novel seems firmly opposed to all that Victoria represents—particularly the tyranny of British rule—Joyce seems keenly aware of the dangers of mindless rebellion. The "Cyclops" chapter of *Ulysses* demonstrates such dangers, as the Citizen and his cronies carry the nationalism and progressivism espoused by Stephen to ludicrous extremes. Joyce counterposes their jingoistic comments with his own linguistic excesses, describing them in pseudo-epic terms not only to parody their grandiosity but also to suggest how far they have themselves fallen. Victoria—whom they drunkenly refer to as "the flatulent old bitch that's dead (p. 186)—significantly figures as an emblem of the rejected magnificence of the past. When Alf O'Bergan pays Terry O'Ryan for a pint of ale, for example, Joyce describes it as an epic gesture of benevolence, despite the uncharitableness and unkindness of the men's comments in the bar. On the coin is engraved the image of a queen of the regal port, scion of the house of Brunswick, Victoria her name, Her Most Excellent Majesty, by grace of God of the United Kingdom of Great Britain and Ireland and of the British dominions beyond the sea, queen, defender of the faith, Empress of India, even she, who bore rule, a victress over many peoples, the wellbeloved, for they knew and loved her from the rising of the sun to the going down thereof, the pale, the dark, the ruddy and the ethiop. (p. 246)

To be sure, Joyce's description ridicules Victoria as the representative of imperial self-importance; yet it also suggests that she stands as a figure for a kind of imaginative excess and authority the tavern nationalists cannot hope to replace.

Joyce was not the only modern writer to exhibit marked ambivalence toward Queen Victoria as a cultural ancestor. Virginia Woolf, who famously proclaimed her own investment in uncovering her literary matrilineage in A Room of One's Own, could not help but note the popularity of the dead queen's published journals and letters among the British reading public. Neither could she ignore that this particular literary foremother seemed to exhibit everything Woolf despised about nineteenth-century sentimental writing. When reviewing the autobiography of Queen Marie of Rumania, Woolf praised it by comparing it favorably to the writing of Marie's grandmother Victoria, noting,

> If we want an example of the difference between writing and non-writing, we have only to compare a page of Queen Marie with a page of Queen Victoria. The old Queen was, of course, an author. She was forced by the exigencies of her profession to fill an immense number of pages, and some of these have been printed and bound between covers. But between the old Queen and the English language lay an abyss which no depth of passion and no depth of character could cross. Her works make for very painful reading on that account. She has to express herself in words; but words will not come to her call.[30]

For Woolf, Victoria's writing belied any recognizable human emotion despite its own claims to the contrary. Instead of conveying genuine sentiment, it demonstrated a bewildering overwrought sentimentality unmediated by any sophisticated means of expression. In her eyes Victoria's writing was not any sort of managed craft but rather the thoughtless exposition of nineteenth-century bourgeois mores.

Woolf might note that Queen Victoria was "entirely unaesthetic," as she did in her 1930 reading notes for the queen's letters, but nonetheless she had to admit the dead queen "knew her own mind. But, mind radically commonplace. Only its inherited force, & cumulative sense of power, making it remarkable."[31] Radically commonplace and yet remarkable, self-confident and yet lacking in aesthetic values, the voice of Queen Victoria somehow bound Woolf to its cultural authority. Although she could mock it, she could not deny the weight of its sanction, any more than could the eponymous heroine of her novel Orlando (1928). Victoria's moral edicts concerning feminine behavior bewilder and even stultify Orlando; nonetheless, she submits to marry, wear crinolines, and even bear a son, as Victoria's domestic example recommends. The queen's example seems identical with the standards of the Victorian era itself, which in Orlando is marked by the wild proliferation of growth—human, vegetative, and municipal—as if to suggest that Victoria's personal fertility extended to her entire age.

Indeed, Woolf suggests that "the life of an average woman" in the period as "a succession of childbirths" led naturally to the expansion of both Britain's political and imaginative might: "Thus the British Empire came into existence," she notes, "and thus—for there is no stopping damp; it gets into inkpots as it gets into woodwork—sentences swelled, adjectives multiplied, lyrics became epics, and little trifles that had been essays a column long were now encyclopaedias in ten or twenty volumes."[32]

Even if Woolf's attitude toward this growth is derisive, it remains unquestioned that the prolific figure of the nineteenth-century matriarch, as typified by Victoria, nevertheless held great attraction. In Woolf's preceding novel, *To the Lighthouse*, (1927), Victoria's maternal authority becomes manifest in the benevolent person of Mrs. Ramsay, whom Woolf famously intended as a tribute to her own mother, Julia Stephen. This identification becomes clear near the novel's beginning, when Charles Tansley observes Mrs. Ramsay standing "quite motionless for a moment against a picture of Queen Victoria wearing the blue ribbon of the Garter; when all at once he realized—she was the most beautiful person he had ever seen."[33] This transfigurative conflation of Mrs. Ramsay with the queen emphasizes the radiant attraction of all that the nineteenth-century matriarch promises, as the protector of male enterprise, the arranger of proposed dynastic marriages, the emotional foundation of a household and culture, and the prodigious wellspring of children and family. For Lily Briscoe, Woolf's prototypical figure in *To the Lighthouse* for the twentieth-century woman artist, such a matriarch offers the inspiration she needs to carry on with her own creative endeavors. We should note that Woolf ended her review of Queen Marie's autobiography by suggesting that Marie's creative imagination, palatable to the modern sensibility, could indeed be traced back to her grandmother's literary ambitions. If women are to think back through their mothers, it seems as if Woolf is grudgingly willing to include Victoria among them.

For Woolf, as for Joyce, the ghost of Victoria could at times be derided, but could never be wholly exorcised. Their inability to work out their attitudes toward her satisfactorily meant that her shade haunted their writings as if they too were gripped in a kind of interminable melancholia for the queen. Because these enormously conflicting responses to Victoria demanded sorting out, it became inevitable that the modern imagination would turn to writing a mythopoeic account of the queen's life. In writing her biography, it could define a metonymized history of its precursor period in consolidated form, with a beginning, a middle, and (particularly) an end. Yet, if it was hoped that writing Victoria's biography would transform the modern melancholia for Victoria into a completed work of mourning, it was to prove as problematic as all other attempts to deal with the dead queen. This became apparent with the first and unquestionably the most important such biography, which was also to prove one of the most influential literary texts of the British modern era: Lytton Strachey's *Queen Victoria* (1921).

IV

If any modernist were to have finished off Queen Victoria successfully and quickly, it should have been Lytton Strachey. After the success of his first book of biographical essays, the notorious *Eminent Victorians* (1918), it seemed inevitable that Strachey, in furthering his work of debunking the sacred cows of the Victorian period, would turn his biographer's gaze next to Her Late Majesty. "We want your method for some stately Victorians who have waited long for it," Walter Raleigh wrote to him in May 1918, "First the great panjandrum—Victoria herself. This is obvious. How can an adjective have a meaning that is not dependent on its substantive?"[34] By writing Victoria's life, Strachey clearly had the opportunity to redefine Victorianism once and for all. So easy a target did Victoria seem that, significantly, Strachey's own mother wrote to her son begging him not to complete this act of cultural matricide. "No doubt she lays herself open to drastic treatment which is one reason I think it better left alone," Lady Strachey wrote her son. "She has won a place in public affection and a reputation in our history which it would be highly unpopular, and I think not quite fair, to attempt to bring down."[35]

Lady Strachey's concerns were no doubt justified, given her son's reputation as a quick and efficient dispatcher of his own biographical subjects. He notoriously suggested in his essay on Macaulay that one of the greatest qualities necessary for a historian was an antipathy to his subject matter.[36] In his artistic manifesto, the preface to *Eminent Victorians*, Strachey had even described his own work in explicitly martial terms and had announced the importance of attacking his enemies with sudden ferocity:

> It is not by the direct method of a scrupulous narration that the explorer of the past can hope to depict that singular epoch. If he is wise, he will adopt a subtler strategy. He will attack his subject in unexpected places; he will fall upon the flank, or the rear; he will shoot a sudden, revealing searchlight into obscure recesses, hitherto undivined.[37]

The dead queen would have seemed hopelessly outgunned when Strachey chose her as the subject for his second work and first full-length biographical study. When *Queen Victoria* was published in 1921, however, it was generally agreed that it was Victoria rather than Strachey who had routed the opponent. Rather than devastate the queen as he had successfully demolished Cardinal Manning, Thomas Arnold, Florence Nightingale, and General Gordon in his earlier work, Strachey, most critics felt, had maintained a curious sympathy with Victoria, and they delightedly agreed that the scourge of the Victorians had himself been defeated by his subject. Raymond Mortimer observed in a 1929 article in *The Bookman*: "Those who had been appalled by [Strachey's] treatment of Gordon and Arnold feared that the Queen would be set up as an Aunt Sally for his irony. Perhaps Mr. Strachey thought so himself when he began the book. But by the end of it he had obviously become subjugated by his subject. He was almost in love with the Queen."[38] This sort of observation had become such a critical cliché by the late 1920s that that same year André Maurois could wryly observe in his Clark lectures to an assembled group of Cambridge undergraduates, "It was one of you who told me the other day that the most remarkable phenomenon of modern biography was the conquest of Mr. Strachey by Queen Victoria."[39]

Strachey himself could hardly disagree. He was very aware during the composition of *Queen Victoria* that he was being overwhelmed by his subject, and becoming himself subject (to use Maurois's metaphor) to her will. He was especially disturbed while writing the book in 1920 by his inability to complete it, which engendered within him a sense of losing a war between Victoria and himself. Although he had planned the book to be roughly one hundred thousand words,[40] he found himself unable to finish his discussion of Victoria's early married years. In a series of letters written to his friends during that year, his fears of losing this battle with his biographical target became increasingly evident:

> Victoria drops a lengthening chain, damn her. It is not so easy to be sprightly with such a Majesty.[41]

> Up to the end of this month I must sit here, struggling with Victoria, who's proving a tougher mouthful than even I had expected. I must masticate and masticate with a steady persistence—it's the only pain.[42]

> Here I sit, over the fire, trying to nerve myself for the coup de grace on Victoria; but I hesitate. . . . she quells me with her fishy eye.[43]

Finally, he wrote to John Maynard Keynes in November of that year: "It seems to me still rather doubtful whether I shall kill Victoria or Victoria me."[44]

If Strachey's rhetoric here seems overdramatic, we must keep in mind the aesthetic stakes he believed were involved in completing Victoria's biography in a timely fashion. In his preface to *Eminent Victorians*, Strachey had written that the first task of the biographer was "to preserve . . . a becoming brevity" (p. 10). In revising the art of the biographer, Strachey had castigated the logorrhea of his Victorian predecessors, praising instead the work of the French, "with their incomparable *éloges*, compressing into a few shining pages the manifold existences of men" (p. 9). As Strachey conceived it, his own task involved eschewing the melancholia espoused by Victorian biographers in their own multivolume accounts of the dead in favor of a work analogous to the Freudian *Trauerarbeit*:

> Those two fat volumes, with which it is our custom to commemorate the dead— who does not know them, with their ill-digested masses of material, their slipshod style, their tone of tedious panegyric, their lamentable lack of selection, of detachment, of design? They are as familiar as the *cortège* of the undertaker, and wear the same air of slow, funereal barbarism. One is tempted to suppose, of some of them, that they were composed by that functionary, as the final item of his job. The studies in this book are indebted, in more ways than one, to such works—works which certainly deserve the name of Standard Biographies. For they have provided me with much indispensable information, but with something even more precious—an example. (p. 10)

In writing *Queen Victoria*, however, Strachey worried that he would not be able to avoid following the example of his Victorian predecessors—especially, it would seem, that of Victoria herself, the great arch-melancholic. Only by finishing the biography quickly could Strachey avoid reenacting Victoria's own interminable melancholia for her beloved Prince Consort, the onslaught of which Strachey sees as her life's turning point. *Queen Victoria* thus reads as a text at war with itself in its attempt to exorcise this possessive, melancholic spirit and complete its own *Trauerarbeit* for her.

As Strachey's own letters quoted earlier suggest, however, harnessing Queen Victoria was not such an easy task. In Strachey's biography many are the figures who, like the biographer, attempt to restrain the queen and appropriate her voice and authority: her mother, her governess, her uncle Leopold, her ministers, even her husband, the Prince Consort. All of these assume they can manipulate Victoria and indirectly commandeer her authority; and all, in Strachey's text, ultimately pay the penalty for this mistaken assumption. In his depiction of an unending war to determine who is the controller and who is the controlled, Strachey suggests the stakes of his own battle to shape the life and times of Victoria for his own purposes.

Obsessed with issues of appropriation, manipulation, and seduction even before the actual birth of its title character, *Queen Victoria* draws the battle lines in these relentless maneuverings for power directly according to gender. Most of the male characters in the text behave much as Strachey might describe himself in his own role as biographer: as reserved and sardonic figures who operate largely behind the scenes. "The satisfaction of his essential being lay in obscurity, in invisibility—in passing, unobserved, through a hidden entrance, into the very central chamber of power," Strachey writes of Albert's adviser the Baron Stockmar, "and in sitting there, quietly, pulling the subtle strings that set the wheels of the whole world in motion."[45] This description might serve for Strachey himself, of course, in his role as manipulator of the nineteenth-century world; but so too could it serve to describe Lord Melbourne, Lord Palmerston, Disraeli, Leopold of the Belgians, and even the Prince Consort himself. In contrast, the women in Strachey's text eschew subtlety in favor of direct confrontation. They are emotional Vesuviuses, ruled by their passions and ready to explode whenever their fearsome wills are thwarted, such as Victoria's cousin the Princess Charlotte, who we are told "had very little of that self-command which is especially required of princes; her manners were abominable" (p. 3). The Duchess of Kent, Victoria's furious and determined mother, often erupts as she does at the birthday party for her brother-in-law William IV, leaving "in a tornado of rage and mortification" (p. 44). Even the demure Baroness Lehzen, Victoria's beloved governess, cannot control her appetites; at one point we are told, "[H]er passion for carraway [sic] seeds . . . was uncontrollable" (p. 46).

The first portion of *Queen Victoria* is largely a series of encounters between these cool male manipulators and the maddened, passionate women of the Hanover court. The attention to the question of succession allows the women the means of power as the inheritors (or the procreators of inheritors) of the throne, but the men consistently act to outmaneuver them. For example, Charlotte, the second in line to the throne before Victoria's birth, is successfully wooed by the scheming Leopold, who "had shown considerable diplomatic skill at the Congress of Vienna; and . . . was now to try his hand at taming a tumultuous Princess" (p. 3). Melbourne shrewdly manipulates women (including his own wife) to further his plans, and even the erratic King William outschemes the Duchess of Kent over her designs for consolidating power.

By establishing this pattern, the text invites us to expect that Victoria herself will also be outmaneuvered by the many men who seek to use her political authority to their own ends. Indeed, Strachey largely structures his biography around these male figures in his title character's life; many chapters take their titles from the names of these men, as if to suggest they were struggling to control Victoria's destiny. Most of them make concerted attempts to take advantage of the queen's romantic nature and appropriate her authority. The biography reads in part as a series of courtships of its title character by smooth manipulators such as Lord Melbourne, who charms Victoria by behaving to her like a young swain to further his secret political agenda, or later Disraeli, who takes the same method with Victoria, successfully winning her over by offering blandishments and allowing her to send him flowers from her palace gardens. In reality, however, no matter how assiduously the men surrounding the queen successfully solicit her feelings of ardor, she ultimately thwarts all efforts to control her. Victoria remains the only female character who is unbowed by masculine manipulation.

Victoria's success in avoiding such control occurs not because she is less emotional than the other more tractable Hanover women in the text but rather because she is *more* so: Victoria, in Strachey's eyes, is Victorian emotionalism at its purest, its most chaotic, and undeniably its most potent. Carolyn Heilbrun has regretted Strachey's "so very mediocre depiction of the Queen's character,"[46] but although Strachey's Victoria is utterly bourgeois in outlook, and even intellectually limited, Strachey is careful to emphasize that Victoria is anything *but* mediocre. Throughout he pays particular attention to her exceptional character. Her piety, her simple demeanor, her keen sense of propriety all receive special note (p. 25), and so perfect does Victoria seem, according to nineteenth-century standards for feminine behavior, that "[o]ne seems to hold in one's hand a small smooth crystal pebble, without a flaw and without a scintillation, and so transparent that one can see through it at a glance" (pp. 35–36). Nonetheless, if Strachey's implication here is that Victoria's character is easily grasped, he quickly amends himself to note her greatest distinction: "Yet perhaps, after all, to the discerning eye, the purity would not be absolute. the careful searcher might detect, in the virgin soil, the first faint traces of an unexpected vein" (p. 36). This "unexpected vein" in Victoria, which resists all easy attempts to read and master it, and which makes her character most remarkable, is her peculiar and inexhaustible passionate nature.

Even more than the character of the other women in Strachey's biography, Victoria's is determined entirely by her ferocious emotionality. Even from childhood the future queen harbors this extraordinary temperamental streak, which can manifest itself with lightning speed as rage or repentance. "From time to time," Strachey notes, "she would fly into a violent passion, stamp her little foot, and set everyone at defiance; whatever they might say she would not learn her letters—no, she would not; afterwards, she was very sorry, and burst into tears . . ." (p. 24). After she becomes queen, Victoria's inability to restrain her volcanic passions becomes even more pronounced. Frequently her emotionality manifests itself in the form of writing: throughout the text Victoria is seen taking pen in hand to ease the burdens of her heart. Although Strachey repeatedly quotes from Victoria's letters and journals to highlight her stylistic artlessness, he nonetheless seems awestruck and even threatened by the torrent of her words, noting that "ecstasies seemed to gush from her pen unceasingly and almost of their own accord" (p. 127). Her letters, Strachey notes in another passage, in the surprising jet of their expression, remind one of a turned-on tap. What is within pours forth in an immediate, spontaneous rush. Her utterly unliterary style has at least the merit of being a vehicle exactly unsuited to her thoughts and feelings; and even the platitude of her phraseology carries with it a curiously personal flavour. (p. 312)

Victoria's writing is thus the exact opposite of Strachey's own style: unmediated and artless, to be sure, but also sincere, spontaneous, and—most important—ceaseless, pouring out from her as an expression of a kind of sentimental *jouissance*.

Victoria's emotionalism is closely wedded in Strachey's text to the dominant ideology of her day. As the figurehead for her nation, she fittingly seems nothing so much as the living embodiment of the national mood. When she accedes to the throne, he notes the approval she finds among her own people: "Sentiment and romance were coming into fashion; and the spectacle of the little girl–queen, innocent, modest, with fair hair and pink cheeks, driving through her capital, filled the hearts of the beholders with raptures of affectionate loyalty" (p. 53). As Perry Meisel has pointed out regarding this passage, "Whether Victoria is cause or effect is left manifestly open."[47] Victoria becomes both producer and product of her age and its sentimental ideology: she is the Victorian temper made flesh. Strachey writes that although with surprising modesty she thinks of herself soon after her marriage as merely Albert's wife, "she was more—the embodiment, the living apex of a new era in the generations of mankind. The last vestige of the eighteenth century had disappeared; cynicism and subtlety were shrivelled into powder; and duty, industry, morality and domesticity triumphed over them. . . . The Victorian Age was in full swing" (pp. 144–45). Although Victoria's importance to her country stems from her public visibility as its national representative, she is beloved by her people because she values the private virtues of "duty, industry, morality, and domesticity" so dear to their hearts. Strachey himself notes that "the distinction between what is public and what is private is always a subtle one; and in the case of a reigning sovereign . . . it is often imaginary" (p. 57). Because she is herself so thoroughly a creature of emotion, Victoria repeatedly privileges private sentiment over public governance.

At first, such privileging makes the queen seem easy prey to her manipulative ministers and male relations; yet always the strength of her feelings begins to surprise and then exhaust her would-be controllers. Most often, and most obviously, Victoria's conquering feelings manifest themselves as rage, as when during the Bedchamber Plot she resists the attempts of Robert Peel's Whig cabinet to replace the ladies of her royal bedchamber: Strachey writes, "[The cabinet's] considerations vanished before the passionate urgency of Victoria. The intensity of her determination swept them headlong down the stream of desire" (p. 91). Victoria's ardor proves every bit as deadly to the men around her as her displeasure. Even those who wish to divert Victoria's streams of passion for their own ends find themselves incapable of controlling their force and urgency. Although Disraeli woos the queen successfully by addressing her with unabashed Spenserian flattery as "the Faery," perceiving "that personality was the key that opened the Faery's heart" (p. 259). Nevertheless, he finds himself hindered rather than empowered by his closeness to the queen. Inundated by her "feverish" outpourings of letters and telegrams demanding his adherence to her personal feelings on political matters, he decides, "This was no longer the Faery, it was a genie whom he had rashly called out of the bottle, and who was now intent upon showing her supernal power" (p. 273). Ultimately, Strachey suggests, Disraeli was hastened to his grave by the demands of his ravenous and wanton genie, "worn out with age and maladies, but moving still." Disraeli is eventually left "an assiduous mummy" by the queen's impossible demands (p. 274).

Even Albert, the beloved Prince Consort, finds himself no match for Victoria's inexhaustible emotional energy. Initially Victoria resists the notion that she might be subservient to Albert's authority after their marriage; Albert, however, success-fully conquers Victoria by simply relying on the depth of her overwhelming conjugal ardor. Indeed, he can remain almost wholly passive in the battle for her heart: Stra-chey suggests that Victoria's struggles are purely internal:

> Her vitality, her obstinacy, her overwhelming sense of her own position, might well have beaten down before them his superiorities and his rights. But she fought at a disadvantage; she was, in very truth, no longer her own mistress; a profound preoc-cupation dominated her, seizing upon her inmost purposes for its own extraordinary ends. She was madly in love. (p. 118)

For many years this works to the Prince Consort's advantage: "Albert was supreme," Strachey notes (p. 125), and for most of his marriage he acts as the de facto sover-eign of the United Kingdom. Even Albert's character, however, crumples before his wife's untiring strength. Strachey makes the causes for Albert's decline somewhat unclear, yet he suggests quite strongly that Victoria may be unconsciously responsi-ble for it. "England lumbered on," Strachey notes, "impervious and self-satisfied, in her old intolerable course. [Albert] threw himself in the path of the monster with rigid purpose, but he was brushed aside" (p. 213). The implications of the sentence's striking anthropomorphic imagery become clear when we recall that Victoria herself *is* England. Strachey suggests that no man can possibly withstand being married to this juggernaut of national temper. Indeed, as Albert declines, Victoria significantly prospers, as if she were vampirically draining her husband's energies out of him, despite her conscious wishes:

> Beside Victoria, he presented a painful contrast. She, too, was stout, but it was with the plumpness of a vigorous matron; and an eager vitality was everywhere visible— in her energetic bearing, her protruding, enquiring glances, her small, fat, capable, and commanding hands. If only, by some sympathetic magic, she could have con-veyed into that portly, flabby figure, that desiccated and discouraged brain, a measure of the stamina and the self-assurance which were so pre-eminently hers! (p. 216)

We are reminded here of Strachey's anxieties that Victoria would drain his own energies in the writing of her biography. A personality no minister or husband can hope to contain can thwart her biographer as well. Much of Strachey's humor in *Queen Victoria* derives from the fun he has at Victoria's expense, describing her boundlessly energetic, spontaneous, and willful behavior in his coolly detached prose. But Victoria, as Strachey's critics bemusedly noted, resists even these attempts to contain her: she proves too much for him just as she proved too much for her hus-band, uncles, and ministers.

Significantly in that Strachey saw his work as a kind of completed and brief "*éloge*," Victoria's greatest sentimental weapon of resistance is her boundless melancholia. Strachey dramatically begins *Queen Victoria* with the death of Princess Charlotte,[48] as if to suggest that death will continually shadow Victoria's biography as she comes to outlive almost all of her allies and opponents. The Duchess of Kent's passing in 1861 first brings out Victoria's penchant for excessive bereavement. Strachey notes the "morbid intensity" with which Victoria "filled her diary with pages of minute descriptions of her mother's last hours, her dissolution, and her corpse, interspersed with vehement apostrophes, and the agitated outpourings of emotional reflection" (p. 218). It is as if Victoria's imaginative and emotive proclivities finally find their meet object in her mother's death. Strachey even suggests that the event allows her to prepare for her emotional apotheosis in her mourning for the Prince Consort: "Her lamentations continued with a strange abundance, a strange persistency. It was almost as if, by some mysterious and unconscious precognition, she realized that for her, in an especial manner, that grisly Majesty had a dreadful dart in store" (p. 218).

In Albert's death the two Majesties—Death and Victoria—find their grandest moment of coalescence. Indeed, the queen's melancholia for the Prince Consort sweeps her to her greatest moments of majesty in affording her her most sustained and extreme venue for sentimental expression. Strachey contends that Victoria threatened to lose all sense of decorum after Albert's death, endangering not only her own well-being but that of the entire nation. "[T]here were moments," he notes, "when her royal anguish would brook no restraint" (p. 226). Strachey suggests that despite her protestations of misery, Victoria's mourning affords her a kind of autonomy she had never enjoyed before, even during her reign. Her repeated insistence that her ministers and her nation allow her to mourn as and when she sees fit keeps her forever immune from the demands of public life; her privileging of private feeling over public responsibility has now become complete. Strachey repeatedly transcribes Victoria's letters justifying her supreme authority through her position as Albert's chief mourner: "I am anxious to repeat *one thing*," he quotes her as writing to her uncle the King of Hanover, "and *that one* is *my firm* resolve, my *irrevocable decision*, viz. that *his* wishes—*his* plans—are to be *my law!* And *no human power* will make me swerve from *what he* decided and wished" (p. 227). In a neat twist, it is Victoria herself—more usually the figure from whom others attempt to appropriate power—who borrows final authority from the figure of her dead husband.

Strachey's implication here, of course, is that Victoria's mourning may be seen as more than a little self-serving. Previously Victoria had left all her youthful "romances" with her manipulative ministers with largely tearless eyes. Albert's death allows Victoria to dwell on memories of the past, and thus gives her an excuse to avoid whatever political responsibilities she wishes; she can forsake London and Parliament for her vacation homes at Balmoral and Osborne whenever she so chooses. "She was the devoted guardian of a sacred trust," he notes. "Her place was in the inmost shrine of the house of mourning—where she alone had the right to enter, where she could feel the effluence of a mysterious presence, and interpret, however faintly and feebly, the promptings of a living soul" (p. 229). Although she describes her duty as Albert's sibyl as "terrible," Strachey is also clear that she understands it as the apotheosis of her power and glory, as when she declares, "I am on a dreary sad pinnacle of solitary grandeur" (p. 229).

Strachey's attitude toward Victoria's surmounting of this dreary, sad pinnacle is decidedly ambivalent. He naturally takes great pleasure in mocking Victoria's role as Albert's elegist, in that her aims are almost counter to his own in writing her biography. Whereas his task was to work from an antipathetic viewpoint in writing his biographies, the task Victoria sets for herself is "to impress the true nature of [the Prince Consort's] genius and character upon the minds of her subjects" (p. 235). Strachey goes out of his way to criticize the blameless porcelain angel stellified in Sir Robert Martin's official hagiography of Albert, which opposes Strachey's own biographical work not only in tone but in sheer mass as well. Strachey's disapprobation of the multivolume Martin biography is such that it prompts him to characterize Victoria, the prime mover behind the textual memorial, as nothing less than a failed elegist:

> [T]he public was the loser as well as Victoria. For in truth Albert was a far more interesting personage than the public dreamed. By a curious irony an impeccable waxwork had been fixed by the Queen's love in the popular imagination, while the creature whom it represented—the real creature, so full of energy and stress and torment, so mysterious and unhappy, and so fallible and so very human—had altogether disappeared. (p. 237)

Strachey's implication here cannot be missed: in contrast to Martin's and Victoria's artificial, inferior, and (in spite of itself) unsympathetic depiction of Albert, he suggests his own portrayal of the Prince Consort is both sincere and sympathetic in its depiction of all of Albert's flaws and failings. Strachey clearly considers himself here the superior elegist, the more honest and artful depictor of the dead.

Yet Strachey does not turn a blind eye toward the peculiar powers of Victoria's decades-long melancholia. He does not fail to credit her energy in promoting her cult of the Prince Consort, and once again links her effulgence of sentimentality with her ability to write fluently and unremittingly. Strachey, whose own writing came only with great hesitancy, effort, and mental distress, must have been tremendously impressed in retrospective consideration of how Victoria's melancholia loosened her prodigal pen even further: "Unceasingly the pen moved over the black-edged paper," he notes, as she pours out her sorrows in her diaries and letters, and promotes Albert's supposed intentions in her official communiqués (p. 234). Victoria's vitalism in her sentimental expostulation translates once again directly into the national mood, as her grief for Albert prompts a colossal commissioning of cenotaphs and memorial sculptures. Although Strachey makes great sport of the aesthetic deficiencies of the Albert Memorial in Hyde Park, his elaborate cataloguing of its physical statistics testifies to how impressed he is with the prodigality of Victorian sentiment made manifest in the memorial.

What strikes Strachey most profoundly about Victoria's melancholia, however, is not its effect on her ministers or her populace but rather its effect on himself as her biographer. As I noted earlier, Albert's death was the point where Strachey decided to curtail significantly the length of his biography, and Victoria's subsequent mourning prompts an admission of a curious lacuna within the text:

> The death of the Prince Consort was the central turning-point in the history of Queen Victoria. She herself felt that her true life had ceased with her husband's, and that the remainder of her days upon earth was of a twilight nature—an epilogue to a drama that was done. Nor is it possible that her biographer should escape a similar impression. For him, too, there is a darkness over the latter half of the long career. The first forty-two years of the Queen's life are illuminated by a great and varied quantity of authentic information. With Albert's death, a veil descends. Only occasionally, at fitful and disconnected intervals, does it lift for a moment or two; a few main outlines, a few remarkable details may be discerned; the rest is all conjecture and ambiguity. . . . [T]hough the Queen survived her great bereavement for almost as many years as she lived before it, the chronicle of those years can bear no proportion to the tale of her earlier life. (pp. 221–22)

Victoria's insistence on the privacy of her pain resists Strachey's work of bringing her life's events to public exposure. As the teasing image of the drawn veil suggests, she ultimately frustrated his task through her insistence on private feeling. Victoria's unending bereavement cannot be contained in Strachey's shortened *Trauerarbeit* for her; part of her forever eludes his grasp. Her melancholia keeps her from being wholly apprehended by the modern gaze, and indeed ensures that any "mourning" for her cannot be completed. Victoria's melancholia thus becomes transmitted not only within her own culture but also to later descendants such as Strachey himself. It becomes no wonder, then, that he felt he was losing his "war" against her, and was in danger of becoming subject to his own biographical subject.

Despite his repeated mockeries of the queen, Strachey's parting gesture to her shows his keen awareness of his generation's profound indebtedness to the Victorian energy and sentimentalism she typified. In the famous long sentence that closes the work, the dying monarch in effect recapitulates the events of the entire biography in reverse chronological order (beginning with her most recent memories of Disraeli and continuing backward through her life with Albert, her ministers, her mother, and finally to her childhood at Kensington Palace). In its smoothly flowing succession of impressionistic clauses, this final sentence decidedly departs stylistically from the rest of the biography's sentences, which partake of Strachey's typical Gibbonian measure.[49] Rather, as many commentators have remarked, it seems more akin to modernist stream of consciousness.[50] In dying, Victoria not only retroactively assumes agency for her life's events, making herself her own biographer (as if to counteract Strachey's authority to the last), but also dreams them up in a manner similar to the very form that most famously distinguishes the succeeding literary generation. Victoria's overflowing sentimental melancholia becomes recognized as the progenitor of an *écriture féminine*: her last sentence recalls the flowing monologues of a Molly Bloom, or of a Virginia Woolf—the latter in fact the dedicatee of *Queen Victoria*. The biography ends as it began, with a death that is also a birth; but this time the death makes possible not a new sovereign but a new mode of discourse. Only in death can Victoria become the mother to British modernism.

Conversely, Victoria also became, through Strachey's biography, herself a modernist creation. Even Virginia Woolf, who privately felt tremendous misgivings about Strachey's facetiousness in the biography, listed his Queen Victoria along with Prufrock and Ulysses as one of the quintessential modern character studies in her essay "Mr. Bennett and Mrs. Brown."[51] Later she would predict that "[i]n time to come Lytton Strachey's Queen Victoria will be Queen Victoria, just as Boswell's Johnson is Dr. Johnson."[52] Maurois would echo this statement, claiming in his Clark lectures that Strachey's creation was "more like Queen Victoria than the Queen Victoria of history."[53] Such a superseding of "the Victoria of history" is itself highly significant in that for the moderns Queen Victoria stood as the very metonymy of history—and of course to be "modern" meant in large part to deny history. Supplanting the Victoria of history with a fabricated queen of their own meant creating history in their own image. Even this new modernist Victoria, however, inevitably became another kind of "Victoria of history," constituted of the constellation of bourgeois attitudes and mores the moderns had come to think of as the Victorian past. In this she remained a potent figure, filled with the maternal authority and weight the moderns wished simultaneously to deny and to reclaim. What their ambivalent relation to Queen Victoria shows is the impossibility of modernism's wish to become free of its heritage.[54] Despite their intentions, the moderns remained, like their nineteenth-century bourgeois antitypes and antecedents, Victoria's subjects, thus preempting the conditions of their own "modernity."

Notes

1. As its very name implied, the "modern" movement in literature always assumed the priority of its own historical moment; thus it became important to assert a date when the present made an irrevocable rupture with the past. This propensity to suggest a key date has extended even to modernist criticism: Richard Ellmann has suggested that "1900 is both more convenient and more accurate than Virginia Woolf's 1910," while Harry Levin has famously proposed 1922 (the year of Proust's death as well as of the publication of Ulysses and The Waste Land) as the annus mirabilis of the movement. See Richard Ellmann, "Two Faces of Edward," in Golden Codgers (New York: Oxford University Press, 1973), p. 115; Harry Levin, "What Was Modernism?," in Refractions: Essays in Comparative Literature (New York: Oxford University Press, 1966), p. 283. For an excellent overview of the need of the modernists to periodize their own movement, see Malcolm Bradbury and James McFarlane, "The Name and Nature of Modernism," in Modernism, 1890–1930, ed. Malcolm Bradbury and James McFarlane (1976; rpt. New York: Penguin, 1991), pp. 19–55.

2. Virginia Woolf suggested December 1910 in her famous essay "Mr. Bennett and Mrs. Brown." See Virginia Woolf, "Mr. Bennett and Mrs. Brown," in The Captain's Death Bed and Other Essays (1950; rpt. London: Hogarth, 1915), p. 91.

3. D. H. Lawrence asserted in Kangaroo, "It was in 1915 the old world ended." D. H. Lawrence, Kangaroo (1923; rpt. New York: Viking, 1960), p. 220.

4. Edmund Gosse, "Queen Victoria," in More Books on the Table (London: William Heinemann, 1923), p. 3.

5. For an informative overview of the chaotic events surrounding Victoria's death, see Stanley Weintraub, Victoria: An Intimate Biography (New York: Dutton, 1987), pp. 632–43.

Jerrold M. Packard, *Farewell in Splendor: The Passing of Queen Victoria and Her Age* (New York: Dutton, 1995), also affords a useful account of Victoria's funerary procession from Osborne House through London to Windsor.

6. Gosse, "Queen Victoria," p. 3.

7. *The Parliamentary Debates, Fourth Series, Second Session of the Twenty-Seventh Parliament of the United Kingdom of Great Britain and Ireland*, vol. 89 (London: Wyman and Sons, 1901), pp. 19–20.

8. Samuel Hynes, *The Edwardian Turn of Mind* (Princeton: Princeton University Press, 1968), p. 15.

9. J. A. Hammerton, "Editor's Note," in *The Passing of Victoria: The Poet's Tribute* (London: Horace Marshall and Son, 1901), p. 5.

10. Weintraub, *Victoria*, pp. 639–40.

11. John Galsworthy, *The Forsyte Saga* (1918; rpt. New York: Charles Scribner's Sons, 1933), pp. 609–10.

12. Ibid., p. 610.

13. Hynes, *The Edwardian Turn of Mind*, p. 15.

14. Miss A. Farr, untitled poem, in *Poetical Tributes to the Memory of Her Most Gracious Majesty Queen Victoria*, ed. Charles F. Forshaw (London: Swan Sonnenschein and Co., 1901), p. 111.

15. Hynes, *The Edwardian Turn of Mind*, p. 15. Although usually in these poems Victoria's goddess aspect is benevolent (as in Arthur Sykes's "Victoria's Star," in Hammerton, *The Passing of Victoria*, p. 97), Flora Annie Steel actually conflates Victoria in one poem with the Indian death goddess Kali, terming both "Mothers-of-Many for Death or Life-giving." See her untitled poem in Forshaw, *Poetical Tributes*, p. 259.

16. Henry James to Oliver Wendell Holmes, Jr., February 20, 1901, in *Letters of Henry James*, vol. 4, *1895–1916* (Cambridge, Mass.: Harvard University Press, 1984), p. 184. James had earlier made a similar statement to his friends Clare and Clara Benedict on the very day of Victoria's death: "I feel as if her death will have consequences in and for this country that no man can foresee. . . . [T]he Queen's magnificent duration had held things magnificently— beneficently together and prevented all sorts of accidents. Her death, in short, will let loose incalculable forces for possible ill" (p. 181).

17. Mrs. B. Hailes, untitled poem, in Forshaw, *Poetical Tributes*, p. 154. See also, for example, F. Harald Williams, "It Is Well," in Hammerton, *The Passing of Victoria*, p. 46: "And she reigns indeed at length / In the calm of conscious strength— / *We* are dead, / And *we* are dreaming."

18. See Arthur A. Sykes, "Victoria's Star," in Hammerton, *The Passing of Victoria*, p. 98: "This night there shall be seen a sign / To mark the Empire-Mother's love / Continuing in the Land above, / A new star in the heav'ns will shine!"

19. Elizabeth Kirlew, untitled poem, in Forshaw, *Poetical Tributes*, p. 167; see also Captain Henderson's untitled poem, ibid., p. 151; Ella M. Dietz Glynes, "At Rest," and Arthur G. Symons, "Re-united," in Hammerton, *The Passing of Victoria*, pp. 92–96 and 136.

20. Galsworthy, *The Forsyte Saga*, p. 612. This is clearly a somewhat romanticized vision of the day of Victoria's funerary procession through London; even the *Times* reported that many of the thousands of spectators lost their tempers in the crush. A few observers reported being shocked by the absence of proper decorum: Arnold Bennett noted that "the people were not, on the whole, deeply moved, whatever the journalists may say, but rather serene and cheerful," while Max Beerbohm complained, "I have never seen such an air of universal jollity," adding, "[I]t is a city of ghouls." Still, by most accounts, the Londoners did their best to observe a respectably mournful air, and even the souvenir hawkers who reg-

ularly swept down upon such public spectacles kept entirely away; the *Times* congratulated the citizens of the empire for quelling their restlessness when the funerary bier approached, at which point "[their] demeanour was all that could be wished, all that could be expected of Englishmen and English women." See Packard, *Farewell in Splendor*, pp. 248–49. Whatever the actual reaction to Victoria's funeral, the accounts of Galsworthy and Gosse point to the necessity for Londoners at least to *remember* themselves as behaving with singular shock and decorum.

21. See Sigmund Freud, "Mourning and Melancholia," in *General Psychological Theory: Papers on Metapsychology*, ed. Philip Rieff (New York: Macmillan, 1963), pp. 164–79.

22. Thomas Hardy, "V.R. (1819–1901): A Reverie," in Hammerton, *The Passing of Victoria*, p. 15.

23. Gosse, "Queen Victoria," pp. 3–4.

24. George Bernard Shaw, "The Ugliest Statue in London" (1919), in *Bernard Shaw on the London Art Scene: 1885–1950*, ed. Stanley Weintraub (University Park: Pennsylvania State University Press, 1989), p. 428.

25. Elinor Glyn, *Romantic Adventure* (New York: E. P. Dutton, 1937), p. 98.

26. Ibid., pp. 98–99.

27. Laurence Housman, *Victoria Regina: A Dramatic Biography* (New York: Charles Scribner's Sons, 1934), pp. 11–12.

28. Leonard Woolf, *Sowing: An Autobiography of the Years 1880–1904* (London: Hogarth, 1970), p. 151–52.

29. James Joyce, *Ulysses*, ed. Hans Walter Gabler (New York: Random House, 1984), pp. 5, 36; subsequent citations are given in the text.

30. Virginia Woolf, "Royalty (I)," in *The Moment and Other Essays* (1947; rpt. London: Hogarth, 1981), p. 188.

31. Virginia Woolf, *The Diary of Virginia Woolf*, vol. 3, ed. Anne Olivier Bell (New York: Harcourt Brace Jovanovich, 1977), pp. 340–41.

32. Virginia Woolf, *Orlando* (1928; rpt. San Diego: Harcourt Brace Jovanovich, n.d.), pp. 229–30.

33. Virginia Woolf, *To the Lighthouse* (1927; rpt. San Diego: Harcourt Brace Jovanovich, n.d.), p. 25.

34. Quoted in Michael Holroyd, *Lytton Strachey: The New Biography* (New York: Farrar, Straus, and Giroux, 1944), p. 440.

35. Quoted ibid., p. 441.

36. Lytton Strachey, "Macaulay," in *The Shorter Strachey* (1980; rpt. London: Hogarth, 1989), p. 93.

37. Lytton Strachey, preface to *Eminent Victorians* (1918; rpt. London: Penguin, 1986), p. 9; subsequent citations are given in the text.

38. Raymond Mortimer, "Mrs. Woolf and Mr. Strachey," *The Bookman*, 68, no. 6 (February 1929): 626.

39. André Maurois, *Aspects of Biography*, trans. S. C. Roberts (Cambridge: Cambridge University Press, 1929), pp. 21–22. It should be noted that this rhetoric of Victoria conquering Strachey continues again and again in almost every review of the work; see, for example, Edgar Johnson, *One Mighty Torrent: The Drama of Biography* (1937; rpt. New York: Macmillan, 1955), p. 517; R. A. Scott-James, *Lytton Strachey* (London: Longmans, Green, and Co., 1955), p. 25; and David Cannadine, *The Pleasures of the Past* (London: Collins, 1989), p. 24. Don Marquis makes amusing reference to this battle between biographer and subject in his 1927 *Archy and Mehitabel*, where he describes the ghost of Queen Victoria arising every night "with the ghost / of a sceptre in her hand / to find mr lytton strachey / and bean him it seems she

beans / him and beans him and he / never knows it." See Don Marquis, *Archy and Mehitabel* (1927; rpt. Garden City, N.Y.: Doubleday, Doran, and Co., 1930), p. 171.

40. Holroyd, *Lytton Strachey: The New Biography*, p. 477.

41. Lytton Strachey to Ralph Partridge, July 26, 1920, quoted in Michael Holroyd, *Lytton Strachey: A Biography* (1971; rpt. London: Penguin, 1987), p. 783.

42. Strachey to Mary Hutchinson, August 14, 1920, quoted in Holroyd, *Lytton Strachey: The New Biography*, p. 475.

43. Strachey to Mary Hutchinson, October 4, 1920, quoted in Holroyd, *Lytton Strachey: The New Biography*, pp. 476–77.

44. Strachey to John Maynard Keynes, November 11, 1920, quoted in Holroyd, *Lytton Strachey: The New Biography*, p. 477.

45. Lytton Strachey, *Queen Victoria* (1921; rpt. San Diego: Harcourt Brace Jovanovich, n.d.), p. 59; subsequent citations are given in the text.

46. Carolyn Heilbrun, *Toward a Recognition of Androgyny* (New York: Knopf, 1973), p. 144.

47. Perry Meisel, *The Myth of the Modern: A Study of British Literature and Criticism After 1850* (New Haven: Yale University Press, 1987), p. 205.

48. Most subsequent biographers of Victoria have followed Strachey's lead (as they have in many things) by commencing the queen's story with the expiration of a member of the royal family, as if to underscore the importance of death to her life and her reign. Edith Sitwell, for example, opens her *Victoria of England* with the death of Victoria's father, the Duke of Kent, while E. F. Benson begins his narrative somewhat inexplicably with the death of Victoria's grandmother Queen Charlotte. Stanley Weintraub (*Victoria*, p. 25) returned to Strachey's model by beginning his biography of the queen (after a short prologue) with the death of the Princess Charlotte. See Edith Sitwell, *Victoria of England* (Boston: Houghton Mifflin, 1936), p. 1; E. F. Benson, *Queen Victoria* (London: Longmans, Green, 1935), p. 1.

49. The one significant exception to this is Victoria's breathless apprehension of the Great Exhibition, which also links this style of discourse to the onslaught of modernity. See Strachey, *Queen Victoria*, p. 148.

50. In "English Prose Between 1918 and 1939," for example, Forster alludes to its decidedly Freudian style: "[T]his last long lovely drifting sentence, with its imaginings of the subconscious, could not have been created at an earlier date." See E. M. Forster, "English Prose Between 1918 and 1939," in *Two Cheers for Democracy* (New York: Harcourt, Brace and World, 1951), p. 283. Herbert Read compared the sentence to Joyce to the detriment of Strachey, whom he accused of using clichés, although perhaps the genius of the sentence is its retranslation of tired Victorian phrases in this new modern syntax. See Herbert Read, "English Prose" (1926), in *A Coat of Many Colours* (New York: Horizon, 1956), pp. 87–99. Carolyn Heilbrun has complained that Victoria, "[b]eing too wholly feminine . . . has become only the passive rememberer of too-powerful men," although memory is hardly a "passive" enterprise for any writer in the age of Proust and Woolf, and none of the men Victoria remembers is ever much of a match for her in any case. See Heilbrun, *Toward a Recognition of Androgyny*, p. 146.

51. See Woolf, "Mr. Bennett and Mrs. Brown," p. 117.

52. Virginia Woolf, "The Art of Biography," in *The Death of the Moth and Other Essays* (London: Hogarth, 1942), p. 122.

53. Maurois, *Aspects of Biography*, p. 170.

54. Paul de Man has argued that modernity's assumption of a break with history only makes it, paradoxically, more dependent upon it since it must define itself against it. See Paul de Man, "Literary History and Literary Modernity," in *Blindness and Insight: Essays in the Rhetoric of Contemporary Criticism*, 2d ed., rev. (Minneapolis: University of Minnesota Press, 1983), pp. 142–65.

Major
and Minor
Reputations

T. S. Eliot and Hart Crane

✻   ✻   ✻

DAVID BROMWICH

B y 1940 T. S. Eliot had emerged as the representative English poet of modernism. This was one of those transitions that feel natural after they have happened—that can seem to settle a reputation once and for all with a finality mysterious to readers who witnessed the struggle for fame. Of such a moment it is always fair to ask how far the climax it affords is a trick of retrospect, a shadow we mistake for a necessary part of the landscape. What if Eliot's assimilation had occurred much faster? What if it had occurred more slowly, or on a more idiosyncratic basis? Eliot's letters and occasional criticism are sown with doubt and wonder at the definitive quality of his triumph. The way a few of his poems joined with a few of his polemical essays to secure a unique place for his poetic achievement is one of those inspired accidents that history casts up from time to time to challenge our determinisms. Of course, this was the outcome Eliot desired all along. But the readers who first cared for his poetry must have seen the possibility of a different development.

Suppose that his poetry had been spurned in every quarter of the literary establishment for a decade or two after *The Waste Land*. What then? Eventually he might have found a place among the unassimilables, the recessive geniuses of English poetry—the company of Collins and Beddoes rather than Donne and Dryden. There would have been much justice in this. The author of *Prufrock and Other Observations* was felt by his contemporaries to be an elusive and not an imposing presence. His charm lay most of all in the relief he offered from importance.[1] Nor did *The Waste Land* seem at first a drastic departure from the earlier sources of his appeal. It commanded respect as an experiment with voices, like "Prufrock" and the Sweeney poems. To think of it in that light may still be more pertinent than to honor it teleologically for the qualities it shares with *Ash Wednesday* and *Four Quartets*. The passing characters of the poem—Mrs. Porter, Mr. Eugenides, the Young Man Carbuncular—these figures were hardly notable for their continuous gravity. They were phantoms of a mind delicately questing after sensations, and their aim was "a new art emotion," to adapt a phrase from Eliot's criticism. Their creator appeared to be a poet averse to no stimulus, however morbid—a cautious welcomer of any experience, however drab—whose peculiarities of temperament had much to do with the dignity of his art.

Some of Eliot's essays of the period lend themselves to a similar description. "Hamlet and His Problems," now commonly read as a manifesto for dramatic objectivity, was a paradox in the vein of *The Authoress of the Odyssey*, a fit of character criticism against the character critics. Eliot's bogus primerlike title (which could be added to the books on the shelf in Beerbohm's caricature of Yeats: *Short Cuts to Mysticism, Half Hours with the Symbols, Reality: Its Cause and Cure, Hamlet and His Problems*) mocked the orderliness of his clinical tone. Even "Tradition and the Individual Talent," to a reader who weighed the chemical analogy in the second part as carefully as the axioms of culture in the first, could seem a late flower of the dandyism of Poe.[2] These essays were, among other things, deliberate curiosities, out-of-the-way solutions to problems the reader was meant to see as in no way impersonal. The solemn reception of Eliot's criticism in the next generation, as if it had been written by a more judicious Matthew Arnold, enhanced his stature in the short run only, and on dubious terms.

I have been trying to convey the susceptible mood in which the young Hart Crane would have approached the poetry of Eliot. But the obstacles to an adequate view of the subject have been placed by Crane as much as by Eliot. Open and impulsive as Crane's letters generally are, they give a misleading impression of this particular debt. His quotable statements of general aims and theories, which align his poetry with Eliot's, tend to take an adversarial stance when Eliot himself is in the picture. This happened, I think, in part because Crane had resolved early to write *The Bridge* as an answer to *The Waste Land*. Another motive may have been that his frequent correspondent in matters concerning Eliot was Allen Tate, a contemporary who shared Crane's advocacy of Eliot's poems but who was already, in their exchanges of letters in the 1920s, on the way to admiring Eliot as a prophet of civilization. The influence of "Gerontion" on the "Ode to the Confederate Dead" differs in character from the influence of *The Waste Land* on *The Bridge*. In the first case the relation is that of principle and illustration, in the second that of statement and counter-statement. Affinity seems a truer word than influence to describe the latter sort of kinship—a point I can bring out by comparing the early poems "La Figlia che Piange" and "My Grandmother's Love Letters."

Both poems address a feminine presence that is not quite maternal, and that is touched by erotic warmth; a presence whose memory must be appeased before the poet can venture into his own acts of love and imagination. Yet the poems exhibit, and exemplify for the sake of each poet's future, distinct uses of sympathy. Eliot's is a tenderness that will at last be detached from erotic passion, whereas Crane is seeking a temporary freedom from familial piety, earned by an intense avowal of such piety. Notwithstanding this divergence of motives, the poems share a single story and a music. The wish of the poets to serve as guardians at a scene of their former lives, protectors of something that was suffered there, is curiously blended with a self-command that makes them stand back from the scene. The result is a tone at the brink of an irony that neither poet entirely wants to formulate. The revealing point for comparison, it seems to me, is the "turn" of the poems—the place in each where the poet speaks of his seclusion from the image with which he began. In "La Figlia che Piange" that image is the glimpsed attitude of a woman at the top of a stair, holding a bunch of flowers; in "My Grandmother's Love Letters" it is the poet's view of a nook by a corner of the roof, where the letters have long been stored. Self-conscious in their bearing toward the women they write about, both poets are also safely hidden in their watching; and a sense of memory as a sheltering medium, protective for the rememberer and the image, touches with regret their knowledge of the person whose life cannot be recovered.

From this fortunate position—a voyeur but one not in search of a voyeur's pleasure—Eliot imagines a meeting with a possible consummation between the woman and a man. (The man, we are free to imagine, is the speaker himself in a different life.)

> So I would have had him leave,
> So I would have had her stand and grieve,
> So he would have left
> As the soul leaves the body torn and bruised,
> As the mind deserts the body it has used.
> I should find
> Some way incomparably light and deft,
> Some way we both should understand,
> Simple and faithless as a smile and shake of the hand.
>
> She turned away, but with the autumn weather
> Compelled my imagination many days,
> Many days and many hours:
> Her hair over her arms and her arms full of flowers.
> And I wonder how they should have been together!
> I should have lost a gesture and a pose.
> Sometimes these cogitations still amaze
> The troubled midnight and the noon's repose.[3]

The compromised interest of the observer has much in common with the attitude of a Jamesian narrator, though even by the terms of that analogy the speaker of "La Figlia che Piange" is evasive—calling his anxiety and bewilderment "cogitations" and his shadowy desire a concern with "a gesture and a pose." He is troubled most by an intimation that the woman is morally innocent, as he somehow is not. And yet her life will be filled to a depth of experience he does not hope to share.

A larger impulse of ordinary sympathy is at work in Crane's poem. He tries— one can feel the pressure of the effort—to associate his fancies with the actual life of the woman he writes about. Yet as his ingenuity stretches to cover the distance between them, the questions his poem asks take on a careful obliqueness like Eliot's. The love that his grandmother felt seems now so far off that, if he should cross the house to retrieve her letters, each step would feel like a passage of countless years:

Over the greatness of such space
Steps must be gentle.
It is all hung by an invisible white hair.
It trembles as birch limbs webbing the air.

And I ask myself:

"Are your fingers long enough to play
Old keys that are but echoes:
Is the silence strong enough
To carry back the music to its source
And back to you again
As though to her?"

Yet I would lead my grandmother by the hand
Through much of what she would not understand;
And so I stumble. And the rain continues on the roof
With such a sound of gently pitying laughter.[4]

I would, the phrase that governs the last several stanzas of Eliot's poem, is displaced by Crane to the last four lines; the entire closing montage of "La Figlia che Piange," with its surprising sudden exterior (a scene of both pathos and indifference), has been miraculously condensed. Crane has the same need to find "Some way incomparably light and deft, / Some way we both should understand" to connect person with person and present with past. Hence the difficult question he asks himself: whether he is strong enough "To carry back the music to its source / And back to you again / As though to her?" The phenomenal life of the world, which continues untroubled as before, at the ends of both of these poems may be a sign that the connection has not been achieved.

"La Figlia che Piange" and "My Grandmother's Love Letters" are linked more subtly by a seasonal counterpoint, Eliot's poem starting in spring and passing into autumn, Crane's set in an autumn that looks back on someone else's spring. There are resonances too between the sunlit and moonlit spaces in which the poems create their distinctive moods of stillness. And (the detail that feels most like conscious allusion) the separate line of "My Grandmother's Love Letters,"

It is all hung by an invisible white hair

recalls a line repeated in Eliot's opening stanza,

Weave, weave the sunlight in your hair

and never returned to in the later stanzas, the weight of which nevertheless carries implicitly through the rest of Eliot's poem. The closing notes of the poems differ perhaps by a nuance of decisiveness. Eliot ends with the amazement or bemusement that was for him at this period a familiar and almost a reassuring motif: one hears it in nearly the same key at the end of the monologue "Portrait of a Lady." By contrast, the sympathy Crane had begun with deepens, as he turns from this memory to other memories.

The sense that is rich in "My Grandmother's Love Letters," of a pity that touches the poet unaccountably from a slight but charged detail of the setting, has its own precedent elsewhere in Eliot. The penultimate stanza of "Preludes" confesses:

I am moved by fancies that are curled
Around these images, and cling:
The notion of some infinitely gentle
Infinitely suffering thing.

Three further lines close "Preludes" in a vein of average irony ("Wipe your hand across your mouth, and laugh. . . ."), but "My Grandmother's Love Letters" includes the fancies as if they would do without a retraction.

"Preludes" is the poem by Eliot that seems most steadily resonant in Crane's early work. Comprising discrete impressions of a city—several perspectives, offered by a "consciousness" or "conscience" not easily distinguishable into a single person—this poem's montage tries out the shifts of tense and mood that will be more gravely performed in *The Waste Land*. It covers a matter-of-fact range, not the intensities of Tiresias, without a claim of supervening authority and without the cues of false or true guidance which would come later, with the demand of Eliot's poetry that it be read as prophetic speech.[5]

For Crane I think the appeal of "Preludes" lay in its intuition of the city's unemphatic routine as an incitement to the poet.

The morning comes to consciousness
Of faint stale smells of beer
From the sawdust-trampled street
With all its muddy feet that press
To early coffee stands.
With the other masquerades
That time resumes,
One thinks of all the hands
That are raising dingy shades
In a thousand furnished rooms.

This landscape was often in Hart Crane's mind when he wrote his shorter poems of the 1920s; hints of it appear as late as the subway entry sequence of "The Tunnel." He remembered the same passage once in a sort of private joke in a letter: arrested drunk one night in 1927, "the next I knew the door crashed shut and I found myself behind the bars. I imitated Chaliapin fairly well until dawn leaked in, or rather such limited evidences of same as six o'clock whistles and the postulated press of dirty feet to early coffee stands."[6] The casual echoes have a wider meaning here. The most difficult task of Crane's poetry, as he comes close to saying elsewhere in his letters, is to connect the thought of an "infinitely gentle, infinitely suffering thing" with some surmise about the emotions proper toward the hands in those "thousand furnished rooms."

His first full response was "Chaplinesque":

We make our meek adjustments,
Contented with such random consolations
As the wind deposits
In slithered and too ample pockets.

For we can still love the world, who find
A famished kitten on the step, and know
Recesses for it from the fury of the street,
Or warm torn elbow coverts.

We will sidestep, and to the final smirk
Dally the doom of that inevitable thumb
That slowly chafes its puckered index toward us,
Facing the dull squint with what innocence
And what surprise!

And yet these fine collapses are not lies
More than the pirhouettes of any pliant cane;
Our obsequies are, in a way, no enterprise.
We can evade you, and all else but the heart:
What blame to us if the heart live on.

The game enforces smirks; but we have seen
The moon in lonely alleys make
A grail of laughter of an empty ashcan,
And through all sound of gaiety and quest
Have heard a kitten in the wilderness.

The poem answers directly with the poet's voice an experience "Preludes" reported as occurring once to someone, the experience that brought "Such a vision of the street / As the street hardly understands."

The "smirk" can seem a mystifying detail even to a reader who feels its rightness. It suggests the improbability of human contact in the city's crowds, where the "squint" looking for the main chance blots out every other concern. The tone is a good deal like "Wipe your hand across your face, and smile"; and maybe for a moment this poem is testing a similar note of scorn. Then the gesture is looked at differently: "The game enforces smirks; but we have seen / The moon in lonely alleys make / A grail of laughter. . . ." The game may be the one Walt Whitman spoke of in *Song of Myself*; "Looking with side-curved head curious what will come next, / Both in and out of the game and watching and wondering at it." Crane's mood suggests something of this poise and inquisitiveness. The kitten, a child of the city, has wandered in from outside the game, a chance embodiment of the "suffering thing." To keep it safe from the fury of the street is a charity worthy of Chaplin's tramp.[7]

The modern artist exists to invent a shelter for the most vagrant of sympathies. Crane said so in the letter to William Wright in which he also declared his interest in Chaplin:

I am moved to put Chaplin with the poets (of today); hence the "we." In other words, he, especially in "The Kid," made me feel myself, as a poet, as being "in the same boat" with him. Poetry, the human feelings, "the kitten," is so crowded out of the humdrum, rushing, mechanical scramble of today that the man who would preserve them must duck and camouflage for dear life to keep them or keep himself from annihilation. . . . I have tried to express these "social sympathies" in words corresponding somewhat to the antics of the actor.[8]

This summary brings to light the active impulse Crane speaks of missing in Eliot. But one must resist the temptation to suppose that either poet was aiming for effects the other accomplished. I doubt that Eliot, given the diffusive emotions that matter to him, would have thought of offering a setting to lines such as

> Recesses for it from the fury of the street

or

> And through all sound of gaiety and quest,

lines that are touchstones of the confidence and isolation of the man who wrote them. A certain striding eloquence seems natural to Crane, and fits with the truth he speaks to the antagonist of "Chaplinesque" (the boss or agent of the state, the character in Chaplin's films who sizes up the tramp with a lowering grimace): "We can evade you, and all else but the heart: / What blame to us if the heart live on." It is the reverse of Eliot's sentiment at the end of "Preludes": "The worlds revolve like ancient women / Gathering fuel in vacant lots." The steps of the women may look random as they cast about for bits of fuel, but a capricious determinism governs their smallest movement. At times the steps of the tramp will look no different. But "Chaplinesque" takes its buoyancy from a resolve—the mood of someone going somewhere—which the tramp asserts at irregular intervals. The forward motion is an illusion, of course, but one that Crane brings to enchanted reality by siding with this hero.

My comments on Eliot and Crane are shaped by an aesthetic judgment as personal as any other, but more widely shared, I believe, than historians of modern poetry have noticed. Prufrock and Other Observations and White Buildings seem to me among the greatest achievements of modernity, quite as original in what they accomplish as The Waste Land and The Bridge. One of the cheats of modernist theory, abetted by Eliot in "Ulysses, Order, and Myth" and embraced by Crane in the conception of his longer poems, was the supposition that the virtual order of human knowledge must stand in some interesting relation to literary form. It followed that one could make the modern world systematically intelligible for art by respecting and executing the proper form of a knowledge special to art—by viewing the novel, for example, as the genre of the "transcendent homelessness of the idea" (the phrase is Lukács's, from The Theory of the Novel). With modernism, genre itself briefly and misleadingly became, as it had been in the eighteenth century, a master clue to the earnestness of the author's claim to represent reality. To poets like Eliot and Crane, this suggested the tactical propriety of expanding the lyric to claim again the scope of the epic. Of the pretensions of high modernism, none has dated so badly as this.

The Waste Land and The Bridge were not assisted imaginatively by the encyclopedic ambition to which they owe their conspicuous effects of structure. The miscellaneous texture of the poems is truer to their motives. A little more consistently than Eliot's early poems, The Waste Land divides into two separate registers for the portrayal of the city, the first reductive and satirical, the second ecstatic and agonistic—the latter, in order to be released, often seeming to require the pressure of a quotation. At any moment a detail such as "The sound of horns and motors, which shall bring / Sweeney to Mrs. Porter in the spring" may modulate to a style less easily placed:

> O City city, I can sometimes hear
> Beside a public bar in Lower Thames Street,
> The pleasant whining of a mandoline
> And a clatter and a chatter from within
> Where fishmen lounge at noon: where the walls
> Of Magnus Martyr hold
> Inexplicable splendour of Ionian white and gold.

Although the transitions of *The Bridge* are less clear-cut, part of Crane's method lies in a pattern of allusions to *The Waste Land*. This plan had emerged as early as his letter of September 11, 1927, to Otto H. Kahn, and later, piece by piece, in the echoes he found of Phlebas and Phoenician, who "Forgot the cry of gulls, and the deep sea swell / And the profit and loss"—lines that haunted him already in "For the Marriage of Faustus and Helen."

Let us turn to a kind of allusion more precisely dependent on context. Eliot in *The Waste Land*, himself looking back to Shakespeare's *Tempest*, overhears a character in "The Fire Sermon" in an unexplained trance of thought,

> While I was fishing in the dull canal
> On a winter evening round behind the gashouse
> Musing upon the king my brother's wreck
> And on the king my father's death before him.

Pondering those lines in "The River," Crane added to the Old World image of destiny the local accretions of a childhood in the American Midwest. The effect is a startling recovery and transformation:

> Behind
> My father's cannery works I used to see
> Rail-squatters ranged in nomad raillery.
> The ancient men—wifeless or runaway
> Hobo-trekkers that forever search
> An empire wilderness of freight and rails.
> Each seemed a child, like me, on a loose perch,
> Holding to childhood like some termless play.
> John, Jake or Charley, hopping the slow freight
> —Memphis to Tallahassee—riding the rods,
> Blind fists of nothing, humpty-dumpty clods.

The allegory of both poets tells of a child set loose from his moorings; but discrete elements of erotic feeling are at work in the two passages.[9] The poet's distance from the allegory is widened by Eliot as far as possible. It is narrowed by Crane to an unembarrassed intimacy with the humble materials from which any cultural myth can be made.

The Bridge, like *The Waste Land*, is spoken by a man reluctant to conquer a landscape he imagines in the form of a woman, a landscape which itself has suffered the assault of earlier generations of men. The king of *The Waste Land* owns an inheritance that has shrunk to nothing. At its outer reach he is dimly conscious of the Thames maidens who "can connect / Nothing with nothing." The same intimation of despair is in the familiar landscape of the child Hart Crane as he watches the hobo-trekkers, but in *The Bridge* the possibility of connection is not despised:

> They lurk across her, knowing her yonder breast
> Snow-silvered, sumac-stained or smoky blue—
> Is past the valley-sleepers, south or west.
> —As I have trod the rumorous midnights, too.

The narrator of the last line is noticeably mortal, and idiosyncratic in what he confides, unlike the Tiresias of *The Waste Land*.

Tiresias was fated to endure sexual experience as a man and a woman, then punished with blindness by Hera for his report that woman's pleasure was greater, and, in compensation, rewarded with the gift of prophecy by Zeus. His self-knowledge, as the poem presents it, is a version of all knowledge. "As I have trod the rumorous midnights, too" implies a more local and personal claim. It is possible that this narrator, too, has known experience in both sexes. If so he has evidently derived feelings of potency from both. And if the word *rumorous* is a further memory of Eliot—"aetherial rumours / Revive for a moment a broken Coriolanus"—the roughs of the "empire wilderness of freight and rails" connect the memory with a different nostalgia.

The paths a single echo may suggest are a consequence of disparate conceptions of poetic authority. When the speaker of "The Fire Sermon" sits down and weeps "by the waters of Leman," he imagines a fraternity shared with the lamenter of Psalms, a kind of fellowship that is possible only across time. The rail-squatters "ranged in nomad raillery" speak of a casual traffic among the traditions of the living; and American folk songs, some of them named in "The River," are a reminder of the energy of such traditions. You make a world in art, Crane seems to have believed, out of fragments knowable as parts of the world.[10] With his submission to the sundry data of life—a gesture unmixed with contempt—the speaker of "The River" admits a fact of his personal life, namely, that he has had a childhood: something (odd as it feels to say so) that cannot be said of the narrator of *The Waste Land*. Crane is able here to discover a pathos foreign to Eliot, even in a line,

> Blind fists of nothing, humpty-dumpty clods,

which itself has a strong foreshadowing in Eliot's "I will show you fear in a handful of dust" (as also in "other withered stumps of time"). "Blind fists of nothing" implies an energy in purposeless action that Eliot withholds from all his characters. The defeats or casualties in *The Bridge* are accepted as defeats without being accounted final. Sex is the motive of this contrast, with Eliot's plot steadily allying sexual completion and disgust—an event and a feeling that Crane may link incidentally, as he does in "National Winter Garden" and "The Tunnel," without implying that these show the working out of an invariable law.

Crane wrote several letters about *The Bridge* and *The Waste Land*. Only one of them says his purpose is the antithesis of Eliot's, and he offers the comparison as a hint rather than an assertion: "The poem, as a whole, is, I think, an affirmation of experience, and to that extent is 'positive' rather than 'negative' in the sense that *The Waste Land* is negative."[11] Because of its use by the pragmatists James and Dewey, "experience," in the 1920s, was a word charged with specifically American associations. It was apt to serve a common argument that the individual—most of all the individual in a democracy—possessed among his inward resources a field of experiment sufficient to define an idea of freedom. Thus, the kind of potency Crane would ascribe to the Mississippi River belonged also to personal consciousness and imagination:

> The River, spreading, flows—and spends your dream.

Eliot's preoccupations were closer to metaphysical realism, and likely in the 1920s, as they were later, to allude with some urgency to a claim on behalf of reality. Knowledge of reality was, by definition, almost impossible to obtain, and that made the requirement of such knowledge all the more pressing. Eliot's usual metaphors when these concerns are in view—metaphors that have a source in the philosophy of F. H. Bradley—picture a realm where knowledge is complete, intelligible and integral, yet by its nature undisclosed to individual consciousness. The nearest one can get to a sense of solidarity in experience is by imagining a sequence of identical privations, each knowing the character of the others because its contents mirror the contents of all others:

> I have heard the key
> Turn in the door once and turn once only
> We think of the key, each in his prison
> Thinking of the key, each confirms a prison.

The comfort this thought brings may be a sort of knowledge, but it is knowledge at the cost of experience, and what it confirms is a negation of freedom.

These theoretical self-definitions would have come home to Crane implicitly enough; I think he understood how much was at stake when he talked of "positive" and "negative." *The Waste Land* is a progress poem of a sort: it moves continuously through its series of sure-to-be-missed connections, in which every episode must prove to have been foresuffered. The structure of the poem is that of a theme and variations. The apparently chance encounters, improvised meetings, and assignations disclose themselves as versions of a single story which underlies the adventitious shifts of age and custom. A truth thus lies in wait beneath the accumulation of masks—a truth not susceptible to the inflections of personal will. There is no aspect or coloring of life that will not be known in advance to Tiresias. The progress of *The Bridge* feels just as repetitive but is harder to follow since it aims to resemble a process of growth. The poem loses what can be lost for the sake of a gain in experience; its recognitions have ceased to be an affair of the guilty living and the unburied dead:

> "Stetson!
> "You who were with me in the ships at Mylae!
> "That corpse you planted last year in your garden,
> "Has it begun to sprout?"

Eliot's style is dramatic and satirical—a choice emphasized in his splendid recording of the poem, with its dryness and air of continuous command. Whereas, in *The Waste Land*, nothing can come of any memory that is reengaged, *The Bridge* offers another kind of memory: a meeting of eyes in which "the stubborn years gleam and atone," as the ranger's mother says in "Indiana."

It is an American hope to seek atonement through experience alone. For that reason I think Yvor Winters was right to associate *The Bridge* with *Song of Myself* (Crane's poem, he observed, "has no more unity than [Whitman's]"),[12] though he was wrong to suppose that this description entailed a self-evident rebuke. *The Bridge* and *Song of Myself* have the same kind of unity—of mood, texture, urgency and enterprise. Crane was conscious early of this link to Whitman, one token of which appears in "For the Marriage of Faustus and Helen." The poet presents himself in the midst of a crowd, anonymous and loitering until his name is called; the passage mingles the thought of Whitman with an echo of Eliot forgetting "the profit and loss":

> And yet, suppose some evening I forgot
> The fare and transfer, yet got by that way
> Without recall,—lost yet poised in traffic.
> Then I might find your eyes across an aisle,
> Still flickering. . . .

The traffic makes it possible to lose oneself "without recall," shorn of a past, and yet to get by, to be on the move and somehow poised. The flickering carries a range of suggestions: of a face in back of a blind; a face suggestive by its lines, though hard to see in the glancing lights of the traffic; a face in which the eyes themselves may be blinking. The aisle seems a metaphor for the canyons dividing the facades of New York's skyscrapers, or the passage between the rows of a cinema—which in turn would give a further sense to the flickering.

In "Faustus and Helen," as in *The Bridge*, eyes know more than they are conscious of; and Crane's thought once again comes from Whitman: "Who knows, for all the distance, but I am as good as looking at you now, for all you cannot see me?" From "Prufrock" on, the eyes in Eliot's poetry are uncertain that knowledge is to be desired. His eyes alight gently but do not fix; they are cast down or averted—part of a face they help you to prepare "to meet the faces that you meet." It is fitting that Crane's most tormenting poem of love should have been a countersong to "Prufrock." There are other antithetical features of "Possessions," the title of which (with its overtones of demonic possession) works against the sense of material property or furnishings. It might have been called "Dispossessions":

> Witness now this trust! the rain
> That steals softly direction
> And the key, ready to hand—sifting
> One moment in sacrifice (the direst)
> Through a thousand nights the flesh
> Assaults outright for bolts that linger
> Hidden,—O undirected as the sky

> *That through its black foam has no eyes*
> *For this fixed stone of lust . . .*
>
> *Accumulate such moments to an hour:*
> *Account the total of this trembling tabulation.*
> *I know the screen, the distant flying taps*
> *And stabbing medley that sways—*
> *And the mercy, feminine, that stays*
> *As though prepared.*
>
> *And I, entering, take up the stone*
> *As quiet as you can make a man . . .*
> *In Bleecker Street, still trenchant in a void,*
> *Wounded by apprehensions out of speech,*
> *I hold it up against a disk of light—*
> *I, turning, turning on smoked forking spires,*
> *The city's stubborn lives, desires.*
>
> *Tossed on these horns, who bleeding dies,*
> *Lacks all but piteous admissions to be spilt*
> *Upon the page whose blind sum finally burns*
> *Record of rage and partial appetites.*
> *The pure possession, the inclusive cloud*
> *Whose heart is fire shall come,—the white wind rase*
> *All but bright stones wherein our smiling plays.*

The first line ends with a pun on "tryst," and the entreaty here of a witness or accomplice is ventured with much of Prufrock's urgency: "Oh do not ask what is it." But this scene of turmoil has obstructions that not only impede but chafe and penetrate; compare the lines of "Prufrock,"

> *It is impossible to say just what I mean!*
> *But as if a magic lantern threw the nerves in patterns on a screen:*
> *Would it have been worth while*

with the unreluctant answer of "Possessions":

> *I know the screen, the distant flying taps*
> *And stabbing medley that sways,*
> *And the mercy, feminine, that stays.*

The contrast follows from Crane's determination to write of a desire on the other side of satisfaction, to make a "Record of rage and partial appetites." So the wariness of

> *The eyes that fix you in a formulated phrase,*
> *And when I am formulated, sprawling on a pin,*
> *When I am pinned and wriggling on the wall,*
> *Then how should I begin*
> *To spit out all the butt-ends of my days and ways?*

gives way to an agonized embrace:

I, turning, turning on smoked forking spires,
The city's stubborn lives, desires.

Crane's speaker has grown old with the spent vehemence of youth, but it is Eliot's who has the lighter step: "Prufrock" is a young man's poem about age.

And yet in "Possessions" the language of "Prufrock" has been so assimilated that its ending can seem to occur the moment after "human voices wake us and we drown." The spray of the sea, in which Prufrock's mermaids were glimpsed, is taken up in "The pure possession, the inclusive cloud" that marks the conquests and surrenders of the later poet, now burnt forever into the city's memory. "Possessions" is a homosexual poem, defiantly so. But the remarkable uncollected lyric "Legende," written when Crane was nineteen, gives a feminine motive to the same image of erotic possession and erasure. The woman there "has become a pathos,—/ Waif of the tides"; the poet closes by saying, "even my vision will be erased / As a cameo the waves claim again." This sense of the good of rendering a life permanent, even as its detail is burned away, would be constant in Crane's work: that is a reason for the *we* of "Possessions" to imitate the Dantesque *we* of "Prufrock," though with a shift of emphasis. Prufrock's companion had to be knowledgeable in the ways of erotic hunger, regret, and repetition, but was largely a pretext for dramatic confidences. Crane's use of the word includes himself and his lover.

A last comparison will bring out the delicacy with which Crane could portray erotic contact as a hint of some larger acknowledgment that was never to be spoken. For his provocation he turned again to *The Waste Land* and particularly to the lines that follow the imperative "Datta":

The awful daring of a moment's surrender
Which an age or prudence can never retract
By this, and this only, we have existed. . . .

Crane's echo, at once violently explicit and curiously tacit, speaks of

       sifting
One moment in sacrifice (the direst)
Through a thousand nights the flesh
Assaults outright for bolts that linger
Hidden.

There had always been in Eliot a need to cherish the personal relation as an enigma, which by its nature belonged to a realm of untouchable grace and self-sacrifice. The anxiety of physical surrender is lest you be given something that was not yours to take: "That is not what I meant at all, / That is not it, at all." But Crane's interest is always to take everything. What survives his experience will be preserved elsewhere—it is not for him to say where—as elusive as "bright stones wherein our smiling plays." The ironic phrase at the point where memory hopes to recover something more palpable—"Accumulate such moments to an hour: / Account the total of this trembling tabulation"—suggests the view of a dry impartiality that will dispense with the work of recovery. For the idea of counting such moments is bound to be false; they are really one moment "that stays / As though prepared."

I have been discussing Crane's poetry and his temperament and personal traits as if these things were plainly related. Yet he is one of those poets who can persuade many readers much of the time that his poetry has shed any empirical relation to a life. One might tell a convincing story about his writing in which the ordinary elements, including the feelings he had for other writers, almost vanished. He would appear then as a romantic hero, uneasily committed in his early years to the "tremorous" moments he invoked in "Legend"—the first poem and in many ways the signature of *White Buildings*—but gravitating at last to a poetry unconfined by chance encounters with the actual world. No poet has written many poems outside those limits. Coleridge did it in "Kubla Khan," and Swinburne in "At a Month's End." Crane may have felt he was crossing a similar threshold when he wrote "Voyages VI." It is something to be the kind of writer for whom such a thought is possible.

On this view of his career, its fable of initiation is "Passage." For, like no other poem by Crane, "Passage" signals a break from experience. But what is impressive is how far even there the landscapes of Eliot, his cadences, and his imaginative predicament become for Crane a prophecy of what he himself must and must not become. In the allegory of the poem, the author is challenged to account for his life by an unnamed figure of admonition. The presence of such a figure is an artistic given—his life from the start has been a scene of risk. "Dangerously the summer burned / (I had joined the entrainments of the wind)," he declares, translating *entraîne-ment* as rapture or enthusiasm. The inquest continues as the weight of the landscape intensifies:

> The shadows of boulders lengthened my back:
> In the bronze gongs of my cheeks
> The rain dried without odour.
> "It is not long, it is not long;
> See where the red and black
> Vine-stanchioned valleys—": but the wind
> Died speaking through the ages that you know
> And hug, chimney-sooted heart of man!
> So was I turned about and back, much as your smoke
> Compiles a too well-known biography.

As in "Emblems of Conduct"—where we are told, of any present moment in art, "By that time summer and smoke were past"—smoke is a figure for a life whose pathos can be captured in a story. The Crane of "Passage" was turning away from such stories, as Eliot, at the end of *The Waste Land*, had done in the hope of subduing his inheritance. But there is no such hope and no acceptance in "Passage": its pledge is to master a fate that will elude any witness or historian of conduct. The poem bequeaths the poet to desires without a possessor, desires harbored and acted upon, to which writing will be a weak secondary clue. *Your* smoke—the possessive pronoun is impersonal, its grammar that of Hamlet's "There are more things in heaven and earth, Horatio, / Than are dreamt of in your philosophy." More is at stake in a life than the smoke that tells the story will ever compile.

Here is his source in Eliot:

> *What are the roots that clutch, what branches grow*
> *Out of this stony rubbish? Son of man,*
> *You cannot say, or guess, for you know only*
> *A heap of broken images, where the sun beats,*
> *And the dead tree gives no shelter, the cricket no relief,*
> *And the dry stone no sound of water. Only*
> *There is shadow under this red rock,*
> *(Come in under the shadow of this red rock),*
> *And I will show you something different from either*
> *Your shadow at morning striding behind you*
> *Or your shadow at evening rising to meet you;*
> *I will show you fear in a handful of dust.*

The passage, from "The Burial of the Dead," offers the first sign that the dread of the Waste Land has a metaphysical dimension. That poem ends with a gesture of reserve that commits the poet to an ordering of life, however provisional; a gesture honorable in its modesty, when considered beside the fear and apathy the poem as a whole has described. At the end of "Passages" Crane, too, breaking one spell to cast another, faces a barren sea from the land's end where memory has set him down. It is here that he asks:

> *What fountains did I hear? what icy speeches?*
> *Memory, committed to the page, had broke.*

He may yet be released into a life more intoxicating than anything memory could yield.

What that life will be the man who prays for it "cannot say, or guess," not because he has ceased to exist, but because the thing he will be is unwritten. Crane lived to make few examples of the poetry that here beckons to him. After "Voyages VI" one can count "The Dance" and perhaps "O Carib Isle!" as efforts of an unexampled pressure of purpose. These are poems of agony—"I could not pluck the arrows from my side"—a record of suffering that testifies against the healing of the sufferer:

> *Let not the pilgrim see himself again*
> *For slow evisceration bound like those huge terrapin*
> *Each daybreak on the wharf, their brine-caked eyes;*
> *—Spiked, overturned; such thunder in their strain!*

But from the first there was another order of poetry that mattered to Crane, and that represents him as faithfully. An agnostic naturalism persisted from "Repose of Rivers" to "The Broken Tower." As one looks back on that span of work, its dominant note comes, one cannot fail to see, not just from the city but from the city of Eliot. What is true of "Chaplinesque" and "Possessions" is also true of "Recitative" and "To Brooklyn Bridge" and "The Tunnel." To say these poems were achieved in dialogue would be to assert too little for the poems and too little for both poets. Crane wrote poetry of a kind unimaginable without Eliot; and the accomplishment of Eliot feels somehow larger in this light.

Notes

1. E. M. Forster tells of reading Eliot's early poems during the First World War and getting from them the kind of satisfaction he found in À Rebours: "Oh, the relief of a world which lived for its sensations and ignored the will. . . . Was it decadent? Yes, and thank God. Yes; here again was a human being who had time to feel and experiment with his feelings, to taste and smell and arrange books and fabricate flowers, and be selfish and be himself." The difference between Eliot and Huysmans was that

> the poems were not epicurean; still, they were innocent of public-spiritedness: they sang of private disgust and diffidence, and of people who seemed genuine because they were unattractive or weak. The author was irritated by tea parties, and not afraid to say so, with the result that his occasional "might-have-beens" rang out with the precision of a gong. . . . Here was a protest, and a feeble one, and the more congenial for being feeble. For what, in that world of gigantic horror, was tolerable except the slighter gestures of dissent?

See E. M. Forster, "T. S. Eliot," in *Abinger Harvest* (New York, 1955), pp. 84–85.

2. Yvor Winters interpreted the essay this way in "T. S. Eliot, or The Illusion of Reaction," in *The Anatomy of Nonsense*, reprinted in *In Defense of Reason* (Denver, 1947), one of the few original-minded estimates of Eliot from a critic of the next generation.

3. All quotations from Eliot's poetry are from T. S. Eliot, *The Complete Poems and Plays 1909–1950* (New York, 1962).

4. All quotations from Crane's poetry are from Hart Crane, *Complete Poems and Selected Letters and Prose*, ed. Brom Weber (New York, 1966).

5. Richard Poirier, *Robert Frost: The Work of Knowing* (New York, 1979), chap. 1, has a pertinent appreciation of "Preludes."

6. Quoted in John Unterecker, *Voyager: A Life of Hart Crane* (New York, 1969), p. 518. "Limited evidence" seems also an echo of the phrase "Or other testimony of summer nights," from "The Fire Sermon."

7. On the relation between "Chaplinesque" and Chaplin's film *The Kid*, see P. Adams Sitney, "The Poet as Film Viewer: Hart Crane's 'Chaplinesque,'" *Motion Picture*, no. 1 (1986).

8. Letter of October 17, 1921, in *The Letters of Hart Crane*, ed. Brom Weber (Berkeley, 1952), p. 68.

9. In *Transmemberment of Song* (Stanford, 1987), p. 211, Lee Edelman notices, in a different connection, Crane's allusion to the passage from "The Fire Sermon."

10. On "The River" and its incorporation of motifs from the popular culture of the time, see John Irwin, "Back Home Again in Indiana: Hart Crane's *The Bridge*," in *Romantic Revolutions*, ed. Kenneth Johnston et al. (Bloomington, Ind., 1990), pp. 269–96.

11. Letter to Selden Rodman of May 22, 1930, in *Letters*, p. 351.

12. The judgment occurs in his review of *The Bridge* entitled "The Progress of Hart Crane," reprinted in *The Uncollected Essays and Reviews of Yvor Winters*, ed. Francis Murphy (Chicago, 1973), p. 75. For an excellent discussion of Crane's poetic and ethical relationship to Whitman, see Langdon Hammer, *Janus–Faced Modernism* (Princeton, N.J. 1993), chaps. 5–7.

Remaking Marxist Criticism

Partisan Review's
Eliotic Leftism, 1934–1936

▦　　　▦　　　▦

HARVEY TERES

I

It has now been a quarter century since the publication of Fredric Jameson's *Marxism and Form* (1971), arguably the most important volume of Marxist criticism published in the United States in the postwar period. Brought out by Princeton University Press at a time when Marxist criticism had little influence among American critics, the book at first did not gain a wide audience. Only gradually, as the 1970s wore on, and it became one of the most important critical texts to a generation of young scholars politicized by the antiwar, feminist, and minority movements of the 1960s. Jameson's book inaugurated a new phase of Marxist criticism in this country, in which the orientation became Continental, the subject literary form rather than content, the mode theoretical, and the manner complex and technical, yet at its best lucid and urbane. The contributions of this criticism have been substantial: it has reconsidered and revised our understanding of nearly every major category of traditional Marxist thought, including class, causation, base and superstructure, production, ideology, and form; and it has expanded other categories such as culture, gender, and race. This has earned for Marxist and materialist criticism unprecedented stature within the academy. Compared with the last great heyday of Marxist criticism in the United States in the 1930s, the current efflorescence is already of greater duration, although threats from inside and especially outside the academy continue to make its existence controversial if not precarious.

Ironically, one factor that has helped neo-Marxism gain respectability within the academy has been its amnesia with regard to earlier, indigenous efforts at Marxist criticism. In his prefatory appeal to a largely academic audience to consider Marxism anew, Jameson himself quite seriously misrepresented this earlier tradition. By ignoring its actual diversity, and the degree to which it was vilified if not suppressed by New Critics during the postwar period, he lost an opportunity to recover examples of accomplished, engaged, and indigenous left-wing criticism that were analogous to the European examples he attended to.[1] Jameson is worth quoting at length:

> When the American reader thinks of Marxist literary criticism, I imagine that it is still the atmosphere of the 1930's which comes to mind. The burning issues of those days—anti-Nazism, the Popular Front, the relationship between literature and the labor movement, the struggle between Stalin and Trotsky, between Marxism and anarchism—generated polemics which we may think back on with nostalgia but which no longer correspond to the conditions of the world today. The criticism practiced then was of a relatively untheoretical, essentially didactic nature, destined more for use in the night school than in the graduate seminar, if I may put it that way; and has been relegated to the status of an intellectual and historical curiosity. . . . (p. ix)

Jameson's condescension, however auspicious it turned out to be for the institutionalization of Marxist criticism, nonetheless did a disservice by classifying an entire era of left-wing criticism on the basis of its most vulgar expressions. By dismissing American criticism with a close connection to actual political movements as tendentious and reductive, and by claiming elsewhere that Anglo-American criticism as a whole was suffused with bourgeois empirical modes both myopic and reactionary, Jameson's turn to Europe, with its own series of binarisms, did not escape the Manichaeanism he deplored in others. This turn seemed to preclude the possibility of comparative study and certainly discouraged further exploration into native left-wing criticism.

There was another problem with the new academic variety of Marxism. Aside from a suggestive, penultimate sentence about criticism's obligation to remain critical and "to keep alive the idea of a concrete future" (p. 416), Jameson remained silent on the question of commitment. Indeed, one of the interesting paradoxes of the dramatic politicization of theory and criticism during the past decade or so is that it has often been confined to the politics of criticism alone, as if this could be separated from the politics of the critic as citizen—as voter, as activist, as an individual with active political beliefs and commitments. The highly politicized debates taking place over modernism and postmodernism, discourse and ideology, "high" and "low" culture, canons and conventions, and even issues of race and gender have occurred largely without crucial reference to political events, movements, causes, or constituencies outside the academy. Thus, many academic critics who espouse a generally leftist or progressive perspective have done so with little regard for the actual consequences their views have for a democracy of informed citizens. Fortunately, there have been exceptions to the rule. An increasing number of studies have explored the achievements and the limitations of the native tradition of left-wing criticism, whose connections to nonacademic constituencies were relatively strong by comparison with current left-wing criticism. The so-called New York intellectuals have been a focus of a good deal of this interest, largely because in their early years their commitments were to radical politics, literary experimentalism, and rigorous literary and cultural criticism.[2]

In what follows I hope to contribute to this renewed interest by examining the changes in critical concepts, values, and language which constituted *Partisan Review*'s subtle critique of orthodox Marxist criticism during the mid-1930s. I look specifically at the appropriation of key concepts from T. S. Eliot's early criticism by William Phillips and Philip Rahv, the founders and chief editors of *Partisan Review*, who were attempting to turn their fledgling "little" magazine into a forceful critical and experimental center of the proletarian literary movement. I make two claims for the importance of this short-lived but nonetheless important critical project. First, historically it has interest for us as a relatively neglected moment in American left-wing criticism when Marxism was injected with non-Marxist critical concepts in order to render it more supple and complex. Second, Phillips's and Rahv's flawed but nonetheless compelling attempt to revise orthodox Marxist criticism bears comparison with European and neo-Marxist analogues. With regard to this latter claim, given the limitations of space, I shall have to be content to suggest but a few pertinent analogies rather than to spell them out at length. My hope is that I might interest others in pursuing specific connections, as well as in pursuing the broader comparative project that is necessary in order to better understand left-wing criticism past and present.

As to the Eliotic sources of Phillips's and Rahv's critical project, it is no secret that they and many other New York intellectuals were heavily indebted to Eliot: every historian of the New York intellectuals has commented on the connection, and Phillips in his memoirs explicitly states that Eliot, and especially *The Sacred Wood*, served as his earliest introduction to modernism and "the new, complex questions of criticism."[3] Although Eliot was not the only major influence on Phillips and Rahv— Edmund Wilson, Van Wyck Brooks, James T. Farrell, and obviously Marx himself were also highly influential[4]—Eliot was nonetheless for them the critic to be reckoned with, as indeed he was for so many writers and critics from the 1920s through midcentury. Yet it remains to explore in detail just how systematic Phillips's and Rahv's appropriation was, and what the results were for their renewal of Marxist criticism during the first two years of *Partisan Review*'s long life.[5]

To readers familiar with the many attacks on Eliot's crypto-fascism, his antisemitism, his misogyny, his traditionalism, and his mandarinism, attacks that have contributed to a discernible decline in his reputation, it may come as a surprise that his contributions had anything to do with renewing left criticism. But the politics of Eliot's early criticism, and by implication that of many modernist texts, have never been as transparent as many make them out to be. In truth their ideological valences have been multiple and shifting, and although reactionary ideology has played no small part in helping to shape their politics, it has not necessarily been determinate. A text's politics depends on a complex interplay between embedded ideological configurations and possibilities on the one hand, and groups of readers responding to both these textual pressures and the pressures and limits of an ensemble of social relations on the other. No text, I argue implicitly, contains its own determinate ideological identity; it contains only dispositions, which are either developed or altered according to the desires and interests of contingent readers.

II

Had the twentieth-century likeness of Meyer Schapiro's urban promenader walked the streets of New York in the winter of 1934, he might have happened upon one of the increasing number of newsstands in the city to carry leftist publications.[6] There he would perhaps have noticed among the assortment of magazines the first issue of *Partisan Review*, then a tiny proletarian "little" magazine and only later, of course, the powerhouse of literary and cultural criticism of the 1940s through the 1960s. Had this wanderer not been possessed of some knowledge of leftist political circles, he would undoubtedly have been confused about this new magazine's outlook, for all indications were that it was assiduously avant-garde. In its physical makeup and design, it resembled a makeshift product of the Soviet constructivist style of the 1920s. Its cover was of coarse, poor-quality paper, pale white in color. Rising across the cover, outlined in pencil-thin blue ink and dynamically aslant to the left were the three-dimensional block letters "JRC," for the little-known John Reed Club. Superimposed over these was the magazine's name, urgently proclaimed in a banner headline. And at the lower right, the contents and contributors were listed in a smaller typeface.

Taking in these details, the wanderer would no doubt have concluded that here was another "highbrow" magazine offering difficult, experimental writing; had the term by then gained wide currency, he might have assumed that he was looking at another "modernist" little magazine. Nor would the magazine's subtitle, "A Bi-Monthly of Revolutionary Literature," have revealed that the new publication considered itself revolutionary in the literary *and* political sense, if only because during the first several decades of the twentieth century most serious literary magazines proffered themselves as revolutionary.

But any misconception about its outlook would have been immediately corrected had he bothered to read the magazine's opening editorial statement, for here its affiliation with the Communist party and the proletarian literary movement was openly declared. The statement began by alluding on the one hand to the worldwide crisis of capitalism and on the other to the example of the Soviet Union, which was said to be embarked headlong on the epochal task of socialist construction. The Soviet Union was furthermore said to be in the vanguard of a worldwide revolutionary movement, of which the project to create a new and revolutionary art in the United States was a part. It was within this political context of intensified class struggle that the editors addressed their audience on the role of their new magazine:

> *Partisan Review* . . . has a specific function to fulfill. It will publish the best creative work of its members as well as of non-members who share the literary aims of the John Reed Club.
>
> We propose to concentrate on creative and critical literature, but we shall maintain a definite viewpoint—that of the revolutionary working class. Through our specific literary medium we shall participate in the struggle of the workers and sincere intellectuals against imperialist war, fascism, national and racial oppression, and for the abolition of the system which breeds these evils. The defense of the Soviet Union is one of our principal tasks.

The editors next turned to cultural matters:

> We shall combat not only the decadent culture of the exploiting classes but also the debilitating liberalism which at times seeps into our writers through the pressure of class-alien forces. Nor shall we forget to keep our own house in order. We shall resist

every attempt to cripple our literature by narrow-minded, sectarian theories and practices.[7]

By now our flaneur would no doubt have long since left the scene, a fact that would not have fazed the new magazine's chief editors, William Phillips and Philip Rahv, in the least, for they intended their magazine for a proletarian audience, or at least a proletarianized audience, of which *les flâneurs* most definitely were not a part. Thus, he could not have known that hidden within the formulaic language of Stalinist orthodoxy—in phrases such as "We propose to concentrate on creative and critical literature," "our specific literary medium," and "We shall resist . . . narrow-minded sectarian theories and practices"—was the beginning of a new critical project for the American literary left, one that has had a powerful influence on American culture and politics as a whole.

What did this project consist of at its most hopeful and salutary? It was, first of all, a challenge to key notions of Stalinist orthodoxy, and it eventually led to a rigorous reevaluation and then a rejection of Marxism. Second, it aspired to and attained an unprecedented degree of autonomy, tolerance, and rigor for literature and criticism—one could say intellectual work in general—within left discourse. Third, it created a compelling, highly unstable union between modernism and political radicalism. This union began to coalesce even as *Partisan Review* championed the cause of proletarian literature, and it was defended most strenuously during the late 1930s and early 1940s as the magazine shifted its allegiance from the Communist party— which itself had abandoned the idea of proletarian literature in 1935—to "independent" socialism. Following several years during which the *Partisan Review* group moved toward Trotskyism, its members were thrown into disarray by World War II, as Rahv, Sidney Hook, Clement Greenberg, and Dwight Macdonald debated the issue of support for the Allies.[8] The decision to support the war effort, combined with a virulent hatred of Stalinism and the Soviet Union, were among several factors that led many within the circle to moderate and in some cases repudiate their political radicalism in the postwar period. By the 1950s, of course, the *Partisan Review* circle had attained its greatest influence, contributing powerfully to the canonization of modernism and to the shape of American culture generally. By then, with some notable exceptions, the politics of the circle was liberal anticommunism.[9]

When *Partisan Review* made its appearance in the winter of 1934, its critical project was at best an incipient one. Within a matter of months, however, the editors had begun their attack on doctrinaire literature and criticism—what they called "literary leftism." In response to critical positions that demanded that literature make explicit appeals for socialist revolution, or present a dialectical-materialist world outlook, or render working-class life in a favorable light,[10] Phillips and Rahv offered a comprehensive reassessment of a range of critical problems and terms. They did so in numerous exploratory essay–articles on aesthetics and form, several of which they coauthored. Here they elaborated their most important critical ideas, and it was here also that Eliot's influence was most pronounced. "The imaginative assimilation of political content," "literature as a way of living and seeing," "specific content," form as a "mode of perception": these were the critical phrases that denoted a major departure from doctrinaire Marxism. But the idea that informed each of them—Phillips referred to it as the "hub" of the problem of literature's relation to politics—was the idea of *sensibility*, also taken from Eliot.

The term *sensibility* has had a long history within the non-Marxist critical tradition, most notably as a term signifying literary effeminacy, as Janet Todd has amply documented with regard to the eighteenth century.[11] Eliot, of course, like Phillips and Rahv after him, chose to bury this particular meaning when he revived the term for twentieth-century criticism, thereby eschewing any attempt at feminization. In fact all three men, by suppressing this background and attempting to universalize the term, were significantly less thorough in their revisions than they might have been. As for American or European Marxism, neither made any serious use of the term before Phillips and Rahv employed it. Indeed, the term seems to have held no special importance for either critic in their pre–*Partisan Review* criticism; only with Phillips's 1934 essay "Sensibility and Modern Poetry" did it acquire its strategic place in his rethinking of Marxist criticism. Phillips announced as much by concluding his essay with the unambiguous appeal for the proletarian movement to adopt as its slogan "Let sensibility take its course."[12] By giving the term such prominence, he meant to counterpose it to the terms of the dominant reflectionist epistemology and corresponding social realist aesthetic of doctrinaire Marxism. The idea of sensibility represented a complex, mediated version of subjectivity in place of the reified antithesis of behaviorism and a spurious voluntarism that beset the Communist International's analysis of the "subjective factor" during its sectarian third period.[13] Much was at stake according to Phillips: understanding the relationship between a poet's beliefs and the merits of his or her poetry; assessing the textual interaction between form and content; and responding productively to "bourgeois" literature, especially as it impinged on the shaping of the new proletarian literature.

As Eliot had before him, Phillips alternately referred to three types, or manifestations, of sensibility: that of the writer, that of the literary work or form, and that of a tradition or historical period. These corresponded, respectively, to different aspects of the literary enterprise: the creative process, the individual work's effect, and the development of literary movements based on shared sensibilities. As for the writer's sensibility, Phillips described it in Eliotic fashion as a medium, or solvent, by which specific opinions, programs, or ideologies are transformed by the writer into something more indirect, subtle, and affective: "We do not respond directly to a poet's beliefs for the simple reason that unless these beliefs are dissolved in his sensibility the poet has not created a poem" (p. 20). As a faculty that amalgamates both cognitive and affective experience, the writer's sensibility is the most important element in the creative process, not to be equated with either class consciousness, stressed by doctrinaire Marxism, or depth of feeling, emphasized by what he took to be the romantic view. Literary production demands a receptivity to all forms of experience, Phillips claimed, and it is precisely the sensibility that is able to assimilate these disparate forms. Without elaborating, he noted that in its turn sensibility is conditioned by a range of historical and biographical factors.

Like a writer's sensibility, a work's sensibility cannot be reduced to a single dimension, whether it be ideological or personal. This, I believe, is the idea behind the atmospheric passage, "[W]hat we recognize as the quality of any poem is its timbre and its condensation of moods and attitudes which float in the world above us" (p. 22). Thus, *The Bridge* by Hart Crane possesses "the sense of . . . the machine," and *The Waste Land* "conveys . . . a feeling of restlessness, tension, and futility" by attempting to "span our cultural traditions" (p. 22). Significantly, Phillips was not concerned with Eliot's or Crane's politics, in or out of their poetry. Rather, as he indicated, his interest was with the feel of the poems, but the feel as it sublates the voice and the author through immersion in what would seem to be epochal subjectivities shaped by capitalism and class conflict.[14]

Finally, groups of poems can share a sensibility if history seems to have the same feel to them. Thus, Phillips referred to Auden, Lewis, Spender, and Horace Gregory as the "transition group" because their common "humanist" sensibility—their "sensibility of choice"—placed them in the camp neither of the bourgeoisie nor of the proletariat but rather "in transit" between traditional and proletarian verse. Employing language from Eliot, Phillips claimed that this sensibility was the "poetic correlative of the intellectuals' sense of conflict and the necessity of taking a position" (p. 22).

The notion of literature "as a way of living and seeing" was another means of pointing out the irreducibility of literature to any single realm of experience, whether purely subjective or purely ideational. The phrase was first used on the occasion of Phillips's review of Henry Hazlitt's *Anatomy of Criticism*. Here Phillips took exception to Hazlitt's dismissal of proletarian literature because, in Hazlitt's words, it "attempts to enforce a specific article in the conventional moral code [and] bring about a specific reform." But Phillips effectively disarmed his opponent by defining proletarian writing in a rather unexpected way: "These are certainly not the kind of beliefs which Marxists advocate for literature. Proletarian literature does not 'enforce a specific article'; it introduces a new way of living and seeing into literature. It does not enforce the new view, it embodies it."[15] "A new way of living and seeing" was a far cry from "the dialectical-materialist point of view." It emphasized the necessary adjustment of subjective life to the new revolutionary situation and, like the idea of sensibility, involved perceptions and values more than beliefs. Its particular resonance was to stress the necessary transformation of the entire individual as part of the transformation of a whole way of life.

The idea of literature as "a new way of living and seeing" encompassed many categories of experience that literature as ideology or literature as imagination at the time excluded: perceptions, attitudes, habits of mind, moods. Although Phillips and Rahv left out of their discussions of this period any reference to the unconscious, it should nonetheless be kept in mind that they assigned to literature's proper province a much wider range of experience than that encouraged by more orthodox critics. Thus, literature might incorporate discursive, propositional, or even topical modes, as the orthodox critics tended to emphasize, but it should not be *expected* to do so. There was in fact an array of rhetorical modes, conventions, and forms by which writers might convey experience. The important thing was that these experiences be communicated so that their social significance is experienced subjectively by the reader. Felt experience must carry more than personal signification; it must bring the reader face to face with broader social contradictions. Viewing literature as a way of living and seeing is at once to call attention to the web of relations that connect literature to a historically constituted "whole way of life" and also to affirm the necessarily subjective way in which these connections are most effectively depicted. Here Phillips's and Rahv's views generally correspond with those of Raymond Williams concerning the individual/social nexus at the heart of culture. All three attempt to describe the play of personal and social, subjective and objective elements that go into the active making and reproduction of culture. Just as for Phillips and Rahv the notion of sensibility was meant to retain the quality of constitutive experience at both the individual and collective levels, so too, as I have indicated, Williams's concept of "structures of feeling" is meant to include the feelings, values, moods, and judgments of those actively engaged in making culture in the aggregate. All three insist that the affective dimension of collective life is part of its material dimension.

The idea of "specific content" was introduced by Phillips and Rahv in "Criticism," their second coauthored essay. Here they addressed the fact that in many works, especially modernist works, there existed little if any *direct* reflection of ruling-class ideology. They made their point with reference to Faulkner's *Sanctuary*, basing it on a distinction between specific content and ideology:

> Evidently the book does not present the author's "ideology" in the sense that it does not tell us about his general political opinions, his economic beliefs, his attitude to all the questions stirring in the South; in fact, it does not even give us anything like a complete view of his esthetic opinions. What it does give us is not ideology directly, but *specific content* in the shape of attitudes toward character, painting of moods, patterns of action, and a variety of sensory and psychological insights. These patterns naturally contain within themselves the implications of a larger world-view (ideology), which the critic may deduce. But the point must be made that *this specific content is not identical with any immediately recognizable reactionary or progressive non-literary program operating in the South today*.

The editors concluded that it is "confusing" to attribute to a work a general ideology "with all its philosophical and political connotations." Its specific content is very much the product of an individual sensibility, historically conditioned to be sure, but exceptional in ways that matter to the reader and certainly to the critic.[16]

Despite the fact that Phillips and Rahv, like nearly all leftists during the 1930s, accepted the narrow definition of ideology as an explicit, socially powerful system of belief, and despite their highly qualified and evasive definitions—"*immediately* recognizable"; "*all* its philosophical and political connotations"—such that it is unclear whether the authors would make the same conclusions about ideology minus the qualifications, their remarks nonetheless spoke to the need for leftists to complicate the processes of literary analysis and valuation. As remains the case today, leftists were sometimes given to measuring the worth of a text largely on the basis of political conviction. Proletarian critics might demand that an author portray working-class life in a favorable light, call for socialist revolution, or exemplify the dialectical-materialist worldview. Even sophisticated progressive critics such as V. L. Parrington and Granville Hicks insisted that the best authors expose the abuses of capitalism and/or validate democratic traditions and values. Phillips and Rahv, in their remarks on Faulkner, called attention to the reductive outcome of such criticism. By focusing their attention on the textual force field as well as the social force field (to borrow and extend Adorno's term), they opened the way to discussing the interplay between dynamic linguistic and formal elements that in successful texts are every bit as resonant and consequential as the complex social forces shaping them. One might say, of course, that diminishing the importance of systematic belief served to depoliticize criticism; I would argue instead that by suggesting ideology may be deduced from a combination of textual and social phenomena by critics working through several intermediary levels of analysis, Phillips and Rahv anticipated critical modes that subsequently proved to be fruitful. They helped to create a situation in left criticism such that if critics were going to discuss ideology persuasively, they would in effect have to reinvent the term. it was in fact the similar critique of the limits of the orthodox understanding of ideology that informed the Frankfurt School's practice of *Ideologiekritik*, and later Althusser's significant expansion of the term to incorporate Lacanian and Gramscian insights. What is germane to my discussion of Phillips and Rahv is that they shared with each of these critics not only a belief in the relative autonomy of literature (at least some literature) from dominant systematic belief, but also a belief in the power of this literature to destabilize dominant habits of mind.[17]

The complex, intermediary levels of textual analysis necessary to any adequate understanding of literature's ideological—or better, *social*—function become clearer when we turn to Phillips's and Rahv's discussions of form. We have seen in the passage on Faulkner that they considered specific content and form to be inseparable: specific content includes point of view ("attitudes toward character"), modes of description ("painting of moods"), and plot devices ("patterns of action"). Not surprisingly, they argued elsewhere that form was actually a "mode of perception," that is, something intimately connected to a writer's and a work's sensibility. Addressing the form/content debate, the major conundrum of Marxist criticism during the 1930s, the editors further extended the idea of sensibility. Generally speaking, the Marxist view of the form/content question has always been problematic. Its premises have been that form and content are dialectically related, and that, in the last instance, content is the primary category. For those within the proletarian literary movement of the 1930s, the discrepancy between these views (which are either contradictory or at best partially incompatible, depending on one's definition of dialectical) was magnified by the repeated belittling of literary form and questions pertaining to it. For some critics, "in the last instance" became "in each instance" as they diagnosed capitalism's cultural condition as decadent, and perfunctorily labeled each modernist innovation in form as a particularly egregious symptom. And yet, inexplicably, these same critics insisted that the proletarian movement learn from past movements, including modernism, and not discard useful formal innovations. Phillips and Rahv pointed out, as did others, that this could not be an acceptably dialectical view of the problem. If form and content were dialectically related, how could Marxists justify preserving certain forms while rejecting their content? And what exactly was meant by these terms, so frequently, yet vaguely employed?

The most complete response to these questions was given in Phillips's essay "Form and Content." He lost little time in rejecting the manner in which the question was being posed by critics within the movement—Phillips charged them with failing to define their terms and failing to explain what they meant by the "separation" of form and content. He then proceeded to critique the reified notions of form and content that contributed to their dilemma. He pointed out that "the shape or structure of a literary work" is often thought of as a king of "mould" into which the writer pours his ideas. But "forms" in this sense, such as the sonnet or lyric, are better described as traditional "patterns of writing" rather than as receptacles. But even here, form as pattern, technique, or method speaks only to the "verbal surface," insofar as linguistic methods, though important in themselves, are nevertheless inseparable from the writer's "purposes and perceptions." Content, by contrast, is depicted as "something solid, organized, and completely philosophical. . . . A more significant definition," hazarded Phillips, would reveal form and content "as two aspects of a unified vision," for if we try to point to the content of a particular work, then by the very act of identification we tear the object of our attention from its context. Consider Hamlet's soliloquy.

> As sheer content it asks whether it is nobler to yield to adverse fortunes or to resist them. As such, it is, of course, banal and silly. But the question takes its meaning from Hamlet's person and state of mind, in short, from Shakespeare's complete perception of the play of human motives and of the character of Hamlet. And this is given not only in the working out of the plot, in the innuendos of action, but in the very idiom of the soliloquy which imparts Shakespeare's grasp of behavior in his time. In saying this, the idea of form is included in that of content.

Since "any suggestive idea of *form* would have to include the elements which give shape and quality to content," a more accurate way of defining form would be as a "mode of perception." Thus, form serves to constitute content just as content shapes form—as is perhaps most readily seen in modernist poetry. Phillips added, however, that the more formally innovative modernist schools emphasize form to the point of "narrow[ing] the range of explicit meaning to the point of extinction." After all, "while form should be regarded as a mode of perception, it cannot be forgotten that it is a way of perceiving a specific literary content."[18] Perception, and ultimately the sensibility that underlies it, is thus the magnetic factor in the creative process: attracting, animating, and setting in tension elements of form and content, the intrinsic and the extrinsic, the existential and the historical.[19]

Phillips's and Rahv's dialectical, interpenetrating rendering of the form/content problem anticipated similar efforts by neo-Marxists and New Historicists. What was innovative about their handling of the problem was that for the first time they laid open a range of formal elements that previously had been considered beyond the pale of American Marxist criticism. Moreover, they fashioned a way of discussing formal questions that avoided formalism, substituting for autotelism a kind of modulated materialism of the text. We recall that for them a work's meaning is produced through the manipulation of its technical possibilities in rendering action, character, style, tone, and so on according to the writer's perceptions. These in turn are products of his or her sensibility, the "agent of selection." And of course the writer selects from a larger range of possibilities set by broad social factors, including politics, economics, and ideology. Thus, a work's final form embodies both intrinsic and extrinsic phenomena. It is open to analysis on a local level, but the critical movement must ultimately be outward, toward a wider social horizon. The positive effect of this approach, broadly shared by the New York intellectuals (Fred Dupee, Elizabeth Hardwick, Irving Howe, Alfred Kazin, Mary McCarthy, Lionel Trilling, William Troy, and so on) and others such as Edmund Wilson and F. O. Matthiessen, can be fully appreciated only by rereading the work of these critics in context. Although in retrospect we are naturally apt to note telling absences and to dissent from particular judgments, alongside the orthodox Marxist critics and orthodox New Critics the work produced by these critics spoke, and continues to speak, with greater subtlety and insight regarding literature's social basis.

At its best, Phillips's and Rahv's criticism also constituted an effective revision of the doctrinaire interpretation of the base/superstructure relationship. Not only did they in effect replace unidirectional determination with the idea of reciprocity and complex causation, but they also drew out some of the consequences of these concepts for literary judgment. Orthodox Marxism had for some time been committed to a reflectionist theory of knowledge, in which ideas come to the mind as phantoms, sublimates, or reflections of real objects. This corresponded to the notion that the superstructure invariably "reflects" the base, and that consciousness "reflects" being. And it led directly to a realist criterion for literature, the best of which was thought to achieve an accurate reproduction of real life. But Phillips and Rahv were ambivalent about socialist realism. They first of all rejected any simplistic notion of mimesis. Rahv explicitly rejected the idea of reflection and preferred to speak of "a deflection with crooked mirrors," which suggests that literature is not one but two removes from the object it purportedly "reflects." Not only is the original object "deflected" or altered by the act of mirroring it, but also the distortions of the mirror itself compound the discrepancy. In other words, both the practice of writing and the material used in writing—one thinks of language itself—cause the original object to be reimagined. This revision of orthodox reflectionism compares favorably with that of Lukács, whose theory of realism did not so much reject reflectionism as alter it so that it applied to processes rather than to objects. Whereas the socialist realism of the proletarian movement often called for the replication of objects, Lukács demanded that forces, trends, and contradictions be elaborated, all of which he thought constituted objective, verifiable historical processes. Whereas Lukács's aesthetic valued those works that most convincingly depicted the totality of objective historical forces, Phillips and Rahv tended to emphasize the ingenuity, resonance, and depth of a fully realized sensibility operating within the work. Their idea of realism, being less epochal than Lukács's, was also less insistent on nineteenth-century forms and methods that served to render society panoramically. They could afford to be more receptive toward literature of less breadth, perhaps, but of more concentrated focus and more various means. Their criticism was thus conceptually better disposed toward modernism, a fact that invites comparison to the anti-Lukácsian impulses in Brecht, Adorno, and Benjamin.

III

Looking at Eliot's early criticism, we can see that his famous comments on the creative process were an important source for the editors' criticism. I refer in particular to the well-known related discussions of the poet's impersonality in "Tradition and the Individual Talent," of sensibility in "The Metaphysical Poets," and of the "objective correlative" in "Hamlet and His Problems." In these essays Eliot attempted to find syntheses for several of the reigning antinomies of criticism: the "inspired poet" versus the "world"; the creative versus the critical, or intellectual, faculties; and, more generally, the subjective versus the objective world. Although Phillips and Rahv could not have known it at the time, Eliot's synthetic, dialectical impulse was grounded in his earlier studies of idealist philosophy. In his dissertation, a critical evaluation of F. H. Bradley's neo-Hegelian idealism and its relation to the realism of Moore, Meinong, and Russell, he had already worked out a meticulously balanced view of the relationship between objective and subjective reality, between mental and physical worlds. It was therefore neither coincidental nor capricious that two young proletarian critics should seize upon the dialectical aspects of Eliot's early criticism.[20] Following Eliot, Phillips and Rahv appealed to partisan writers to transmute their deeply felt opinions into persuasive literary emotion by laboriously mastering techniques and by striving for greater equanimity during the writing process. Thus, Rahv praised Hemingway for his "impersonality of method,"[21] and the proletarian novels of William Rollins, Jr., and Arnold Armstrong because the solution to the class conflict was resolved "not externally, through the well-known device of preaching and finger-pointing, but internally."[22] Even Eliot's *Murder in the Cathedral* was rather courageously acclaimed (in very Eliotic language) because "it is precise, contemporary, sustained by a sensibility able to transform thought and feeling into each other and combine them in simultaneous expression"—this, remarkably enough, in the teeth of the controversy that followed the publication of *After Strange Gods* in 1934.[23]

Eliot's double-edged notion of sensibility provided Phillips and Rahv with a way of responding to critics of both the right and the left. In the face of those who in their fulminations against Marxism reduced literature to the immediacy of pure feeling, they could evoke the cognitive function of sensibility. To the doctrinaire critic who insisted on confusing literature with documentary or propagandistic writing, they could point out the need for felt ideas. In this new context, quite different certainly from Eliot's, his concept of sensibility served as a flexible tool for helping to fashion new forms of proletarian literature and Marxist criticism.

Several other of Eliot's concepts helped shape Phillips's and Rahv's thinking as well. Especially pertinent was a portion of Eliot's discussion in "The Possibility of a Poetic Drama" concerning the complex relationship that obtains between literary forms and society. To those who would simply manufacture a new form or copy an old one, he replied:

> To create a form is not merely to invent a shape, a rhyme or rhythm. It is also the realization of the whole appropriate content of this rhyme or rhythm. The sonnet of Shakespeare is not merely such and such a pattern, but a precise way of thinking and feeling. The *framework* which was provided for the Elizabethan dramatist was not

merely blank verse and the five-act play and the Elizabethan playhouse; it was not merely the plot—for the poets incorporated, remodelled, adapted or invented, as occasion suggested. It was also the . . . "temper of the age" (an unsatisfactory phrase), a preparedness, a habit on the part of the public, to respond to particular stimuli.[24]

As we have seen, traces of this passage appear throughout Phillips's and Rahv's early criticism. Eliot's "precise way of thinking and feeling" became "a way of living and seeing," the dynamic understanding of form remaining the same. Form for all three critics became a "mode of perception" as opposed to a shape needing to be filled. And the public's "preparedness," its "habits of response," the "temper of the age": these fairly well describe what the editors meant by the sensibility of an age.

In addition, there was the issue of *systems* of ideas in literature. As I have shown, this was no small matter for proletarian critics, many of whom demanded that literature reflect a dialectical-materialist viewpoint or support the party's political program. Here Eliot was enormously helpful to Phillips and Rahv, who opposed placing the burden of ideological correctness on literature. Eliot had dealt with the problem of systematic belief in "Dante," the final essay in The Sacred Wood. He defended what he called "philosophical" poetry against Valéry's claim that such was no longer acceptable as modern poetry. Eliot based his defense largely on the evidence of The Divine Comedy, which he maintained demonstrated that "the author, more than any other poet, has succeeded in dealing with his philosophy, not as a theory . . . or as his own comment or reflection, but as something *perceived*" (pp. 170–71). Dante did so, according to Eliot, by integrating his system of beliefs with the structure of the poem. The structure in turn was made essential to each of the parts. Eliot observed further that "the examination of any episode in the *Comedy* ought to show that not merely the allegorical interpretation or the didactic intention, but the emotional significance itself, cannot be isolated from the poem" (p. 165). By "realizing" ideas rather than merely evoking them; by "inspecting" them rather than arguing them, the poet can indeed deal successfully with philosophical ideas. As Sanford Schwartz has perceptively observed, Eliot here reverses the emphasis on objectifying feeling found in his discussions of impersonality and the objective correlative—the lone emphasis we have unfortunately come to associate with him. In the essay on Dante he provides the other element in his dialectical treatment of the subject/object problem by praising the poet for enlivening overly objective doctrine through transmuting it into sensation.

The relevance of these passages to Phillips's and Rahv's situation is clear: to the extent that late medieval religious belief and twentieth-century orthodox Marxist belief were codified and official, the issues at stake for religious and proletarian poetry were the same. Like Eliot, the editors argued that for systems of ideas to operate successfully, they have to be thoroughly embedded in the structure and feeling of the work. Their idea that through the operation of a perceptive sensibility a proletarian writer could transform political doctrine into a work of imaginative power was a direct application of Eliot's insights into successful religious verse.

Finally, in assessing the direct and indirect results of Eliot's influence on Phillips and Rahv, we must not forget that their most passionate writing was that in which they defended criticism and theory against those within the movement who mini-mized their importance or in some cases rejected them outright. By the spring of 1935, not long after the appearance of their most important early essays, ominous allusions to "bourgeois aestheticism" and to "academicism" were cropping up, and not long afterwards Mike Gold, the party's best-known spokesperson, charged them with "mandarinism." These attacks prompted them to make a vociferous reply in "Criticism." Elaborating on comments they had made in their first coauthored piece, "Problems and Perspectives in Revolutionary Literature," in which criticism was likened to Lenin's notion of a vanguard,[25] the editors claimed that criticism was indispensable to the revolutionary literary movement. Only criticism, they declared, could "clarify the aims and premises" of the different schools and currents within the movement, and only criticism could relate these tendencies to one another and ensure that the more promising among them would succeed. To accomplish this, crit-icism would need to elaborate "a considerable body of aesthetic theory" in order to "relate the problems of art and literature to the larger body of Marxist theory." With-out theory, practical criticism must lose its bearings, giving itself over to "empirical observations, estheticism, or crude applications of politics to literature" (pp. 16–17).

Perhaps the most interesting part of their article was that devoted to refuting their critics' claims of academicism. Here Phillips and Rahv were unyielding in their defense of standards, maintaining that too much criticism was being performed by amateurs "who lack the critical temperament and a knowledge of Marxism." Rather, "recognized Marxists" with a command of both literary theory and Marxist theory ought to be writing the reviews and essays. Theory was not to be judged by its acces-sibility to a wide audience. That is a fair expectation for practical criticism, they allowed, "which simplifies for the purpose of daily reviewing." But more serious crit-icism, meaning theory, demands different criteria, and here they were defiant:

> [C]riticism is in the main a form of conceptual analysis, and is primarily directed at readers familiar with the problems of literature. "Criticism is not the passion of the intellect, but the intellect of passion" (Marx). It is to be judged by its validity, by its generalizing power, and not by its temperature, or by the number of readers who can easily digest it. Its effect is a slow one. . . . [I]t finally reaches its mass audience in an indirect form. (p. 17)

A "cult of popularity," the editors maintained, had caused some to stigmatize theory as "academic." "But what is academic writing?" they asked. "It is not so much a qual-ity of style as a content marginal to important literary problems" (p. 17).

Finally, the editors addressed the problem of "the servile role that many writers have assigned to criticism." For some, criticism is to be narrowed down to little more than "publicity for new proletarian novels and plays." To this they gave a stinging reply, in which they elevated criticism's status to a then-unprecented height. "Crit-icism," they proclaimed,

> is by no means obligated to herald each third rate poem as a boon to the proletariat. Its main concerns are with creating a new esthetic, with revaluating literary history, and with advancing proletarian art. The search for new creative methods so promi-nent in a new literature puts the stress on the critical faculty, not only in critics but

in every poet and novelist. In this sense, the tasks of the critic in this particular
period are perhaps even more complex than those of the creative writer. (p. 17)

Within the boundary of a purportedly mass-based popular movement, Phillips and
Rahv had reaffirmed the need for a vanguard of critics—well trained, expert even—
whose profession was "criticism and not something else" (p. 18). For a moment at
least, the possibility loomed of an unlikely alliance between Eliot's professional critic
and Lenin's professional revolutionary.

IV

Phillips's and Rahv's Eliotic criticism of the mid-1930s constituted the most ambitious exploration of proletarian literary concepts undertaken within the proletarian
literary movement, then under the auspices of the Communist party and more
broadly the Communist International. The very example of their dogged pursuit of
literary and cultural questions represented a repudiation, in practice, of the prevailing view that culture, and specifically literary criticism, could not be a high priority
for the revolutionary movement. Indeed, Phillips's and Rahv's early work draws our
attention beyond the limited confines of the proletarian movement toward other
developments in Marxist theory contemporary with it and subsequent to it. Their
early criticism can profitably be seen as a preliminary enunciation of important
themes taken up by other Marxist revisionists. I emphasize *preliminary* for two reasons. First, their work represented an initial excursion into certain practical problems
faced by an ongoing political movement with little theoretical rigor of its own. It did
not offer finished theoretical arguments. And second, at this point in their careers,
Phillips's and Rahv's criticism was heterodox as opposed to unorthodox. That is, for
every group of insights that seemed to show them embarking on a serious restatement
of the dominant views of their movement, a seemingly discrepant opinion would
reestablish them on conventional orthodox terrain. When it came to evaluating
modernist texts, for example, ideological content alone sometimes shaped their critical response.

In other ways Phillips and Rahv failed to free themselves from traditional perspectives. After they rejected the idea of proletarian literature following their acri-
monious split with the Communist party in 1937,[26] they failed to maintain their earlier connections, tenuous as they were, with popular constituencies. Instead of
developing new ties, they in effect substituted themselves for the masses, claiming
that as adversarial intellectuals *they* were the revolutionary class. This encouraged
them to put Eliot to new and often detrimental uses: professionalization sometimes
became an excuse for elitism, and the dissociated sensibility was superimposed on the
American tradition, creating several unfortunate binarisms which have only recently
been deconstructed.[27] With regard to the humanist ideal of a unified sensibility lending stability to a reader, writer, or text, there are grounds for concluding that Phillips
and Rahv underestimated the destabilizing force of the unconscious, of desire, and of
language itself, all of which, as we are now well aware, partially undermine even the
kind of provisional dialectical, and historicized equilibrium they sought.

Given their proximity to the public and their specific social and political obligations, however, I would argue that Phillips's and Rahv's critical humanist reformulation of Marxist criticism was remarkably resistant to essentializing the self—or any other category for that matter, whether it be class, revolution, truth, or beauty. Their relationship to a dynamic and popular political movement, with its culture in a state of flux, forced them to construct ideals and goals whose effects must be judged pragmatically and in context. That context was the attempt by writers and critics, often encumbered by the party apparatus, to create a thriving proletarian literature that would be the center of a general cultural revival. Their commitment stemmed from their disdain for capitalism's separation of critical culture from the everyday lives of ordinary Americans. Proletarian literature was seen as a response to what was perceived as an elitist and increasingly specialized idea of literature within capitalism's class-determined organization of learning and acculturation. The editors rejected the view that the solution to the divisions of bourgeois society lay in a new arrangement in which the masses could passively enjoy classical or "serious" culture. Advocating a unique vision of proletarian literature, Phillips and Rahv prescribed a new kind of literature that would close the gaps existing within capitalist culture. They assumed that, given access to culture, especially high culture, the masses would inevitably reshape it according to their own experiences and needs. Moreover, because these experiences and needs were inevitably linked to the struggle to make a living, their new culture could be expected to concern itself with material as well as spiritual dimensions of life. By combining a full treatment of objective factors with subjective ones—in the editors' words, the "habits" and "psychological relationships" existing within the "unexplored continent of fiction" that was working-class life[28]—proletarian literature would become the basis for a whole new conception of literature. No longer would literature be thought of as being imprisoned in individual consciousness, separated from its real grounding in social, even economic life. Literature would properly be seen as deeply embedded in the historical process, yet not to such an extent that it would become a mere simulacrum of "real" social or historical forces. It would provide a common ground where an eminently social self might be explored.

This idea of a popular proletarian literature no doubt goes against the grain of Eliot's traditionalism and elitism—although Eliot's passionate love for such "lowbrow" forms of culture as the music hall complicates matters. Yet Phillips and Rahv were not stymied by the acknowledged limitations of Eliot's views; their sense of urgency propelled them beyond the common leftist dismissals of Eliot in order to gain sustenance from others of Eliot's views. Thus, the creation of a new, distinctly proletarian sensibility would be the means of achieving a new level of working-class cultural output. Unlike many of their colleagues on the left, they were willing to grant that an active individual sensibility capable of assimilating a range of social processes might arrive at a substantially new vision within the limits of what the social range makes possible. This was an advance, certainly, over criticism that overemphasized the reproductive aspects of creation. Yet, against aesthetic theories premised on the separation of the social and the personal and clinging to notions of genius, inspiration, or some innate talent for "getting it right," Phillips and Rahv asserted the inescapably social nature of all experience, including literary creation. Raymond

Williams's term "active reproduction" best captures the dialectical impulse behind their thinking.[29]

Why would Phillips and Rahv have appropriated key terms from a critic considered a class enemy by many on the left at the time? Certainly such borrowing was not without its risks. One must remember that by the mid-1930s the disproportionate interest in reactionary politics among modernists had caused much of the American left to consider the entire literary and artistic movement anathema; those who lacked the political acumen to endorse modernism without the necessary and ritualistic qualifications were soon suspected of aestheticism, decadence, and petty-bourgeois vacillation.[30] The deep skepticism toward modernism expressed by the doctrinaire left meant that young proletarian critics such as Phillips and Rahv had to conceal their debt to Eliot in order to maintain their status within the proletarian movement. If the debt now seems relatively obvious, this was certainly not the case for many mid-1930s party functionaries and fellow travelers, many more of whom, one may safely hazard, knew of *The Sacred Wood* than had actually read it. It was thus rather remarkable that the two editors forged ahead with a critical strategy that, though it took its bearings from the literary and cultural life of an ongoing political movement, still managed to assert its independence from that movement's shibboleths. This was no small accomplishment, short-lived though it may have been. It offers some insights into what form engaged, worldly criticism might take today.

Notes

A version of this essay first appeared in *American Literature* 64, no. 1 (March 1992):127–53 and comprises portions of chapter 3 of *Renewing the Left: Politics, Imagination and the New York Intellectuals* (Oxford: Oxford Unversity Press, 1996).

1. Throughout I suggest comparisons between William Phillips and Philip Rahv and their better-known European analogues. The best general treatments of what Perry Anderson has termed "Western Marxism" (though none deals with British Marxism) remain Anderson's own *Considerations on Western Marxism* (London: Verso, 1979); Fredric Jameson, *Marxism and Form* (Princeton, N.J.: Princeton University Press, 1971); Martin Jay, *The Dialectical Imagination* (New York: Little, Brown, 1973); and Eugene Lunn, *Marxism and Modernism: An Historical Study of Lukács, Brecht, Benjamin, and Adorno* (Berkeley: University of California Press, 1982). References to Jameson's *Marxism and Form* are cited by page in the text.

2. Certainly an abundant amount has been written on the New York intellectuals, most of it by the New Yorkers themselves. These include Lionel Abel, *The Intellectual Follies: A Memoir of the Literary Venture in New York and Paris* (New York: Norton, 1984); William Barrett, *The Truants* (New York: Doubleday, 1982); Sidney Hook, *Out of Step: An Unquiet Life in the 20th Century* (New York: Harper & Row, 1987); Irving Howe, *A Margin of Hope* (New York: Harcourt, 1982); Alfred Kazin, *New York Jew* (New York: Random House, 1978); Mary McCarthy, *Intellectual Memoirs* (New York: Harcourt Brace Jovanovich, 1992); William Phillips, *A Partisan View: Five Decades of the Literary Life* (New York: Stein and Day, 1983); Norman Podhoretz, *Breaking Ranks: A Political Memoir* (New York: Harper & Row, 1979); and Diana Trilling, *The Beginning of the Journey* (New York: Harcourt, 1993). In addition, there are several general historical accounts, including Alexander Bloom, *Prodigal Sons: The New York Intellectuals and Their World* (New York: Oxford University Press, 1986); Terry Cooney, *The*

Rise of the New York Intellectuals: Partisan Review and Its Circle, 1934–1945 (Madison: University of Wisconsin Press, 1986); James Gilbert, *Writers and Partisans: A History of Literary Radicalism in America* (New York: Wiley & Sons, 1968); Neil Jumonville, *Critical Cross: The New York Intellectuals in Postwar America* (Berkeley: University of California Press, 1991); and Alan Wald, *The New York Intellectuals: The Rise and Decline of the Anti-Stalinist Left from the 1930s to the 1980s* (Chapel Hill: University of North Carolina Press, 1987).

3. William Phillips, *A Partisan View* (New York: Stein and Day, 1983), p. 29.

4. Terry Cooney argues that Edmund Wilson exerted an influence greater than that of Eliot, especially with *Axel's Castle* (*Rise of the New York Intellectuals*, pp. 28–29). Brooks in *America's Coming of Age* (1915) and James T. Farrell in *A Note on Literary Criticism* (1936) both provided the two critics with compelling models of socially conscious criticism.

5. As the reader will suspect, their appropriation of Eliot also had implications for their subsequent drift away from Marxist criticism in the early 1940s. I touch on this aspect of Eliot's influence as space permits; for a fuller discussion, see my *Renewing the Left: Politics, Imagination, and the New York Intellectuals* (New York: Oxford University Press, 1996).

6. Schapiro's discussion of the relevance of the city stroller to modern art predated Benjamin's discussion of the flaneur by two years. See Meyer Schapiro, "The Nature of Abstract Art," *Marxist Quarterly* 1, no. 1 (January–March 1937): 77–98 (reprinted in *Modern Art, Nineteenth and Twentieth Centuries: Selected Papers* [New York: George Braziller, 1979], pp. 185–211; see especially pp. 192–93).

7. Wallace Phelps [William Phillips] and Philip Rahv, "Editorial Statement," *Partisan Review* 1, no. 1 (February–March 1934): 2.

8. For a concise summary of these debates, see S. A. Longstaff, "*Partisan Review* and the Second World War," *Salmagundi* 43 (Winter 1979): 108–29.

9. The exceptions included Irving Howe, who throughout the postwar period defended democratic versions of socialism in *Dissent*; Macdonald, who embraced various forms of oppositional politics, most notably pacifism; Rahv, who during the 1960s returned to the Marxism of his earlier years, becoming a "born-again Leninist," as one commentator put it; and Mary McCarthy, who actively opposed the Vietnam War.

10. The range of more or less officially sanctioned views on the correct definition of proletarian literature can be found in Henry Hart, ed., *The American Writers' Congress* (New York: International Publishers, 1935). Some critics insisted on more than one of these prerequisites if literature was to be considered authentically proletarian. This said, it must be kept in mind that the proletarian literary movement was far from monolithic. Phillips and Rahv collectively represented one example among many of critics, and especially writers, sympathetic to the idea of proletarian literature yet who dissented from the semiofficial pronouncements and produced committed work of genuine originality. Significantly, a large proportion of writers willing to dissent from the orthodoxies of dissent were women and people of color, whose experiences differed from those of "typical" workers. These included Tillie Olsen, Meridel LeSueur, Muriel Rukeyser, Richard Wright, and Langston Hughes, to name a few. For other exemplary cases, see Constance Coiner, *Better Red: The Writing and Resistance of Tillie Olsen and Meridel Le Sueur* (New York: Oxford University Press, 1995); Barbara Foley, *Politics and Form in U.S. Proletarian Fiction, 1929–1941* (Durham, N.C.: Duke University Press, 1993); Charlotte Nekola and Paula Rabinowitz, eds., *Writing Red: An Anthology of American Women Writers, 1930–1940* (New York: Feminist Press, 1987); Cary Nelson, *Repression and Recovery: Modern American Poetry and the Politics of Cultural Memory, 1910–1945* (Madison: University of Wisconsin Press, 1989); and Paula Rabinowitz, *Labor and Desire: Women's Revolutionary Fiction in Depression America* (Chapel Hill: University of North Carolina Press, 1991).

11. See Janet Todd, *Sensibility: An Introduction* (New York: Methuen, 1987).

12. Wallace Phelps [William Phillips], "Sensibility and Modern Poetry," *Dynamo* 1, 3 (Summer 1934): 25; hereafter cited by page in the text.

13. This was the period from 1927 to 1934, when the main international danger to the working class was said to be not fascism but liberalism, social democracy, and democratic socialism, all of which were alleged to represent petty-bourgeois forces of capitulation within the working-class movement. The Comintern contemptuously labeled this trend "social fascism."

14. One is reminded of Raymond Williams's useful term "structure of feeling," which describes a similar phenomenon. In both cases there is an attempt to ground the idea of the "spirit of the age" in material conditions; at the same time, subjectivity is freed from the reductive encumbrances of a single "worldview" or ideology. See Raymond Williams, *Marxism and Literature* (Oxford: Oxford University Press, 1977), pp. 128–35.

15. Wallace Phelps [William Phillips], "The Anatomy of Liberalism," review of *Anatomy of Criticism* by Henry Hazlitt, *Partisan Review* 1, no. 1 (January–February 1935): 49. It is worth noting that the art critic John Berger has profitably employed the notion of "ways of seeing" in similar fashion.

16. Wallace Phelps [William Phillips] and Philip Rahv, "Criticism," *Partisan Review* 2, no. 7 (April–May 1935): 20; hereafter cited by page in the text.

17. See, for example, Raymond Geuss, *The Idea of a Critical Theory: Habermas and the Frankfurt School* (Cambridge: Cambridge University Press, 1981), pp. 26–44; Theodor Adorno, *Aesthetic Theory*, trans. C. Lenhardt (New York: Routledge, 1984), pp. 320–69; and Louis Althusser *Lenin and Philosophy*, trans. Ben Brewster (New York: Monthly Review Press, 1971), pp. 127–86, 221–27. To suggest further comparisons, like Gramsci, Phillips and Rahv, refused to equate consciousness with a single system of signification. They shared his premise that bourgeois culture was heterogeneous and contradictory, and that the orthodox model of a monolithic, economically determined culture failed to explain the complex character and function of "hegemonic" culture in the industrial democracies. Like Raymond Williams, in their comments on Faulkner's *Sanctuary* Phillips and Rahv devalued the importance of ideology. They certainly considered formally held systematic beliefs to be relevant; but like Williams, they believed that neither bourgeois culture nor bourgeois literature was reducible to them (see Williams, *Marxism and Literature*, pp. 108–14).

18. Wallace Phelps [William Phillips], "Form and Content," *Partisan Review* 2, no. 6 (January–February 1935): 33–34.

19. I have employed Jameson's terms here. See pp. 306–416 of *Marxism and Form* for his highly influential and still useful discussion of the form/content problem.

20. Eliot's dialectical philosophical inquiries in both his dissertation and his early criticism have been explored in Michael Levenson, *A Genealogy of Modernism* (Cambridge: Cambridge University Press, 1984); Walter Benn Michaels, "Philosophy in Kinkanja: Eliot's Pragmatism," *Glyph* 8 (1981): 170–202; Sanford Schwartz, *The Matrix of Modernism* (Princeton, N.J.: Princeton University Press, 1985); and Richard Shusterman, *T. S. Eliot and the Philosophy of Criticism* (London: Gerald Duckworth, 1988). Schwartz makes some very interesting comparisons between Eliot's subject/object dialectic and Lukács's analysis of reified subjectivity and objectivity.

21. Philip Rahv, review of *Winner Take Nothing* by Ernest Hemingway, *Partisan Review* 1, no. 1 (February–March 1934): 58.

22. Philip Rahv, "The Novelist as a Partisan," review of *Parched Earth* by Arnold Armstrong and *The Shadow Before* by William Rollins, Jr., *Partisan Review* 1, no. 2 (April–May 1934): 50.

23. Philip Rahv, "A Season in Hell," review of *Murder in the Cathedral* by T. S. Eliot, *Partisan Review* 3, no. 5 (June 1936): 10. Phillips had reviewed the notorious volume when it first

appeared in 1934. Although he joined the leftist chorus of denunciation, claiming that "only the blind would hesitate to call Eliot a fascist," he sounded an unusually elegiac note as he mourned the loss of the critic whose early work had "won him a large following among young American and English writers." "Eliot Takes His Stand," review of *After Strange Gods* and *The Use of Poetry and the Use of Criticism* by T. S. Eliot, *Partisan Review* 1, no. 2 (April–May 1934): 52.

24. T. S. Eliot, *The Sacred Wood* (1920; rpt. New York: Methuen, 1980), pp. 63–64; hereafter cited by page in the text.

25. Specifically, they had stated that "the critic is the ideologist of the literary movement," and followed this with a long passage from Lenin that began "[An ideologist] is worthy of that name only when he marches at the head of the spontaneous movement, points out the real road [and solves] all the theoretical, political, and tactical questions." Wallace Phelps [William Phillips] and Philip Rahv, "Problems and Perspectives in Revolutionary Literature," *Partisan Review* 1, no. 3 (June–July 1934): 5.

26. The break was publicly announced in Rahv's insightful but ultimately reductive attack "Proletarian Literature: A Political Autopsy," in which he claimed that "proletarian literature is a literature of a party disguised as the literature of a class" (*Southern Review* 4 [Winter 1939]: 623). Rahv barely acknowledged that many others, like himself and Phillips, had struggled to reshape the movement from within.

27. The most notable examples are Philip Rahv, "Paleface and Redskin" and "The Cult of Experience in American Writing," in *Essays on Literature and Politics, 1932–1972* (Boston: Houghton Mifflin, 1978), pp. 3–22; Lionel Trilling, "Reality in America," in *The Liberal Imagination* (1950; rpt. New York: Harcourt, 1978), pp. 3–20; and Richard Chase, *The American Novel and Its Tradition* (Garden City, N.Y.: Doubleday, 1957). Along with Eliot's notion of the dissociated sensibility, Van Wyck Brooks's highbrow/lowbrow dualism was also influential.

28. Phillips and Rahv, "Criticism," pp. 223.

29. See Williams, *Marxism and Literature*, pp. 206–12.

30. One might contrast this prevailing attitude toward modernism with that of the British left, for which modernism generally did not present nearly the same kind of threat. W. H. Auden, Louis MacNeice, Cecil Day-Lewis, and Stephen Spender, among others, were all popular poets of the left whose debt to modernism was profound and openly acknowledged. There were many reasons for the difference, two of the most important being the relative strength of British cultural and intellectual traditions—hence the greater confidence and autonomy of its writers—and the relative weakness of the British Communist party compared with the American Communist party during the 1930s. See Samuel Hynes, *The Auden Generation* (Princeton, N.J.: Princeton University Press, 1972); and Valentine Cunningham, *British Writers of the Thirties* (New York: Oxford University Press, 1988).

Florence Farr

A "Transitional" Woman

❖   ❖   ❖

A. WALTON LITZ

When the letters written to Florence Farr by George Bernard Shaw and William Butler Yeats were first published in 1941, the *Times Literary Supplement* reviewer assumed that she was unknown to a younger generation who probably needed a footnote to identify Shaw's "Mrs. P.C." as Mrs. Patrick Campbell.[1] Farr had been at the center of the "New Drama" of the 1890s, playing Rebecca West in the first English production of *Rosmersholm*, Blanche Sartorius in Shaw's *Widower's House*, and Louka (a part written for her) in *Arms and the Man*. In 1899 she took the role of Aleel, the poet, in the Dublin performance of Yeats's play *The Countess Cathleen*. She also wrote, with Olivia Shakespear, two occult plays, *The Beloved of Hathor* and *The Shrine of the Golden Hawk*; published several novels and dramas of her own; and was in the early part of the century an active contributor to avant-garde journals such as *The New Age* and *The Mint*. But the *TLS* reviewer of 1942 was surely right in assuming that only an older generation would remember Florence Farr.

Today, after a half century of investigations into early literary modernism, Farr is firmly placed in the margins of literary history.[2] Her shadowy role in the formation of Imagism has been explored, although none of her published poems (if there were any) has been discovered. She lives in the biographies of Shaw and Yeats, and is one of the "ghosts" of Yeats's "All Souls' Night" that require a footnote for the contemporary reader, who needs to be reminded of her interest in the occult, of her role in the creation of Yeats's theories about the relationship between poetry and music, and of her isolated death in Ceylon. (Like most of her friends, Yeats remembered her as Florence Emery, although she returned to her maiden name after her painful divorce from the actor Edward Emery in 1895).

> *On Florence Emery I call the next,*
> *Who finding the first wrinkles on a face*
> *Admired and beautiful,*
> *And by foreknowledge of the future vexed;*

> *Diminished beauty, multiplied commonplace;*
> *Preferred to teach a school*
> *Away from neighbour or friend,*
> *Among dark skins, and there*
> *Permit foul years to wear*
> *Hidden from eyesight to the unnoticed end.*[3]

Here the real Florence Farr has been completely absorbed into the Yeatsian mythology of idealized love and heroic gestures. More accurate is Ezra Pound's "Portrait d'une Femme" (1912). It had long been rumored that this poem was based on Farr's life, but the specific occasion was not known until the publication of the letters between Pound and his future wife, Dorothy Shakespear, in 1984. In July 1912, after reading Farr's recently published novel *The Solemnization of Jacklin: Some Adventures on the Search for Reality*, Dorothy Shakespear wrote to Pound: "Such a Sargasso Sea muddle. Every body divorced several times, & in the end going back to their originals: & a young man called 'Dorus Callando' who lay among lilies all night & is Oscar [Wilde], without the bitter-sweetness."[4] Pound's well-known poem, one of the first in his freely cadenced "modern" style, opens:

> *Your mind and you are our Sargasso Sea,*
> *London has swept about you this score years*
> *And bright ships left you this or that in fee:*
> *Ideas, old gossip, oddments of all things,*
> *Strange spars of knowledge and dimmed wares of price.*
> *Great minds have sought you—lacking someone else.*
> *You have been second always. Tragical?*
> *No. You preferred it to the usual thing:*
> *One dull man, dulling and uxorious,*
> *One average mind—with one thought less,*
>   *each year . . .*[5]

Pound's portrait is much more accurate than Yeats's romantic mythologizing, but it still leaves Farr in the margin, a passive receptor to the age's ideas and ideals. It is of a piece with his late half-affectionate, half-satirical portraits of the world of the "nineties" in *Hugh Selwyn Mauberley*. And it poses the question: Was Farr more than Shaw's "lover" and chosen mouthpiece, Yeats's musical muse, Pound's passive sitter for his twentieth-century version of a Jamesian portrait? Farr seems to have been one of those women that men love to shape, to re-form into some imagined ideal. Yeats wished to rescue her from the vulgarity and lack of "style" in Shaw's dramas, while Shaw was disgusted by her participation in Yeats's "cantilations":

> Remember that even in singing, it is an Irish defect to lose grip and interest by neglecting the words and thinking only of the music. Cats do the same thing when they are serenading one another. . . . Yeats is heaping fresh artificialities and irrelevances and distractions and impertinences on you instead of sternly nailing you to the simple point of conveying the meaning and feeling of the author.[6]

Farr now has a lasting place in the subcanon of annotations and secondary criticism, and also in the irrepressible subculture of the occult (*The Beloved of Hathor* and

The Shrine of the Golden Hawk were revived in London by the Rudolf Steiner Theatre; the printed program contains, among other wonders, an advertisement for the Mandrake Press, "The World's Number One Publisher of the Works of Aleister Crowley"). But does she have a life worth remembering beyond her associations with the great and the famous? If she does, that life is not to be found in her novels or plays, such as *The Dancing Faun* (1894), *The Mystery of Time* (1907), or *The Solemnization of Jacklin* (1912). Rather we must turn to her journalistic social criticism, where her voice escapes from the control of those powerful, patriarchal ventriloquists who sought to incorporate her into their own high dramas.

Florence Farr's most extended presentation of her views on woman's role in society can be found in *Modern Woman: Her Intentions* (1910). The chapter headings are a summary of her lifelong agenda as representative of the "New Woman":

1. The Vote
2. Women's Incomes
3. The Variations of Love
4. The Sordid Divorce
5. The Green Houses of Japan (a defense of prostitution)
6. Beauty and Motherhood
7. The New Psychology (and the possibilities of a matriarchal society)
8. The Imaginative Woman
9. Experiments (in the relationships between men and women)
10. The Savage, the Barbarian, the Civilized

But the tone of this ninety-four-page monograph is uncertain, and in retrospect we can see that it anticipates her decision to leave England two years later. Farr clearly feels that she belongs to an earlier, "Ibsen" generation, and that the aggressive attitudes of the new feminism which had been building since roughly 1906 have left her behind. In the preface she confesses that "in writing of the women of the first ten years of . . . the Woman's Century" some readers will think her "outrageously advanced," while others will dismiss her as "absurdly conventional." If we are to hear the authentic voice of Florence Farr, freed from the constraints of contemporary opinion and powerful companions, we must turn to her journalism of 1907–8.

In May 1907 Farr returned from a highly successful three-month stay in America, where she had lectured widely on the theories of speaking verse to music which she and Yeats had developed (she was to summarize these two years later in *The Music of Speech*). Her American tour had been sponsored by the New York lawyer John Quinn, a friend of Yeats and Lady Gregory, who was to become the leading patron of modernist art. Farr landed in England, full of energy and self-confidence, at almost exactly the time when A. R. Orage took over *The New Age* (the first issue of the New Series was May 2, 1907). Orage was a remarkable editor who allowed his contributors great freedom, and over the next decade he was to turn his Fabian journal into the most important record of the British cultural and political scene. Between May 23, 1907, and January 4, 1908, Farr contributed eighteen short essays to *The New Age*, giving full and lively expression to her personal opinions. The first essay, "G.B.S. and New York" (May 23, 1907), manages to praise that city's energies while at the same time firmly distancing herself from Bernard Shaw. Shaw is "New York incarnate," sharing a "certain delicate brutality" with the city but not yet appreciating its orna-mental beauties. She concludes: "Mr. Shaw will write about another kind of woman when he has found his own place in New York."

This gesture of independence is followed (May 30, 1907) by a celebration of Mrs. Patrick Campbell's role in the play *Votes for Women*. Arguing from current theories of eugenics, Farr claims that women should be active outside the home and in poli-tics for the sake of the race: "Indiscriminate pity is the danger that threatens the race and women ought to remember this when they start life as innocent enchantresses." This theme is developed further in her article "The Silence of Adolescence" (June 6, 1907), where she argues for "Socratic" guidance to guard against "permanent ado-lescents"; and in "Innocent Enchantresses" (June 20, 1907), where—once again fol-lowing the cues of the New Eugenics and Luther Burbank—she concludes that "[g]reat men must be the children of enthusiasm, and the great question for women is how they are to inspire and be inspired with right enthusiasms and exultations." (Almost in an aside Farr suggests that "girls should be asked seriously to think about the future of the race before they are too old and ugly," thus anticipating Yeats's romantic theory in "All Souls' Night" that Farr left England for Ceylon when she found "the first wrinkles on a face / Admired and beautiful").

In "The Shrine of the Jester-Critic" (July 4, 1907) and "The Sword of Laughter" (July 18, 1907), Shaw with his "preaching" is the hidden target, and Farr calls for a laughter that will clarify the soul and promote social decency: "[W]hen women have a sense of humour, they will laugh at men instead of loving them." Her reaction to "Marie Corelli and the Modern Girl" (August 1, 1907) is more mixed. Corelli calls for "delicate chastity, gentle reserve, modesty, and intellectual force," but Farr is aware that most of these qualities play into the hands of a patriarchal society. Her attitude toward sexuality is, as always, a conflicted one, caught between the old expectations and the new views of liberated women.

> It seems most important in these days, when so many thinking women are revolt-ing against the tyranny of the home and the patriarchal law that girls should realise that Alexandre Dumas spoke the exact truth when he said: "There is always one thing a man can do to console a pretty woman who loves him." That "one thing" is the very act which a woman would never willingly allow unless she was passionately attached to a man. . . . The fact is women can be friends with many men and love very few; men can love many women and be friends with very few. Until this fact is clearly acknowledged the sexes will continue their mutual deceptions.

As if to resolve (or avoid) her ambivalence about the sexual role of the New Woman, Farr turns next to "The Rites of Astaroth" (September 5, 1907), anticipat-ing in some ways the anthropological argument that Pound was to employ years later in Canto XLV. She praises the ancient rites that made sexuality sacred, and contrasts these ceremonial passions with the modern West, where "men have seen fit to drag the veil of the flesh away from the temples and leave it in the gutter to fare as well as it can." Although it "is certain from recent researches that all women are not by any means capable of being healthy mothers; it is still a matter of speculation whether a good mother can be a good wife, that is to say a sympathetic companion to a man." As always, Farr is torn between her Victorian past and her recognition of present-day reality, defending prostitution as an unsatisfactory but necessary alternative. But of one thing she is sure: sexuality must be purged of economic forces. She is convinced that "a race is likely to become degenerate so long as the sex question resolves itself ultimately into the question how women can make the best economic bargain and, in so doing, deny themselves the liberty of free choice."

This qualified argument is carried on in "Man" (September 19, 1907) and "Goth and Hun" (September 26, 1907), the latter a commentary on Laurence Binyon's play *Attila*. Passion would not be "so immoderate and so dangerous if cultivation and transmission of passion were taught instead of suppression and concealment in dishonour." Binyon's tragedy is cold and "impersonal," like the modern restoration of a Gothic building. "We must come into contact with what we call the savage spirit" (a Yeatsian phrase) and recapture the mystery of ancient rites.

Farr's drift into semimysticism continues in "Our Evil Stars" (October 3, 1907) and her review of *The Medea of Euripides*, translated by Gilbert Murray (October 24, 1907). Reformation of the marriage laws and public health is not enough: "We must kill the force in us that says we cannot become all that we desire, for that force is our evil star which turns all opportunity into grotesque failure. . . . So let us each recognise the truth that our first business is to change ourselves, and then we shall know how to change our circumstances." Farr wishes to recover the force and mystery of Medea, who "performed all [Jason's] heroic deeds for him" and was "the goddess incarnate." In these two essays Farr's deep interest in the occult mingles uneasily, as always, with her sense of the need for practical reform.

Farr's stint as a regular contributor to *The New Age* ended with her six essays on "Ibsen's Women": Hedda Gabler (October 17, 1907), Rebecca West (October 31, 1907), Nora Helmer (November 14, 1907), Ellida Wangel (November 30, 1907), Rita Allmers (December 21, 1907), and Hilda Wangel (January 4, 1908). These six essays are the most coherent statement she ever produced of her personal views. She had played the role of Rebecca West in the first English production of *Rosmersholm* (February 23, 1891), and she belonged to the "Ibsen generation," not to the newer generation of suffragettes (a term first coined in 1906). Like her more powerful male companions, she tended to interpret life through art, and for her Hedda Gabler was the great type of "transitional womanhood," rebelling against the "mere facts of middle-class life," while Rebecca West, "who will not submit to be degraded by her misfortunes," is the true modern heroine: "The tragedy of the woman who refuses to 'give life to evil by remembering it' and the man who forces her to end everything in the feeble protest of suicide makes 'Rosmersholm' a play of strange power."

In her catalogue of Ibsen's women all of Farr's deepest beliefs, so scattered in her other writings, come into focus. Nora Helmer "was swept out into the open jaws of the world away from the little corner she thought so beautiful," and discovered that reality was "a hideous mockery of her ideal." Ellida Wangel wants only what the modern woman desires—"freedom to choose for ourselves," a "mental transference from servitude to responsibility that is good for the development of human intelligence." Rita Allmers finally discovers that her true mission, "the noblest that a woman could undertake, is to disclose the real nature of the fetish of home," while Hilda Wangel is "Ibsen's greatest affirmation": "Candid, direct, unspoiled by complexities or contradictions, she is that most delightful of beings, a wild child–woman." In the midst of her own complexities and contradictions, Farr can cherish Ibsen's women as clear archetypes of the modern woman's life in a difficult environment, her frequent failures and occasional successes.

After her work for *The New Age* had ended, Farr continued to write for other journals, but she never regained the confident and authentic "voice" we hear in *The New Age* essays. The excitement and self-confidence generated by her visit to America; the generous encouragement of Orage; the chance to take up each interest as it arose—all these factors contributed to a moment of independent power. Looking back over Farr's career, it seems that in the six essays on Ibsen's women she expressed her most profound feelings, so that after that series nothing was left but summary and repetition. Ibsen, not Shaw or Yeats or Pound, was her true mentor, and through his dramas she came to understand herself and her ambiguous place in the women's movement. Ezra Pound must have sensed this, and he made it explicit years later in Canto XXVIII. In this canto he memorializes Farr's abrupt departure from London to Ceylon, where she taught in a College for Girls until her death in 1917.

> *And they wanted more from their women,*
> *Wanted 'em jacked up a little*
> *And sent over for teachers (Ceylon)*
> *So Loica [Shaw's Louka] went out and died there*
> *After her time in the post-Ibsen movement.*[7]

Notes

1. *Florence Farr, Bernard Shaw and W. B. Yeats*, ed. Clifford Bax (Dublin: Cuala Press, 1941). Reviewed in *Times Literary Supplement*, March 7, 1942, p. 118.

2. See Wallace Martin, *The New Age Under Orage* (New York: Barnes & Noble, 1967); Josephine Johnson, *Florence Farr: Bernard Shaw's "New Woman"* (Totowa, N.J.: Rowman and Littlefield, 1975); Cassandra Laity, "W. B. Yeats and Florence Farr: The Influence of the 'New Woman' Actress on Yeats's Changing Images of Women," *Modern Drama*, 28 (December 1985): 620–37; Ronald Schuchard, "'As Regarding Rhythm': Yeats and the Imagists," in *Yeats: An Annual*, ed. Richard Finneran, vol. 2 (1984), pp. 209–26; and material throughout *Yeats and Women*, a special issue of *Yeats Annual*, no. 9, ed. Deirdre Toomey (London: Macmillan, 1992).

3. William Butler Yeats, "All Souls' Night," in *The Collected Poems*, ed. Richard Finneran (New York: Macmillan, 1989), pp. 228–29.

4. *Ezra Pound and Dorothy Shakespear: Their Letters, 1909–1914*, ed. Omar Pound and A. Walton Litz (New York: New Directions, 1984), p. 132.

5. Ezra Pound, "Portrait d'une Femme," in *Personae: The Shorter Poems* (New York: New Directions, 1990), p. 57.

6. *Florence Farr, Bernard Shaw and W. B. Yeats*, pp. 22–23.

7. Ezra Pound, Canto XXVIII, in *The Cantos* (New York: New Directions, 1986), p. 136.

Appendix
Ibsen's Women By Florence Farr

No. 1 Hedda Gabler

There is a wonderful music in the name of Hedda Gabler, an almost magical music. It is one of the best remembered sensations of my life driving rapidly down the Knightsbridge Road after the first epoch-making performance of the play on April 20th, 1891, with the words of the name wailing and singing to me and crowding my mind with all the tragedy of a woman who is not quite enough a woman.

Hedda Gabler's nerves are set on edge by the mere facts of middle-class life. She dreams of men in livery and riding-horses, because she wants to put a stately retinue between herself and natural necessities. She feels acutely the agony of the ideal in the presence of the real; the disgusting contrast of animal functions with the outward beauty of flowers and birds, and the contrast of the genteel poverty which she has fallen into, with the social ideals she believed would mean escape from the boredom of facts.

The background Ibsen has provided for her is perfect. She stands out from it as the woman who failed to find the vine crown of Dionysus and bound instead the purple fillet of her own life blood upon her temples. Tragic and beautiful, yet linked to her surrounding by an inexpressible meanness of outlook, we perceive in her a never-to-be-forgotten picture of the under-sexed woman. She is there among the fussy well-meaning little family so content to shed tears and laugh and accept death and birth and marriage in the regular course of things without thought of impossible wonders which the rich imagination can enjoy and the poor imagination can only crave. For imagination and its creations, the great potencies of art, of oratory, of invention, of empire are the heritage of the childless more often than of the fathers and mothers of our race.

Hedda is especially described as a cold type, a morbid curiosity taking the place of any kind of interest in passion as passion. On the stage I have never seen Ibsen's idea of Hedda Gabler, restrained, thin-haired, a little anæmic, with her steel grey eyes and deadly whisper as she thrusts Lovbörg's MSS. into the flames: "Now I am burning—am burning your child; you woman with beautiful hair." I have seen Elizabeth Robins and Eleonora Duse, but both of them are full to overflowing of a kind of power which it was Hedda's tragedy not to possess. They can feel life, but Hedda cannot. Nothing short of death really thrills her—nothing short of the Dionysus of her imagination with vine-leaves in his hair could have stirred a real pulsation of passion in her heart; anything short of that bores her.

Anyone who has a moderate amount of brain can perceive the incongruities, the gross absurdities, the impossible pretensions of human life—we have to become a little blinded by the light of our life-work before we can really forget such facts. Hedda was clever enough to see through the illusion of the things that are apparent, but she had not enough force to dig into them and to seek the heart of the mystery. She played at life a little while—long enough to hurt her self-respect

—then killed herself rather than contemplate her own incompetence, her own lack of vitality.

The physiology of the sexes appears to be undergoing extraordinary modifications. Co-incident in time with the over-population question there have arisen in our midst women who hate motherhood. These beings are filled with emotional ideals. They are eloquent and clever; they are often the most conspicuous members of their families; they go through life exciting strong enthusiasms and strong antipathies; they look upon average men and women as indecent swine. Hedda Gabler is the great type of this transitional womanhood. The curiosity which Hedda displays about the extravagant details of passion is a curiosity which is tinged with disdain as she wonders at the strange vagaries of human nature. She herself finds nothing to tempt her to join in the throng. She is bored by marriage and driven to desperation by the ignominy of losing her looks and of passing through the other unpleasant details of motherhood. Her position is so logically sound that those who sympathise with it cannot understand how any woman can be found willing to help to increase the population. And it is to be hoped that before long it will only be those women who really hear their unborn children crying imperatively to them that will be expected to become mothers of a generation that may surpass in quality if not quantity this generation of unwilling wives and unmated mothers. If there were not in Hedda Gabler's tragedy this background of the tragedy of the transitional woman it would be mean enough. To listen to the aspirations of a young woman who wants to ride in the Row with a liveried servant and a fashionable habit would be futile indeed—but that is the mere blind expression of the needs of a highly-strung woman who cares neither for sex nor for motherhood. She has dim yearnings for an intellectual comradeship with men; but she has not learned to stand up to life enough to succeed. When a woman's social ambition is bounded by suburban ideas she must be very careful to keep within the bounds prescribed by suburban opinion. To be mixed up in any kind of scandal, to have to appear in any public capacity, let alone in a law court, to have to take a part of any kind in a matter that is likely to be commented on by the newspapers is a thing not to be thought of by a real lady in Suburbia. And up to a certain point that is all poor Hedda Gabler is; she is a real lady of the suburbs. Then comes the quaint touch of poetry that justifies her beautiful name, that almost makes her of one kin with the goddesses who demanded not love but great deeds from their heroes: the goddesses created in an age before woman had learned to be abject and amorous, when instead she was half-mother, half-lover, with a touch of the patron saint. Hedda dimly feels that some such relation is possible between a man and a woman. The despised Thea, with the beautiful hair, has achieved something of the kind in her own little trembling way. Somehow her very weakness has been an inspiration to men. Hedda longs for a more positive influence, and she invokes Dionysus and his vine-leaves. But Dionysus and the mighty huntress of men, the red-haired Diana, are too over-coloured for Hedda's taste. Just as so many others have done who sought ecstasy and found drunkenness, sought illumination and found darkness, Hedda sought excitement and found hideous dissipation. Her romance, her cold savagery, when she destroys the great book written by the man who loved her, and confided in her his love for other women, redeem her character from meanness.

She shoots herself finally for many reasons, but chief among them was probably the abiding sense that women of her temperament must have of the mediocre ugliness of the only life they know.

Matthew Arnold has put the case of Hedda Gabler in a haunting quatrain:—

> "An aching body, and a mind
> Not wholly clear, or wholly blind,
> Too keen to rest, too weak to find,
> Are God's worst portion to mankind."

The very meanness of this tragedy of Norwegian Suburbia is the thing that cuts us to the heart. We know that thousands and thousands of girls in every part of the world are being trained into just these little purposeless grooves of thought. They are realising the unpleasant details of motherhood; they want to imitate the fine ladies they see driving in the park; they want to amuse themselves by flirting with a dozen men; they want to escape all that touches the disgusting aspects of life; they want to keep the hem of their skirts white. In pursuit of these ideals they harden their hearts until they are like dead things without sympathy or understanding, harbouring the strange perverted jealousy of the dog in the manger and the aimless conceit of a foolish tradition which tells them perpetually: "My dear, people don't do these things." Hedda's case makes us realise the futility of conventionality, for she was conventional in all her ideals; only her selfish instincts broke through and shattered her system of morals. She would not hear of "any kind of unfaithfulness"; she was ready to flirt and lead men on; but some innocent critics have even gone the length of supposing that she "preferred death to dishonour." Why Hedda really preferred death is, I believe, simply because she was proud enough to feel the ignominy of the situation which was forced upon her by Brack's knowledge of her secret. She was ready to commit any crime that amused her if she did it of her own free will and was sure it would not be found out; but she was not willing to be forced into a mean intrigue. That was what surprised Brack, who had not reckoned on the pride of General Gabler's daughter.

Pride is a very effective substitute for virtue, and has much the same effect on our actions; but if the nature has innate nobility it will remain noble, however much it may outrage social standards; so, perhaps, Hedda's chastity was rather a poor affair after all.

No. 2 Rebecca West

One of our contemporaries, a woman who has fought through every kind of slander and kept her self-respect, has written the words: "Do not give life to evil by remembering it." That is the most revolutionary doctrine that can be preached. Carried out faithfully it would put such a stir into feeble wills and crushed-down spirits that Heaven might be experienced at any moment in the hearts of all mankind. If we could realise what it would mean to put away from our memories all our grievances, all our downfalls, all our regrets, we should spend the rest of our lives in striving to control our memories and destroy the hells we each one of us has created with so much earnestness of purpose.

Rebecca West started life with a sound faith in her own capacity to keep her conscience in order. When she was a young girl she fell a victim to an old admirer of her mother's, and she remained faithfully nursing him through two years of paralysis until she was about twenty-five. He died, leaving her quite unprovided for, and she turned her fascination to account by charming a very hysterical lady who was the childless wife of the principal landowner in the neighbourhood.

Like many another woman who has an unpleasant secret of the kind, Rebecca knew other people would look upon her as an outcast if they had the chance, and she possessed all the freedom of the hopeless vagabond. Rosmer, on the contrary, belonged to the best old family in those parts, he was a student, and liked a pleasant quiet companionship. A wife with some hysterical aberrations had made him feel a loathing for any kind of violent passion. He had all the charm, therefore, of a man who does not pursue women. Added to this, his taste, his intellectual speculations, and his social position overwhelmed the clever girl fresh from two years of self-sacrifice at the bedside of a paralytic. I do not think that any other training has such an effect on the young as that long watching of a case of senile paralysis: to see some capable strong-minded man or woman gradually change; the body just a little feebler month by month, but the intellect evaporating and the friend one knew vanishing and needing nothing but the attentions that a one-year-old child requires of its nurse. To watch this heart-rending disease saps all one's belief in the immortality of intellect and in the value of individual endeavour. A young man or woman leaves such a death bed with only one firm faith, and that is the necessity of taking all he or she can get out of life while it is day, "or ever the silver cord be loosed or the golden bowl be broken."

Rebecca belonged to the democracy; she was a daughter of Finland, strong with the strength of those who have nothing to lose; relentless as a young bird of prey she descended upon the dark joyless household where a passionate miserable woman brooded at the fireside opposite a refined sensitive gentleman.

It was not long before Rebecca's womanhood overtook her. She was at the dangerous age when women suddenly awake; when the old easy life of acceptance ceases, when they desire to choose for themselves instead of submitting eternally to being chosen. She chose Rosmer, who was the incarnation of all she herself could never hope to achieve. Of gentle blood, of assured position, of exceptional and sensitive good-taste, he was by temperament and possession all that represented to her the unattainable. She spread her nets for him in vain—he was not capable of underhand action, his breed was pure, and he lived up to the ideals of his profession.

Then the battle began. She meant to win. She thought life was such a simple thing. She thought one had only to take what one desired. She had not the smallest warning that desire fails us all at the moment of accomplishment, and leaves nothing but a vacancy in the place of the burning will and striving intellect.

The hysterical Beata irritated her at first with her passionate affection; by degrees she took a delight perhaps in torturing this incubus-woman who was always demanding exuberant demonstrations from those she loved. She began to see that unhappy nature through Rosmer's eyes; she began to take warning by the example and to sympathise with his desire for quiet comradeship; but at the same time she "wanted Beata away," and she hinted and hinted until she finally attained her desire and Beata drowned herself. But Beata was more powerful in death than life. Rosmer was staggered by the tragedy and Rebecca's will was broken by her success. She made no further attempt to capture her prey; the Rosmer view of life had penetrated her heart and she was content to wait and serve.

From that time her only care was to try and shield Rosmer from self-reproach, and she urged him to take an active part in social propaganda. When the play begins she is still hoping that the two of them together will do some good work in the world. She has realised the soul-purging effect of kindness and tenderness. She has committed a horrible and malignant crime, but all the horror and malignity have melted away in the real tenderness of her love for Rosmer. Peace descends upon her, a stillness like the stillness of the northern cliffs and quiet of the birds under the midnight sun. So it was she gave life to good by forgetting evil.

But their Revolutionary propaganda roused all the powers that be. Vested interests hand in hand with the blindness that will not see was at their doors and all their little world was in arms. The politicians took up their usual weapons and Rosmer was gagged by fear of public opinion and his passion for innocence.

The "immature dream of innocence" passes away and he descends into the hell of his own heart. He realises that he too is capable of a passion that would break down all barriers. He gives up his convictions one by one in order that he and his comrade may be united—then with a blow of a sledge hammer he feels—she is no longer the comrade he believed in. He has lost his faith in himself and his faith in her.

Like a mother she indulges him in whim after whim—with only one shudder of horror she consents to die the death she had forced upon Beata—she gives up the game. Then she finds she has won him altogether. He cannot live without her; he has killed her will and she has killed his faith. They have no further hope but in an expiation which may sanctify their first and last embrace as they fling themselves together into the mill-race.

Sin seems a simple thing to the people whose duty it is to punish crime. Someone is murdered, all that has to be done is to murder the murderer, now—just as they used to do when the Jewish lawgiver claimed inspiration. I cannot see very much difference between a human sacrifice under the auspices of the law and a human sacrifice under the auspices of religion. Murder fills us all with a shuddering horror; it is impossible to think of oneself killing a man, or a sheep, or a snail, or anything larger than a fly without unutterable disgust. Yet one knows perfectly well that there have been moments in one's life when one would gladly have gripped with fang and claw if it had been possible. The longing to throw a heavy glass inkstand at the heads of one's relations is familiar to most of us. Needless to say the rage in our hearts generally finds vent in some such phrase as "How very annoying!" Still we should all deserve hanging if thoughts could kill and desires could punish, and it seems as if that did happen with the thoughts and desires of the dead. The dead Beata broods over the House of Rosmer, bringing no blessing, but a curse. Everyone is more comfortable without her, but slowly out of the darkness her sorrow rises up and drags down to death the man and the woman who were made to give each other that mysterious exchange of influence which is one of the greatest mysteries of life.

Rosmer had been almost awakened to a feeling of inspiration. He felt he could rouse the sleepers round him and stir them into some kind of thought so that the chains of folly and ignorance might be loosened. Rebecca had learned the hardest of lessons. She was a woman who, having once sacrificed herself as the nurse of a para-lytic man, sacrifices herself again and dies—the victim of the man who had no faith in her. She evidently is born a mother-woman, created for devotion and sacrifice to someone or something. Doubtless the old Ibsen maxim that "a woman who has once sacrificed herself for others does not do so again" was hers when she started her cam-paign; but she was a woman made for self-sacrifice, made to tend and care for a man even to the extent of creating some luminous ideal for his imagination to play with. For a little time, after her martyrdom to the exacting old sinner, Dr. West, she felt ready to fight for her own hand. But soon love caught her and forced her on her knees once more. In one day she is brought face to face with the sacrifice of honour Dr. West, like Cenci, has exacted from his own daughter and the sacrifice of life Rosmer, the sensitive scholar, the man of breeding, exacts. Like Beatrice Cenci, after one throb of terror she faces death bravely.

The tragedy of the woman who refuses to "give life to evil by remembering it" and the man who forces her to end everything in the feeble protest of suicide makes "Rosmersholm" a play of strange power. But the gloomy household and the gradual deadening of the living woman counterbalance the charm and poetry that must always surround the brave daughters of Finland, or any woman like Rebecca West who will not submit to be degraded by her misfortunes.

No. 3 Nora Helmer

Every man, woman and child among us is Nora Helmer. Many critics have written about that play as if it was possible to go out of our front doors into a world that will reveal us to ourselves. Yet who among us had learned that secret? Did Ibsen himself see it with his eyes like gimlets peering out at men and women, peering into his own heart, peering into the hearts of others and noting down the psychic and physical symptoms of his patients? What is the greatest among us that he should say: "I know myself. I have found myself?" We are all dolls, puppets, and toys, and he who thinks himself wisest is the greatest fool.

"Know thyself,"—the everlasting riddle dangled before us all by the Principali-ties and Powers that they may laugh at our efforts and make merry on the fruit we bring forth.

Once in a dream I stood with those Principalities and Powers before the Tree of Life. One of the branches was dead, with five, ripe, beautiful fruit still hanging to their exhausted stalks. And the Powers whispered to each other, "Let us cut off the dead branch and cry aloud that we take it away to plant it in the earth so that in its turn it may become a Tree of Life." And they said those words as they cut through the wood and carried the branch away. Then they ate the fruit and threw away the branch. I said: "Why did you utter those words?" and they replied: "In order that the other branches may do likewise. The fruit brought forth at the price of the death of the bringer is the fruit we eat with most relish." Perhaps the vision is cynical, but such it was, and it is a symbol of man's hope.

Poor little Nora Helmer goes out into the world full of hope; she is going to face facts for herself; she thinks that if she makes up her own mind about religion and facts she will be nearer the truth. She feels she must go outside the ready-made ideas of her husband and father—outside the region of unjust law—outside the region where abstract principles, such as justice and order, are called in to justify the majority, and put the thoughtless, or rather, those who have trained themselves to think for their own advantage, in an unassailable position of authority and trust. But the truth is that at the beginning of the play she knows and sees far more clearly than Helmer. She is as wise as Omar Khayyam, who was only second in wisdom to the author of Ecclesiastes. She sees laws are man-made, morals are man-made, convention—good taste, is man-made; and that the prestige which all of them have borrowed from religion and divine right is vanity of vanities. She sees nature is cruel as the grave, exacting in retribution, shedding sunlight and punishment alike on the just and the unjust. But she thinks she will discover new secrets; she thinks there is some master-key to the mystery, and she desires liberty and loneliness that she may find it.

Here, of course, she agrees with all the great sages of the world. One and all have declared that the first step in the degrees of wisdom is to fast in the wilderness; to acquire some sense of our own instinct, our own tendencies, apart from the stimulus of attractions and repulsions. Even the least-loved member of a family cannot know himself until he has gone out from the hatred which surrounds him. We are influenced through hatred even more powerfully than we are influenced by love; because hatred is a cutting off, a concentration of malignity; and love is only a kind of expansion of tenderness. It acts in every direction, while hatred focuses itself in one direction. But Nora Helmer was loved by everyone, just as a pretty kitten is loved by everyone because it is young and merry and full of little guiles and tricks to keep ugly things out of sight. It will never gobble up its food like a puppy; it is discreet and charming from the first, and does not require the whip to teach it good manners.

Every man has an impulse to act the father to his beloved, just as every woman wants to pet her lover as if she were a mother cossetting a baby. I cannot see that Helmer is to be blamed for his attitude towards his wife; the only thing that one can say about him is that he is an intolerable prig. He is a man of principle, and it seems a very difficult thing for a man honest enough to merit an appointment as bank-manager not to be a prig; any business man is brought up in such an atmosphere of cheating and bribery that it is quite natural he should take a pride in a probity which is his private capacity would be a matter of course. We have not enough mercy on people who struggle to be good and do their duty. It seems such an absurd attitude—still, we must remember that society is a ladder, and those at the bottom who have set out to climb to the top have to cheer themselves after each toilsome step by a complacency which amuses those who have abandoned the social ladder in favour of the ladder of the intellect or the ladder of the emotions.

After all, in spite of Ibsen's special pleading for Nora, she has been mothering Helmer quite as much as he has been fathering her. She has deceived him for his

good, and indulged his foolish prejudices against sweetmeats and his prudent prejudice against debt. He has deceived her into thinking him a very fine fellow, ready to
risk his honour and liberty in defence of helpless woman; just as readily as she was
ready to risk her honour and life in defence of helpless man. The family was a particularly merry one under this system of mutual illusion, and it is possibly the only
way to hope for merriment in family life. The husband and wife that respect each
enough to keep up each others' illusions have a better chance than the frankly brutal couple who respect neither each other nor themselves. Without illusion no one
but That which understands everything can forgive everything. And what man or
woman can be sure of having attained to That?

Ibsen wrote the "Doll's House" early in his career. At that time, no doubt, he
himself was playing the part of Greger Werle in "The Wild Duck,"—the apostle of
the ideal and of Truth. Later on Ibsen saw that family life must be founded on mutual
forbearance, that is to say, on mutual deception. No human being can live in the
presence of Jehovah, and no human being could live in the presence of Truth or any
other absolute abstract principle. It is a condition of manifest life that it should be
concrete and limited, one-sided, full of prejudices and convictions. When these fail,
desire fails, and the grasshopper is a burden and man goeth to his long home and the
mourners go about the streets.

Half the misery of a young man and woman arises from a pathetic belief in the
absolute. All the inspiration of life arises from the faith that we may attain to it; to
some clear, bright state when all things shall be as verifiable as mathematics. This
faith is ours, side by side with the knowledge that in our hearts we love charm and
fascination and glamour, taste and discrimination, choice, and a power to do good or
evil. When we realise the joy of the absolute, the changeless Seer, it may, as an experience, be known as the supreme ecstasy. Yet it is only an ecstasy because we contrast
it with the ever-flowing panorama of manifest existence.

Nora has lived in the ebb and flow of life; she has set up Helmer as her ideal of
the absolute. He has appreciated the position and taken the place of the Almighty
in her cosmos with the utmost complacency. But, after all, a bank-manager has his
limitations, just as any other man has; and in spite of St. Paul's exhortations to the
contrary, women are beginning to find out that men are not altogether satisfactory
representatives of absolute deity.

Against the general atmosphere of mutual flattery in the Helmer household I
have nothing to say; it is one of my quarrels with the home as an institution that it
makes those who are happy satisfied with a very low standard of social brilliance. No
public society could endure the jokes of a happy and united family any more than
they could endure the quarrels of an embittered family; although any permanent
body of people, such as a theatrical company or a committee, either quarrel a great
deal, like the House of Commons, or do not attend sittings, like the House of Lords.

As far as one can tell, an ideal social state would be one of permanent imper-
manence. The social units constantly subject to change, like the drops of the ocean
purified by the perpetual motion of the waves, would keep a more vivid existence
than if, like the drops of water in a stagnant pool, they are left in their corners to
breed disease and ague. It is coming to this, and the little stagnant pools, beautiful

as they are in their drowsy way, are being swept out into the ocean just as Nora Helmer was swept out into the open jaws of the world away from the little corner she thought so beautiful and found such a hideous mockery of her ideal. The life of a family in the true sense, bound to the soil, inheriting land from generation to generation, was an attempt to stem the savage tides which tear through human beings just as surely as they tear through sea and ocean. But we are beginning to see a new kind of family—the father slaving that the son may spend; the son springing from the gutter becoming the master of men. And the children who will conquer the world lie in the heart of that braver life.

No. 4 The Lady from the Sea

It is a panic fear that Ellida Wangel feels in the presence of the man who has filled her imagination and is to her the incarnation of the mystery and gruesome darkness of the sea. Pan has taken possession of her, and she is in touch with all the strange life of the elemental creatures with which mankind has ceased to have communion. Man is a creature of dust, and it is only natural that he should draw the life he calls "his life" from the dust. Ellida was a creature of the water of the sea, and had her life from that lovely element.

We who care for literature feel a little resentful when our art has to serve its destroyers. We are jealous when we find science, with its words like cast-iron railings, defining and dividing up the old beauty and the old wisdom. In the same way, having been seized with the poetry of the idea of the enchanted lady from the sea, we resent having to follow Dr. Ibsen into the details of pathological research. Still, he has led the way and go we must. Ellida Wangel is subjected to two kinds of attraction, and both of them threaten to take entire possession of her nature; she feels bound to both, yet able to choose neither. Thus she is not so much the type of a wife longing for emancipation as of the human will longing to free itself both from civilisation and from Life itself.

The Stranger from the ship beckons Ellida back to a more elemental life just as Death beckons all of us to cast away the ties which bind us to life.

We who are crying for a re-valuation of all values want, after all, only what Ellida wanted,—freedom to choose for ourselves. We want more scope for the responsibility of human beings; we want it to be possible for a greater variety of social standards to exist in the little stagnant corners of the world. Ellida was oppressed by social convention, and she really only wanted the pressure removed; when that was done she was prepared to act in accordance with convention. All of us have cried out against authority in our time as if it were something driving us against our will. But the great mystery is that the moment we have kicked over the traces and started, as we say, freed from visible control, the law of our own being takes the place of authority; and our sense of responsibility drives us afterwards in the same direction as our sense of servitude drove us before.

It is this mental transference from servitude to responsibility that is good for the development of human intelligence. A sense of responsibility is far more likely to end in right action than the impulse of perverse resistance every real personality experiences in the presence of authority. These perverse experiences of the human mind are very frequent among the leonine types of men; but there are multitudes of men who belong to another type altogether,—dog-like natures which positively rejoice in being controlled. These are the people who almost deserve to have tails, they would take such delight in wagging them as they ask for advice and guidance from their friends. The more you beat them the better they'll be; they tell you so themselves. Just because so many creatures of this breed have found their way into the human race the more leonine natures, rarer and more admirable in every sense, have to live under laws only fit for dogs.

In watching, some years ago, an indifferent performance of the "Lady from the Sea" it was amusing to see the dog-like audience flabbergasted at the mere idea of a husband having the patience to discuss with his wife the question of her infatuation for another man. Such a course of conduct seemed to these faithful creatures so outside reality as to border on farce, and they sniggered through the scene until they were deprived of breath by the climax which comes when Wangel releases his wife from her bond and sets her free to choose. In Mr. Edward Garnett's magnificent study, "The Breaking Point," we have a woman of Ellida Wangel's temperament torn similarly between her father and her lover, but neither of these men has the courage to put Dr. Wangel's prescription to the test, and the woman, in consequence, is broken between the two and driven to seek refuge in death.

That in all probability would have been Ellida's solution also if her husband had not remembered in the nick of time, that the dog will come when it is called, the cat will walk away. For the dog-like public prefer that men should bluster and women submit; so the main thesis of this play is never likely to make "The Lady from the Sea" really popular. It has a lesson for leaders, not for the multitude.

A very interesting question that arises from the study of the psychology of Ellida Wangel is the relation between falling under hypnotic influence and falling under the more personal influence we call love. The results are different, of course, but they start in much the same way. It is well known that even skilled hypnotists cannot influence everybody. It appears as if all the means used by hypnotists, such as flashes of light, concentration of the sight and so on, are powerless in themselves. The operator must make some strong appeal to the imagination in hypnotism as in love.

In ordinary life we should describe the stranger in Ibsen's play as a romantic and mysterious man. Very little is known of him; his influence exists almost entirely in Mrs. Wangel's own mind. Dr. Wangel, on the contrary, is a kind little man, transparent as the day and rather fond of consoling himself with cognac. There is no mystery about him. Ellida sees him every day of her life and he exists entirely in the outside objective world. She has no need to think about him, or imagine him; he is always there.

All the great loves in history have been the loves of lovers divided by death or misfortune; they have grown out of the first overwhelming impression made by the beloved one's face or smile; their development has been entirely in the imagination of the lover. They are, in fact, the result of the magical force of the imagination heated until it glows with that adoring faith which brings miracles to pass. This wonderful flower of love fed upon itself is very different from the ordinary passion of daily life,—the passion that writes the book of happy married love; but it is not very different from hypnotic influence. The ideal love is a creature of the dream world,—the world in which Ellida lived for three years, filling it with the sea and the enchantment of the sea. She was a dreamer, but no great joy and no great art came from her dreams; she only was possessed with the panic dread. The eyes of her child changing with the light, like the sea, terrified her. Her phantom lover standing by her side peered at her also with those changing eyes, and she only trembled as she felt her reason giving way under the stress of vivid dreaming. This power exercised over another is the power that has inspired many great poems, many great deeds; but when it is not an inspiration it is a horrible terror, and we speak of the man or woman who suffers it as possessed or obsessed.

The Stranger exercises a far more powerful authority over Ellida than her own husband, because he has this kind of hold upon her imagination. He loses it because the husband is clever enough to make a further bid. The Stranger says to her: Come to me of your own free will. She says in effect: I would come to you if I were free, but my husband's authority binds me to him. The husband replies: I set you free; follow your own will. And almost immediately her imagination abandons the old *idée fixe* which had tormented her so long and delights itself in the idea of free choice. She turns to her deliverer and bids the Stranger good-bye for ever. Wangel takes her to his arms, and we may presume they are happy ever after.

To bribe a woman by dangling before her the old apple of the Tree of Knowledge of Good and Evil seems a sorry trick. But it serves its turn. The illusion of free-will to choose good or evil is the strongest of all illusions, and we each accept it in our turn. Logic forbids us to believe in it, but life insists on our belief; and Ellida is going to live. Henceforth she will take her part in a nice humdrum little family, reproduce her species, and darn her husband's socks. What more need any woman want?

No. 5   Rita Allmers

As men and women go through life facts that have been symbols, almost without meaning to them, gain a deeper and deeper significance. "Little Eyolf" was written towards the close of Ibsen's career, and we find in it all the profound under-currents of family life treated with the clear insight of the fully ripened intellect. To the superficial playgoer the problem between the husband and wife seems strained and unnatural; any inexperienced person would have thought that having lost their only child the obvious course would have been to consider the possibility of becoming parents a second time, but it is the whole point of the play that Alfred Allmers never even thinks of such a possibility: Ibsen is quite right when he brings out the all-absorbing mystery that men and women cannot and will not be guided by logical reasoning.

Rita is a great lady owning land and gold; she is also tall and fair, entrancingly beautiful and ardent. She and her husband have been married ten years and had never been apart for twenty-four hours until Alfred started on his seven weeks' tramp on the mountains. Alfred, on the other hand, has a deep affection for his half-sister; he has married Rita for her beauty and her money, but always with the thought of providing for Asta. The impression given to the audience is simply that he is wearied of matrimony and longs for solitude and even death. But on carefully reading the play one discovers a far deeper cause for his wandering, groping state of mind. For years he has tried to relieve the boredom of too much affection by teaching his little crippled son and by composing a work on "Human Responsibility." When he goes out on the mountains he is brought face to face with the appalling truths that his ideas are all second-hand, that he has no first-hand knowledge of even the preliminary stage of the metamorphoses of the spirit, and that he is not a servant of the public "whose law is duty, whose aim is service, whose watchword is responsibility." When he finds this out he does not see how he can cure his sense of shame until the idea strikes him that he will renounce the hope of being an author and live out his responsibility for his crippled child.

He comes home so full of the idea of saving himself from despair by a metamorphosis of spirit that he takes no notice of his beautiful, ardent wife; whose desire to possess him entirely, heart and mind and body, has been intensified by his absence. His love is of the kind which men feel in their hearts to be unclean; the feeling, in themselves, which makes them contemptuous of a woman's love when it is openly manifested. Her love is intense and absorbing enough to give her no spontaneous consciousness of selfishness. She is, as far as she can tell, absolutely devoted to her husband; she has given him leisure and luxury, and in return she demands that he shall love her in her way.

When the dramatic crash comes at the end of the first act and little Eyolf is drowned, Alfred sentimentalises with Asta and is irritated beyond endurance by Rita's attempts at reconciliation. The second crash comes when he learns that Asta, on whom he had relied for pure sisterly tenderness, is not his sister at all, and that she also feels a passionate attachment for him. Then he indeed feels the earth clutching at him from all sides, and in his passion for the sea and sky he longs for the utter solitude of mountains, where he can rejoice in the peace and luxury of death.

Towards the end of the play Rita is in despair over her failure as wife and mother; suddenly the screams of children being beaten by drunken fathers and the sounds of women shrieking for help in the hovels on her estate come to her as a revelation. In an instant she flings aside all her old-fashioned ideas, all her old prejudices. She sees her course plainly. Her own homelife has been nothing but a cloak for intemperate sensuality. Down there among the hovels, human lives are being wasted and ruined in order to keep up the wretched mockery of home. She will take all those little children away from their unworthy parents, she will give them good food and clean clothing, she will love them more than she ever loved her own child, the poor little interloper that separated her from her husband, and she will see that the children on her own estate at least have the chance of growing up in health and vigour, with strong bones and pure blood in their veins. She sees clearly that human life is valuable in itself, and that no ideal of home ought to be allowed to prevent us from insisting that the children of the poor shall at least be clean and well-nourished, whatever their parents may be. She had known the unspeakable pain of bearing a child, and she had seen the vision of the "great open eyes" of her child looking up at her through the deep water; and they pierced her heart as they revealed to her that sad hopelessness of the children that are not wanted. Now she knows that her grief shall be fruitful at last. She will do all she can to ennoble the children for whom she makes herself responsible; she knows the uselessness of second-hand ideas. She has no grand educational schemes for stuffing children with trash, but she will feed them so that they may have brains to think with and limbs to work with when the time comes.

Her mission, the noblest that a woman could undertake, is to disclose the real nature of the fetish of home; for she sees that it often demoralises the happy and depraves the miserable. Her husband joins with her gladly in the work, and he looks her straight in the eyes as he says his aim and her aim are alike directed towards the topmost peaks of human possibility. The last word of the play is her thanks to him for his understanding.

The whole power of ignorance is organised against any real social progress. The home used to be only a harmless indulgence; a means for securing the average man the woman of his choice against the fascination of the more dangerous men who are above or below the average. But now the home is no longer a harmless indulgence. We are told that the children of the poor must not be given food and clothing at the public expense because the parents must be taught their duty to the home, and not allowed to spend their incomes in drink and self-indulgence. I would like to know how a generation of healthy children can possibly be reared on an income of a guinea a week for a family of six people. That means exactly sixpence a day for each person for food, clothing, shelter, insurance, amusement, travelling. This is a respectable average for a working man's wage, but a low average for his family.

People who talk glibly about economy among the working classes should try for a little while to see what kind of a life they could lead themselves on such an income, when rents are at 7s. 6d. for two unfurnished rooms in a slum. It seems to me not in the least surprising that the poor give up this and darker problems and spend their sixpence a day on beer to drown the thought of their wretched existence. The physical degeneracy of the poor and the self-indulgent is so terrible at the present time that it is above all important that if money and devotion are to be spent on anything they should be spent in ways that will ensure the health of the rising generation. A system of insurance among prostitutes in order that they need not be driven by starvation to practise their profession when they are out of health is one remedy that has been suggested; another is that the money that is spent on prisons and lunatic asylums should be spent upon the prevention rather than the punishment of crime and imbecility.

But such remedies, merely because they are founded on logical common sense, will never be carried out until passionate women like Rita Allmers, feeling their own motherhood is a failure, stand shoulder to shoulder and say: "We know the sorrow of women in childbirth, and we refuse to bear the waste of that sorrow any longer. The State asks us for children, but we reply that only when the children that have been born already are valued will we do our share in bringing more children into the world." Rita Allmers looked at the straight limbs of the little street urchins, and saw that if they were fed and clothed properly their chance was quite as good as that of her own child, accidentally crippled as he was.

No. 6 Hilda Wangel

Like the north wind—bracing, invigorating, stimulating, Hilda Wangel fills our nostrils with the breath of life. She brings no languorous breeze bearing the spices of the south, no nipping blast from the east full of repentance, regrets, and retributions, no rain-laden storm from the west, but clear and brilliant as frost-crystals she sees and conquers and thrills us. She is Ibsen's greatest affirmation. Candid, direct, unspoiled by complexities or contradictions, she is that most delightful of beings, a wild child-woman. Her man was chosen when she was a child, and when her ten years of waiting were up she came to him to claim him as her kingdom. She surrounded him with ideal attributes, and when he seemed to fall short of her ideals she forced him to fulfil them. To see him great was her ambition, to find him a little mean, a little dizzy, was her supreme tragedy. By comparison his death was no tragedy in her eyes, for it did not imply defeat, and she cried out in triumph even at the moment of his destruction, that he had conquered.

It is said that there are three metamorphoses of the spirit of man: the first is an awakening to responsibility for others; the second is an awakening to the joke of it all; the third is an awakening to the value of life just as it is, without purpose, without discipline, without wisdom, or property, or anything but unbounded faith in the immediate present and one's own royal prerogative. The return, in a word, to the state of the divine child.

We are all attracted and terrified by those whose spirits are undergoing these fermentations. The "responsible" spirits jog along, hoping that something may come of it in the future if they keep their attention sufficiently fixed on the past. They save us trouble, and we generally feel a great weight of gratitude, which burden prevents our feeling the smallest enthusiasm for the kindly souls who do their duty by us from high motives. The philosophers who have heard the second trumpet-blast of the spirit, puzzle us, amuse us, terrify us, attract and repel us by turns. But it is the wild children, the great founders of religions, the simple saints and yogis who have heard the third blast, that are engaged in the real and final transmutation of the spirit. The child-spirits hate good done in a roundabout way for the artificial motive of duty. They hate double-dealing and meanness instinctively. They have no desire to do evil that good may come in the old way of those who make themselves "responsible" for others. They do not care for the divine laughter of philosophy, they mix duty, philosophy, and faith in one melting-pot, and when their work is finished we get the supreme incarnation of spirit in the heart of some divine wanderer. Such beings have been fed on the red tincture of the alchemists which is obtained by overwhelming the dark doctrine of duty in the white laughter of philosophy so often that all the darkness and brightness unite and are born again in the redness of the perfected and perfecting qualities of the little child.

There is always a period in a child's life, roughly from two till six years, when its sayings are full of a profound, direct, and spontaneous wisdom never to be regained. Whether this blessed state is defiled by contact with older people or by the direct influence of education one cannot tell. I have seen one instance in which the child-spirit was carefully fostered by the father, a university professor, who considered that education was a curse. He thought this more especially about women, who, he believed, should be content to learn reading, writing, French, dancing and the use of money. He pleased himself by believing that his girl kept the charm of childhood; but the success of his hope was not so conspicuous as it was in the case of Hilda Wangel, who was born to influence others. To abound in vitality was her way of preserving the child-spirit unspoiled. She was not brought up on any particular system; but no stronger spirit encountered hers. If she was educated she was not influenced by authority, but only, and always, by her affections, and she never questioned their promptings for a moment.

She descends upon Master Builder Solness, and brings with her, as I have suggested, the invigoration of the wind that blows straight from the north. She has no touch of sickly conscience; her mate is to be noble and great. She finds him surrounded by mouldering influences; jealousy of the younger generation; fear of some necessary expiation of his own relentlessness in the past; and above all with one of those deadening relations which form the sombre background of so many homes. A wife and husband who deceive each other are often quite happy together; but a wife and husband who have totally false ideas about each other and who spend their time in weaving imaginary wrongs, imaginary misunderstandings, are hopelessly wretched. Mrs. Solness has been afflicted from the beginning with that terrible kind of rectitude that positively wants things to be disagreeable in order that there may be opportunity for sacrifice and duty-mongering. She sacrificed her children to duty because rather than let them be brought up by hand she nursed them when she was feverish. Solness thinks it is this which preys on her mind; but after all it is not the break with the future which worried her, but the break with all the old family relics, and above all the destruction of the playthings she had cherished. Mrs. Solness is the child-woman, too, but she is ashamed of it, and plays with her dolls secretly; Solness never has the least suspicion how dear they are to her, but the unashamed Hilda wins her confidence in five minutes, and the whole secret is out. It would have been a thrilling problem for all three of them if Solness had lived to come down from the high tower and take his Princess in his arms before the world: for Hilda's conscience had got a little sick. She did not mind carrying Solness off from a woman she did not know, but she found the problem much more alarming after she had had her confidential talk with Mrs. Solness. I cannot help thinking it is probable that, judging by her behaviour about Ragnar, when she insisted upon Solness doing the straight thing by him, she would have cleared away the fogs that clouded Mr. and Mrs. Solness's minds by some equally vigorous touch. It must be remembered that her problem was the same as the problem before Rebecca West, with this difference, that Rebecca found an hysterical, amorous wife united to a refined scholar; whereas Hilda found an elderly man who feels his day is done, who is behaving badly to everyone concerned in his business and family life, united to a wife who is merely a rather faded wreck quite occupied in seeing that he does nothing to risk catching cold. In a single day Hilda spurs on the man to display some kind of courage, and finds out the little homely secrets that fill Mrs. Solness's thoughts. In another week she would have had Mrs. Solness sunning herself and taking an interest in her garden, and getting through her day without making tactless remarks about duty at every turn. But what would she have done about the elderly gentleman, who could hardly have realised the ideal of Hilda's valiant "Master-Builder" for long? Such castles in the air as hers are best built about the absent or the dead, and Ibsen provided us with the only vibratingly happy ending possible by letting Solness crash down to earth ennobled at the hands of Persephone, while Hilda still heard harps in the air and dreamed she had met her hero.

"The Business of the Earth"

Edward Thomas and Ecocentrism

░ ░ ░

EDNA LONGLEY

I

Modernism and Marxism fetishize the city, but in different ways. The one neglects "nature poetry" as having refused a cognitive and aesthetic revolution; the other criticizes "pastoral" as repressing the exploitation not only of urban workers in the present but of rural workers in the past. For example, the unreal city of American poetic modernism—cosmopolitan London or Paris refracted through "the simultaneity of the ambient"—does not meet the political demands that Raymond Williams (in *The Country and the City*) sees cities as making on the literary imagination. To Williams, T. S. Eliot's urban impressions appear "as relentless and as conventional as pastoral . . . neo-urban imagery, of the same literary kind as the isolated neo-pastoral . . . [mediating] a general despair in the isolated observer."[1] Ultimately he diagnoses a continuing, and perhaps necessary, conflict between modernist urban myth making (best represented by the related but disconnected consciousness streams of *Ulysses*) and the collectivist "social ideas and movements" also produced by the modern city. This dialectical model, with its 1930s aura, still excludes most twentieth-century rural writing in the British Isles. Although Williams finds among the texts of that tradition occasional resistance to an "elegiac, neo-pastoral mode," nonetheless "[t]he underlying pattern is . . . clear. A critique of a whole dimension of modern life, and with it many necessary general questions, was expressed but also reduced to a convention, which took the form of a detailed version of a part-imagined, part-observed rural England . . . [a] strange formation in which observation, myth, record and half-history are . . . deeply entwined."[2]

These remarks follow an analysis of Edward Thomas's poetry in which Williams discerns a few unpastoral sparks, but which he accuses of falling back on "inexpressible alienation." Thomas has often been squeezed by a pincer movement of modernist and Marxist preconceptions—not that this has put off his many "common readers." I want to change the perceptual ground by looking at his "alienation" in the light of contemporary environmental theory, an approach that also reinserts him into the Edwardian period. Formerly I have suggested that various factors prevented Thomas (1878–1917) from becoming a poet of 1900, that he became inevitably a poet of 1914. But the late twentieth century may both reopen some of Thomas's Edwardian contexts and link his "critique of a whole dimension of modern life" (Williams) with issues now on the global political agenda. Perhaps Edward Thomas is, in fact, a poet of the year 2000. Perhaps his symbolic "warning" looks much farther ahead than Wilfred Owen's, just as it had a deeper hinterland. His sonnet "February Afternoon," which thrice repeats the phrase "a thousand years," suggests how readily Thomas himself could think in terms of millennia—although the cumulative effect is hardly millenarian:

> Men heard this roar of parleying starlings, saw,
> A thousand years ago, even as now,
> Black rooks with white gulls following the plough
> So that the first are last until a caw
> Commands that last are first again,—a law
> That was of old when one, like me, dreamed how
> A thousand years might dust lie on his brow
> Yet thus would birds do between hedge and shaw.
>
> Time swims before me, making as a day
> A thousand years, while the broad ploughland oak
> Roars mill-like and men strike and bear the stroke
> Of war as ever, audacious or resigned,
> And God still sits aloft in the array
> That we have wrought him, stone-deaf and stone-blind.[3]

Williams finds here "a tension between [a] sense of timelessness and the sense of war in which, in a different sense 'Time swims before me.'"[4] But "February Afternoon" (to be discussed later) may, in fact, introduce a third perspective whereby human actors and constructs share in a larger earthly drama. This perspective defines Thomas's ecocentric sense of history.

In her book *Environmentalism and Political Theory* (1992) Robyn Eckersley sums up ecocentrism as follows: "Ecocentrism is based on a . . . philosophy of *internal relatedness*, according to which all organisms are not simply interrelated with their environment but also *constituted* by those very environmental interrelationships." Ecocentrism perceives the world as "an intrinsically dynamic interconnected web . . . in which there are no absolutely discrete entities and no absolute dividing lines between . . . the animate and the inanimate, or the human and the nonhuman."[5] Or, as Edward Thomas put it more monosyllabically and musically in 1915:

> There's nothing like the sun as the year dies,
> Kind as it can be, this world being made so,
> To stones and men and beasts and birds and flies,
> To all things that it touches except snow,
> Whether on mountain side or street of town . . .

The irony that touches the leveling third line, with its regular iambics, denies humanity a primary or Promethean role in "this world" and its making. I argue, first, that Edward Thomas is a prophet of ecocentrism (cognate terms are biocentrism and geocentrism) not only conceptually but also in terms of poetic structure; and second, that to read his poetry (and prose) in this light is to vindicate its Green politics/poetics against criticism from precisely those theoretical quarters that, for Eckersley, fall short of an ecocentric vision. Thus she finds that the "orthodox eco-Marxist approach turned out to be the most active kind of discrimination against the nonhuman world." This is because of its anthropocentric "focus on the relations of production at the expense of the forces of production, and its uncritical acceptance of industrial technology and instrumental reason."[6] Eckersley also analyzes revisionist forms of eco-Marxism as modified by humanism and eco-socialism. Although she discovers more common ground here with the ecocentric perspective, her conclusion is that anthropocentrism keeps sneaking back in, whether as a benign domestication of nature or as the recruitment of Green politics for an anticapitalist agenda. Ultimately, the need for a paradigm shift that would reorient humanity's relation to the rest of nature is not accepted even by the most heretical Marxist thinkers.

Some of Eckersley's arguments have a literary-critical counterpart in Jonathan Bate's innovative *Romantic Ecology* (1991) and a geographic counterpart in Anne Buttimer's *Geography and the Human Spirit* (1993). Bate says in his introduction:

> The 1960s gave us an idealist reading of Romanticism which was implicitly bourgeois in its privileging of the individual imagination; the 1980s gave us a post-Althusserian Marxist critique of Romanticism. The first of these readings assumed that the human mind is superior to nature; the second assumed that the economy of human society is more important than . . . the economy of nature. It is precisely these assumptions that are now being questioned by green politics.[7]

In arguing that "there is not an opposition but a continuity between [Wordsworth's] 'love of nature' and his revolutionary politics," Bate several times relies on the insights of Edward Thomas. But he limits Thomas's ecocentric radicalism, his metaphysical and political leaps beyond Wordsworth, by highlighting only his "localism" and concern with place names. These emphases should be construed as strands of a larger web which amounts to more than "connecting the self to the environment."[8] Also, no writer more profoundly tested the romantic poets' legacy to modernity than did Thomas in his criticism and poetry—even testing it to destruction. One problem with Bate's tentatively proposed "ecocriticism" might be the soft streak in English readings of the English "nature" tradition. Here a merely personal subjectivity is the anthropocentrism that keeps sneaking back in. Nor should *every* nature or country poem be identified with the Green revolution—or all versified Green propaganda with poetry. Such traps were latent and occasionally articulated in a "Green" issue of *Poetry Review* (London) that appeared in 1990. Yet something more is required than the editor's reassurance that poets "have remained animists . . . [exploring] the mini-Gaia of our daily life" or a reviewer's dismissal of "telling one another how much we care in the worn-out words of greenspeak and sociobabble."[9] The absent element might be historical and critical feeling for where (and how) poetry has pioneered Green themes. Otherwise it will lack the means to carry these themes further.

In her introduction to *Geography and the Human Spirit*, Anne Buttimer calls for freedom from academic and ideological "Faustian frames . . . which are no longer appropriate for the challenge of understanding humanity and earth." She also states (her findings stem from the International Dialogue Project, 1978–88): "Proclamations about the meaning of humanness . . . make little sense geographically until they are orchestrated with the more basic nature of dwelling. . . . Neither humanism nor geography can be regarded as an autonomous field of enquiry. . . . The common concern is terrestial dwelling; *humanus* literally means 'earth dweller.'"[10] Earth, man, and home are crucial and interactive terms in the poetry Edward Thomas wrote from his particular "temporal, geographic and cultural setting" (Buttimer's phrase). By persistently asking what it is to be an "inhabitant of earth" ("The Other"), he anticipates the eco-humanism for which various theorists are arguing today. In "The New Year" he takes a fresh look at the sphinx's riddle, at man the earth dweller:

> *Fifty yards off, I could not tell how much*
> *Of the strange tripod was a man. His body,*
> *Bowed horizontal, was supported equally*
> *By legs at one end, by a rake at the other:*
> *Thus he rested, far less like a man than*
> *His wheel-barrow in profile was like a pig.*

Thomas's historical position and cultural coordinates place him at a nodal point in relation to current ecological issues and their intellectual repercussions. "Mainly Welsh" but brought up in London, he moved physically and imaginatively from city to country, from metropolis to region, border and rural parish, from built to natural environments. He walked all over the south of England at a time when its suburbanization, behind which lay agricultural depression, marked a new frontier, and perhaps limit, of the industrial revolution. The rapid erosion of rural England had no counterpart in any other European country. Thomas saw himself as a product of the London suburbs which had mushroomed without being conceptualized or imagined. One of his personae speaks of "belonging to no class or race and having no traditions" and calls people of the suburbs "a muddy, confused, hesitating mass."[11] This is not just alienation that might have been voiced at any time since industrialization or since the always-lost "golden age." It belongs specifically and oppositionally to Edwardian England. Jose Harris, in *Private Lives, Public Spirit: Britain, 1870–1914* (1993) emphasizes how between 1871 and 1881 "the population of the most heavily urbanised counties increased by 75 per cent—the fastest decade of urban growth for the whole of the nineteenth century." Consequently, the "prolonged building boom of the 1870s and 1880s encircled all towns and cities with the middle- and working-class red or yellow brick suburbs, which remain the most enduring physical monument of the late Victorian age."[12] Thomas's irritation with the title of Edward Marsh's "Georgian" anthologies ("Not a few of these [poets] had attained their qualities under Victoria and Edward") might have extended to his own posthumous periodization in such terms.[13]

Edward Thomas's career as a writer, including its poetic apotheosis from December 1914 until his death, coincides with the trajectory traced by Samuel Hynes in

The Edwardian Turn of Mind: "[T]o think of Edwardian England as a peaceful, opulent world before the flood is to misread the age and to misunderstand the changes that were dramatised by the First World War." At the same time, Hynes exhibits a certain (possibly American, metropolitan, and postmodernist) impatience toward those who failed to swim with tidal waves of social transformation. For example, he criticizes C. F. G. Masterman's literary rural nostalgia—such as his regard for W. H. Davies's *Autobiography of a Super-Tramp* (also promoted by Thomas)—and Masterman's "problem of accepting the idea of a twentieth-century, urban, industrial England."[14] This was not necessarily an idea, a cultural or imaginative accommodation, that could be made overnight. The "shock of the new," as an aesthetic thrill, may bypass culture shocks which literature needs time to absorb. The 1930s, when English society had supposedly got used to the city, saw a back-to-nature movement as striking as that of the 1900s—Louis MacNeice's "hiking cockney lovers." The scenario detailed by *Private Lives, Public Spirit* makes more room for Masterman's hankerings and for Thomas's disquiet with the suburbs. Throughout her study Harris stresses not a Victorian national solidarity beginning to crumble after near-defeat in the Boer War, but a more volcanic and more variegated historical, temporal, and spatial picture. She concludes by underlining "the varying pace of time, the idiosyncrasy of local habits and the frequent conjunction of quite dissimilar or contradictory social structures," and continues:

> Yet my overall point—that the true watershed came at the beginning [1870] rather than the end of the period . . . can be supported on many levels. The shift to a "modern" demographic structure began in the 1870s, and in the eyes of many contemporaries was already alarmingly advanced by 1914. The structural and qualitative transformation of cities did not come with the Industrial Revolution but with the arrival of public utilities and municipal socialism after 1867. . . . It was not the early nineteenth-century factory system, but the onset of mass-production and the retailing and financial revolutions of the 1880s that created the distinctive class, status, and consumer groups that were to characterise British society for much of the twentieth century.[15]

As a reviewer for the *Daily Chronicle* (from 1901) and the *Morning Post*—this was also the period when mass newspapers proliferated—and in his other literary criticism, Thomas was explicit about contemporary instabilities and the challenges they posed to poetry in particular. In 1905, reviewing a book by the feminist Frances Power Cobbe, he describes the present as "an age of doubt and balancing and testing—of distrusting the old and not very confidently expecting the new." In the same year, reviewing new verse, he rebukes both literary arcadianism and arcadian literariness:

> [A] country life is neither more easy nor more simple than a city life. If it were, the world would now be ruled by the brewers, bankers, and journalists who are now taking the place of hops in Kent. And just as, in thinking about life, we cry out for a return to Nature and her beneficent simplicity, so we are apt to cry out for a return to simplicity in literature. . . . A critic has lately spoken of *Tom Jones* and *Pendennis* as unrolling "the infinite variety of human nature before us," and has compared Mr Meredith most unfavourably with them. They are simpler, and they do not disturb.

Nothing could be more false than this attitude. If it were also strong, it might endanger much that is most characteristic of our age. . . . Here, before us, are many views which would seem to have been inspired by a cunning search for simplicity. These men are trying to write as if there were no such thing as a Tube, Grape Nuts, love of Nature, a Fabian Society, A Bill for the reform of the Marriage Laws; nor do they show that they are in possession of any grace or virtue which can be set up against those wonders of our age.[16]

Evidently, however, this is no straightforward hurrah for modernity. Thomas's allusions to economic and demographic change and to "wonders of our age" are as ironic as "cunning search for simplicity." As for the political reformism also glanced at, it featured in his disagreements with his father, and his reaction to the Bedales intelligentsia again suggests dissidence from its ethos, if not its aims. Bedales was the progressive school in Hampshire near which Thomas and his family lived from December 1906. Although Helen Thomas, who taught in the kindergarten, was inspired by the school's staff, she records, "[Edward] frankly did not like them, and to them he was an enigma—a solitary wandering creature . . . who had no political beliefs or social theories, and who was not impressed by the school or its ideals. . . . [T]hey could not like him or rope him in at all."[17]

Helen Thomas may take her husband's lack of politics too literally; but there might be good warrant for a writer's not being impressed by any school and its ideals: Samuel Hynes quotes Beatrice Webb's admission "without apparent regret, that she was 'poetry-blind.'"[18] Yet Thomas then faced the task of developing a literary mode, and perhaps an alternative politics, which would at once interpret what was happening to Kent, remember that Grape Nuts could not be uninvented, and go beyond the false simplicities of the poets under review. It has to be said that it took him nearly ten more years, in the course of which his own "love of Nature" (there is self-irony in the review, too) still perpetrated cunning simplicities: "But at morning twilight I see the moon low in the west like a broken and dinted shield of silver hanging long forgotten outside the tent of a great knight in a wood. . . ."[19] Thomas himself mocked "my soarings & flutterings"[20] over *The South Country* (1909), from which that sentence comes. Yet some parts of the book organize his perceptions in a way that would eventually help to recharge the "nature poem," while other chapters contain literary-critical, sociological, and ecological thinking that tends in the same direction. The literary-critical dimension matters: the Green movement does not always acknowledge its literary origins. Thomas returned to origins (early English and Welsh transactions with nature); read not only all nature poetry up to its romantic apotheosis, but the entire tradition of "country books" culminating in Richard Jefferies and W. H. Hudson: and asked questions about the meaning of this literature in irretrievably complex times.[21] His study *Richard Jefferies* (1909) charts Jefferies's discontent "to some purpose . . . with modernity" and hard-won holistic awareness of "the diverse life of the world, in man, in beast, in tree, in earth and sky, and sea, and stars."[22] Thomas looked for contemporary works "which really show, in verse or prose, the inseparableness of Nature and Man" and approved a modern "diminution of man's importance in the landscape." At the same time, he savaged the "chattering" nature-trash he received for review, and (prefiguring *Romantic Ecology*) regretted the scientific and literary specialization that seemed to "make impossible a grand con-certed advance like that which accompanied the French Revolution."[23]

On the sociological front, Thomas's prose abounds in semidocumentary por-traits of obsolescent, displaced, or potentially displaced country people. These fig-ures flesh out Jose Harris's representation of "a society in which rootlessness was endemic and in which people felt themselves to be living in many different layers of historic time." What Harris terms "a lurking grief at the memory of a lost domain" (also a feature of Irish cultural nationalism) is, of course, partly Thomas's own grief coloring the canvas. But he does not merely foist his feelings on to real casualties of "the 1880s when, alone among European countries, Britain chose not to protect home producers against American wheat, with a consequent collapse of archaic rural communities, an explosion of migration to great cities. . . ."[24] His father's more upwardly mobile migration from Wales enabled Thomas to connect an autobio-graphical deracination with the wider forces whereby the countryman was "sinking before the *Daily Mail* like a savage before pox or whisky."[25] Childhood holidays in Wales and Wiltshire had indelibly, if precariously, reconstituted the lost domain. A central trope in *The South Country*, as in Thomas's other prose, is a passage from country to city; then, usually by a second generation, from city to country in an attempted retrieval of loss. This reflexive narrative occupies Chapter 6, "A Return to Nature," which concludes with a last glimpse of "the man from Caermarthen-shire," back once more in London "ill-dressed" and "thin," amid a pathetic march of the unemployed: "Comfortable clerks and others of the servile realised that here were the unemployed about whom the newspapers had said this and that . . . and they repeated the word 'Socialism' and smiled at the bare legs of the son of man and the yellow boots of the orator."[26]

In *Edward Thomas* (1986) Stan Smith stresses "A Return to Nature" in his inter-esting analysis of Thomas's situation as "a superfluous man," a term that Thomas him-self borrowed from Turgenev. But while Smith highlights the depopulation of the countryside, arguing that some of the natural beauties of Thomas's England depended on dereliction and that Thomas was responsibly aware of this, he may point his sense of superfluousness too much toward class, too little toward the lost domain with its cultural as well as aesthetic pull. For example, he identifies "the crisis of a genera-tion," which Thomas's writings enact, as "the dilemma of a middle-class liberal indi-vidualism under strain, faced with the prospect of its own redundancy in the changed world of a new era, and struggling, with remarkable intensity and integrity, to under-stand the flux in which it is to go down."[27] First, it is not clear that the Edwardian period was such a bad time for middle-class liberalism. Second, even if there never has been a golden age but only "an *imaginary* plenitude, a utopian land of lost con-tent which is precisely nowhere,"[28] Harris's study suggests that Thomas internalized a "crisis" which can be seen as major historical watershed—and not only in the con-text of England. What Smith perceives as Thomas's symptomatic political paralysis, his deadlock between resignation and revolution, may be a search for other parame-ters in addition to class politics. His ultimate discovery of those parameters coincided with his discovery of distinctive poetic forms, and with the impact of the war on his existing sense of crisis.

Thomas's prose is undeniably romantic about "children of earth," about men "five generations thick," about the innocence or earth-motherhood of rural women.[29] Yet his empathy with the London unemployed, which includes their pre-London history, questions whether socialism is the only answer, and whether even rural poverty might not have harbored valuable communal and local meanings now dispersed. (This is not the same as claiming "organicism" for any community: the clearances in the Soviet Union were to prove as socially disastrous as those in the Scottish Highlands.) Similarly, he says of Gypsies: "They belong to the little roads that are dying out."[30] One aspect of Thomas's thought, his inner western rather than southern landscape, understands depopulation, change, obsolescence, dereliction, though not with a consoling nuance: Cornwall's "deserted mines are frozen cries of despair, as if they had perished in conflict with the waste." On a longer time scale the mines consort with "cromlech, camp, circle, hut and tumulus of the unwritten years . . . a silent Bedlam of history, a senseless cemetery or museum, amidst which we walk as animals must do when they see those valleys full of skeletons where their kind are said to go punctually to die." Yet the very intensity of this reaction suggests that Thomas sees the current transformations as uniquely ominous for man. The peril is exemplified by the situation of an old man, living in a London suburb where once his father farmed, and mourning the final loss of elm trees which "had come unconsciously to be part of the real religion of men in that neighbourhood . . . and helped to build and keep firm that sanctuary of beauty to which we must be able to retire if we are to be more than eaters and drinkers and newspaper readers."[31] Today's deep ecologists would endorse that interconnectedness, rephrased in "The Chalk Pit": "imperfect friends, we men / And trees since time began; and nevertheless / Between us still we breed a mystery."

Thomas's prose writings criticize "the parochialism of humanity" with respect to larger evolutionary processes.[32] This critique, which chimes with the Green stress on the short-termism of our species, comes to a head in *The South Country*, where he exclaims: "How little do we know of the business of the earth, not to speak of the universe; of time, not to speak of eternity."[33] Or, as Edward O. Wilson puts it in *The Diversity of Life* (1992): "The biosphere . . . remains obscure."[34] "Earth" in Thomas's poetry is not only a spatial but also a temporal domain. Although (or because) he was a historian himself by academic training, *The South Country* attacks the tunnel vision of orthodox historians, comparing them to "a child planting flowers severed from their stalks and roots, expecting them to grow."[35] This covers not only "the unwritten years" but also the excluded species and ignorance of how our own has survived. Similarly, Wilson observes:

> Humanity is part of nature. . . . The human heritage does not go back only for the conventionally recognised 8,000 years or so of recorded history, but for at least 2 million years. . . . Across thousands of generations, the emergence of culture must have been profoundly influenced by simultaneous events in genetic evolution . . . [and] genetic evolution by the kinds of selection arising within culture. Only in the last moment of human history has the delusion arisen that people can flourish apart from the rest of the living world.[36]

Thomas understands this delusion when he says, "We are not merely twentieth-century Londoners or Kentish men or Welshmen," or appeals for a holistic approach to human and natural history. This would show us "in animals, in plants . . . what life is, how our own is related to theirs . . . in fact, our position, responsibilities and debts among the other inhabitants of the earth."[37] "Digging" is both an eco-historical poem (like "February Afternoon") and a symbolic model for eco-historical research:

> What matter makes my spade for tears or mirth,
> Letting down two clay pipes into the earth?
> The one I smoked, the other a soldier
> Of Blenheim, Ramillies, and Malplaquet
> Perhaps. The dead man's immortality
> Lies represented lightly with my own,
> A yard or two nearer the living air
> Than bones of ancients who, amazed to see
> Almighty God erect the mastodon,
> Once laughed, or wept, in this same light of day.

Thomas's eco-history provides a tough and agnostic basis for his ecocentric philosophy. He anticipated (by eighty years) Andrew Dobson's précis: "The science of ecology teaches us that we are part of a system that stretches back into an unfathomable past and reaches forward into an incalculable future. . . ."[38] Thomas writes in the chapter of The South Country called "History and the Parish": In some places history has wrought like an earthquake, in others like an ant or mole; everywhere, permanently; so that if we but knew or cared, every swelling of the grass, every wavering line of hedge or path or road were an inscription, brief as an epitaph, in many languages and characters. But most of us know only a few of these unspoken languages of the past. . . ."[39] The text of the earth remains to be read, and not all its inscriptions are human. In "November" the speaker exclaims:

> the prettiest thing on ground are the paths
> With morning and evening hobnails dinted,
> With foot and wing-tip overprinted
> Or separately charactered,
> Of little beast and little bird.

II

It is often claimed that any such long-term view is merely a device for discouraging political action and protest. Here I want to bring together Thomas's historical situation and his ecocentrism, at their wartime crisis point, as a preliminary to exploring some of their structural and epistemological consequences in his poetry. Just as Raymond Williams sees "February Afternoon" as simply opposing a sense of timelessness to a sense of war, so Robert Wells has criticized Thomas for being philosophically "unable to protest; not against the destruction of [English rural] culture nor against the mass slaughter of the men who embodied the culture."[40] It all depends on what you mean by "protest." In "In Memoriam (Easter, 1915)" Thomas does not minimize a catastrophe when, rather than comparing the dead to flowers, or ridiculing that comparison, he points to a socio-ecological alteration:

> *The flowers left thick at nightfall in the wood*
> *This eastertide call into mind the men,*
> *Now far from home, who, with their sweethearts, should,*
> *Have gathered them and will do never again.*

Similarly, "February Afternoon" and "Digging" are not really saying it will be or was "all the same in a thousand years" or several thousand years. Both poems are partly framed as ironical questions to *human* powers-that-be—political and religious—in the context of an ecosystem to which they belong and from which they might learn. Anger works through perspectives such as "The dead man's immortality / Lies represented lightly with my own," with the ambiguity of "immortality" (as in "Haymaking," quoted later) and the oxymoronic pun on "represented lightly." Here, you might say, war recruits achieve solidarity beyond the parochialism of the contemporary. Also, "living air" and "light of day" seem ecological accusations. They contrast with the (self-sponsored) reduction of the human element to dead "matter" and the doubt as to whom it matters in another sense. Indeed, "the living air," the biosphere, questions the binary opposition of "tears or mirth." One sign of such questioning is that "Digging" (the first poem Thomas wrote after his enlistment) is a revision of an earlier poem of the same title. Initially he picks up on its final rhyme, given more emphasis and some irony by a rhyming couplet. Thus the rhyme sequence from poem to poem runs as follows: earth, mirth, mirth, earth. "Earth," the key word in common and enclosing term of the chiasmus, shifts in meaning from soil, *humus*, to more global suggestions. The disturbing archaeology of "Digging" [II] upsets a harmony, above ground, in "Digging" [I], whereby "It is enough / To smell, to crumble the dark earth, / While the robin sings over again / Sad songs of Autumn mirth." Here the robin's song is said to integrate what the later poem perceives as a split in (or owing to) human consciousness: we laugh or weep. "February Afternoon" also inquires into the oppositional habits that produce wars in which "men" can be only "audacious or resigned." The sonnet incorporates a political bird fable in its use of a starlings' parliament, perhaps in democratic contrast to imagery of gulls led by rooks. But if the natural world is competitive, too, it seems better regulated. Men who plow (or dig) contribute to the system. Men at war become unable to see or hear what the animal or vegetable creation might be suggesting. This blindness and deafness is totalized in a patriarchal Judaeo-Christian God "aloft," transcendental, out of touch with the earth: "And God still sits aloft in the array / That we have wrought him. . . ." "Array" hits at religious forms lacking the substance that a genuine "humanus" might have put there. ("Almighty God" in "Digging" is a similar construct on the part of our inability to read an evolutionary environment in which we have survived the mastodon.) When "the broad plough-land oak / Roars mill-like" with starlings, like the mastodon it is both an emblem of earth at war and a reminder of older "laws." Thomas's historical sense in the poem functions in the same microcosmic way as his spatial sense. If he uses millennia to get into focus one day in 1916, one day in 1916 also focuses millennia.

Thomas's eco-history is equal to interpreting briefer timespans and individual lifespans. "Man and Dog" and "A Private" complement each other as concentrations of Thomas's earlier rural biographies, which themselves culminated in several articles about rural and urban England preparing or unprepared for war: "I shall write down, as nearly as possible, what I saw and heard, hoping not to offend too much those who had ready-made notions as to how an Imperial people should or would behave in time of war, of such a war. . . ."[41] Robert Wells cites "Man and Dog" when he faults Thomas for merely elegizing a culture, thereby assenting in its "general will to die." This political and critical naïveté suggests that Wells, rather than Thomas, has succumbed to fatalism and "shows little sense of the common tragedy in which Europe was caught by the war."[42] England was a window for Thomas, not an insular limit, and "elegy" is a wide-ranging genre, not an invariably passive lament.

> "'Twill take some getting." "Sir, I think 'twill so."
> The old man stared up at the mistletoe
> That hung too high in the poplar's nest for plunder
> Of any climber, though not for kissing under:
> Then he went on against the north-east wind—
> Straight but lame, leaning on a staff new-skinned,
> Carrying a brolly, flag-basket, and old coat,—
> Towards Alton, ten miles off. And he had not
> Done less from Chilgrove where he pulled up docks . . .

At certain historical junctures the artist's most useful action may be to point the camera. But there is analysis and criticism in this subtly blended elegy. As the speaker attends to oral history stemming from the last third of the nineteenth century, we learn in a seemingly incidental phrase that the man's "sons, three sons, were fighting." This information takes its place in a shifting history of hard work, hardship, and environmental change. Industrial casual labor has encroached on farm laboring, itself grown casual, and the old man, too, has been a soldier:

> His mind was running on the work he had done
> Since he left Christchurch in the New Forest, one
> Spring in the 'seventies,—navvying on dock and line
> From Southampton to Newcastle-on-Tyne.
> In 'seventy-four a year of soldiering
> With the Berkshires,—hoeing and harvesting
> In half the shires where corn and couch will grow.

If the close of the poem moves with an autumnal rhythm, it simultaneously condemns the exploitative ethic that has led to the war and the man's obsolescence:

> "Many a man sleeps worse tonight
> Than I shall." "In the trenches." "Yes, that's right.
> But they'll be out of that—I hope they be—
> This weather, marching after the enemy."
> "And so I hope. Good luck." And there I nodded
> "Good-night. You keep straight on." Stiffly he plodded;

And at his heels the crisp leaves scurried fast,
And the leaf-coloured robin watched, They passed,
The robin till next day, the man for good,
Together in the twilight of the wood.

This counterpoints the histories of man, robin, and trees. All the life in the poem belongs in different but interconnected ways to what is "passing," to the business of the earth. There is, however, an implied question about the accelerating human impact on natural systems and cycles. The old man's relationship to the earth, on balance—and *in* balance—positive, is becoming a thing of the past. And yet, within the politics of this scenario, the nonhuman creation is shown to resist subjugation: mistletoe plays hard to get; couch grass grows with corn; the man can skin a staff but has been lamed by a fall from a tree; the robin appears noncommittal; the leaves "scurry" as if speeding a departure. Meanwhile, humanity's self-destructive tendencies are accelerating too: "shires" have become regiments. Thus the poem's valedictory vista disturbingly implicates all its readers ("the man for good"). According to eco-history, human endings matter but are not all that matter. As the conclusion of another poem, "The Mountain Chapel," reminds us: "When gods were young / This wind was old."

The old man's passing, individually if not culturally, might be seen as a fitting evolutionary return to the earth (compare the death of Lok in William Golding's novel *The Inheritors*). But this does not apply to the swifter recycling implied by "Digging" or grimly encapsulated in Thomas's lines "when the war began / To turn young men to dung" ("Gone, Gone Again"). The death of "A Private" covers the intolerable plight of the old man's sons:

This ploughman dead in battle slept out of doors
Many a frozen night, and merrily
Answered staid drinkers, good bedmen, and all bores:
"At Mrs Greenland's Hawthorn Bush," said he,
"I slept." None knew which bush. Above the town,
Beyond "The Drover," a hundred spot the down
In Wiltshire. And where now at last he sleeps
More sound in France—that, too, he secret keeps.

The war has prematurely violated the ploughman/private's bonds with "Mrs Greenland"—a joke that anticipates Gaia. And his riddle about where he sleeps, together with the poem's own ironic, riddling play on "privacy" and secrecy, further accuses human agencies of usurping earth-mysteries. When Thomas himself got to the front (in January 1917), it is not incongruous that his "War Diary" should have intermingled nature notes and battle log, thus conveying a whole environment under bombardment. The second-to-last entry (April 7) reads: "A cold bright day of continuous shelling. . . . Larks, partridges, hedgesparrows, magpies by O[bservation] P[ost]. A great burst in red brick building in N. Vitasse stood up like a birch tree or fountain. Back at 7.30 in peace. Then at 8.30 a continuous roar of artillery."[43]

III

Thomas's poems are usually spoken by a first-person singular, and both text and author are, of course, inescapably human, inescapably "cultured." Nonetheless, their procedures do much to renew the root meaning of *humanus*—to reinforce "the inseparableness of Nature and Man," to diminish "man's importance in the landscape," and to subvert anthropocentric authority. Thus, David Gervais in *Literary Englands* (1993) misses a fundamental point when he says that "the typical Thomas poem takes place outside human settlement," or exclaims: "How different it is from the England of the novelists! There are no steam trains [wrong] or ocean liners, telephones or suffragettes, garden cities or Labour MPs."[44] In fact, most of Thomas's poems allude to settlement in one way or another; but his margins are, rather, a vantage point from which to criticize "the England of the novelists" and examine earthly tenancies. "Up in the Wind," the first poem he wrote in December 1914, includes the lines:

> Her cockney accent
> Made her and the house seem wilder by calling up—
> Only to be subdued at once by wildness—
> The idea of London there in that forest parlour . . .

Keeping Jefferies's *After London* in his sights, Thomas strategically deflects "the roar of towns / And their brief multitude" ("Roads"). Nor, as we have seen, does he suppress what John Barrell (in his study of English painting 1730–1840) terms "the dark side of the landscape"—the condition of rural England further darkened by war.[45]

Contemporary theory of landscape painting argues that landscape is never "natural," being always viewed through cultural lenses even before its reproduction; that its "prospects" may be complicit with imperialism; and that the forward movement of the colonizing eye, in the words of W. J. T. Mitchell's introduction to *Landscape and Power* (1994), "is not confined to the external, foreign fields toward which the empire directs itself; it is typically accompanied by a renewed interest in the re-presentation of the home landscape, the 'nature' of the imperial center."[46] Thomas was an anti-imperialist: he desired to rescue "the home landscape" from "Great Britain, the British Empire, Britons, Britishers, and the English-speaking world" and from a centralizing metropolis.[47] But the imperialism against which he fought aesthetically was the imperialism of the human, rather than the capitalist, prospect (though the former may beget the latter). His poem "The Watchers" contrasts a carter "[w]atching the water press in swathes about his horse's chest" with "one [who] watches, too, / In the room for visitors / That has no fire, but a view / And many cases of stuffed fish, vermin and kingfishers." That such a detached, prospecting eye implicates a death-dealing human imperium is central to the thrust of the poem. So is progressive self-insulation from the pressure and fire of the nonhuman creation.

"Haymaking" and "The Brook" indicate Thomas's awareness and wariness of the visual arts landscape tradition. The scene in "Haymaking" is very deliberately a scene, one that underlines the specific—radical and demotic—varieties of pastoral to which it subscribes:

The men leaned on their rakes, about to begin,
But still. And all were silent. All was old,
This morning time, with a great age untold,
Older than Clare and Cobbett, Morland and Crome,
Than, at the field's far edge, the farmer's home,
A white house crouched at the foot of a great tree.

Although this freeze-frame suggests the spirit of which Thomas had earlier wished to make "a graven image," "Haymaking" is also self-referentially conscious of frames within frames; and, like most other poems quoted here, moves between "different lay-ers of historical time" (Harris). "Under the heavens that know not what years be," Thomas lays out a vista of beginnings (the moment when agriculture starts), long eco-history (the "great tree"), literary and artistic traditions (agriculture becomes cul-ture), and possible endings. Indeed, the poem ends by enclosing itself within a reced-ing and ambiguous wartime frame: "The men, the beasts, the trees, the implements / Uttered even what they will in times far hence— / All of us gone out of the reach of change— / Immortal in a picture of an old grange." If "Haymaking" ultimately stresses the visual, its collective earthly "utterance" also depends on other kinds of sense impression ("shrill shrieked . . . / The swift," "the scent of woodbine and hay new-mown"). Similarly, "The Brook," written two days later, starts with the speaker "watching a child / Chiefly that paddled," then takes in birdsong and "a scent like honeycomb / From mugwort dull." Yet "The Brook" dramatizes, rather than assumes, the primal epistemology of "gathering sight and sound," and the speaker's peaceable sensory kingdom of birds, flowers, and insects is allied to the "motion, and the voices, of the stream" as well as to the focal stillness of "Haymaking." And this scene edges the human presence to its margin: a butterfly behaves "as if I were the last of men / And he the first of insects to have earth / And sun together and to know their worth."

Several of Thomas's poems establish a working relation between the "natural" and the "human," in which the senses, together or separately, constitute the basis for an "interconnected web" (Eckersley). "Digging" [II] begins: "Today I think / Only with scents." In this present-tense scenario an inseparable "Nature and Man" ecologically cooperate as "a bonfire burns / The dead, the waste, the dangerous, / And all to sweet-ness turns." Elsewhere, the "otherness" of species and natural phenomena can prove challenging. The rain is not always "[w]indless and light, / Half a kiss, half a tear, / Say-ing good-night" ("Sowing"). Or, if the pathetic fallacy is inevitable, Thomas imprints nature not only with human unhappiness but also with human extinctions. In "Rain" the speaker has "no love which this wild rain / Has not dissolved except the love of death." "The Mill-Water" ends with "water falling / Changelessly calling, / Where once men had a work-place and a home." Here local economic change brings the "Bedlam of history" into focus. The voices he assigns to water and wind often appear adverse or inaccessible to consciousness. Similarly, birdsong and human language con-verge in "March" ("Something they knew—I also, while they sang"); diverge in "If I Were To Own" (the thrush's "proverbs untranslatable"). Sometimes concentration on natural sounds is correlated with a salutary loss of human memory. In "The Word" the speaker's obsession with "a pure thrush word," "an empty thingless name," downgrades anthropocentric history: "I have forgot . . . names of the mighty men / That fought and lost or won in the old wars." Thomas's protagonist frequently fails to translate, construe, or utter the earthly text that matters more than those ironically lost "mighty men," or he finds that his eye fails him. In "Birds' Nests" winter trees expose what he has missed, but this does not mitigate the failure: "Since there's no need of eyes to see them with." Chastened and educated, he goes on to discover natural microsystems "deep-hid." In the paradoxically named "First Known When Lost," bearings have to be revised after a woodman fells a copse: "And now I see as I look / That the small winding brook, / A tributary's tributary, rises there." To "see as I look" humbles the prospecting human eye, and true observation socializes the "isolated observer" (Williams) as an inhabitant of earth. John Barrell's essay "Being Is Perceiving" contrasts John Clare's subjectivity, constituted by a "complex manifold of simultaneous impressions," with James Thomson's "subject . . . which needed to announce itself as autonomous, as freeing itself from the determination of the objects it perceived."[48]

Thomas's syntax, more sophisticated than Clare's, takes the reader on destabilizing mystery tours that give the "complex manifold" or interconnected web dimensions in time as well as space. His syntactical maneuvers, allied to changes of angle and vantage point, help to alter power relations between the human element and other perceivers. Take, for example, "Thaw":

> Over the land freckled with snow half thawed
> The speculating rooks at their nests cawed
> And saw from elm-tops, delicate as flower of grass,
> What we below could not see, Winter pass.

"The Path" plays on the constrictions of human sight, human engineering, and, indeed, literary pastoral, as it lures the reader along unbeaten tracks:

> the eye
> Has but the road, the wood that overhangs
> And underyawns it, and the path that looks
> As if it led on to some legendary
> Or fancied place where men have wished to go
> And stay; till, sudden, it ends where the wood ends.

"Fifty Faggots" is a temporal microcosm in which seasonal change interacts with less predictable historical forces set in motion by human beings. It begins with a statement about visual, tangible present-tense presence: "There they stand, on their ends, the fifty faggots," but then introduces history: "That once were underwood of hazel and ash / In Jenny Pinks's copse." The poem continues with a set of variables that will determine relations between present and future:

> Now, by the hedge
> Close packed, they make a thicket fancy alone
> Can creep through with the mouse and wren. Next Spring
> A blackbird or a robin will nest there,
> Accustomed to them, thinking they will remain
> Whatever is for ever to a bird:
> This Spring it is too late; the swift has come . . .

Although bird and animal habitats have been influenced by human actions, the speaker/author is equally subject to the incalculable: "Before they are done / The war will have ended, many other things / Have ended, maybe, that I can no more / Foresee or more control than robin and wren." In the course of the poem, the same (or almost the same) object is consigned to a corresponding range of linguistic variables: faggots/underwood/thicket.

Foresight and control are also problematic when it comes to more elaborate edifices. Settlement, in Thomas's poetry, hovers on the verge of unsettlement: "Where once men had a work-place and a home." The rare "Manor Farm," conjuring "a season of bliss unchangeable," is far outnumbered by precariously placed or ominous dwellings. Thomas's "houses" include: "that forest parlour," "A white house crouched at the foot of a great tree," "road and inn, the sum / Of what's not forest," "the woodman's cot / By the ivied trees," "Chapel and gravestones, old and few," the "fir-tree-covered barrow on the heath." It is striking how many houses are situated close to the mystery of men and trees, with trees as the dominant presence. Ideally this situation should foster the reciprocities latent in the human/animal words "crouched" and "foot" applied to house and tree in "Haymaking." But "The Barn" begins: "They should never have built a barn there, at all— / Drip, drip, drip!—under that elm tree." The barn undergoes what from the viewpoint of agribusiness would be degradation: "Built to keep corn for rats and men / Now there's fowls on the roof, pigs on the floor." ("Rats and men" seems pointed.) From a more holistic angle, the barn's decline has restored it biodegradably to nature. First, "Starlings used to sit there with bubbling throats":

> But now they cannot find a place,
> Among all those holes, for a nest any more.
> It's the turn of lesser things, I suppose.
> Once I fancied 'twas starlings they built it for.

Thomas's forest fixation does not only reflect the tree-covered Hampshire hangers or mourn obsolescent wood trades such as charcoal burning or imply the wilderness of the individual unconscious. Ultimately it symbolizes an evolutionary and eco-historical perspective (the unconscious of the species perhaps) within which all human settlement appears vulnerable. "The Green Roads" outlines this perspective almost diagramatically by layering the lifespans of different species and their individual members:

> The green roads that end in the forest
> Are strewn with white goose feathers this June,
>
> Like marks left behind by someone gone to the forest
> To show his track. But he has never come back.
>
> Down each green road a cottage looks at the forest.
> Round one the nettle towers; two are bathed in flowers.
>
> An old man along the green road to the forest
> Strays from one, from another a child alone.

The diagram includes an "old" thrush, "young" trees, a dead oak that "saw the ages pass in the forest," and the poet–historian's accurate, foreboding footnote: "all things forget the forest / Excepting perhaps me. . . ." Yet, as in "The Mill-Water" and "Tall Nettles," Thomas may partly relish the power reversal whereby nettles come to "tower," "reign," or "cover up." In "The Green Roads" the cottages, with subtextual anxiety, "look at" the forest. In "House and Man" the trees "look upon" a house "from every side." On Thomas's time scales this isolated wood dweller, paranoid about "forest silence and forest murmur," represents more than "an image of poverty"[49] or the disappearance of rural England: "One hour: as dim he and his house now look / As a reflection in a rippling brook. . . ." In "The Long Small Room," one of Thomas's last poems, the house metaphor overtly merges into all earth-dwelling. An earlier poem, "The Other," arrives at a brief moment of poise in which the divided protagonist internalizes "one star, one lamp, one peace / Held on an everlasting lease" and feels himself to be "[a]n old inhabitant of earth." But "The Long Small Room" is spoken retrospectively by a less secure leaseholder, who also speaks on behalf of other natural phenomena:

> When I look back, I am like moon, sparrow and mouse
> That witnessed what they could never understand
> Or alter or prevent in the dark house.
> One thing remains the same—this my right hand
>
> Crawling crab-like over the clean white page . . .

Here the activity of writing figures at a distance from the possibility of deciphering or controlling the earthly text. "Crab-like" further subverts the anthropocentric arrogance of *Homo faber* as author and artist. Thomas's doubts about human constructs extend to the architectural model of the artist (a contrast with some of Yeats's emphases). It is not only "superfluous men," to quote Stan Smith, who "do not own [the house] or share in its significances."[50] Man, in a more generic sense, may be superfluous. And "ownership" here has to do with deeper eco-nomics. In other poems, however, the earth offers its own kind of access to "significances." Raymond Williams gets it exactly wrong when he praises the opening lines of "Swedes" ("They have taken the gable from the roof of clay / On the long swede pile. They have let in the sun / To the white and gold and purple of curled fronds / Unsunned"), but objects to a comparison between this revelation and "going down into an Egyptian tomb."[51] The point is that the artifacts bearing witness to the pharaoh's glory— "God and monkey, chariot and throne and vase, / Blue pottery, alabaster, and gold"— are deathly, unnatural, unrenewable. Like the voyeuristic art associated with the "watcher" in the inn, they contrast with what an ecocentric aesthetic might have to offer: "But dreamless long-dead Amen-hotep lies. / This is a dream of Winter, sweet as Spring." The post-Darwinian conjunction "God and monkey" satirizes the link between art and the transcendental, immortalizing claims of religion. The trenches did not make Thomas less atheistic: "Rubin . . . believes in God and tackles me about atheism—thinks marvellous escapes are ordained. But I say so are the marvellous escapes of certain telegraph posts, houses, etc."[52]

Yet Thomas does not entirely give up on the capacity of humanity to "build" as well as "see": to mediate or inhabit the environment in more ecocentric ways. The interconnected webs of his poetry are sometimes reflexively adduced as evidence that the earth cannot dispense with the spider of human consciousness. Thus, in "Roads," "The hill road wet with rain / In the sun would not gleam / Like a winding stream / If we trod it not again." Only imagination can establish the interconnections of metaphor. Similarly, "The Thrush" updates Keats's nightingale by probing the bird's limitations in the cognitive business of "reading," "knowing," naming, and remembering: "Or is all your lore / not to call November November, / And April April. . . . But I know the months all, / and their sweet names. . . ." This replies dialectically to the "pure thrush word" by valuing the human mind's interconnections with "[a]ll that's ahead and behind." Thomas applies the word "roar" to any unmediated noise— whether of towns, machines, trees, or artillery. "Good-night," a rare effort to connect explicitly with man-made London, is plotted in terms of changing sounds and moves in a (historical?) direction opposite to the usual Thomas trajectory: from skylarks "over the down" to "suburb nightingales" to a city center "noise of man and beast and machine" which submerges birdsong/poetry. But the urban sounds include streets made "homely" by the echo of his childhood in "the call of children . . . Sweet as the voice of nightingale or lark," and the poem itself creates a fleeting community: "homeless, I am not lost . . . it is All Friends' Night, a traveller's good night." This provisional accommodation neither surrenders to nor evades the city. It still insists that the streets are the "strangest thing in the world"[53] because they have yet to be imagined as earth-dwellings, their roar assimilated, even if the poem's own naming begins the process.

Thomas's versions of the artist involve not the builder or maker but the listener, the seeker, the traveler, the receiver of signals from the environment, the apprentice to natural language, the medium of human language: "Will you . . . Choose me, / You English words?" ("Words"). Obviously this receptivity, too, is a strategic construct, though the poetry does not impute invariable success to its self-images. In "Aspens" Thomas elaborates his ecological aesthetic, defining it as a voice intermediary between earth and human beings:

All day and night, save winter, every weather,
Above the inn, the smithy, and the shop,
The aspens at the cross-roads talk together
Of rain, until their last leaves fall from the top.

Out of the blacksmith's cavern comes the ringing
Of hammer, shoe, and anvil; out of the inn
The clink, the hum, the roar, the random singing—
The sounds that for these fifty years have been.

Stan Smith emphasizes "dereliction" and the speaker's own "redundancy like that threatening the blacksmith,"[54] but Thomas again seems to move from a particular historical context to a longer eco-historical perspective, one that includes literary history. The "inn, the smithy, and the shop" represent three perennial kinds of man-made "house": society, manufacture, and commerce. The poem erases these houses in what might be night, war, or a proleptic absence:

The whisper of the aspens is not drowned,
And over lightless pane and footless road,
Empty as sky, with every other sound
Not ceasing, calls their ghosts from their abode,

A silent smithy, a silent inn, nor fails
In the bare moonlight or the thick-furred gloom,
In tempest or the night of nightingales,
To turn the cross-roads to a ghostly room.

Yet this also suggests that the sounds associated with the trees (talk, whisper, call) are more durable, mindful, and meaningful than the mechanistic noise of the smithy or the sublinguistic and "random" sounds attached to the social inn. The poem's own aspen-imitative music obliquely disparages the chime of "ringing"/"random singing," which implies an incoherent or simplistic relation between society and (literary) expression. Once more a third force has entered the arena, and its urgent if disregarded "talk of rain" combines longer historical perspectives with a deeper aesthetic. "Aspens" was written in 1915, so "these fifty years" begin in 1865 and denote not old England but the modern "cross-roads": the period of unprecedented change and now of war. Yet this half-century is itself a blip:

And it would be the same were no house near.
Over all sorts of weather, men, and times,
Aspens must shake their leaves and men may hear
But need not listen, more than to my rhymes.

Evidently Thomas is making Cassandra-like claims for his own "marginal" poetry. "Aspens" aligns it with the tree rather than the house, declares its grief more than personal, and insists on a necessary reciprocity between poetry and earth. Inseparable from "all sorts of weather," the aspens—traditionally the trees with tongues— also symbolize earth's concern that mankind should tune in to its transmissions:

Whatever wind blows, while they and I have leaves
We cannot other than an aspen be
That ceaselessly, unreasonably grieves,
Or so men think who like a different tree.

IV

Ecology, like economy, derives from the Greek *oikos*, home. "Home" is a key word in Thomas's meditation on England (as is "England" in his meditation on home), a much-canvassed topic, to which David Gervais has made a contribution. Gervais stresses the "partial, private," and provisional nature of Thomas's England, criticizes any attempt to recruit his poetry for a pure elixir of Englishness, and says: "We rarely find [Hardy's] *shared* meaning in the rural life Thomas writes about. . . . Thomas did not come to his England from a position sufficiently *inside and of it* to think of it as more than special and local. He was reticent when it came to investing it with any significance beyond itself (as later readers have been tempted to do)."[55] Hardy's kind of "shared meaning" may still be accessible in "the inn, the smithy, and the shop," but the aspen-poet listens to other winds. If Thomas sought and found Englishness most persuasively in particulars, localities, and momentary epiphanies, this in itself deconstructs the totalizing, centralizing propensities that "Great Britain" was beginning to assume in the Edwardian era, and which were eventually to culminate in the Thatcherite project. Commentators such as John Lucas in *England and Englishness* (1990), who maintain that "rootedness is always something wished on others,"[56] unwittingly testify to the success of that century-long hegemonic trend. Thomas's local emphases, including his interest in dialect and folk song, can also be seen as intelligently conservationist. Jose Harris writes: "[An] intense and variegated local and provincial culture was still a major strand in British social life between 1870 and 1914 . . . [although] the late Victorian period saw a subterranean shift in the balance of social life away from the locality to the metropolis and the nation. The elements in this shift were complex and only partly visible to contemporaries. . . ."[57] Evidently they were visible to Edward Thomas, and he looked for countervailing elements in communities farther from the metropolis. Hence his alertness to the literature of "intimate reality" inspired by Ireland as contrasted with Britannia—"a frigid personification."[58] *Beautiful Wales* (1905) devotes half a page of its first chapter to reciting the names of places visited, and attributes extreme and holistic local loyalties to some of the people met. Of course, as *Beautiful Wales* indicates, the suburbs had reached Wales, too, though change was slower there. Thomas's Anglo-Welshness may or may not have involved "contradictions."[59] It certainly gave him insights that dramatized the conflict, throughout the British Isles, between modernization and traditional kinds of communal self-understanding, a conflict that is not quite over yet. I have already argued that, for Thomas, "shared meaning" requires participation in a wider web than the social nexus Gervais finds lacking in his work.

Thomas wrote three poems called "Home," and two of them are unhappy. The first (February 1915) begins "Not the end: but there's nothing more," and turns on an unresolved tension between utopian or arcadian possibility ("That land, / My home, I have never seen") and the "fear [that] my happiness there, / Or my pain, might be dreams of return / Here, to the things that were." On its social level, this parable sticks with the present while registering the lost domain. The third in the series, written in March 1916, after his enlistment, has a more exclusively cultural focus. The title is given in quotation marks, and the poem concerns a walk taken by three soldiers over "untrodden snow" in the "strange" countryside around their training camp:

> The word "home" raised a smile in us all three,
> And one repeated it, smiling just so
> That all knew what he meant and none would say.
> Between three counties far apart that lay
> We were divided and looked strangely each
> At the other, and we knew we were not friends
> But fellows in a union that ends
> With the necessity for it, as it ought . . .

In this poem of division and estrangement, "shared meaning" is precluded because the meaning shared is that "home" means different things, different places, different perceptions. The men have been constrained into a military, and perhaps national, "union" that overrides local particularisms. Thomas's poetry is shaped by the antinomies: familiar/strange; known/unknown or unknowable; solitude/society. These antinomies raise overlapping questions about psychic, cultural, and ecological belonging which are most affirmatively answered in the second "Home" poem (April 1915). Here, to quote Robyn Eckersley, the various "organisms" are harmoniously "constituted by environmental interrelationships," while psychology and culture also achieve equilibrium:

> Often I had gone this way before:
> But now it seemed I never could be
> And never had been anywhere else;
> 'Twas home; one nationality
> We had, I and the birds that sang,
> One memory.
>
> They welcomed me. I had come back
> That eve somehow from somewhere far:
> The April mist, the chill, the calm,
> Meant the same thing familiar
> And pleasant to us, and strange too,
> Yet with no bar.

The extension of "nationality," historical "memory," and shared meaning to birds is a subversive stroke in 1915. It sharpens the similar transferrals, in Thomas's prose, of sociopolitical vocabulary to "this commonwealth of things that live in the sun, the air, the earth, the sea, now and through all time." That phrase occurs in his meditation on "the business of the earth" and on the reality that the "rumour of much toil and scheming and triumph may never reach the stars. . . . We know not by what we survive."[60] The poem ends by including in its local ecosystem a laborer who "went along, his tread / Slow, half with weariness, half with ease," and the "sound of [his] sawing" is given the last word. This construction of "Home" partly endorses, partly qualifies, Thomas's wartime redefinition of "England" as "a system of vast circumferences circling round the minute neighbouring points of home."[61] Its ecosystem is not necessarily a national microcosm but cognitively self-sufficient. Thus the centrifugal implications converge on those of "Home" in quotation marks. "England," as well as "Great Britain," has to be broken down. Thomas's originality in reimagining the "knowable community," however, is to fuse ecology and sociality, to unite environmental and local/regional priorities against the metropolis. Yet, as a poet concerned about the condition of England, Thomas sometimes insinuates that its "system of vast circumferences" becomes the interconnected web of his own poems, which might have various local meanings. In the camp, talking to fellow recruits about England, he was pleased to find "There isn't a man I don't share some part with."[62]

Thomas's poetry destabilizes authority, perception, and time in a spirit often regarded as peculiar to modernist aesthetics. It does so with precise reference to environmental and epistemological issues latent in his immediate historical context. And it exhibits a kind of historical imagination usually precluded by the premises of American and Irish modernism. His antinomial landscape is also compounded of presence and absence: a matter not of theoretical protocols but of lost domains, senseless cemeteries, and human departures—the "flowers left thick at nightfall," "two clay pipes," "a ghostly room." Stan Smith has demonstrated that the "ghost is one of the commonest tropes in Thomas's poetry."[63] But absence in Thomas not only laments or prophesies loss but also marks what ought to be there. The poet returns from the margin, "comes back . . . from somewhere far," with meanings for community.

Thomas is as occupied with meaning and language as modernist writing is supposed to be, and often more disturbingly. "I read the sign. Which way shall I go?" says "The Signpost," one of his first poems, and the poetry that follows reads many ambiguous natural and cultural signs that are missed by contemporary theorists (Robyn Eckersley attacks "The Failed Promise of Critical Theory" from an ecocentric viewpoint).[64] Indeed, Thomas's interest in language pivots on relations between nature and culture: not just the anthropocentric question whether culture seeks to "naturalize" itself for suspect political reasons, but the ecocentric question whether human languages remain in touch with their environmental origins. "The Combe" begins, "The Combe was ever dark, ancient and dark. / Its mouth is stopped with bramble, thorn, and briar." If this suggests the impenetrability of some earth languages, the poem goes on to find the Combe's stopped mouth less dismaying than an ecological violence that bears on England at war, not only with Germany but with itself:

> But far more ancient and dark
> The Combe looks since they killed the badger there,
> Dug him out and gave him to the hounds,
> That most ancient Briton of English beasts.

Thomas's humanizing language for the badger (which invokes Celtic rather than imperial Britain) tries to heal a split in home and in natural man. In "Words" Thomas celebrates the English language for being "as dear / As the earth which you prove / That we love." Language, too, has a long eco-history, being "[a]s our hills are, old." Similarly, the elusive "Lob" represents one language's evolutionary fitness in speech and writing: "Calling the wild cherry tree the merry tree." In this positive linguistic scenario, it is not that "word" exactly or referentially reproduces "thing," but that the *associations* of words, in an ecological sense, testify to the development of language (and literature) as a function of bodily, sensory, local, and earthly existence. The likeness/difference of bird language is not just a sentimentality on Thomas's part. Humanity kept itself in the text through language. And our ability to ensure that language is "Worn new / Again and again" ("Words") depends on recognizing the "lost homes" it harbors.

But the dark alternative is that man's textual inscriptions may wear thin or lose touch. Two of Thomas's first poems, "March" and "Old Man," written on consecutive days, stand in an antinomial symbolic relation to each other. In "March" Thomas identifies his own artistic release with thrushes imposing their song after bad weather has "kept them quiet as the primroses" and postponed spring: "So they could keep off silence / And night, they cared not what they sang or screamed." At the end of

"March" there is a sense that the linked vocal efforts of poet and birds have been productive. "Old Man" begins by holding the human and nonhuman creation in a precarious balance:

> Old Man, or Lad's love,—in the name there's nothing
> To one that knows not Lad's-love, or Old Man,
> The hoar-green feathery herb, almost a tree,
> Growing with rosemary and lavender.
> Even to one that knows it well, the names
> Half decorate, half perplex, the thing it is:
> At least, what that is clings not to the names
> In spite of time. And yet I like the names.

Certainly this does not subscribe to a correspondence theory of language, or suggest that any single verbal formula can get at "the thing it is." The contradictory names of the plant, and the speaker's liking for them, however, belong to a history of proximate if not shared meanings. In contrast, the end of "Old Man" unravels the interconnected web ("I have mislaid the key. I sniff the spray / And think of nothing; I see and I hear nothing") to open up a vista devoid of human presence, history, memory, meaning, and language: "Only an avenue, dark, nameless, without end." Nonhuman creatures can cope with nameless things, or speak "thingless names," but not mankind. This ultimate or original absence is not the silence and night that Thomas sometimes welcomes as an earthly *requiescat*. It forebodes the premature encroachment of "nothingness" if we "mislay the key" to the domain, if we cease desiring to be "not a transitory member of a parochial species, but a citizen of the Earth."[65]

Notes

1. Raymond Williams, *The Country and the City* (London, 1973), p. 240.

2. Ibid., pp. 245–46, 256, 261.

3. Citations of Edward Thomas's poetry are from *The Collected Poems of Edward Thomas*, ed. R. George Thomas (Oxford, 1978).

4. Williams, *The Country and the City*, p. 260.

5. Robyn Eckersley, *Environmentalism and Political Theory: Toward an Ecocentric Approach* (London, 1992), p. 49.

6. Ibid., pp. 182, 86.

7. Jonathan Bate, *Romantic Ecology: Wordsworth and the Environmental Tradition* (London, 1991), p. 9.

8. Ibid., pp. 10, 11.

9. *Poetry Review* 80, no. 1 (Spring 1990): 3, 41.

10. Anne Buttimer, *Geography and the Human Spirit* (Baltimore, 1993), pp. 8, 2–3.

11. Edward Thomas, *The South Country* (1909; rpt. London, 1993), p. 65.

12. Jose Harris, *Private Lives, Public Spirit: Britain, 1870–1914* (1993; rpt. London, 1994), p. 42.

13. Edward Thomas, review of *Georgian Poetry, 1911–1912*, by Edward Marsh, *Daily Chronicle*, January 14, 1913; reprinted in Edna Longley, ed., *A Language Not To Be Betrayed: Selected Prose of Edward Thomas* (Manchester, 1981), pp. 112–13.

14. Samuel Hynes, *The Edwardian Turn of Mind* (1968: rpt. London, 1991), pp. 5, 63.

15. Harris, *Private Lives, Public Spirit*, p. 252.

16. *Daily Chronicle*, August 14, 1905, and August 30, 1905; excerpted in Longley, *A Language Not To Be Betrayed*, pp. 201–2.

17. Helen Thomas, *As It Was and World Without End* (London, 1956), p. 115.

18. Hynes, *The Edwardian Turn of Mind*, p. 126.

19. Thomas, *The South Country*, p. 43.

20. Letter of August 20, 1908, in *Letters from Gordon Bottomley to Edward Thomas*, ed. R. George Thomas (London, 1968), p. 167.

21. See introduction to Longley, *A Language Not To Be Betrayed*.

22. Edward Thomas, *Richard Jefferies* (1909; rpt. London, 1978), p. 294.

23. Edward Thomas, "Some Country Books," in *British Country Life in Autumn and Winter: The Book of the Open Air*, ed. Edward Thomas (London, 1908); reprinted in Longley, *A Language Not To Be Betrayed*, pp. 162–65 (quote p. 164).

24. Harris, *Private Lives, Public Spirit*, pp. 5, 36.

25. Edward Thomas, *The Country* (London, 1913), p. 21.

26. Thomas, *The South Country*, p. 71.

27. Stan Smith, *Edward Thomas* (London, 1986), pp. 18–19.

28. Ibid., p. 19.

29. Chapter 12 of *The South Country* is called "Children of Earth"; see also p. 161 and pp. 18, 131–34, 148.

30. Thomas, *The South Country*, p. 164.

31. Ibid., pp. 121–22, 50.

32. Ibid., p. 26.

33. Ibid., p. 19.

34. Edward O. Wilson, *The Diversity of Life* (1993; rpt. London, 1994), p. 330.

35. Thomas, *The South Country*, p. 20.

36. Wilson, *The Diversity of Life*, pp. 332–33.

37. Thomas, *The South Country*, pp. 116, 110.

38. Andrew Dobson, ed., *The Green Reader* (London, 1991), p. 8.

39. Thomas, *The South Country*, p. 115.

40. Robert Wells, "Edward Thomas and England," in *The Art of Edward Thomas*, ed. Jonathan Barker (Bridgend, 1987), p. 71.

41. Edward Thomas, "Tipperary," from *The Last Sheaf* (London, 1928); reprinted in Longley, *A Language Not To Be Betrayed*, pp. 231–40 (quote p. 232).

42. Wells, "Edward Thomas and England," pp. 72, 66.

43. Entry of April 7, 1917, "Diary of Edward Thomas," January 1–April 8, 1917, Appendix C, in *The Collected Poems of Edward Thomas*, p. 481.

44. David Gervais, *Literary Englands: Versions of "Englishness" in Modern Writing* (Cambridge, 1993), p. 41.

45. John Barrell, *The Dark Side of the Landscape: The Rural Poor in English Painting, 1730–1840* (Cambridge, 1980).

46. W. J. T. Mitchell, ed., *Landscape and Power* (Chicago, 1994), p. 17.

47. Thomas, *The South Country*, p. 55.

48. John Barrell, "Being Is Perceiving," in *Poetry, Language, and Politics* (Manchester, 1988), pp. 126–27.

49. Smith, *Edward Thomas*, p. 67.

50. Ibid., p. 44.

51. Williams, *The Country and the City*, p. 259.

52. Entry of March 23, 1917, in "Diary of Edward Thomas," p. 478.

53. Edward Thomas, *The Heart of England* (London, 1906), p. 4.

54. Smith, *Edward Thomas*, p. 84.

55. Gervais, *Literary Englands*, p. 43.

56. John Lucas, *England and Englishness* (London, 1990), p. 6.

57. Harris, *Private Lives, Public Spirit*, pp. 18–19.

58. Edward Thomas, review of John Cooke, ed., *The Dublin Book of Irish Verse*, in *Morning Post*, January 6, 1910.

59. "That he could himself embrace his Welshness and yet at the same time not feel the strain of reconciling it with his idea of England testifies to the power of ideology to contain contradictions." Smith, *Edward Thomas*, p. 15.

60. Thomas, *The South Country*, p. 19.

61. Edward Thomas, "England," in *The Last Sheaf* (London, 1928); reprinted in Longley, *A Language Not To Be Betrayed*, pp. 222–31 (quote p. 231).

62. Letter of February 11, 1916, in *Letters from Gordon Bottomley*, p. 259.

63. Smith, *Edward Thomas*, p. 66.

64. Eckersley, *Environmentalism and Political Theory*, pp. 97–117.

65. Edward Thomas, "George Meredith," in *A Literary Pilgrim in England* (London, 1917); excerpted in Longley, *A Language Not To Be Betrayed*, pp. 36–37 (quote p. 37).

Edwardian Miscellany

The Edwardian Shaw, or the Modernist That Never Was

NICHOLAS GRENE

In 1970 I went to a production of *Major Barbara* at the Aldwych in London, the Royal Shakespeare Company's first staging of a Shaw play. Clifford Williams directed in post-Brechtian modern style; instead of a curtain rising on a fully represented Edwardian scene, Lady Britomart's library was constructed downstage before the audience by costumed stagehands who unrolled carpets and moved furniture into place as tokens within a space that remained largely empty and unoccupied. This cutaway style, advertising its theatrical temporariness, helped to point up the play's changes of scene, to the stark bareness of the West Ham Salvation Army shelter of act 2, and then to the munitions factory/model town of act 3. It was an interesting and intelligent production, with some fine performances—Judi Dench as Barbara, Brewster Mason as Undershaft—an admirable attempt to rescue Shaw from the comfortable datedness of traditional representational productions. Much in the play seemed to warrant such a modern theatrical idiom: the materialist unmasking of conventional political attitudes, particularly in the last act, with its alienating scenic ironies—the foreground of the munitions factory with dominating cannon and mutilated dummy soldiers leaking straw, and the distant prospect of the flawless model town. And yet it was this last act which I found least satisfactory in the RSC production, which left me most aware of some sort of mismatch between play and playing style. Something in the relentless assurance of Undershaft, the sheer energetic control of his big speeches, a confidence that things were (potentially at least) all for the best in the best of all possible worlds, clashed with the chilling estrangements of the stage set.

Why should Shaw's texts be so resistant to modern treatment? There seems to have been the makings of a modernist in Shaw, particularly the Edwardian Shaw, and there have been recurrent critical attempts to see premodernist modes in his work of this period. Thus, for example, Charles Berst argues that the dream sequence in *Man and Superman*, "Don Juan in Hell," "is second cousin to Strindberg's dream

135

plays."[1] Irving Wardle comments on how frequently Shaw "anticipates styles of the future," even down to the "Ionesco territory" of the skit *Passion, Poison, and Petrification*.[2] *Misalliance*, Michael Holroyd claims, reveals "links with contemporary innovations, from Post Impressionism to Dadaism, that show G.B.S. . . . was familiar with the earlier experiments of modernists and had his own agenda for clearing away the dominance of the well-made play comparable to theirs."[3] As with Williams's production of *Major Barbara*, such critics appear to be trying to retrieve Shaw from the historical freeze-frame of Edwardianism as an old-fashioned thing apart from the styles of international modernism that overtook it. But how much conviction do they carry? If the *Man and Superman* dream sequence is second cousin to Strindberg, it must be many times removed; the jeu d'esprit of *Passion, Poison, and Petrifaction* is philosophically innocent; it sends up the absurdities of stage representation rather than assaulting the principle of representation itself as the absurdists do. And Shaw's strategy for displacing the well-made play was to substitute another sort of well-made play, not the radical deconstruction of form of the modernists. Why did Shaw not become the modernist he might have been? Why did his career not follow the curve of development of other late-Victorians-turned-modernists, his near-contemporary Yeats being the most striking case? I want to look for an answer in the Edwardian Shaw, and in the attitudes toward modernity manifested in the Edwardian Shaw.

From Motorcars to Aeroplanes

Shaw's Edwardian drama begins with the theatrical appearance of a motorcar (*Man and Superman*, written 1901–2, published 1903, produced 1905), and ends with an airplane crash (almost) on stage (*Misalliance*, written 1909, performed 1910). Shaw was nothing if not up-to-the-minute. The introduction of these new machines into his plays was not primarily aimed at theatrical novelty value: *Man and Superman* was not originally written to be produced but was intended to be "unactably independent of theatrical considerations."[4] But Shaw loved new technologies and lived always with a journalist's awareness of the topical. Thus, the car chase in *Man and Superman*, so integral to the perverse narrative design of woman the huntress, Don Juan the hunted, arises out of the atmosphere of the early motor enthusiasms of 1901–2. Straker, Tanner's chauffeur, is stung to rivalry by the challenge of Hector Malone's "new American steam car."[5] At the time of the play's composition, it was by no means clear that the "petroleum spirit motive power" engine would win out over steam. So, for example, the Automobile Club, at motor trials organized in Glasgow in October 1901 in connection with the Glasgow International Exhibition, awarded two gold medals in the class for cars costing less than £250, to "a 5-h.p. Wolseley car and a steam car of the Locomobile Company of America" because, it was reported, "a complete comparison could not be made between two types of vehicles so different as steam cars and cars driven by internal combustion engines."[6] Straker is frustrated by Tanner's unwillingness to allow him to join in the road trials and races which were threatened by the imposition of bans on the Continent as in Britain: "[T]herell be a clamor agin it presently; and then the French Government'll stop it; an our chance'll be gone, see? Thats what makes me fairly mad: Mr. Tanner wont do a good run while he can" (CP 1, 594). Public opinion was indeed moving against the Straker speed merchants, though in December 1901 Europe did still represent a less restricted space for racing: "A race between motor-cars over 110 miles of road for a prize of £1,000 was recently announced. Great opposition was, however, offered to the proposal, and is now stated that, owing to the pressure brought to bear by the Automobile Club ... the race will take place upon the Continent."[7] The spoilsport Automobile Club, according to the report, arguing that "racing on the public highway must always tend towards driving without proper consideration of other users of the road," threatened to expel any of its members who took part in such road racing, and proposed asking clubs on the Continent to do the same—just the development Straker feared.

Shaw believed in hands-on experience of the new forms of transport, becoming a wildly dangerous motorist in 1908 as he had been an accident-prone cyclist in the 1890s.[8] As early as 1904, according to one account, he had gone ballooning, crash-landing in "a country gentleman's treasured greenhouse," as the aviators in *Misalliance* were to do.[9] The writing of *Misalliance* in September–November 1909 was conditioned by the developments in aviation in Britain in the months before it was written. The first cross-Channel flight by Louis Blériot in July, flights by Samuel Franklin Cody (brother of Buffalo Bill), including one in August which had made his wife the first woman to fly in Britain, concern voiced in letters to *The Times* about crashes, and forced landings during cross-country flights all ensured topicality for the surprise entrance by air of Joey Perceval and Lina Szczepanowska into the Tarletons' country house in *Misalliance*.[10] Shaw made his plays of the stuff that lay to hand, the more recent, the more up-to-date, the better. He gloried in the newness of the new.

Shaw was a technological modernist as he was a social and political progressive, and he continually associated the two. In the preface to *Getting Married*, Shaw dismissed those who were disturbed by the higher divorce rate made possible by the relatively liberal laws of the state of Washington:

> When journalists and bishops and American Presidents and other simple people describe this Washington result as alarming, they are speaking as a peasant speaks of a motor car or an aeroplane when he sees one for the first time. All he means is that he is not used to it and therefore fears that it may injure him. Every advance in civilization frightens these honest folk. This is a pity; but if we were to spare their feelings we should never improve the world at all. (CP 3, 524)

Shaw not only links advances in technology with advances in civilization; he positively approves of the related principle of obsolescence. "It is a waste of labor to make a machine that will last ten years, because it will probably be superseded in half that time by an improved machine answering the same purpose" (CP 4, 15). Discarding the obsolete is the key to progress, technological, social, or spiritual, in Undershaft's crucial speech to Barbara in the third act of *Major Barbara*:

> What do we do here when we spend years of work and thought and thousands of pounds of solid cash on a new gun or an aerial battleship that turns out just a hairs-breadth wrong after all? Scrap it. Scrap it without wasting another hour or another pound on it. Well, you have made for yourself something that you call a morality or a religion or what not. It doesnt fit the facts. Well, scrap it. Scrap it and get one that

does fit. That is what is wrong with the world at present. It scraps its obsolete steam engines and dynamos; but it wont scrap its old prejudices and its old moralities and its old religions and its old political constitutions. (CP 3, 170–71)

In Shaw's creed of Creative Evolution, God becomes a sort of super-Undershaft:

> My doctrine is that God proceeds by the method of "trial and error," just like a workman perfecting an aeroplane. . . . To me the sole hope of human salvation lies in teaching Man to regard himself as an experiment in the realization of God, to regard his hands as God's hand, his brain as God's brain, his purpose as God's purpose (CL 2, 858)

With such a model of the world, Shaw could never regard the innovations of the modern as inaugurating a definitively new age, to be greeted with the fascinated horror of many modernist writers. At worst the modern era was only a transitional stage on its purposeful forward way to something better.

Garden Cities and Model Towns

BROADBENT: Have you ever heard of Garden City?
TIM (*doubtfully*):   D'ye mane Heavn?
BROADBENT: Heaven! No: it's near Hitchin. (CP 2, 899)

Writing *John Bull's Other Island* in the summer of 1904, Shaw could have relied on enough of his audience knowing about the garden city to share the joke when the fake stage Irishman Tim Haffigan thinks Broadbent is talking about the great garden city on high. Work on the first garden city at Letchworth in Hertfordshire (at this stage simply called Garden City) had begun earlier in 1904 as the culmination of a movement started by Ebenezer Howard's book *To-morrow: A Peaceful Path to Real Reform* in 1898.[11] It is this publication (or possibly its 1902 revised edition, *Garden Cities of To-morrow*) which Broadbent hands to the bewildered Haffigan—"He gives him a copy of Ebenezer Howard's book"—adding earnestly: "You understand that the map of the city—the circular construction—is only a suggestion" (CP 2, 899).

The circular construction was only one of the many utopian features of Howard's ideal garden city which were not realized in practice. The idea was to build on a green site a wholly planned city that would combine the urban and the rural, residential areas, industrial estates, and an outer agricultural green belt in a self-sufficient community providing a real alternative to the blight of polluted and slum-ridden nineteenth-century cities. Howard had been acquainted with Shaw in the early 1880s when they had both been members of the Zetetical Society, one of the forerunners of the Fabian Society. They had moved in the same circles of advanced political thinking at the time, and had both been strongly influenced by Henry George's *Progress and Poverty*. There was a missionary zeal in Howard's ideas as there was in Shaw's: one of the underlying aims of the garden city was the broad reconciliation of religion and science.[12] But, although a socialist in many aspects of his thought, Howard was deeply distrustful of centralized government control and never followed Shaw into the planned economics of the Fabian Society. It was because of its reliance on the public spirit of private investors that Shaw was initially dismissive of Howard's notions, taking pleasure in demolishing the arguments of "Ebenezer the Garden City Geyser" at a public lecture in Hindhead in 1899 (CL 2, 118–19). Shaw was in some ways quite sympathetic to the notion of a garden city with its planned suburban idyll, and he was to invest in both Letchworth and Welwyn Garden City in due course.[13] His quarrel with the scheme, set out at length in a letter to the chairman of the Garden City Association, the Liberal M.P. Ralph Neville, had to do with the naïveté of expecting capitalists to forgo their rights of property in the communal ownership of land, which was fundamental to the notion of the garden city.[14]

In some ways *John Bull's Other Island* is an illustration of that argument. Broadbent's plan is to "start a Garden City in Ireland" (CP 2, 899). This is plausible at least insofar as Broadbent is a Liberal and most of the prominent politicians who supported the garden city movement were from the Liberal party. He has the necessary site for development because the Land Syndicate which he and his partner Larry Doyle represent have foreclosed the mortgage on the estate of Nick Lestrange, the Anglo-Irish landowner of Rosscullen. Broadbent paints in broad strokes the picture of all the benefits he will bring to the town: "I shall bring money here: I shall raise wages: I shall found public institutions: a library, a Polytechnic (undenominational, of course), a gymnasium, a cricket club, perhaps an art school. I shall make a Garden city of Rosscullen" (CP 2, 1015). Shaw, though, uses Peter Keegan, the unfrocked priest, to unmask the process of capitalist exploitation by which Broadbent's syndicate will take total control of this imagined dream community for their own profit:

> [W]hen at last this poor desolate countryside becomes a busy mint in which we shall all slave to make money for you, with our Polytechnic to teach us how to do it efficiently, and our library to fuddle the few imaginations your distilleries will spare, and our repaired Round Tower, with admission sixpence, and refreshments and penny-in-the-slot mutoscopes[15] to make it interesting, then no doubt your English and American shareholders will spend all the money we make for them very efficiently in shooting and hunting, in operations for cancer and appendicitis, in gluttony and gambling; and you will devote what they save to fresh land development schemes. For four wicked centuries the world has dreamed this foolish dream of efficiency; and the end is not yet. But the end will come. (CP 2, 1017–18)

Keegan's denunciation here goes well beyond what was necessary to show up the capitalist serpent in the notionally Edenic garden city. This is Shaw in one of his relatively rare moods of real revulsion against modernization, its libraries and Polytechnics and what we would now call theme parks. And it is significant that it occurs in relation to Ireland, and to the mutation of political colonialism into cultural and economic colonialism. In many ways Shaw is closely identified with the figure of Larry Doyle in the play, the Irish exile reluctant to return (Larry goes back to Rosscullen after eighteen years; Shaw was to return to Ireland in 1905 after twenty-eight years' absence). Larry, like Shaw, had no time for Irish nationalist separatism; he speaks for his author when he declares, "I want Ireland to be the brains and imagination of a big Commonwealth, not a Robinson Crusoe Island" (CP 2, 914). The extent of Shaw's identification with Larry Doyle can be seen in the number of political ideas voiced by Larry in the play, such as the establishment of the Roman Catholic church in Ireland, which he himself endorses in the "Preface for Politicians." Yet by the end of the play, Doyle's urge to assist in the "modernisation" of Rosscullen is revealed as a bitter self-destructive revenge upon the country of his own provincial origins. There is a kind of self-judgment by Shaw in the creation of Doyle, even as he gave voice to another strain within himself in the "mad" prophet Keegan. Keegan, with his messianic belief in Ireland as "holy ground," with his mystic utopianism of "a country where the State is the Church and the Church the people," makes the limited social engineering of the garden city an inadequate sham, and reveals the supposedly benevolent intentions of liberals like Broadbent as a predatory colonialism of international capital. In the context of Ireland, the modern, with its enforced touristification of Rosscullen, is seen as a coming horror rather than an advance toward a higher civilization.

In *Major Barbara*, the next play after *John Bull*, Shaw portrayed not a putative garden city but an employer's model town. Perivale St. Andrews, "an almost smokeless town of white walls, roofs of narrow green slates or red tiles, tall trees, domes, campaniles, and slender chimney shafts, beautifully situated and beautiful in itself" (CP 3, 157), is like George Cadbury's Bournville or W. H. Lever's Port Sunlight in that it is created and controlled by the employer whose industry provides it with its raison d'être. Both Cadbury and Lever were involved in the garden city movement, though Lever, significantly, resigned his directorship of the First Garden City Company over his opposition to maintaining Howard's principle of communal ownership of the land.[16] Shaw, who went to such lengths to expose the probability of self-interested capitalist control in the garden city, might have been expected to disapprove even more thoroughly of the employer-dominated company town. But Shaw could always be relied on not to do what was expected of him. And so Perivale St. Andrews is portrayed as "horribly, frightfully, immorally, unanswerably perfect" (CP 3, 158). Where Keegan shows up Broadbent's promised benefits to Rosscullen as mere beads for the natives, the audience of *Major Barbara*, like the onstage visitors to Perivale St. Andrews, are intended to be overwhelmingly impressed by its listed amenities: "the nursing home . . . the libraries and schools . . . the ball room and the banqueting chamber in the Town Hall . . . the insurance fund, the pension fund, the building society, the various applications of co-operation" (CP 3, 159). These were the kinds of comforts of working affluence proposed by Ebenezer Howard to the residents of his garden city; Shaw shows them as products of the munitions manufacturer's company town.

The completeness of Undershaft's dominance in *Major Barbara* bothered Shaw's Fabian associate Gilbert Murray, model for Adolphus Cusins, Undershaft's adoptive heir-to-be, and it in fact seems to have bothered Shaw himself. Yet in spite of his rewriting of the last scene to meet some of Murray's criticisms, he concluded, "As to the triumph of Undershaft, that is inevitable because I am in the mind that Undershaft is in the right, and that Barbara and Adolphus, with a great deal of his natural insight and cleverness, are very young, very romantic, very academic, very ignorant of the world" (CL 2, 566). The last is the key phrase because *Major Barbara* is in Shaw's worldly wise mode, teaching its imputed high-minded audience of Barbaras and Cusinses a brutal lesson in the realities of power, money, and gunpowder. There is no point in wringing your hands at the evils of your society, Shaw tells us, and going off and doing "good works" to the poor and starving in London's East End: go where the power is, the power that can produce a Perivale St. Andrews as well as torpedoes and aerial battleships. The play instructs us that we must learn, as Barbara does, that "turning our backs on Bodger [the distiller] and Undershaft is turning our backs on life" (CP 3, 183).

This is in line with Fabian principles of permeation, the strategy of influencing existing institutions and authorities rather than standing off in isolationist opposition, and of the need for political and practical engagement by moral and intellectual leaders. What is characteristically Shavian in the play, or characteristic at least of one side of Shaw, is the idealization of the benevolently despotic capitalist and his imagined alliance with spiritual, moral, and political forces. His triple entente of Undershaft, Barbara, and Cusins at the end of the play is intended as an elite alliance for radical social and political progress, as against the wasteful and ineffective processes of democracy. (If modernist is nothing else, Shaw could be as antidemocratic as the highest of high modernists: it was not the subfascist Yeats of the 1930s but the socialist Shaw in 1903 who called "our political experiment of democracy, the last refuge of cheap misgovernment" [CP 2, 512].) There is a kind of coziness in this Shavian fantasy of power sharing, for all the ferocity of Undershaft's shock tactic rhetoric in which poverty is a crime and killing the final test of conviction. The moral horror of the munitions and the wars they serve is somehow elided in the prospect of the suburban pastoral of Perivale St. Andrews, where Barbara and Cusins, the next Andrew Undershaft to be, are to settle down in happy-ever-after married bliss. The contrast with the ending of *John Bull* could not be greater. Whereas Keegan, the religious visionary in that play, strays off alone with his "dream of a madman" while Broadbent and Doyle remain in possession, choosing the site for the Rosscullen hotel, Barbara, with her evangelical crusade on a new course, "has gone right up to the skies" as she prepares to move into her father's model town. Perivale St. Andrews, and what it may represent for the future, comes out in the end as an almost unironized utopia.

Science and Progress

I was born in the year 1856. That does not seem — if I may judge from the expression of your faces — to convey very much to you; but if you will remember that Darwin's Origin of Species was published in 1859 you will understand that I belong to a generation which, I think, began life by hoping more from Science than perhaps any generation ever hoped before, and, possibly, will ever hope again. I give the date in order to get out of the minds of any of you who may entertain such an idea that I am in any hostile to science. Science will always be extraordinarily interesting and hopeful to me. At the present moment we are passing through a phase of disillusion. Science has not lived up to the hopes we formed of it in the 1860s; but those hopes left a mark on my temperament that I shall never get rid of till I die.[17]

Samuel Hynes cites this passage from a 1909 paper of Shaw's as introduction to his chapter "Science, Seers, and Sex" in *The Edwardian Turn of Mind*, illustrating the mixed feelings about science in the Edwardian period.[18] Shaw is certainly a good example of such mixed feelings. As he goes on to say in this same paper, "I have, more or less, all my life concerned myself with science, because throughout my life-time science has been very largely going wrong on social questions."[19] Not only on social but on ethical, spiritual, and metaphysical questions as well. Shaw followed Samuel Butler in questioning Darwin's theory of evolution by natural selection because, in Butler's phrase, it "banished mind from the universe." His belief in Cre-ative Evolution was an attempt to retain something like the scientific structure of evolutionary theory while restoring to it a teleology of final ends. Shaw was suffi-ciently of his late Victorian generation to use "scientific" as the hallmark of intel-lectual authenticity: his plays were to teach people the need for "a genuinely scien-tific natural history" (CP 1, 385). Yet he remained often skeptical of the science and scientific thought of his time. While he happily saluted advances in technology and equated them with advances in civilization, he was much more doubtful of the asso-ciation of science with progress, especially in the case of medical science. The result in The Doctor's Dilemma was a curiously double set of attitudes.

The Doctor's Dilemma is in many ways a classic medical satire in the tradition of Molière. Shaw, as might be expected, has a specific political case to make for social-ized, as against private, medicine, arguing that private medicine gives positive finan-cial incentive to malpractice. In this play the doctors are all more or less shown up as quacks, blinding their lay patients with pseudo-science, each with his own pet remedy, whether it be the surgeon Cutler Walpole's recommended removal of the "nuciform sac," or Sir Ralph Bloomfield Bonington's splendid and unfailing cry, "[W]e will stimulate the phagocytes." The nearest we get to a Shavian spokesperson or Molièrean raisonneur in the play is the old Irish doctor Sir Patrick Cullen. He is used to voice many of the criticisms of contemporary medicine expressed by Shaw in the preface, from the craze for useless minor surgery to the (in Shaw's view) quite mis-taken identification of the bacterial origin of diseases such as diphtheria. It is Sir Patrick, speaking to the play's protagonist, Sir Colenso Ridgeon, who expresses the most general skepticism about advances in medical science:

> SIR PATRICK: . . . Modern science is a wonderful thing. Look at your great discovery! Look at all the great discoveries! Where are they leading to? Why, right back to my poor dear old father's ideas and discoveries. He's been dead now over forty years. Oh, it's very interesting.
> RIDGEON: Well, theres nothing like progress, is there?
> SIR PATRICK.   Dont misunderstand me, my boy. I'm not belittling your discovery. Most discoveries are made regularly every fifteen years; and it's fully a hundred and fifty since yours was made last. (CP, III, 329).

Yet it is crucial for the plot of The Doctor's Dilemma that the audience should believe in the reality and significance of Ridgeon's discovery; otherwise the supposition that he can save Dubedat from death by tuberculosis is destroyed. Not only that, but "opsonin," Ridgeon's supposed discovery in the play, was the actual discovery of Shaw's friend Sir Almroth Wright. Wright, an Irishman and graduate of Trinity Col-lege, was an eminent bacteriologist whose work had been recognized by the award of a knighthood in the Birthday Honours of June 1906. Writing *The Doctor's Dilemma* just six weeks later, Shaw began his play on the day that Colenso Ridgeon's knighthood is announced.[20] As with the use of Gilbert Murray for Cusins in *Major Barbara*, Shaw took an extraordinary liberty in modeling Ridgeon so closely on Wright, especially in view of the fact that he makes the doctor in the play a murderer, but Wright, though he had his misgivings—and walked out of the play when he finally saw it— did not attempt to stop its staging.[21]

"Opsonin," discovered by Wright with a collaborator in 1903, is defined in the *OED Supplement* as "a substance (usu. an antibody) in blood serum which combines with bacteria or other foreign cells and renders them more susceptible to phagocytosis," or more graphically by Shaw, via Ridgeon, as "what you butter the disease germs with to make your white blood corpuscles eat them" (CP 3, 331). Shaw's initial reaction when Wright had sent him a pamphlet about his work in 1905 had been as skeptical as Sir Patrick Cullen's: "Oh, bother your pamphlets" (CP 3, 331).[22] Shaw's long-standing opposition to vaccination had made him prejudiced against any form of serum therapy. But a visit to Wright's laboratory in St. Mary's Hospital seems to have helped to change his mind, particularly when he came to see the understanding of opsonin as part of a natural pattern. Ridgeon expounds it as follows:

> What it comes to in practice is this. The phagocytes wont eat the microbes unless the microbes are nicely buttered for them. Well, the patient manufactures the butter for himself all right; but my discovery is that the manufacture of that butter, which I call opsonin, goes on in the system by ups and downs—Nature being always rhythmical, you know—and that what the inoculation does is to stimulate the ups and downs, as the case may be. . . . Everything depends on your inoculating at the right moment. Inoculate when the patient is in the negative phase and you kill: inoculate when the patient is in the positive phase and you cure. (CP 3, 332)

This makes possible the play's plot: Dubedat, turned over to the egregious Bloomfield Bonington, who blithely inoculates without understanding about Ridgeon's discovery, is swiftly killed, whereas the humble and worthy Dr. Blenkinsop, treated by Ridgeon, is completely cured. In fact, according to Wright's biographer, all this was based on a Shavian misinterpretation:

> Wright had reported (it was not a new discovery) that following an innoculation of vaccines, a patient's "resistance" would sometimes drop ("the negative phase") and later rise ("the positive phase"). Shaw interpreted this as a discovery that there are rhythmical fluctuations of immunity—irrespective of inoculations. . . . It was quite a different proposition from what Wright had intended—and one for which Wright had no evidence.[23]

Shaw was in the end indifferent to the scientific truth or otherwise of the alleged medical facts on which he based *The Doctor's Dilemma*. When, years later, Wright confessed that "his ideas about phagocytosis in those early days had been all wrong," Shaw exclaimed, "Never mind; they enabled me to write a jolly good play."[24] What is significant is the way he uses science, and the attitudes he adopts toward it. In spite of Shaw's disclaimer that he was "in any way hostile to science," he tended to be antiscientific, with the characteristic layman's distrust of anything which he could not fully understand. His opinions on medical matters were largely formed by personal experience: things he had heard as a young man in Dublin such as the identification of hydrophobia with tetanus,[25] the smallpox he himself suffered in 1881 in spite of having been vaccinated in infancy, the time he spent convalescing with his doctor uncle in Leyton in Essex,[26] and the tuberculosis from which one of his sisters died while the other recovered.[27] His political viewpoint inclined him to emphasize the social causes of disease, and adequate sanitation was his favorite remedy for most illnesses. It is typical that Shaw should have misinterpreted Wright's work as a discovery of a naturally therapeutic pattern—"Nature being always rhythmical, you know." This holistic or vitalist strain is a part of Shaw's skepticism about the supposed advances of most modern medical science.

And yet Wright in real life, and Ridgeon in the play, are exempted from this general distrust. Many of science's claims to originality are fraudulent, most of its supposed steps forward may be illusory, but not all. The idea of progress is maintained in relation to certain great advances, certain great men, of which opsonin and Almroth Wright are examples. The greatness of the man here is more important than his discovery. So, in the preface to *The Doctor's Dilemma*, Shaw allows for the possibility that opsonin may not prove as significant as it is made to appear in the play, but implies that it would be Wright's own future researches that might overtake it. "By the time this preface is in print the kaleidoscope may have had another shake; and opsonin may have gone the way of phlogiston at the hands of its own restless discoverer" (CP 3, 316). True advances in science, as in other fields of thought, come from the few really original thinkers in any generation, and it takes one, like Shaw, to recognize another, like Wright. To that extent science did remain "extraordinarily interesting and hopeful" to Shaw, and, for all his iconoclastic exposure of "doctor's delusions" in *The Doctor's Dilemma*, the play does contain a belief in the possibility of undeluded scientific progress.

Shaw, the Modern, and Futurity

Shaw was familiar with the phenomenon of yesterday's radicals becoming tomorrow's reactionaries. He pillories such a person in the figure of Roebuck Ramsden in *Man and Superman*: "You pose as an advanced man," splutters Ramsden to the enfant terrible John Tanner. "Let me tell you that I was an advanced man before you were born." "I knew it was a long time ago," replies Tanner (CP 2, 547). Shaw was determined never to become a Roebuck Ramsden but to remain "advanced" even as he moved in the reign of Edward VII from his forties into his fifties. Socially and politically, the Edwardian Shaw did indeed stay well in advance of his audience. In *Getting Married* and its preface, for example, he argued for what we would now call "no fault" divorce, freely available on request by either married party. The Royal Commission on Divorce and Matrimonial Causes, reporting in 1912, was unable to have even its very limited recommendations for liberalization put into law by the government because of the opposition of the church.[28] In the "Treatise on Parents and Children," which was the preface to *Misalliance*, Shaw exposed the psychopathology of the parent–child relationship and the perniciousness of the authoritarian education system that buttressed it. Formally, too, Shaw challenged his Edwardian audiences and critics. In *Man and Superman* he created a new form of disquisitory comedy for the stage by ignoring the requirements of the stage. *John Bull's Other Island* was solemnly proclaimed "no play" by the reviewers before going on to be the sensational success that established Shaw's theatrical reputation. If the "tragedy" of *The Doctor's Dilemma*, cheekily so categorized, retained a plot and a conventional five-act structure, these were spectacularly abandoned for the ceaseless tides of talk of the sui generis discussion plays *Getting Married* and *Misalliance*.

Yet in the end his political and social radicalism, his formal experimentation, did not move Shaw on into modernist modes. The attitudes toward modernity which I have been looking at in Shaw's Edwardian work are perhaps best seen finally in the context of his Victorian provincial formation. That formation was provincial in the sense that Shaw came to London at the age of twenty in search of "a metropolitan domicile and an international culture" which would allow him to fulfill his destiny as the important figure he believed he would become.[29] As a young Irishman without money, higher education, professional training, or influence, confronting the daunting hierarchies of class and power which declared his insignificance, he adopted a double strategy. One part of that strategy was an idiosyncratic self-making which permitted him to rule himself *hors concours*, utterly his own man, from his all-wool Jaeger suit to his flamboyantly mixed bag of opinions, ideas, and convictions. To be that outré was to exclude oneself as unclassifiable in the variety of available class systems. This was G.B.S., Hyde Park corner orator, quirky journalist, conversational clown. The other part of the strategy was to prepare, long and laboriously, and to wait, patiently and confidently, for his hour to come. Essential to his defense against discouragement was an armor of unconcern about the defeats of the present. All was to be made good in some imagined future state in which he would be transcendently successful. Shaw did desperately want and need ultimate recognition; he wanted eventually to be acknowledged by majorities, not just coteries. This is where the provincial formation was of key importance: the need for validation by the metropolitan big world. In the scheme of things by which everyone was currently out of step but our G.B.S., it was vitally important that, in some future time, the pace and direction of the march would change and that Bernard Shaw would be seen to be out there leading the troops. Michael Holroyd calls the volume of his biography which includes the Edwardian Shaw *The Pursuit of Power*. In his graph of Shaw's psychological development, the pursuit of power in the middle years was a substitute for a failed search for love driven by the hungers of a loveless childhood, and the repeated frustrations in attaining such power led on to the lure of fantasy in the later period of Shaw's career, where he fictionally remade the world which in its uncontrollable actuality had eluded his grasp. Whether we accept this thesis or not, from first to last Shaw believed in what could be called a deferred power principle. He was right, and he would—at last—be shown to be right: even if power were not attained now, power would be attained in some longest-term perspective. Although the need to invent the long-livers of *Back to Methuselah*, the projections forward as far as thought can reach, may indeed testify to Shaw's decreasing confidence in achieving authority in any immediately foreseeable future, the faith in futurity nonetheless remains a constant.

The matrix of looking forward faithfully to the future underpins Shaw's thinking and practice as writer and thinker, and made much of modernism necessarily unavailable to him. Shaw took pleasure in the advances of technology; he had mixed emotions about capitalist-driven modernization; he was partly skeptical of the advances of science; but he never saw modernity as some radically new dispensation. There could be for him no epoch-changing moment of annunciation like Yeats's famous reaction to *Ubu Roi,* "After us the Savage God."[30] With the possible exception of *Heartbreak House,* and only partially there, Shaw was never attracted to the vision of apocalypse now which so obsessed the modernist imagination. Instead, for all his denunciations of the evils of his own time, he kept a nineteenth-century belief in what he called "the general march of enlightenment' (CP 3, 700). Shaw was a modern materialist insofar as he insisted that the grounds of all human behavior had to be sought in the socio-economic conditions in which people lived. But his materialism was designed to lead on and up to a higher supramaterialist metaphysic. Therefore we never find in his work either the exhilaration in pure material reality which is one strain in modernism, nor yet the horrified reaction against a mindlessly material universe which is another.

Shaw vehemently denied that he was a rationalist; he saw himself as a prophetic visionary. Yet such manifestations of mystic irrationalism as we find in the Edwardian plays—in the dreaming "mad" Keegan, say, or the oracular Mrs. George in *Getting Married*—speak for a greater rationalism to come. "Every dream is a prophecy," says Keegan, "every jest is an earnest in the womb of Time" (CP 2, 1021). Visionary dreams thus prefigure a literal reality to come, unlike the nonrational associative forms of modernist writing which uncover truths buried in the unconscious of the present or the primitive consciousness of the past. Formally Shaw remained committed to a forward-moving dialectic of thesis–antithesis–synthesis. If his plays have been much misunderstood as simply didactic plays with a purpose, they were always purposeful plays, bringing an audience on in measurable stages toward new understanding. It was this need for a formal teleology to match his ultimate teleology of the world which precluded Shaw from producing modernist forms that actively declared their own fragmentary and arbitrary nature. Where Stephen Dedalus saw history as a nightmare from which he was trying to awake, Shaw believed that it was a comedy whose happy ending for the human race we were all more or less consciously striving to attain. The modern for Shaw was not something incomparably new and different in essence; it was just one more installment of futurity.

Notes

1. Charles A. Berst, *Bernard Shaw and the Art of Drama* (Urbana, Ill., 1973), p. 128.

2. Irving Wardle, "The Plays," in *The Genius of Shaw,* ed. Michael Holroyd (London, 1979), p. 145.

3. Michael Holroyd, *Bernard Shaw,* vol. 2, *1898–1918: The Pursuit of Power* (London, 1989), p. 245. Abbreviated references to the first two volumes of Michael Holroyd's five-volume biography in the rest of this essay are as follows: Holroyd 1 = *Bernard Shaw,* vol. 1, *1856–1898: The Search for Love* (London, 1988); Holroyd 2 = *Bernard Shaw,* vol. 2, *1898–1918: The Pursuit of Power* (London, 1989).

4. Bernard Shaw, *Collected Letters, 1874–1897*, ed. Dan H. Laurence (London, 1965), p. 222. All quotations from Shaw's letters are from this edition, and are cited parenthetically in the text as *CL* 1 (ibid) or *CL* 2 = Bernard Shaw, *Collected Letters, 1898–1910*, ed. Dan H. Laurence (London, 1972).

5. Bernard Shaw, *Collected Plays with Their Prefaces*, vol. 2 (London, 1971), p. 587. All quotations from Shaw's plays are taken from this seven-volume Bodley Head edition (London, 1970–74), and are cited parenthetically in the text in the form *CP* 2, 587.

6. *The Times*, October 18, 1901, p. 3, col. 6.

7. *The Times*, December 6, 1901, p. 11, col. 4.

8. See Holroyd 2, 206–8. On Shaw's cycling, see Holroyd 1, 267–68.

9. The account is that of Eleanor Robson Belmont, cited in Rodelle Weintraub, "A Parachutist Prototype for Lina," *Shaw: The Annual of Bernard Shaw Studies*, 8 (1988): 77–84. There seems, however, to be no other evidence for this incident, and Shaw's first ascent in a balloon is generally given as 1906. See Holroyd 2, 187–88.

10. For the background, see Robert G. Everding, "Bernard Shaw, *Misalliance*, and the Birth of British Aviation," in *Shaw: The Annual of Bernard Shaw Studies*, 8 (1988): 69–76.

11. For detailed information, see Robert Beevers, *The Garden City Utopia: A Critical Biography of Ebenezer Howard* (Basingstoke, Hampshire, 1988). I am grateful to my colleague Fred Aalen of the Geography Department, Trinity College, for referring me to this book.

12. Ibid., pp. 40–42.

13. Ibid., pp. 78, 181.

14. Ibid., pp. 74–77.

15. A mutograph is "an apparatus for taking a series of photographs of objects in motion"; hence, a mutoscope is "an apparatus for exhibiting a scene recorded by the mutograph, which may be seen by looking through an aperture and turning a handle at the side of the instrument" (*OED*), both inventions of 1897.

16. Beevers, *The Garden City Utopia*, pp. 93–94

17. Bernard Shaw, "Socialism and Medicine," in *Platform and Pulpit*, ed. Dan H. Laurence (London, 1962), pp. 49–50.

18. Samuel Hynes, *The Edwardian Turn of Mind* (Princeton, N.J., 1968), p. 132.

19. Shaw, "Socialism and Medicine," p. 50.

20. For reasons I have not been able to discover, Shaw set the actual date of the play back to June 15, 1903.

21. For the background, see Holroyd 2, 157–64.

22. See Holroyd 2, 158.

23. Leonard Colebrook, *Almroth Wright: Provocative Doctor and Thinker* (London, 1954), p. 190.

24. Ibid., p. 195.

25. See Shaw, "Socialism and Medicine," pp. 65–66.

26. See Holroyd 1, 91–93.

27. A letter from Shaw to Almroth Wright in 1905, cited in Holroyd 2, 158, suggests that his sister Lucy's experience of tuberculosis (see Holroyd 2, 305–6), the disease from which his other sister, Agnes, had died, had made him especially skeptical that it was curable by vaccination.

28. See Hynes, *The Edwardian Turn of Mind*, pp. 208–11.

29. Bernard Shaw, preface to *Immaturity* (London, 1931), p. xxxiv.

30. W. B. Yeats, "The Tragic Generation," in *Autobiographies* (London, 1955), p. 349.

Kipling in the History of Forms

LOUIS MENAND

Rudyard Kipling has a role in everyone's notion of the history of modern British literature, but no one's notion of the history of modern British literature depends on the role that Kipling plays. This has been the case pretty much universally since Kipling's death in 1936. Many mighty engineers of critical taste since then have taken Kipling as a topic for serious appreciation, of course: in the early 1940s George Orwell, T. S. Eliot, and Edmund Wilson all proposed ways in which, by shortening the horizon of our critical expectations just enough, we might find rewards for taking an interest in Kipling's work. More recently, and with a somewhat clearer conscience, Angus Wilson, Irving Howe, and Craig Raine have found admiring things to say about Kipling. But none of these considerations makes a historical claim about Kipling's importance. What they make are taste claims.

This is not to say that taste claims do not matter, for they matter a great deal, and Kipling is one of the classic problems in taste criticism. Taste criticism begins when you like something a little bit more than your better judgment feels comfortable with—or, sometimes, a little bit more than everyone else's better judgment feels comfortable with. Some people like Ezra Pound in this way; some people like Trollope in this way. You then proceed to take this conflict for an ethical issue, and attempt to justify your pleasure to your principles. A great deal of Kipling criticism has been built up from this ground, and the consequence is that when Kipling's importance is asserted, it tends to be asserted in an ahistorical or decontextualized way. Kipling is declared to be an artist by virtue of qualities detachable from his circumstances. The detachment is especially desirable in Kipling criticism because the circumstances—late Victorian chauvinism and its ideological impedimenta—are understood to be the very things that make Kipling a problem in the first place.

But is there a version of Kipling that makes a difference to our understanding of the history of modern literature—or, possibly more interesting, is there a version of the history of modern literature that makes a difference to our understanding of

Kipling? There is one mighty engineer of critical taste whose evaluative judgments about writers are always to some degree historical, since they are always comparative: Harold Bloom. In the introduction to the anthology of Kipling criticism in the Chelsea House series he edits, Bloom makes some assertions about Kipling's literary relations with other writers, and these point the way toward a fresh approach to the problem of estimating Kipling's importance.

Bloom proposes the following:

> Kipling, with his burly imperialism and his indulgences in anti-intellectualism, would seem at first out of place in the company of Walter Pater, Oscar Wilde, and William Butler Yeats. Nevertheless, Kipling writes in the rhetorical stance of an aesthete, and is very much a Paterian in the metaphysical sense. The "Conclusion" to Pater's *Renaissance* is precisely the credo of Kipling's protagonists.
>
> [Bloom here reprints two longish quotations from the "Conclusion."]
>
> Like Pater, like Nietzsche, Kipling sensed that we possess and cherish fictions because the reductive truth would destroy us. "The love of art for art's sake" simply means that we choose to believe in a fiction, while knowing that it is not true, to adopt Wallace Stevens's version of the Paterian credo. And fiction, according to Kipling, was written by daemonic forces within us, by "some tragic dividing of forces on their ways." Those forces are no more meaningful than the tales and ballads they produce. What Kipling shares finally with Pater is a deep conviction that we are caught always in a vortex of sensations, a solipsistic concourse of impressions piling upon one another, with great vividness but little consequence.[1]

This is a little casual, and one looks in vain in the rest of Bloom's introduction, or in any of the essays by other critics that follow it, for some substantiation of these claims about Kipling's aestheticism. When Bloom says that Kipling is Paterian "in the metaphysical sense," the phrase sounds, in the context, uncomfortably like "in the Pickwickian sense," since metaphysics is precisely what is left out of the intellectual disposition that Kipling and Pater are supposed to share. It might be more accurate to say that an indifference to metaphysics, or a choice to do without metaphysics, is what they have in common. And Pater's phrase "the love of art for art's sake" does not seem correctly paraphrased as "we choose to believe in a fiction, while knowing that it is not true." The problems of belief and of truth versus nontruth are the very problems that Pater thought he was better off not trying to deal with. Pater did not *want* to get into a philosophical tussle about the nature of truth or belief; what he seems to be saying is more along the lines of: "We choose to experience art and reality as though there were no essential difference between them—that is, as sensory stimuli—and the consciousness of the pure materiality of those phenomena lends a tragic frisson" (it is hard to know any other way to characterize Pater's thought here, since everything in Pater reduces to a frisson) "to that experience." It is the quality of an experience that interests Pater, not (as in, for example, Stevens) the degree of fictionality.

But it is odd, as Bloom concedes, to think of Kipling in the company of Pater, Nietzsche, Yeats, and Wilde—odd in spite, I think, of its being essentially correct. The reason this group strikes us as an unlikely one to imagine Kipling hanging around with has to do with the need to tie aesthetic dispositions to extra-aesthetic values, a need that infects criticism at many levels. We find, for example, that the disruption of the reader's expectations is a common feature of many works of literature. But we cannot stop there, for we must satisfy an impulse to assign a value to this device. We find ourselves wanting to say something like: a piece of literature that disrupts expectations works to subvert, rather than flatter, received opinion, and therefore counts as progressive in the politics of consciousness. This habit is one of the things that makes taste criticism such an exciting business. For we run into all sorts of writers whose equipment includes the full range of techniques we have identified as, let's say, progressive (or whatever extra-aesthetic value is important to us), but whose actual views are disappointing. Eliot and Pound are familiar cases in point. Criticism of these writers then tends to turn on whether the form of, say, *The Waste Land* is understood as dehistoricizing imagism (probably bad) or decentering polysemy (probably good). Naming the technique produces the judgment.

The reason we get into these kinds of discussions about the connection between technique and tendency has to do with the formalist bias that naturally follows from the isolation of the literary object for attention. Once we extract the text from its circumstances, we almost invariably find ourselves generalizing from the form outward, attempting to associate the use of a particular literary technique, or form, with some extraliterary tendency. We tend to pursue—and this is the nub of the difficulty—a paradoxical strategy in this endeavor: we want to be able to describe the form in neutral terms, detached from content, but then, having accomplished that, we want to be able to say that content is implicated inexorably in the technique. As professional students of literature, we cannot just say we don't like Eliot's politics; we have to say that we have discovered through formalist analysis (informed by years of professional training in these matters) that Eliot's poetic technique conduces to undesirable political attitudes.

The surprise in Bloom's claim about Kipling's filiations with Nietzsche, Pater, and Wilde, therefore, comes from finding ourselves compelled to apply a value judgment (generally sympathetic) that contemporary criticism has already made about Nietzsche, Pater, and Wilde to a writer who looks very much *not* like an ally. We feel that once we accept Bloom's suggestion that there is a common metaphysical (or antimetaphysical) ground that Kipling walks in the company of Pater, Nietzsche, and Wilde, we will have to raise our estimation of Kipling's value, and revise our judgment of his political tendencies. But we do not need to do those things. *The Waste Land* shares many modernist techniques with *Ulysses*; it shares many thematic interests with *Ulysses*. But it is perfectly possible to acknowledge this and to conclude nevertheless that *The Waste Land* and *Ulysses* have radically different bearings in their views of life, and without ascribing the difference to form.

What is true of form is true of theory. There is virtually no theoretical difference between Oscar Wilde and the young T. S. Eliot, for instance. They seem to have shared roughly the same philosophical principles. But Eliot despised, and not even cordially, Oscar Wilde, and he probably had perfectly honest reasons for doing so. No doubt he also had honest reasons for disliking Pater, too, whom he certainly *was* influenced by. To suppose (as some readers of Eliot have been tempted to suppose) that Eliot's expressions of distaste for Pater and Wilde merely amount to an effort to obscure the nature of his debt to their views about originality, style, and interpretation is to suppose more than the case requires. Within the same episteme, people differ. Abstraction from context is the deathbed of judgment.

The "theoretical" view that Wilde shared with the young Eliot is easily summarized because many of its features are familiar in contemporary intellectual culture. It was a view that elected not to make an issue of truth claims; that held fundamentally skeptical views on the autonomy and integrity of the subject and the possibility of originality; that accepted a generally materialistic and deterministic account of phenomena; that understood meaning to be a function of relation and value to be a function of interest. These views unite any number of writers and artists of the late nineteenth and early twentieth centuries, and unite them without requiring them all to speak in the same voice or to the same ends. Wilde and Pater, Nietzsche and William James, Peirce and Saussure, Conrad and Joyce and Duchamp, Croce and Dilthey and Eliot—these names represent a very diverse culture. They belong to a common intellectual tradition; but that does not mean they embrace a common set of values.

This is the tradition in which Bloom means to place Kipling. Without inquiring about the extent to which Kipling gave explicit assent to every one of the philosophical views associated with this tradition, we can fairly claim that as an artist, Kipling worked within the boundaries of its aesthetic assumptions and implications. And the only conclusion we need to draw from this observation—that Kipling was, as a writer, very much of his time—is that it gave him a range of effects to work toward, and a set of expectations to rely upon. The enthusiasm for Kipling in England coincided exactly with the enthusiasm for Wilde, and we do not need to deny that the two writers exhibited very different personalities, and attracted very different admirers, to say that they worked out of a common feeling, pervasive in their time, for the nature of the aesthetic experience. Understanding what this common feeling was is a way of understanding how Kipling fits into modern literary history.

Kipling quickly acquired a reputation as an establishment writer. He was regarded at first as an antidote to the decadents and later as an antidote to the modernists. This makes it easy to forget that Kipling was raised as an heir to the Pre-Raphaelites, and an heir in a fairly genealogical sense. He was related through his mother, Alice Macdonald, to Edward Burne-Jones, whom he knew as Uncle Ned, and during the part of his childhood he spent in England he was exposed to Pre-Raphaelite art and artistic ideals, which he absorbed precociously and thoroughly. His headmaster at Westward Ho!, Cormell Price, another family intimate, had been a member of William Morris's circle at Oxford. Kipling was given the run of Price's library at the school, where he was directed particularly to the poetry of Dante Gabriel Rossetti and Swinburne and to FitzGerald's translation of the *Rubáiyát*. His favorite poem as a schoolboy and as a young man was James Thomson's "City of Dreadful Night." One of his own earliest poems, "Ave Imperatrix," in honor of Queen Victoria, was an imitation of a poem by Oscar Wilde. There is, in Kipling's temperament, a good deal of the outsider's resentment, which is explained in part by his brutal upbringing at the hands of his guardians, by his truncated education, and by his having to serve his apprenticeship in India. But Kipling was no more of an outsider in the world of English letters than Virginia Woolf was.

After Westward Ho! Kipling returned to India, where he worked as a newspaperman and produced enough stories to fill six volumes in a series called the Indian Railway Library—as the name suggests, train reading material. When he returned to London, in 1889, he was twenty-three years old, but he had been a professional writer for six years, he had established a reputation among the Anglo-Indians, and he had already written a number of the stories that would later be his most celebrated. In 1890 he burst upon the domestic literary scene with the first of the poems eventually published as *Barrack Room Ballads*—"Danny Deever," on February 22. This was followed by "Tommy," published on March 1; "Fuzzy-Wuzzy," published on March 15; "Gunga Din," on June 7; and "Mandalay," on June 22. Meanwhile, the stories that had appeared in the Indian Railway series were being reissued and new stories were being composed, so that in 1890 no fewer than eighty stories by Kipling were published in England. And he was all the time working on the novel that contemporary critics regarded as the true test of his literary powers: this was *The Light That Failed*, first published serially in *Lippincott's Monthly Magazine* in late 1890, and then reissued in volume form, with a different ending, in 1891.

It is easy today to understand why Kipling was regarded as a prodigy in 1890. Here was a very young man who had arrived from the other side of the empire with a subject matter all his own and a style already fully formed. It is easy to understand, too, what it was about that style and subject matter that appealed to Tories such as W. E. Henley, who edited the *Scots Observer*, and his associate Charles Whibley, who would much later become one of T. S. Eliot's conservative friends, earning a pat on the back in one of the essays in *The Sacred Wood*. But Kipling also impressed contemporaries whose opinions are likely to carry more weight today. His early stories enjoyed serious critical attention; an enthusiastic review of the Indian Railway series in the *Times* in March 1890 did much to promote public interest in his work. Wilde, in "The Critic as Artist," published in September 1890, referred to Kipling—condescendingly, but not disrespectfully—as "a genius who drops his aspirates."[2] Henry James, in the same year, named Kipling "the star of the hour,"[3] and two years later called him "the most complete man of genius (as distinct from 'fine intelligence') that I have ever known."[4] This praise from Henry James startles us; it certainly startled his brother William, who, when he heard of it from William Dean Howells, wrote to Henry in great relief to say "that I have been ashamed to write of my adoration of that infant phenomenon, not knowing, with your exquisitely refined taste, how you might be affected by him and fearing to *jar*. . . . He's more of a Shakespeare than anyone yet in this generation of ours, as it strikes me. . . . Distinctly the biggest literary phenomenon of our time."[5] (One can imagine how Henry took this particular way of putting the matter.)

William James had particular admiration for what he called the "new effects"[6] Kipling had managed in *The Light That Failed*, but the critical reception of the novel, when it appeared in 1891, was mixed, and its standing has not improved with time. *The Light That Failed* is not a long book—Kipling seems to have written it in under nine months—but even at fifty thousand words the length proved too great for him to manage successfully. Kipling knew it, for he was professional enough to realize when he had pushed too hard against the limits of his talent. "It will always be one of the darkest mysteries to me," he confessed to Mrs. Humphrey Ward, the author of *Robert Elsmere*, a novel about five times as long as *The Light That Failed*, "that any human being can make a beginning, end *and* middle to a really truly long story. I can think them by scores but I have not the hand to work out the full frieze."[7] The worm of inadequacy seems never to have stopped gnawing at Kipling on this subject, for in the very last pages of his autobiographical fragment *Something of Myself*, composed in the final months of his life, he returned to the topic. *The Light That Failed*, he explained, was really "only a *conte*—not a built book." And *Kim* "was nakedly picaresque and plotless—a thing imposed from without. . . . Yet," he confessed, "I dreamed for many years of building a veritable three-decker out of chosen and long-stored timber . . . an East Indiaman worthy to lie alongside *The Cloister and the Hearth*."[8]

In fact, as Charles Carrington points out in his life of Kipling, the era of the Victorian three-decker had come to an end by 1890, and Kipling was one of the writers who ended it.[9] *Robert Elsmere*, published in 1888, was one of the last successful three-volume novels. And if we think of the characteristic British fiction of the end of the nineteenth century, we can see that a much shorter narrative form had begun to dominate. The two serials that preceded *The Light That Failed* in *Lippincott's Monthly Magazine* in 1890 were Arthur Conan Doyle's *Sign of Four* and Wilde's *Picture of Dorian Gray*. Many of Henry James's shorter fictions—*The Europeans* (1878), *Washington Square* (1881), *The Aspern Papers* (1888)—had already appeared; *Daisy Miller* made its author famous when it came out in 1879. *An Outcast of the Islands* appeared in 1896, *The Nigger of the "Narcissus"* in 1897, and *Heart of Darkness* in 1899.

There is no commonly accepted name for the genre these works belong to. Criticism has decided that *The Light That Failed* should be called a novel, despite Kipling's suggestion that we regard it as a *conte*, and it is probably true that at the time it was published he hoped it *would* be taken for a novel. *The Sign of Four* is pretty clearly not a novel; it is a story like the other Holmes stories, though the atmospherics are highly intensified (which, given the quantity of atmospherics in every Holmes story, is to refer to a considerable thickness of atmosphere). But we do not get very far considering *The Picture of Dorian Gray* and *The Nigger of the "Narcissus"* as novels. We have the term *novella*; but the trouble with novella is that although these works are, relative to *Robert Elsmere* or *Middlemarch*, "little" enough, they are pretty clearly not "little novels," for there is nothing novelistic about them.

This trouble with terms is a nice example of the trouble with nonsubstantive formal definitions generally. Prose fiction is not a continuous bolt of cloth cut to various sizes; it is a highly heterogeneous family of forms. The members of the family cannot be arranged according to some neutral measure like length, which would be like categorizing the members of a family of people by height. They can be arranged only by substance—as we naturally categorize people, even and especially people in the same family, by character. And even then we are aware (as we are when we describe people) that we are naming only attributes. There are, very strictly speaking, no novels; there are only texts that are novelistic, and a definition of *novelistic* which is something more than a list of formal features is therefore more useful than a formal, or content-neutral, definition of *novel*.

Those generally shorter works that began to emerge in the late nineteenth century are not little novels; they are long stories. They are not "novel-like" but "story-like." They belong to the great period of the story form, the period that runs from the 1870s, when Henry James's stories began appearing, into the 1920s, when Hemingway began writing his stories, and that includes the stories of Hardy, Chekhov, Conrad, Crane, Lawrence, Joyce, and, of course, Kipling. There is an argument for saying that the story is the representative genre of the period, and that its importance has been obscured by its tendency to be regarded as the novel's shorter sibling. To see what makes the story distinctive as a genre, we need to see what makes it different from the genre whose authority it supplanted, the realist novel—the sort of book Kipling could not write.

The classic analysis of the realist novel was published in 1916. The circumstance puts us in mind of the flight habits of the owl of Minerva, and properly so, for Georg Lukács's *Theory of the Novel* is a work saturated in Hegel. "The novel," Lukács said, "is the epic of an age in which the extensive totality of life is no longer directly given, in which the immanence of meaning in life has become a problem, yet which still thinks in terms of totality."[10] Lukács was talking about what we now call the nineteenth-century realist novel, and he later offered reasons for refusing to consider what we call the modernist novel properly novelistic. *The Theory of the Novel* is a eulogy for a genre that modernism killed.

The essential difference between the short late nineteenth- and early twentieth-century fictional narrative and the realist novel as Lukács describes it is that the story form lacks irony. Of course there is plenty of local irony in James's and Conrad's and Joyce's stories—irony directed at the characters, at the narrators, at the reader. But irony is not present as a principle of form; and the reason is that the story writer no longer chooses to think, as Lukács says the novelist does, in terms of totality. For to think in terms of totality is to make a problem of objectivity. "The objectivity of the novel," says Lukács, "is the mature man's knowledge that meaning can never quite penetrate reality, but that, without meaning, reality would disintegrate into the nothingness of inessentiality."[11] It is the defining feature of the novel that the heroic labor of objective form giving is not abandoned in the face of this mature knowledge. The certainty that the labor will fail is inherent in the novelist's understanding of the conditions of modern life; it is the source of the irony; and it is therefore (with thanks to the helpful operation of the dialectic at this difficult point) the reason why the realist novel achieves objectivity in spite of itself. This is why the realist novelist is so readily identified with the typical realist hero—the young man or woman who enters the social realm in the hope of penetrating the heart of the mystery, of solving the riddle of the world's unmeaning. For, like the novelist, this character can realize his or her quest only by failing in it.

Objectivity—this whole metasubjective ambition—is not a problem in the story form. It is no part of the story writer's intention to achieve an objectivizing form, and he or she is therefore released from the responsibilities of reflexive irony. This is not to say that the story writer does not aspire to get it right. It is that what he or she aspires to get right is no longer fact; it is impression. "To make you hear, to make you feel . . . before all, to make you see," as Conrad, running down the list of sensory stimulations available from print, put it in the preface to *The Nigger of the "Narcissus."*[12] This ambition comes with its own bundle of epistemological complications. These are reflected most repeatedly in the story genre by the use of double-frame narrations—not just narrators who tell a story someone else told them, but narrators who tell a story in which *another* narrator tells a story someone else told him, a device James uses in *The Turn of the Screw* (1898) and Conrad uses in *Heart of Darkness*. Conrad employed a version of it in *Lord Jim* (1900), as well, with famously awkward results. It takes most people two days (and most students two weeks) to read some of the passages Marlow is supposed to narrate in a few hours after dinner on a verandah somewhere. But *Lord Jim* was begun as a story—Conrad told his editors he expected to produce a 20,000-word tale, and ended up writing 150,000 words—and the framing device can probably be regarded as one of the husks of the story form that the book eventually outgrew.

Lukács discusses the story form briefly in *The Theory of the Novel*, by way of stressing one of the polemical points of his book: that prose fiction is not simply a generic tree bearing narrative fruits of different sizes but similar flavors. He classes the story with what he calls the minor epic forms, such as the idyll. "Completeness in the minor epic forms," he explains, "is subjective: a fragment of life is transplanted by the writer into a surrounding world that emphasizes it and lifts it out of the totality of life; and this selection, this delimitation, puts the stamp of its origin in the subject's will and knowledge upon the work itself: it is, more or less, lyrical in nature." In the short story, Lukács goes on to say, which is "the narrative form which pin-points the strangeness and ambiguity of life, such lyricism must entirely conceal itself behind the hard outlines of the event; here, lyricism is still pure selection."[13]

And then Lukács makes a striking claim:

> The short story is the most purely artistic form; it expresses the ultimate meaning of all artistic creation as *mood*, as the very sense and content of the creative process. . . . It sees absurdity in all its undisguised and unadorned nakedness, and the exorcising power of this view, without fear or hope, gives it the consecration of form; meaninglessness *as meaninglessness* becomes form; it becomes eternal because it is affirmed, transcended and redeemed by form.[14]

Now it is easy enough to see how the story form, as it was thus understood by Lukács in the period of its florescence, is a genre responsive to the view of experience for which Bloom names Pater the spokesman. There is, to begin with, the emphasis placed on the strength of the impression, as against some sort of conceptual grasp of the totality of experience. This is nicely complicated in the story form by the counteremphasis, through framing devices and so forth, on the difficulty of transmitting impressions from one center of consciousness to another. The absurdity or pointlessness of the flux is redeemed by the operation of subjective selection, but only because experience is being frankly drawn up into the realm of art: "meaninglessness as meaninglessness becomes form." And the brevity of the story promises an experience that is both intense and complete.

Sounds great. But how does it actually work? In his brief study of the genre, John Bayley calls the story effect a "special effect."[15] He means that the effect a story produces is traceable to nothing in the story itself, and has nothing to do with anything the story says. The effect is the effect of life itself, but life as it is experienced *outside of* the experience of art—the experience of life being explicitly defined, in fact, as the opposite of the experience of art. A formalist analysis cannot get at the causes of this effect, Bayley argues, because the effect is carefully left outside the boundaries of the literary artifact itself. Here is another, somewhat cruder, way to put it. The novelist actually has a better chance of creating in the reader's mind the illusion of real experience than the story writer does for the banal reason that novels are longer. You have time to forget that it's only a book; in fact, the more you put down a novel and return to it, the more strongly you feel the sense of involvement in a real experience you want to get back to. Stories are not long enough to work this trick. In the short amount of time required to read a story, you forget to remember to forget (as, in a different context, Elvis Presley once put it) that you are just reading a book. The magic has to be managed by other means.

The notion that the story's aesthetic is aimed exclusively at an "effect" dates from a text generally regarded as the primal document of the modern story era, Edgar Allan Poe's 1842 review of Hawthorne's *Twice-Told Tales*. "A skillful literary artist has constructed a tale," Poe says.

> If wise, he has not fashioned his thoughts to accommodate his incidents; but having conceived, with deliberate care, a certain unique or single *effect* to be wrought out, he then invents such incidents—he then combines such events as may best aid him in establishing this preconceived effect. . . . In the whole composition there should be no word written, of which the tendency, direct or indirect, is not to the one pre-established design.[16]

Two features of the classic story help conduce to the "effect" cited by Poe and Bayley (and, in his letter on *The Light That Failed*, by William James). The first is the use of elaborate narrative machinery, already mentioned as one of the consequences of the difficulty understood to attach to the business of conveying "what it felt like" to someone who was not there. The second is the persistent use of melodramatic and frequently supernatural situations, sometimes subtly alluded to and sometimes frankly described, situations that seem outside the experience of real life. These two features work in a very simple way: by advertising the artificiality of the story, they leave room for the sensation you have when the reading is done and the book laid aside that something quite real, something having nothing to do with the literary car wash you have just been driven briefly through, has been evoked. This is the story "effect." It is the ringing in your ears after the noise of the radio is turned off, the image that persists on the retina after the object has been turned away from. The production of this effect is what the story form is all about. This is why, for example, it was surely entirely beside the point for Edmund Wilson to go to all that trouble to prove that the governess's story in *The Turn of the Screw* is a hallucination. Doubt about the governess's account of what she saw is part of the form; but no more than doubt about her account of how her food tasted would have been. For the governess's account of

ghosts no one else can see is just an allegory for my account of a sensation you cannot feel. The phantoms that are my present sensations and memory images are real
enough to me, even though they must always remain a rumor to everyone else.

It was, in a sense, a great convenience to the writers of this period that the most
prominent ancestor of the late nineteenth-century story form was the ghost story;
and it is hard to think of a story from the classic period that does not involve the
appearance of a ghost. Some, like James's story "The Jolly Corner" or Kipling's tale
"The Phantom Rickshaw," are clearly ghost stories. Others are teasingly ambiguous
ghost stories. If in *The Turn of the Screw* you read of apparitions and wonder if they
are real, in "The Secret Sharer" you read of someone real and wonder if he is an
apparition. But many, many of the stories are, though not technically ghost stories,
stories about ghosts. "The Dead" is a story about a ghost. "The Beast in the Jungle"
is a story about a ghost—even, it can be argued, a story about a vampire (and it is
worth mentioning that Bram Stoker's volume-length story *Dracula* was published in
1897). "The Snows of Kilimanjaro" features a ghostly experience; even "The Indian
Camp," with the fish leaping out of the water at the end, is a story with a ghost.

The ghost is a melodramatic allusion to the interiority of experience—experience as it is represented in the model so central to the Paterian view of mind: the
inner flashings forth in image and sensation of the data transmitted by the neural
machinery. The elaborate and slightly hokey stage mechanisms of the story form, by
contrast, are the writers' tribute to the sheer materiality of phenomena. Experience
is the accidental product of Pater's "forces on their ways": its origins are mechanical,
not providential. We do not contribute to the event (this is a tiny but fatal problem
for Pater, since if everything is determined, how are we to *choose* to love art?), since
consciousness is only the toy of matter. But for Pater, that is the hidden advantage
of accepting a materialist account of the universe. Given the material from which
they are generated, mental phenomena—the inner picture we have of a complete,
coherent, blooming and buzzing world—are as mysterious as an apparition (and
more mysterious than divine intent, which explains too much). The universe spins
its atoms, and the mind stupidly but miraculously churns out its illusion of a world.
The writer rattles his props, and the ghost appears—except that it is not the ghost
the governess says she sees but the apprehension of something utterly real which is
left with us after the story is over.

If anything is an allegory for this view of mental activity, it is the cinema. We can see
one way of understanding the historical coincidence, in the late nineteenth century,
of the movies and the story form in Peter Galassi's essay "Before Photography,"
printed in the catalogue for the show of that name, exhibited in 1981 at the Museum
of Modern Art. Galassi's argument is that photography could have been invented at
any time after 1727, which is the year it was discovered that silver halides turn dark
when they are exposed to light. But photography was invented when it was—around
1839—because that was about the time that painters began to invert their notion
of perspective. In a painting by Ucello, for example, the principles of perspective
are employed to give the illusion of three-dimensionality to a scene that has already
been composed in two dimensions, so that you can see each horse or dog or man as

a complete figure whose size is relative to its position on the apparently receding horizontal plane of the canvas. But in a painting by Degas, the figure is partial, or obscured, by virtue of the accident of where the painter's eye happens to be. The picture is not composed first and the perspective added; perspective is already there in the world, and the painter reproduces it "automatically"—that is, like a camera.

Galassi puts it this way:

> Initially . . . perspective was conceived only as a tool for the construction of three dimensions out of two. Not until much later was this conception replaced—as the common, intuitive standard—by its opposite: the derivation of a frankly flat picture from a given three-dimensional world. Photography, which is capable of serving only the latter artistic sense, was born of this fundamental transformation in pictorial strategy.[17]

The conclusion Galassi draws is that we should understand the invention of photography not as a technological phenomenon exogenous to the development of art, but as an episode in the history of painting. "The new medium was born," he says, "into an artistic environment that increasingly valued the mundane, the fragmentary, the seemingly uncomposed—that found in the contingent qualities of perception a standard of artistic, and moral, authenticity."[18]

In order for cinema to be invented, a few elements were needed in addition to those required for photography—notably, a transparent film through which light could be projected. But the physiology of cinema—the manner in which the brain perceives a succession of still images as a continuous moving picture—was understood long before (possibly millennia before) movies were actually invented, and so, of course, was the technology of photography. So if it makes sense to call the invention of photography an episode in the history of painting, we might call the invention of the cinema an episode in the history of narrative.

Two Frenchmen are commonly associated with the creation of the commercial cinema: Louis Lumière and Georges Méliès, both of whom began showing motion pictures theatrically in the same year, 1895. Lumière (who worked with his brother Auguste) and Méliès chose to exploit the possibilities of film as a popular art form in fundamentally different ways. Lumière shot what we would call documentary film—a man watering a garden or a train pulling into a station. He set the camera down in the world and recorded what happened. Méliès, who was a professional magician, made his movies in the studio, and he used editing techniques to produce fantasy sequences—characters materializing and vanishing in front of our eyes, and so forth. His best-known film is a science fiction movie, *Voyage to the Moon*, produced in 1907.

If you were asked to imagine, in 1895, the artistic direction that seemed most promising for cinema, the direction that made use of its special technology most fully, you would probably have decided in favor of the direction chosen by Méliès. For the ability to represent what is physically impossible as though it had really happened is surely one of the most astonishing qualities of the cinematic medium. But cinema developed instead in the direction chosen by Lumière: most movies represent the real, not the fantastic. The fantastic has always been a minor genre within cinema; but, until a period of self-conscious indulgence in special effects technology began in the mid-1970s, the mainstream of commercial motion pictures was overwhelmingly within a realist narrative tradition. What Lumière discovered, in effect, was that you don't need to add magic to film because film is already a magical medium. When audiences watched his short film of a train pulling into a station, *L'Arrivé d'un train*, the people in the front rows ducked. Movies do not need special effects because film is itself a special effect.

Lumière hardly knew what he had started. He imagined that the movies were a passing fad, a mechanical gimmick that people would tire of, and he is supposed to have told Méliès that film had "no commercial future whatsoever."[19] Within twenty years movies were a major industry and moviegoing a worldwide activity. All it needed to be a recognized as an art form was a theory, and in 1916 this was supplied by a Harvard professor called Hugo Münsterberg.

Münsterberg was a German psychologist who had been brought to Harvard by William James in the 1890s, when James wanted to leave the psychology lab and return to the philosophy department. The two departments were closely allied in those years, and Münsterberg's work in psychology reflects to some degree the view of consciousness found in the writings of James and, more particularly, of their colleague Josiah Royce. Münsterberg's book on cinema, published in the last year of his life, is called *The Photoplay: A Psychological Study*. It undertakes to answer the question: "Do the moving pictures brings us an independent art, controlled by aesthetic laws of its own, working with mental appeals which are fundamentally different from those of the theater, with a sphere of its own and with ideal aims of its own?"[20] Münsterberg's answer is yes to all of the above. Cinema, he concludes, is an autonomous art form that cannot be understood by analogy with any other art form—which is the first step in generating a theory for any artistic medium.

Most of *Photoplay* is taken up with itemizing the distinctions between theater and cinema as artistic media. The argument is detailed, but the main point is straightforward enough. Theater is a representation achieved by the reproduction of physical reality; cinema is a representation of mental activity. The psychological trick of the cinema lies in its ability to invest a succession of two-dimensional shadows with the qualities of reality—with depth, solidity, and movement. "We see actual depth in the pictures," says Münsterberg,

> and yet we are every instant aware that it is not real depth and that the persons are not really plastic. It is only a suggestion of depth, a depth created by our own activity, but not actually seen, because essential conditions for the true perception of depth are lacking [because the screen is flat]. Now we find that the movement too is perceived but that the eye does not receive the impressions of true movement [because a movie is really a rapid succession of still photographs]. It is only a suggestion of movement, and the idea of motion is to a high degree the product of our own reaction. Depth and movement alike come to us in the moving picture world, not as hard facts but as a mixture of fact and symbol. They are present and yet they are not in the things. We invest the impressions with them. The theater has both depth and motion, without any subjective help; the screen has them and yet lacks them. We see things distant and moving, but we furnish to them more than we receive; we create the depth and the continuity through our mental mechanism.[21]

Münsterberg's point is that although film appears to be a medium for the mechanical and literal reproduction of the world of objects, it is in fact a medium for the representation of purely subjective experience. "The photoplay," he says, "tells us the human story by overcoming the forms of the outer world, namely, space, time, and causality, and by adjusting the events to the forms of the inner world, namely, attention, memory, imagination, and emotion." On this basis Münsterberg is prepared to make an exalted claim for the cinema. The ideal of all art, he argues, is the complete removal of experience from the sphere of the practical world into a sphere where the mind enjoys perfect freedom to remake experience according to its own laws. The purest art, therefore, is music. In the cinema, "the mind has triumphed over matter and the pictures roll on with the ease of musical tones. It is a superb enjoyment which no other art can furnish us."[22] In short, Immanuel Kant goes to Hollywood.

It is not necessary to make much of the accident that Münsterberg's *Photoplay* appeared in the same year as Lukács's *Theory of the Novel*, in which the story form is described in terms strikingly parallel to those used by Münsterberg in his analysis of the cinema. For we have, as well, the early accounts of the movie experience left by the inventors themselves. W. K. L. Dickson, the Englishman who did most of Thomas Edison's movie work for him, described his sensations watching his first movie this way:

> The effect of these somber draperies [black curtains to shut out the light], and the weird accompanying monotone of the electric motor attached to the projector [like breathing?] are horribly impressive, and one's sense of the supernatural is heightened when a figure suddenly springs into [one's] path, acting and talking [Edison was using a synchronous phonographic sound system] with a vigor which leaves [one] totally unprepared for its mysterious vanishing.[23]

(It's the word "vigor" that communicates the thrill: a ghost is a shadow with life.) And we have our own memories of going to the movies to help us see the resemblance between the cinematic experience and the story effect: the cinema is a frankly mechanical form of representation which generates an illusion experienced as real— and usually as most real at the moment of walking out of the theater. The movie theater is a large-scale reproduction of the Paterian model of the inside of the human head, and the inside of the human head, in that model, is a haunted house.

What this suggests is that when we read a short story by Kipling, we can help ourselves to find a way through it by keeping in mind Pater's view of experience, and at the same time by understanding that view of experience to inform a far wider range of expression than the art and literature conventionally associated with the aesthetic movement. The obvious place to try out this claim is a story of Kipling's that makes one of the earliest references in literature to the cinema, "Mrs. Bathurst," first published in 1904.

Stories are often riddles without quite enough clues; that is one of the ways they achieve three-dimensionality, one of the ways they accomplish their gesture toward the life-outside-art. Still, for many readers "Mrs. Bathurst" is a little too clueless.

Kipling liked to take time cutting away bits of his stories before he published them (a very Paterian notion of craft), and some critics have complained that in "Mrs. Bathurst" he got carried away and left too much material on the cutting room floor. This is the story we are given. Our narrator is an unnamed Englishman with some time to kill in South Africa. He runs into a friend called Hooper, a railway inspector who has just returned from a tour of duty to the north, having gone as far as Rhodesia. The two pick up the South African equivalent of a six-pack and retreat to a quiet railway siding on the beach to swap stories and while away the time. Hooper is just preparing to tell the narrator about something that happened during his recent trip, and is reaching into his waistcoat pocket to show him an object connected with the incident, when he is interrupted by the appearance of two slightly dissolute representatives of His Majesty's merchant marine, Pyecroft and Pritchard. Pyecroft and Pritchard accept the beer that is offered them and join the party. Casual gossip about various matters leads to the story of a man named Vickery, a sailor who goes by the nickname Click, after a set of false teeth imperfectly installed, and who has recently gone AWOL. The story is narrated chiefly by Pyecroft, who knew Vickery best, with additional dialogue supplied by Pritchard.

It seems that there is a woman in Vickery's story, and her name is Mrs. Bathurst. Mrs. Bathurst is the proprietress of a saloon in Auckland, and a woman whom most men find unforgettable for certain personal qualities, in particular for her long memory for her favorite clients and for what is described as a certain "blindish" way of looking at men which is evidently extremely fetching.[24] Much of the evidence for Mrs. Bathurst's singular and ineffable attraction is provided by the testimony of Pritchard, a man who has an impressive history of intimacy with various women around the empire. Some sort of relationship has developed between Mrs. Bathurst and this Vickery, though just what sort of relationship is the mystery of the tale.

That the two had a relationship was learned by Pyecroft, who was once stationed in a South African port with Vickery. One night Vickery asks Pyecroft to accompany him to the cinema, where the show includes Lumière-style movies of London Bridge and of a train pulling into Paddington Station. Vickery wants Pyecroft to confirm something he sees in this latter film. This is Pyecroft's account:

> "We were in the front row, and 'Home an' Friends' came on early. Vickery touched me on the knee when the number went up. 'If you see anything that strikes you,' he says, 'drop me a hint'; then he went on clicking. We saw London Bridge an' so forth an' so on, an' it was most interestin'. I'd never seen it before. You 'eard a little dynamo like buzzin', but the pictures were the real thing—alive and movin'."
>
> "I've seen 'em," said Hooper. "Of course they are taken from the very thing itself—you see."
>
> "Then the Western Mail came in to Paddin'ton on the big magic-lantern screen. First we saw the platform empty an' the porters standin' by. Then the engine come in, head on, an' the women in the front row jumped: she headed so straight. Then the doors opened and the passengers came out and the porters got the luggage—just like life. Only—only when any one came too far towards us that was watchin', they walked right out o' the picture, so to speak. I was 'ighly interested, I can tell you. So were all of us. I watched an old man with a rug 'oo'd dropped a book

an' was tryin' to pick it up, when quite slowly, from be'ind two porters—carryin' a little reticule an' lookin' from side to side—comes our Mrs. Bathurst. There was no mistakin' the walk in a hundred thousand. She come forward—right forward—she looked out straight at us with that blindish look which Pritch alluded to. She walked on and on till she melted out of the picture—like—like a shadow jumpin' over a candle, an' as she went I 'eard Dawson in the tickey seats be'ind sing out: 'Christ, there's Mrs. B.!'"[25]

Vickery then asks Pyecroft to confirm the identification of the woman on the screen as Mrs. Bathurst, which Pyecroft does. This brings a look of dread to Vickery's face. They leave the cinema, and Vickery leads Pyecroft on an intense drinking spree all around Cape Town. For five nights the scenario is repeated: the two visit the cinema, Pyecroft identifies Mrs. Bathurst, and Vickery and Pyecroft proceed to boil an owl. Pyecroft's requests for enlightenment from Vickery yield just two pieces of information: first, that Vickery believes Mrs. Bathurst is in London looking for him, Vickery, and, second, Vickery's statement: "[R]emember that I am *not* a murderer, because my lawful wife died in childbed six weeks before I came out. That much at least I am clear of."[26] After the fifth night of this, Vickery requests a private audience with the captain of his ship, the details of which are not learned by Pyecroft. The consequence is that he is assigned duty that takes him up north, alone. He leaves the ship, performs his mission, but fails to return. That is the last Pyecroft has heard of Click.

Now it is Hooper's turn, and he returns to the incident he had been about to relate to the narrator at the beginning of the story. Hooper's business up north had taken him on a train ride through a teak forest. He had been asked to look out for two tramps walking along the railroad line. But when he came upon the tramps, one was standing by the railway siding and the other was squatting down looking up at him. "What did you do for 'em?" asks Pritchard. Hooper's answer is that there was not much he could do, for there had been a thunderstorm in the teak forest, and the two tramps had been struck by lightning; they were stone dead and as black as charcoal. "They fell to bits," Hooper says, "when we tried to shift 'em. The man who was standing up had the false teeth. I saw 'em shining against the black. Fell to bits he did too, like his mate squatting down an' watchin' him, both of 'em all wet in the rain." It seems the standing corpse had a tattoo, which Pyecroft confirms was Vickery's. Then Hooper says:

"We buried 'em in the teak and I kept . . . But he was a friend of you two gentlemen, you see."

Mr. Hooper brought his hand away from his waistcoat pocket—empty.

A few sentences later the story ends, as a party of picnickers from the beach goes by singing a romantic song, and Pyecroft observes that "'avin' seen 'is face for five consecutive nights on end, I'm inclined to finish what's left of the beer an' thank Gawd he's dead!"[27]

The riddle of "Mrs. Bathurst" is usually solved by one of two interpretations. The first is that the love of Vickery and Mrs. Bathurst is a great *Liebestod* whose pathos is heightened by its contrast to the vulgar world of the British tar and his casual romances. (In this version the squatting figure in the teak forest is Mrs. Bathurst.)

The second reading is that Mrs. Bathurst has been tricked into a bigamous marriage by Vickery, who fears, when he sees her hunting him down in London, that she will catch up to him and vent upon him the full fury of a woman scorned; and so he stands up in the teak forest to attract lightning and avoid a grimmer fate. It doesn't matter entirely which solution is the "correct" one. For Kipling's purpose is clearly to evoke, behind the yarn spun by these four idle men, some complication of real emotion that not merely their gossipy and patchwork tales but Kipling's art itself cannot reach. You have simply to feel the sensation; you have to be haunted by something indefinable in the story. And if it isn't indefinable, it won't haunt.

"Mrs. Bathurst" is set up by the characteristic story frame. As in so many stories, the narrator is an anonymous character whose presence become the occasion for someone else to tell a story. Our story, "Mrs. Bathurst," is *a story about the telling of a story* about Mrs. Bathurst, just as *Heart of Darkness* is a story about the telling of a story about Marlow's meeting with Kurtz. Kipling's narrator takes the trouble to cast the circumstances in which he hears the story as vaguely dreamlike: with the sun, the surf, and the beer, he says, he felt cast into a "magical slumber."[28] Mrs. Bathurst's story requires, in fact, not one but three other characters for its telling, and there are several broad hints about the gullibility and unreliability of Pyecroft and Pritchard. All this is familiar as the sort of complication the evocation of an impression requires: tribute has to be paid to the epistemology of the impression. We are given the authority to fill in the lacunae and to correct the misleading inferences precisely because such authority is withdrawn from the story's narrators.

The genius of the story is the role Kipling assigns to the cinema. Pyecroft's account of the experience reflects wonderfully the double nature of the cinematic experience—the sensation that what he is seeing is both perfectly real ("they are taken from the very thing itself—you see," as Hooper reminds him) and perfectly magical, "like a shadow jumpin' over a candle." The combination of incredulity and horror that characterizes Vickery's response to the movie image of Mrs. Bathurst is easily explained: he has seen a ghost. His dread, and the reason he insists on drawing Pyecroft into his private trauma, is simply a version of the dread that has always accompanied a view like Pater's of mental operations: the fear of solipsism. Fantasizing about Mrs. Bathurst on the hunt for him, Vickery one night sees that fantasy projected on a movie screen. If his mental image has become virtually real to him, how can he know that the cinematic image is not its projection? In the same way we know that what we see is real, that we are not brains in a vat: by asking another person to confirm our experience by matching it with his own. We say, as Vickery says to Pyecroft: "Do you see what I see?"

The neatest touch occurs at the very end of Kipling's story, when Hooper, who has been fingering something in his waistcoat pocket, withdraws his hand and reveals—nothing. The nothing in Hooper's hand is the nothing of art, the absence that stands for what-cannot-be-imitated. And the opening of the empty hand is the precise moment when we believe the whole story, for every reader has been hypnotized to see what is not there. It is impossible to read the sentence and not see, lying in Hooper's hand, Vickery's false teeth. This little technical coup recalls the ending of another famous Kipling story, "The Man Who Would Be King," in which the believability of a fantastic yarn about two adventurers in some land across the Khyber Pass turns on the moment when the returned adventurer, who tells the tale, pulls from his sack the severed head of his former companion. The effect is exactly and strikingly the opposite: you see the head, and you don't believe the tale. You don't see the teeth, but you believe "Mrs. Bathurst." The paradox is Pater's: empirical reality is the only reality, but it is never real enough.

In discussions of literature, the term *cinematic* is sometimes used to name a technique; and avant-garde high modernist literature, with its discontinuities, its emphasis on the image, and so forth, is therefore sometimes characterized as "cinematic." The invention of the cinema consequently tends to appear alongside the discovery of the unconscious and the discovery of the relativity of time and space on the list of clichés about the emergence of the conditions necessary for high modernism in literature and art. Cinema gets taken, in this way, for an inherently modernist form.

But high modernism tries to create a new medium within the art form as it is given: it is committed (programmatically, at least) to the creation of adequate form. Film, however, like the short story, depends for its effect entirely on the inadequacy, on the very conventionality, of the medium as it is given. For the sensation movies and stories produce is the effect precisely of what the form cannot manage—as our notion of the world always exceeds the materials it is constructed from. The belief that the cinema is allied with literary modernism is based on an abstraction of the formal properties of a medium from its history, and in particular on a neglect of the contemporaneous emergence of the story form. The movies were invented at almost exactly the moment when general literary taste turned from the realist narrative to the story, and in that aesthetic tradition, which runs up to our own day, high modernism looks like a relative blip.

This does not mean, though, that the effect movies and stories produced a century ago is the effect they produce today. For although, if we want to understand the meaning of an artistic form, we need to ask what effect is intended, the question of what effect is intended is always a historical question.

Notes

1. Harold Bloom, introduction to *Rudyard Kipling: Modern Critical Views* (New York: Chelsea House, 1987), pp. 2–3.

2. Oscar Wilde, "The Critic as Artist," in *The Artist as Critic: Critical Writings of Oscar Wilde*, ed. Richard Ellmann (New York: Random House, 1969), p. 402.

3. Henry James to Mr. and Mrs. Robert Louis Stevenson, March 21, 1890, in Henry James, *Letters*, vol. 3, 1883–1895, ed. Leon Edel (Cambridge, Mass.: Harvard University Press, 1980), p. 272.

4. Henry James to William James, February 6, 1892, in *The Correspondence of William James*, vol. 2, *William and Henry*, 1885–1896, ed. Ignas K. Skrupskelis and Elizabeth M. Berkeley (Charlottesville: University Press of Virginia, 1930), p. 200.

5. William James to Henry James, February 15, 1891, ibid., pp. 174–75.

6. Ibid., p. 174.

7. Rudyard Kipling to Mrs. Humphrey Ward, ca. 1895, in Janet Penrose Trevelyan, *The Life of Mrs. Humphrey Ward* (New York: Dodd, Mead, 1923), p. 117.

8. Rudyard Kipling, *Something of Myself for My Friends Known and Unknown* (Garden City, N.Y.: Doubleday, Doran, 1937), p. 245.

9. See Charles Carrington, *Rudyard Kipling: His Life and Work* (London: Macmillan, 1955), pp. 166–67.

10. Georg Lukács, *The Theory of the Novel: A Historico-Philosophical Essay on the Forms of Great Epic Literature*, trans. Anna Bostock (Cambridge, Mass.: MIT Press, 1971), p. 56.

11. Ibid., p. 88.

12. Joseph Conrad, preface to *The Nigger of the "Narcissus": A Tale of the Sea*, in *The Works of Joseph Conrad*, 18 vols. (Garden City, N.Y.: Doubleday, Page, 1920), 3:xiv.

13. Lukács, *The Theory of the Novel*. pp. 50–51.

14. Ibid., pp. 51–52.

15. John Bayley, *The Short Story: Henry James to Elizabeth Bowen* (New York: St. Martin's, 1988), p. 9.

16. Edgar Allan Poe, review of *Twice-Told Tales* by Nathaniel Hawthorne, in Poe, *Essays and Reviews*, ed. G. R. Thompson (New York: Library of America, 1984), p. 572.

17. Peter Galassi, *Before Photography: Painting and the Invention of Photography* (New York: Museum of Modern Art, 1981), p. 18.

18. Ibid., p. 28.

19. Quoted in David Robinson, "Georges Méliès," in *Cinema: A Critical Dictionary*, ed. Richard Roud, 2 vols. (New York: Viking), 2:676.

20. Hugo Münsterberg, *The Photoplay: A Psychological Study* (New York: D. Appleton, 1916), p. 43.

21. Ibid., pp. 70–71.

22. Ibid., pp. 173, 220.

23. W. K. L. Dickson and Antonia Dickson, "Edison's Invention of the Kineto-Phonograph" (1894), in *The Movies in Our Midst: Documents in the Cultural History of Film in America*, ed. Gerald Mast (Chicago: University of Chicago Press, 1982), p. 16.

24. Rudyard Kipling, *Traffics and Discoveries*, in *The Writings in Prose and Verse of Rudyard Kipling*, 36 vols. (New York: Scribner's, 1907), 22:392.

25. Ibid., pp. 397–98.

26. Ibid., p. 405.

27. Ibid., pp. 407, 408.

28. Ibid., p. 380.

How Lawrence Corrected Wells;
How Orwell Refuted Lawrence

▨　　　▨　　　▨

EDWARD MENDELSON

The first reader who recognized the stature of *Tono-Bungay* was D. H. Lawrence. "You *must, must* read *Tono-Bungay*," he wrote to his friend Blanche Jennings in 1909, a few days after *The English Review* finished its serialization of the book: "It is the best novel Wells has written—it is the best novel I have read for—oh, how long? But it makes me so sad. If you knew what a weight of sadness Wells pours into your heart as you read him—Oh, Mon Dieu! He is a terrible pessimist. But, Weh mir, he is on the whole, so true" (1.119).[1] Two months later Lawrence again urged his friend to "read, *read Tono-Bungay*; it is a great book" (1.127).

Literary history has consistently divided Lawrence from the popular, reputedly conventional novelists of his time by drawing an artificial border between modernist experimental energy and conservative Edwardian safety. Lawrence drew a similar border between himself and his contemporaries as a means of isolating and focusing the energies that he used in writing his novels. Yet he felt free to exploit the resources he had taken from the other side of the border, even if he no longer admitted to himself where he had found them. Recent attempts by literary historians to erase the barriers between high modernism and low culture seem embarrassed by Wells's wholesale use of settings and subjects from the lower-middle class; it is the one class that most resists being idealized. Lawrence, in contrast, was too busy hating one class or another to bother being embarrassed by any of them. After his early burst of praise for *Tono-Bungay*, he seldom mentioned it again. But unlike almost all later critics and interpreters of the book, he understood its pervasive apocalyptic dread, and he continually wrestled with the images and implications of the book during the apocalyptic years from 1914 to 1918.

Around 1914, when he felt haunted by an impending universal doom—effectively the doom predicted at the end of *Tono-Bungay*—he wrote his first sketches for a novel that confronted the coming horror by specifically refuting Wells's vision of disaster. Lawrence's novel answered the apocalyptic pessimism of Wells's novel with

166

a vision of apocalyptic hope, and it adopted and then transformed the most characteristic images of the earlier book. He considered underlining the apocalyptic atmosphere of his book by giving it the title *The Latter Days* or *Dies Irae*, before he settled on *Women in Love*. The enticing title did not conceal the prophetic content. "The book frightens me: it is so end-of-the-world," he told a friend. "But it is, it must be, the beginning of a new world too" (3.25–26).

Lawrence initiated his argument with Wells in his first letter to Blanche Jennings about *Tono-Bungay*:

> One thing Wells lacks—the subtle soul of sympathy of a true artist. He rigidly scorns all mysticism; he believes there is something in aestheticism—he doesn't know what; but he doesn't do his people justice. To be sure George Ponderevo's uncle is a little bladder, but Wells need not scoff at the little fellow's feelings when he is stirred to the full depth of his soul. Everybody is great at some time or other—and has dignity, I am sure, pure dignity. (1.119)

Wells had done more than deny his people dignity. George Ponderevo, his narrator, had seen "this immense process of social disorganisation in which we live" as one that reduced sexual love to irreversible isolation and futility. "Love," he wrote, was now "a thing adrift, a fruitless thing broken away from its connections." He told the story of his final love affair "because of its irrelevance, because it is so remarkable that it should mean nothing, and be nothing except itself. It glows in my memory like some bright casual flower starting up amidst the *débris* of a catastrophe" (pp. 303–4).[2]

That catastrophe was final and absolute. George Ponderevo, and therefore the whole plot and atmosphere of *Tono-Bungay*, is

> haunted by a grotesque fancy of the ultimate eating away and dry-rotting and dispersal of all our world. So that while man still struggles and dreams his very substance will change and crumble from beneath him. . . . Suppose indeed that is to be the end of our planet; no splendid climax and finale, no towering accumulation of achievements but just—atomic decay! I add that to the ideas of the suffocating comet, the dark body out of space, the burning out of the sun, the distorted orbit, as a new and far more possible end—as Science can see ends—to this strange by-play of matter that we call human life. (p. 268)

But in Lawrence's apocalyptic prophecy the central love affair is the one event that matters. Everyone in the book is vaguely aware of the impending chaos that Lawrence's representative, Rupert Birkin, alone fully understands: "Dissolution rolls on just as production does. . . . It is a progressive process, and it ends in universal nothing—the end of the world" (p. 173).[3] But Lawrence's visionary mysticism lets him foresee a time *after* the time of chaos: "Supposing this old social state *were* broken and destroyed, then, out of the chaos, what then?" (p. 102). He awaits the phoenix that Wells never imagined, and its place of rebirth from the ashes is the new sexual conjunction that Birkin seeks with Ursula Brangwen.

At the start of George Ponderevo's last love affair, when he and Beatrice Normandy sit in a canoe on a lake, she suddenly kneels forward and cries, "Who cares if it upsets? . . . If you say another word I will kiss you. And go to the bottom clutching you. I'm not afraid of that" (p. 306). When Lawrence needed a metaphor for the lethal constraints of possessive sexual love, he transformed Beatrice's words into an action. In the "Water-Party" chapter of *Women in Love*, Diana Crich falls from a boat and drowns herself and the young man who tries to save her. "The bodies of the dead were not recovered till towards dawn. Diana had her arms tight round the neck of the young man, choking him. 'She killed him,' said Gerald" (p. 189). (Near Nottingham, during Lawrence's childhood, a young man and a six-year-old girl had drowned while the man tried to hold the girl above the water, but the essential detail of the woman drowning the man came from Wells.)

In 1917, while Lawrence was working on *Women in Love*, he listed his contemporaries, "Wells Bennett Galsworthy Compton Mackenzie and Gilbert Canaan," and added: "They all bore me, both in print and in the flesh" (3.166). But his refutation of *Tono-Bungay* in *Women in Love* was a disguised tribute to the powers of the first of the writers on his list—and as late in 1926 he dismissed one of Wells's later novels, *The World of William Clissold*, by contrasting it with the earlier one: "If *Tono-Bungay* is a novel, then this is not one."[4]

The central symbol of dissolution and decay in George Ponderevo's narrative is the radioactive isotope quap, found only on an island off West Africa. Lawrence remembered this substance when he made Gudrun in *Women in Love*, at the start of her affair with the doomed Gerald Crich, sense "the field of his living, radio-active body" (p. 332). This was apparently Lawrence's first use of the word *radioactive*, and his only use of it in his fiction. (Lawrence may have responded to quap's African source and its excretory name when he gathered the end-of-the-world metaphors that in the London chapters of *Women in Love* link an African fetish and dung-eating beetles.)

The episode in which George steals quap from Mordet Island is one of the greatest moments of moral imagination in modern literature. Wells signals its centrality through the ironic technique of making his narrator describe it as disconnected from everything else—just as he describes his final love affair as irrelevant and incidental. Under the influence of quap, George kills an African native who observes the theft. He mentions this murder at the start of the book in a one-sentence paragraph: "And once (though it is the most incidental thing in my life) I murdered a man" (p. 9).

The moral dissolution of the murder, far from being incidental, violently enacts the social dissolution that George recognizes in twentieth-century England and the physical dissolution that he predicts for the universe of matter. In 1908, before anyone had guessed at the dangers of radioactivity, Wells, with startling prescience, imagined it as both medically and morally lethal:

> [T]here is something—the only word that comes near is *cancerous*—and that is not very near—about the whole of quap, something that creeps and lives as a disease lives by destroying. . . .
>
> To my mind radioactivity is a real disease of matter. Moreover it is a contagious disease. . . . It is in matter exactly what the decay of our old culture is in society, a loss of traditions and distinctions and assured reactions. (p. 268)

When the crew of George's ship shovels quap from the island to the ship, they succumb to a feverish malaria that, unlike ordinary malaria, does not respond to quinine.

Then "the men's hands broke out in sores." Later, after they set out with the quap on board, "the ship began to go to pieces," until it simply disintegrates—an event that, as George speculates, results from quap's "rapid rotting effect upon woody fibre." It has the same effect on moral fiber:

> I found out many things about myself and humanity in those weeks of effort behind Mordet Island. I understood now the heart of the sweater, of the harsh employer, of the nigger-driver. I had brought these men into a danger they didn't understand, I was fiercely resolved to overcome their oppositions and bend and use them for my purpose, and I hated the men. But I hated all humanity during the time that the quap was near me. (p. 270)

The whole expedition, in which adventurers from one European power steal a lethal substance from a "forbidden zone" proscribed by another European power, displays a mordantly anti-imperialist irony highlighted by the presence of a sea captain whose attitudes and accent spoof those of Joseph Conrad. A joke lightly concealed in the texture of the narrative treats the theft from a "forbidden zone" as a repetition of the fall of man as told in *Paradise Lost*: "But I cannot now write the history of those days of blundering and toil, of how Milton, one of the boys, fell from a plank to the beach, thirty feet perhaps, with his barrow and broke his arm and I believe a rib . . ." (p. 269).

One of the strongest motives that impels a writer to add a new novel to the mass of existing ones is the conviction that an earlier novel violates a truth that insists on being told. Writers compete with their predecessors not only by asserting greater technical and imaginative power, but also by asserting a more accurate and thorough comprehension of the world. Every literary plot is a thought experiment in the science of consequences: if people who are circumstanced in a certain way perform certain actions, what follows? As in science, many of these experiments are attempts to disprove results reported by earlier experimenters. When the attempt to disprove is conscious and deliberate, the later book is a satire of the earlier one, and depends on the early one for its interest. You probably won't finish *Shamela* if you know nothing about *Pamela*, or if you don't enjoy the literary puzzle of reconstructing the genre of *Pamela* by reading a parody of it. But when the attempt to refute the earlier experiment is unconscious—when an author argues not so much with an earlier book as with the understanding of reality that informed the book, an understanding whose entangled limits and powers make it a persistent irritant no longer directly associated with the book itself—then the result can be a book whose insight and argument strike both author and reader as original and autonomous. Hardy was probably unaware that *Tess of the d'Urbervilles* is a refutation of the thought experiment in *Jane Eyre*, but he nonetheless chose much of Tess's misery as a means of demonstrating what would occur, in the world of ordinary human unhappiness, when a girl educated above her station found herself desired first by a hypermasculine lover and then by an overethereal one.

Wells's thought experiment in *Tono-Bungay* began with the premise that England had entered the first stage of apocalyptic decline: "It is like an early day in a fine October. The hand of change rests on it all, unfelt, unseen. . . . One frost and the whole face of things will be bare, links snap, patience end, our fine foliage of pretences lie glowing in the mire" (p. 14). The erotic history of George Ponderevo—the disconnected sequence of his failed marriage, his affair with a worker in his office, his futile love for the Honorable Beatrice Normandy—is the consequence in the private sphere of the dissolution in the public one. But Lawrence sought to refute Wells's results by correcting his exclusion of mysticism and dignity. When Lawrence repeated Wells's experiment, he retained *Tono-Bungay*'s central question but included the essential factors of mystical energy and psychological force that Wells had omitted. The chapter in which George Ponderevo takes over the manufacture of Tono-Bungay and offhandedly invents the assembly line, decades before Henry Ford, flowered into Lawrence's symbolically charged chapter "The Industrial Magnate," in which "the miners were reduced to mere mechanical instruments" (p. 230). Lawrence took over Wells's calculatedly casual metaphors and converted them into the unsettling dissociations of his narrative technique. George Ponderevo perceived his life as a mass of fragments—"One gets hit by some unusual transverse force, one is jerked out of one's stratum and lives crosswise for the rest of the time, and, as it were, in a succession of samples" (p. 9)—and that succession of samples became the means by which *Women in Love* (in Frank Kermode's words) "proceeds by awful discontinuous leaps," entirely unlike the "extended arcs" of its immediate predecessor, *The Rainbow*.[5]

Lawrence, like Wells, knew that an apocalyptic era tears a unique rift in the fabric of time, and breaks the steady procreative stream from one generation to the next. Love in *Tono-Bungay* is "fruitless"; after the first few pages no one has parents or children; the absolute break in the genealogical chain is not a matter of choice but a sign of universal discontinuity. In *Women in Love* the apocalyptic disaster that cannot be averted can at least be escaped by the new sexual conjunction between Birkin and Ursula, but their "star-equilibrium" involves an active repudiation of children, a deliberate break with the cycle of generation. Ursula is a schoolteacher, Birkin a school inspector; both begin with social responsibility to nurture the minds of the young, and Birkin, in an early classroom scene, takes their education seriously enough to demand crayons so that he can indicate on a drawing of flowers the "one fact to emphasize," which is the fact of the flowers' sexuality. (Ursula, not yet initiated into Birkin's sexual vision, can only answer: "I haven't any crayons" [p. 36].) Yet when their relation begins, in the "Excurse" chapter, they instantly abandon the younger generation. "We must drop our jobs, like a shot," Birkin says, as "a new understanding dawned" in Ursula's face (p. 315). Lawrence wrote in the "Foreword to *Women in Love*": "The people that can bring forth the new passion, the new idea, this people will endure. Those others, that fix themselves in the old idea, will perish with the new life strangled unborn within them" (p. 486). Those who are saved from the apocalypse bring their faith along with them. Their family stays behind.

A novelist's argument with an earlier book is always a sign of a parallel argument between two aspects of the writer's self. The earlier writer's errors take the blame for that part of the later writer's knowledge that the later one most hopes to evade. The autobiographical narrative in *Tono-Bungay* is a thought experiment that refutes both the meliorism of *David Copperfield* and the commercial optimism and ultimately triumphant moral self-education portrayed in *Great Expectations*. But Wells used the apocalyptic pessimism of *Tono-Bungay*, and George Ponderevo's conspicuous failure to understand his own story, as a means of refuting a more pernicious enemy than anything in Dickens. The novel was written by Wells's private self to demolish the meliorist optimism tirelessly promoted by his public self. The strategies of his inner argument were complex and devastating. In most arguments that erupt within a divided self, we can find comfort by choosing to believe one side or the other; the part of the self that makes the accusations can be reassured by taking pride in its own clear-sighted judgment. But in *Tono-Bungay* Wells created a double self-portrait in which he divided himself into two separate characters, and made it impossible to take comfort in the merits or pretensions of either one.

George Ponderevo, whose history parallels that of Wells the scientific experimenter and theorist, is superficially the more self-flattering half of Wells's divided portrait. Edward Ponderevo, whose history parodies that of Wells the public figure who dined with prime ministers, is the other. George finds in science a singleness of purpose that eluded Wells, and when he celebrates scientific truth as "the remotest of mistresses," who "*is always there!*," the note of Wells's frustration with the tempests of his erotic life can be heard beneath his exaltation: "She is reality, the one reality I have found in this strange disorder of existence. She will not sulk with you nor misunderstand you nor cheat you of your reward upon some petty doubt." But George's sense of scientific truth includes the darker understanding that while *it* is always there, its objects are subject to final dissolution and decay, "so that while man still struggles and dreams his very substance will change and crumble from beneath him" (pp. 316–17, 268).

George's dialectic of aspiration and pessimism casts an ironic shadow over his uncle's commercial ambitions for the product he sells under the intriguing name Tono-Bungay. (Critics seem not to have noticed that the dangerous ingredients and questionable marketing of Tono-Bungay are modeled precisely on the early history of Coca-Cola.) That overadvertised, overstimulating beverage is Wells's ironic parody of the scientific utopianism that he advocated daily in speeches and essays and books. His insistence that the world could be saved only if its government were taken over by scientists was ultimately as false as Edward Ponderevo's pseudoscientific advertisements with their instructive drawings of happy phagocytes.

Like every imaginative writer, Wells simultaneously held official and unofficial positions: beliefs that he held in his journalism and essays and very different beliefs that he held in his fictions. In the same way T. S. Eliot, for example, simultaneously wrote official utterances that described poetry as impersonal and described himself as an orthodox Christian, and unofficial utterances in which his unique personal dilemmas ran riot and in which he espoused, under the name of Christianity, a Manichaean and anti-Christian Platonism in which the incarnation was a "still point" instead of a living body. Wells stated his optimistic, improving, and official views in public utterances about the benefits of scientific planning, world government, rational politics, and the new republic. He stated his uncomfortable, subversive, and unofficial views in his novels and stories, which, at their best, as in *The Time Machine* and *Tono-Bungay*, saw human aspiration decline into hopeless chaos. Dur-

ing the 1930s Stephen Spender told Wells that he intended to write an essay arguing that Wells was in fact a poet whose vision was darker than anything suggested
by his official statements. Wells replied: "I forbid you to write that essay."[6]

Women in Love is Lawrence's most harrowing novel precisely because it is the one
in which his argument between his official and unofficial positions rises to its greatest fury. Lawrence's official position is that of his Puritan self, who disdains established order and serves the higher truth that assures his salvation. The voice of the
official Lawrence speaks in essays such as "Pornography and Obscenity":

> The sex functions and the excrementory functions in the human body work so close
> together, yet they are, so to speak, utterly different in direction. Sex is a creative flow,
> the excrementory flow is towards dissolution, de-creation, if we may use such a word.
> In the really healthy human being the distinction between the two is instant, our
> profoundest instincts are perhaps our instincts of opposition between the two flows.
>
> But in the degraded human being the deep instincts have gone dead, and then
> the two flows become identical. *This* is the secret of really vulgar and pornographi-
> cal people. . . . It happens when the psyche deteriorates, and the profound control-
> ling instincts collapse. Then sex is dirt and dirt is sex. . . .[7]

The official Lawrence makes effortless distinctions between the opposites of creation and de-creation. But the unofficial Lawrence, the more tangled and contradictory voice of the novelist, cannot make the distinctions hold. Ursula savages
Birkin precisely for his confusion of dirt and sex: "What you are is a foul, deathly
thing, obscene, that's what you are, obscene and perverse.—You, and love! You may
well say you don't want love. No, you want *yourself*, and dirt and death—that's what
you want . . ." (p. 307). Birkin admits to himself that "he knew she was in the main
right. He knew he was perverse, so spiritual on the one hand, and in some strange
way, degraded, on the other" (p. 308). The best solution Lawrence can find is the des-
perate one of declaring the flow toward dissolution and de-creation ultimately to be
the most creative flow of all. A few pages after Ursula's denunciation of Birkin, "she
closed her hands over the full, rounded body of his loins," and feels the "overwhelming, outflooding from the Source of the deepest life-force, the darkest, deepest,
strangest life-source of the human body, at the back and base of the loins" (p. 314).
Lawrence is consciously referring here to a mystical doctrine that located the focus
of cosmic energies at the base of the spinal cord. (In an earlier chapter, as Gerald
Crich sits next to the mistress of a London acquaintance, "[h]er being suffused into
his veins like a magnetic darkness, and concentrated at the base of his spine" [p. 72].)
But Lawrence's language suggests that he is sublimating, with only partial success,
Ursula's language of obscenity and dirt: "the Source of the deepest life-force, the
darkest, deepest, strangest life-source of the human body, at the back and base of the
loins." The deepest anxiety in the later chapters of Women in Love is Lawrence's fear
that Birkin and Ursula may not be among the saved, that they may be subject to the
same destructive doom that leads George Ponderevo to his final career as a builder
of destroyers, and leaves Beatrice Normandy, in the word she uses against herself,
"spoiled" (p. 308).

Lawrence's refutation of Wells was inevitably partial and inconclusive. One fiction can set out to be more truthful than another, but it can never escape its own status as fiction; and the accumulated thought experiments of fiction do not asymptotically approach the truth as the accumulated experiments of Baconian science aspire to do. *Women in Love* experimented with the connection between sexuality and apocalypse in the first of the twentieth century's great apocalyptic moments. The novel that argues most pointedly against the conclusions of Lawrence's novel was written in the second.

George Orwell's moral imagination was continually stimulated to argue for the truths that a powerful opponent had concealed through falsified evidence and falsifying language. The greater his opponent, the more powerful was his reply. The same argumentative impulse drove his fictional imagination. "*A Passage to India* is not the perfect novel about India, but it is the best we have ever had and the best we are likely to get," he wrote in 1936.[8] But Orwell had published a novel two years earlier in which every major event represents his sense of what would have been, in reality, the more probable consequences of the events in the novel that Forster had published in 1924.

In *A Passage to India* the muddle that results when a young Englishwoman visits India gets sorted out without serious damage being done to anyone. A private vision of emptiness in the Marabar Caves prompts Mrs. Moore to her gradual withdrawal from her own life, but no one suffers permanent harm from anyone else's ill will. In *Burmese Days* the muddle that results when a young Englishwoman visits Burma ends in violent death, and every man's hand is against everyone else. Orwell's mild Englishman Flory and Flory's Burmese friend Dr. Veraswami correspond to Forster's Fielding and Dr. Aziz. But where Fielding and Aziz end prosperously in a half-fulfilled reconciliation, Flory ends in suicide and Veraswami, as a direct result, ends in disgrace. Whereas Adela Quested, Forster's visitor from England, discovers the unworthiness of the colonial official whom she had expected to marry, Orwell's Elizabeth Lackersteen pursues the swinish colonial policeman only to see him flee in selfish panic. Instead of the mysterious terror that Adela endures in the cave, a terror that others interpret as a sexual attack, Orwell has Elizabeth fight off Flory's unambiguous approaches. Whereas Forster portrays a crowd of Indians marching inconclusively against the English, Orwell has a crowd of Burmese besiege the English camp until routed by gunfire. The well-meaning, harmless disorder of Forster's India is refuted by Orwell's corrupting, lethal struggle between brutish colonials and degraded natives. Yet Orwell acknowledged Forster's novel as the best ever written about India. It was precisely its lucidity and intelligence that made it so urgent for Orwell to refute its generous falsehood.

Later, in the early years of the cold war, when democracy and law seemed threatened by atomic war and totalitarian power, Orwell wrote another novel that argued against an earlier one. As Lawrence did in *Women in Love*, Orwell imagined in *Nineteen Eighty-four* an apocalyptic era of universal moral decay, an era in which the sexual instincts are everywhere corrupted and deflected, where work and community are reduced to mechanical emptiness. Like Lawrence, he imagined a man and woman who sought to escape the culture of death through the free impulses of sex. But unlike

Lawrence, Orwell knew that sexual instinct could not be freed from the world in which it found its outlet. Birkin and Ursula can escape to the Tyrol, but the world around Winston Smith and Julia permits no escape, and their hopes and lives are subsumed in the general apocalyptic rout.

Orwell's most insistent theme in the last dozen years of his life was the failure of writers, politicians, and thinkers to comprehend the methods and appeal of totalitarianism. In 1941 he had attacked Wells for underestimating Hitler by regarding him merely as the enemy of rationality and progress, "all the war-lords and witch-doctors in history rolled into one," who therefore "is an absurdity, a ghost from the past, a creature doomed to disappear almost immediately." By setting up "the supposed antithesis between the man of science who is working towards a planned World State and the reactionary who is trying to restore a disorderly past," Wells had rendered himself incapable of understanding that his antithesis was false, that men of science had helped build the German state: "Much of what Wells has imagined and worked for is physically there in Nazi Germany." A few lines later Orwell asked himself, "[I]s it not a sort of parricide for a person my age (thirty-eight) to find fault with H. G. Wells?" Wells's vision of the scientific and technological future had shaped "the minds of us all, and therefore the physical world. . . . Only, just the singleness of mind, the one-sided imagination that made him seem like an inspired prophet in the Edwardian age, make him a shallow, inadequate thinker now."[9]

Orwell had made himself forget that Wells's mind had always been double and his imagination always divided against itself. When Orwell wrote *Nineteen Eighty-four*, the book was in part a parricide committed against Wells's official vision of a World State, but, as in many literary parricides, the son wielded a weapon that the father had forged. The systematic, planned world divided between the Party and the Proles that Orwell imagined in *Nineteen Eighty-four* derived many of its terrifying details from a similar future in Wells's novel *The Sleeper Wakes*. And when Orwell, by destroying the intimacy of Winston and Julia in *Nineteen Eighty-four*, rebuked Lawrence for imagining a personal escape from social disaster, he vicariously defended Wells against Lawrence's earlier rebuke with all the impassioned energy of a faithful son.

Notes

1. Lawrence's letters are quoted from the Cambridge University Press edition of *Letters of D. H. Lawrence*, vol. 1, ed. James T. Boulton (1979), and vol. 3, ed. James T. Boulton and Andrew Robertson (1984). Citations are given in the text.

2. Quotations from *Tono-Bungay* are from the text edited by Bernard Bergonzi, first published with his introduction (Boston: Houghton Mifflin, 1966), later republished without it (Lincoln: University of Nebraska Press, 1978). Citations are given in the text.

3. Quotations from *Women in Love* are from the Cambridge University Press edition, edited by David Farmer, Lindeth Vasey, and John Worthen (1987). Citations are given in the text.

4. D. H. Lawrence *Phoenix*, ed. Edward D. McDonald (New York: Viking, 1936), p. 436.

5. Frank Kermode, *D. H. Lawrence* (New York: Viking, 1973), p. 65.

6. Information from Sir Stephen Spender.

7. D. H. Lawrence, *Selected Literary Criticism*, ed. Anthony Beal (New York: Viking, 1966), p. 39.

8. Review of *Black Spring* by Henry Miller and other books, in George Orwell, *The Collected Essays, Journalism, and Letters*, 4 vols., ed. Sonia Orwell and Ian Angus (New York: Harcourt, Brace & World, 1968), 1:232.

9. George Orwell, "Wells, Hitler, and the World State," ibid., 2:139–45.

The Lowly Art of Murder
Modernism and the Case of the Free Woman

▨   ▨   ▨

MARIA DiBATTISTA

> He was a realist. He knew women.
>
> —Graham Greene
> *A Gun For Sale*

Modern Entertainments

When Graham Greene designated his dark detective thrillers as entertainments, he was, perhaps, being commercially shrewd in soliciting a certain kind of popular readership. He was also being aesthetically quite correct. Nowhere is the boundary line between high and low culture more finely drawn than at the crossover between "literature" and detective fiction. Does anyone speak, except in provocation or misprision, of a detective novel? Crime thriller, detective *story*, murder mystery, yes, but even in common parlance, *detective* and *novel* keep their distance, even if they do not completely part company.

What is a detective story? Perhaps Gertrude Stein's definition is still the best because, like the detective story itself, it resolves all difficulties in a self-evident demonstration that confounds, even as it satisfies, logic: "[W]ell detective stories are what I can read."[1] Detective stories are what we all, with the notable exception of Edmund Wilson,[2] can read, presumably, because they are—Stein's word again—"soothing." They assure their readers that reality will yield its secrets and that good and evil will definitely declare themselves. Within their pages one can escape the world of mixed motives and complicated or unresolved outcomes. Opaque mysteries fade to pallid transparencies under the illumined gaze of the detective's analytic mind, their solutions untroubled, as life is often troubled, by loose ends, imperfect understanding of human relations, unmotivated or random evil. It is worth recalling that Poe's Dupin solves the most baffling crimes by aligning himself with a deliberate superficiality. "By undue profundity we perplex and enfeeble thought": such is Dupin's guiding principle.[3] Attention to the surface of things, on which the solution of "The Purloined Letter" depends, is the first rule of detection, which dismisses as unprofitable any philosophic rummaging in the murky depths.

The distinction between the shallow arts of detection and the deeper perturbations of literature is not a critical afterthought, but dates from the detective story's emergence as a distinct genre of popular entertainment. Dr. Watson, in first presenting Sherlock Holmes's character to the world (A *Study in Scarlet* [1881]), notes the deliberate specialization of Holmes's cultural literacy. Two items in particular warrant our attention:

> Item 1: Knowledge of Literature. Nil.
> Item 9: Knowledge of Sensational Literature.—Immense. He appears to know every detail of every horror perpetrated in this century.[4]

Watson's inventory of Holmes's mental attainments assumes that the study of human life might be pursued by consulting the records of two different, if adjacent, realms of written expression: literature, whose knowledge is not specified, presumably because whatever knowledge it possesses or communicates does not easily yield or appeal to Holmes's applied "science of deduction"; and "Sensational Literature," which is literature only in the loosest sense of writings devoted to a particular subject—in this instance the horrors men and women inflict on one another. We might hazard, after Stein, that sensational literature is what Holmes can read, or rather what he *must* read, just as he must experiment with poison compounds or calculate the rates at which ashes form and fall from different tobacco blends. In its sordid archives he may research the ingenious villainies, diabolical schemes, and treacherous liaisons by which evil is accomplished. Sensational literature is Holmes's index to reality if reality is understood, as Conrad's Kurtz ultimately and sensationally understood it, as "the horror, the horror."

Holmes, as Watson subsequently discovers, intends to present his findings to the world in the grandiloquently titled magnum opus *The Book of Life*. The organizing premise of this work is astounding, and indisputably antinovelistic. As Watson reports, Holmes's intent is to "show how much an observant man might learn by an accurate and systematic examination of all that came in his way," so that, for example, it is possible "that by a momentary expression, a twitch of a muscle or a glance of an eye, to fathom a man's inmost thoughts. Deceit, according to him, was an impossibility in the case of one trained to observation and analysis."[5] Such a book, had it been published, would have rivaled Freud's *Psychopathology of Everyday Life* (1901) and would have rendered the new science of psychology, for all practical if not clinical purposes, obsolete. If we can fathom a man's inmost thoughts by a twitch of a muscle, why delve into his dreams, listen to his talk, or note telltale slips of the tongue for unwitting, vital clues to the story he carries within him? Such a book might unmask deceit of both conscious and unconscious intention, but would embolden the complacent belief that no one need be a mystery to others or to oneself. Romance would wither and die under its analytic glare. The "inner life" would no longer be the great unknown which we might explore with the novel as our guide, but a familiar neighborhood we visit from time to time. Holmes's book, we might surmise, would eliminate the need not only for a modern psychology but for modern literature.

Of course, in this would lie much of its appeal. Some such sentiment inspired Marjorie Hope Nicolson when she championed detective fiction precisely because it provided an escape not from life but from "high" modernist literature:

> We have revolted against an excessive subjectivity to welcome objectivity; from long-drawn-out dissections of emotion to straightforward appeal to intellect; from reiterated emphasis upon men and women as victims either of circumstances or of their glands to a suggestion that men and women may consciously plot and consciously plan; from the "stream of consciousness" which threatens to engulf us in its Lethean monotony to analysis of purpose, controlled and directed by a thinking mind; from the sophomoric to the mature; most of all, from a smart and easy pessimism which interprets men and the universe in terms of unmoral purposelessness to a rebelief in a universe governed by cause and effect.[6]

Nicolson rallies to the detective story as the welcome Counter-Reformation to the modernist revolution. One need not be a partisan of literary reaction to appreciate how Nicolson's prepossessing description identifies one of the most soothing elements of detective fiction as a "low" genre: its morally assured analysis of human character. Detective fiction displays a healthy suspicion of the high modernist's preoccupation with a besieged, often purposeless and erratic subjectivity. Its interest in human beings is sensibly confined to the question, Whodunit—and then, of course, how he or she went about doing it. We do not pick up a detective story to overhear characters droning on in Lethean monotony, nor to observe them irresistibly driven by glandular compulsions or mangled in the social machinery meticulously reassembled in the "pessimistic" fictions of the naturalist school. Detective fiction offers us the entertaining as well as instructive spectacle of men and women acting true to type, busily plotting their lives—or alibis—according to calculable self-interest and discernible motives. In the Holmesian book of life, human beings are presented as ultimately, thoroughly knowable.

To such imperturbable assurance, contrast the humbling uncertainties that afflict the ostensibly omniscient narrator of *A Tale of Two Cities*, a novel that anticipates, as does much of Dickens, the modern use of the devices of detective fiction to expose public evils and private wrongs either too lurid or too plain to be convincingly dramatized by conventional novelistic means. The narrator confesses himself awed and baffled, however, by the larger, insoluble mystery of human character:

> A wonderful fact to reflect upon, that every human creature is constituted to be that profound secret and mystery to every other. A solemn consideration, when I enter a great city by night, that every one of those darkly clustered houses encloses its own secret; that every room in every one of them encloses its own secret; that every beating heart in the hundreds of thousands of breasts there, is, in some of its imaginings, a secret to the heart nearest it! Something of the awfulness, even of Death itself, is referable to this. No more can I turn the leaves of this dear book that I loved, and vainly hope in time to read it all. No more can I look into the depths of this unfathomable water, wherein, as momentary lights glanced into it, I have had

glimpses of buried treasure and other things submerged. It was appointed that the book should shut with a spring, for ever and for ever, when I had read but a page. . . . My friend is dead, my neighbour is dead, my love, the darling of my soul, is dead; it is the inexorable consolidation and perpetuation of the secret that was always in that individuality, and which I shall carry in mine to my life's end.[7]

A defining feature of authentic mystery is that it gestures toward an irreducible knowledge that can be neither dispelled nor assimilated into a reality other than or apart from itself. The novel recognizes that this knowledge comprises all the mystery and majesty of Death. Death in the novel is not so much a natural fact whose causes can be determined as the impenetrable, untellable secret that lies at the heart of each individual's life. Such mystery lingers and suffuses consciousness, dyeing it with strange, usually somber colorations. The detective story, in contrast, typically leaves no such residues at its conclusion to irritate or fret the mind. Holmes aspires to collect his findings into a definitive book of life, but Dickens dare not presume to decode but a page in the dark tome in which the secrets of each human creature are written. A detective story is what I can read; the novel is what I hope I am able to read, page by mysterious page.

The ease with which detective fiction dispatches with its mysteries in thoroughly readable, transparent solutions prompts Tzvetan Todorov to insist that the defining characteristic of detective fiction as a popular entertainment is that it incarnates rather than transcends the generic conventions that constitute it. The great book, according to Todorov, "establishes the existence of two genres, the reality of two norms: that of the genre it transgresses, which dominated the preceding literature, and that of the genre it creates." Popular literature is "the happy realm" where the "dialectical contradiction between the work and its genre does not exist."[8] Greatness is sacrificed in pursuit of the primary satisfaction derived from seeing the typical reembodied with ingenuity as well as precision.[9]

It is precisely such gratifications that a socially minded critic such as Franco Moretti finds suspect.[10] For Moretti, the affinity of detective fiction for the stereotypical depreciates the novelistic investment in *Bildung*, in detailing the slow, complex formation of character. Characters are either suspects or detectives, but in either case, Moretti objects, they never are shown progressing toward a state, or, less grandly, a moment, of enlightenment in which the individual comes to see himself in relation to the world. But there is an even more sinister plot at work in such fictions that Moretti finds troubling. The detective, in uncovering facts, extracts and alienates them from their social and historical context, thus rescinding the "real" connection between causes and effects and substituting a soothing, quasi-mythical representation of the current state of things. Holmes's method of "reasoning backwards" appears, in this light, as a mystification of determining causes, not their elucidation. Detective fiction, according to this view, is a form of antiliterature, since it provides mythical solutions rather than reproducing for us the tangled web of causes and effects in which the novel nets the intractable reality of the world.

Yet literary history exposes, as is its wont, the thinness of the boundary line separating great from popular books, mythical from novelistic representations of the way things are and how they have come to be that way. Defenses on both sides of the divide are neither adequately fortified nor energetically maintained. For one thing, "serious" novels have made such frequent and open crossings over the border into popular entertainments that it no longer seems remarkable for a highly intentioned author to descend from his ivory tower and trespass into the torrid zone of mass culture. From Dickens through the reputed golden age of British detective fiction in the first third of this century, this low form has attracted the imagination of the biographer of Saint Francis of Assisi, a writer of children's stories, and a translator of Dante.[11] Even Beckett, the great modernist solitary, cannot fully map "Molloy country" without the hysterical (and hilarious) ratiocinations of the hapless detective Moran. The generation that came into literary ascendancy after the Second World War, especially the advocates of the *nouveau roman*, had a special fondness for the hermeneutics of detection, which served them well in discrediting the "myth" of character as a deep structure while providing them with a logically elegant paradigm for narrative construction. They were attracted, as Robbe-Grillet noted, to the principled antipsychologism of the form and its mandate of graphic description and precise measurement.[12] Even when things are at their most baffling, we *know* that all mysteries will be accounted for at story's end. How different, then, from the modern novel, with its perspectivism and indeterminacy in the presence of the Real. Detective fiction pretends to a certain knowledge of reality otherwise debarred writers of high cultural persuasion. It can entertain the "lower" forms of life without being either impressed or intimidated by the bad company it keeps. In its sensational pages the neglected, discredited, and ultimately revengeful spawn of the Social Unconscious surface for their deadly sport with the forces of light.

The Sex of Detection

But what precisely is this "reality" known primarily to the "lower" orders of literary art, and how are we to be sure we have succeeded in capturing it? "The Murders in the Rue Morgue," conventionally regarded as the first detective story, offers some clues to the enduring fascination and popularity of the form. Even before the mystery is unveiled, we are presented with a clue to its original nature in the story's gnomic epigraph from Sir Thomas Browne: "What song the Syrens sang, or what name Achilles assumed when he hid himself among women, although puzzling questions, are not beyond all conjecture." The epigraph is oddly soothing, since it suggests that even though the story will introduce us to mysteries as puzzling as those perennial enigmas whose solutions seem lost in history, these mysteries are not beyond unraveling. Poe intriguingly associates the ratiocinations of the detective, remarkable for his "mental features" (the first words of the story) rather than his physical attributes, moral character, or social status, with conjectures about the seductive arts and hidden life of women. In some way not beyond all conjecture, the crimes that intrigue the detective are akin to, or direct offspring of, the persisting mysteries of the sexual life, which men and women share but experience and fantasize differently.

Such mysteries reconnect us to the primal life of nature, in perpetual enmity with civilization and the laws of the tribe. G. K. Chesterton, in one of the first artistic defenses of the genre, thought detective stories a popular modern revival of

romance, with the police force cast in the role of knights-errant. But detective stories could legitimately boast a more ancient lineage. In their crafted plots, the creative agon Nietzsche discerned between Apollo and Dionysus, between dreaming
intellect and ecstatic instinct, is revived as modern, popular entertainments. Poe
seems aware of this genealogy in describing Dupin and his narrator–companion as
Apollonian beings "busying [their] souls in dreams—reading, writing, or convers-
ing."[13] Nor is it incidental, but paradigmatic, that the first case Poe imagines for
Dupin involves a particularly baffling mystery surrounding the Dionysian "fate" of
women—the brutal slaughter and dismemberment of a mother, who is beheaded,
and a daughter, whose body is stuffed up the chimney. There is no sign of forced entry
to their locked apartments.[14] Those who overheard the distressed cries of the victims
agree that the assailant spoke in a gruff voice in a language unknown to them. The
official in charge of investigating the crime, Le Bon, considers plausible motives—
money or fanatical politics—and even apprehends a suspect, but it is Dupin who,
imaginatively reflecting on the import of the linguistic rather than forensic clues
reported to him, ultimately alights on the real culprit—an orangutan.

It is easy to see why this story has attracted, nay demanded, psychoanalytic readings, the first and still most dazzling offered in Marie Bonaparte's 1949 study of Poe.
Bonaparte traces the origin of the crime to Poe's infantile sexual researches, particularly the riddle he perceived in the dubious paternity of his sister Rosalie. Poe's
failed sexual researches, she argues, are resumed—with a happier outcome for the
horrified ego—in a detective tale in which Poe "splits" his ego and projects himself
into the following characters: Dupin, the fantasy projection of the "infallible ratio-
cinator"; the friend who narrates the story and allows Poe to observe, as it were, his
own triumph; and, most cunningly, the sailor in whom Poe revives "the infant present at the parental sex act, sadistically conceived." Bonaparte thrillingly concludes:
"Thus, part of Poe's ego has attached itself to the father–figure orangoutang in his
desire to identify himself with the father to whom the mother belongs. But only the
merest allusion indicates this—the creature's youth."[15] One might quickly comment
here, in the best detective tradition of collaborative speculation, that the orangutan's
guttural, prehuman language may more explicitly allude to the infantile source of this
murder fantasy, since presumably the young creature who witnesses the "crime" of
parental intercourse has not yet been inducted in the symbolic order of language
(psychoanalytically denominated as the realm of the Father and his Law). We shall
return to this crucial point a little further on. For now, let us note that Bonaparte's
local reading is later elaborated by Geraldine Pederson-Krag, who argues, on the basis
of both clinical and literary evidence, that the detective story is generically disposed
to the sadistic reenactment of primal scene fantasies. The reader of detective fiction
may thus satisfy an unconscious voyeurism without arousing a corresponding fear of
being punished for aggressively libidinous Oedipal urges: "In an orgy of investigation,
the ego, personified by the great detective, can look, remember, and correlate without fear and without reproach in utter contrast to the ego of the terrified infant witnessing the primal scene."[16]

That there exists a link between the infant's alleged amazement at the (imagined) sadism in sexual intercourse and the adult's subsequent enjoyment of seeing

sadistic crimes brought to light seems to be a plausible, though hardly definitive, conjecture that accounts for one distinguishing feature of the classic detective story that Raymond Chandler sardonically remarked—that it "has learned nothing and forgotten nothing."[17] It is both the expectation and the rule of the detective story that no renegade detail be allowed to intrude upon and disturb its complete "remembrance" or reconstruction of past crimes. At story's end there should be no "inconvenient" remainders to queer the logically elegant resolution mandated by the form. Stein succinctly identifies the moral and psychic elements harmonized by the formal economy of the detective story at the conclusion of her one venture at a murder mystery, *Blood on the Dining-Room Floor*: "Forgive forget, forewarn foreclose foresee."[18] Everything that happens in a detective fiction is included within a self-contained system of moral (forgive, forget) and hermeneutic (forewarn, foreclose, foresee) directives. One might add, in perfect(!) justice, foredoom, since it is the "good genius" of the form that its resolution is a foregone conclusion. The knowledge it sedulously garners is fundamentally a redundant knowledge, since it was first ascertained, although in a very crude and imperfect form, in the early sexual researches of childhood.

We would do equally well to recall that Dupin solves the mystery of the rue Morgue by recognizing that the unidentified "language" of the culprit is a species of oracular gibberish issuing from those sybilline quarters—the locked bedroom. He notes that all witnesses comment on the incomprehensibility yet uncanny familiarity of the sounds coming from the death chamber, which they attribute to the fact that the worlds are part of a language unknown to them. The key to decoding this other, "foreign" language lies not so much outside as within them. It is the language of a creature in the grips of its animal nature, whose grunts and cries find their original in the "primal sonorities," as Nabokov's Humbert Humbert calls them, of the primal scene. It is the language, humanly considered, of reversion. Positioned just on the threshold of "literature," the detective story is particularly well situated to record and interpret this unreasoning language in which instinct has its violent, often incomprehensible say.

It is arguable, then, that murderers are also revivalists. They resurrect the dormant animality we thought we had left behind in the dim reaches of our infancy, or, even further back, in the first ages of mankind. The detective may thus be regarded as an Apollonian healer–therapist who exorcises or otherwise subdues the Dionysian specter of atavism. Chesterton understood this early on in arguing that the detective story morally regards "the agent of social justice [as] the original and poetic figure, while the burglars and footpads are merely placid old cosmic conservatives, happy in the immemorial respectability of apes and wolves."[19] Detective fiction is not spooked by the bogeys of atavism that haunted fin-de-siècle and early modernist culture. Chesterton's Father Brown, for example, not only solves crimes but also clarifies religious mysteries, banishing superstitions and similar survivals of pagan fancifulness. In a more secular vein, Dorothy Sayers's Lord Peter Wimsey possesses the genealogical tree, Agatha Christie's Hercule Poirot the dandified culture, to verify that the cultivated man need not be morally decadent or sexually debauched. Such characters oppose what is arguably the most modern element in modern literature[20]:

the discontent with civilization and consequent attraction to the feral energy of instinct, an attraction that displays itself in all literary registers, from the genteel savageries of Saki's satiric bestiary to the bestial utterances of the dream-creatures into which Joyce's Dubliners metamorphose in the "Circe" episode of *Ulysses*.

Thus, to stress the intellectual relation binding the detective to the "mastermind" or cunning criminal misleadingly exalts the human image with which detective fiction is concerned. Detection may rely on the latest scientific knowledge to interpret the world, but its subject is always, in the larger sense, retrograde humanity. The case that Holmes, on the brink of solving, regards as "one of the most singular and sensational crimes of modern times"[21] *is* sensational, but precisely because in its origins and in its cultural significance it is neither singular nor modern. I refer, of course, to Holmes's most sustained piece of detection, *The Hound of the Baskervilles*. The specific challenge facing Holmes in this bizarre case is to reconstruct the "missing links" that connect the dead Baskerville, to all appearances murdered by a monstrous hound, to the actual murderer, Stapleton, the unscrupulous Baskerville in line to inherit the estate, who masquerades as a benign "naturalist." Tellingly, Stapleton's real identity is confirmed when Holmes recognizes his physical resemblance to an ancestral portrait, a resemblance that reveals the telltale features of hereditary degeneracy.[22]

Stapleton, however, is not the only "throwback" in this mystery. A major snare in the plot involves Watson's mistaking "the man on the tor"—presumed to be a caveman persisting in the physical and moral condition of Neolithic man—for Holmes himself. Here is a comic instance of how Holmes's "reasoning backwards" also entails retracing the evolutionary path of the mind as it rises out of the unreflective animal existence of the "first ages" of life. Dr. Mortimer, who brings the case to Holmes's attention, simultaneously introduces the scientific culture concerned with solving such "mysteries" of human evolution—or retrogression. The titles of his publications—"Is Disease a Reversion?," "Some Freaks of Atavism," and "Do We Progress?"—allude to popular scientific theories, promulgated in works such as Nordau's *Degeneration* and Lombroso's criminology, that individual and social ills are the manifestations of imperfect or thwarted evolution. Instances of "sensational" reversion were frequent subjects of fin-de-siècle literature, from the lurid sensationalism of Stevenson's "Dr. Jekyll and Mr. Hyde" to Conrad's sardonic parodies in *The Secret Agent* of how "advanced" scientific thinking posed the problem of good and evil. In discovering the links between a murderous brute and a brutish murderer, Holmes is not only solving a crime but also retracing an unflattering but scientifically "sound" (i.e., current) genealogy of morals.

The particular genealogy of Baskerville morals is traced to a handwritten manuscript in which is recounted how, at the time of the Great Rebellion, Sir Hugo Baskerville abducted a yeoman's daughter and, when she escaped, pursued her in a frenzied lust until he himself was killed by an avenging hellhound. In Sir Hugo, wellhead of the "masterful Baskerville strain" (p. 22), we confront the genotype of sexual evil; in the hound, the beast in whom the family's sexual transgressions are totemistically bound up. It should therefore come as no surprise to the addicted reader of classic detective fiction that Holmes's researches into a crime apparently originating in this "curious, old-world narrative" (p. 9) would eventually lead to a locked room. In pursuit of the murderer, Stapleton, Holmes and Watson enter a locked chamber, where they find "an object so strange and so unexpected" that both are reduced to amazement. The room resembles a museum where Stapleton, like Conrad's Stein in *Lord Jim*, dotes over his specimens, the finest of which is exhibited, bound and gagged, in the center of the room. It is a figure "so swathed and muffled in the sheets which had been used to secure it that one could not for the moment tell whether it was that of a man or a woman" (p. 158). This sexual indeterminacy is quickly resolved (although we should note how common such confusions are to primal scene fantasies, when the "sex" of the "beast with two backs" is precisely what needs to be determined). Only when the figure, released from bondage, falls weakly to the floor do Holmes and Watson notice "the clear red weal of a whiplash across her neck" (p. 158). The sight of this weal, symbolic mark of castration and the traumatizing knowledge of sexual difference, provokes Holmes, in an atypical outburst of sexual gallantry, to consign his criminal quarry to the category of brute.

Yet it must be said that Holmes, who has successfully identified the villain, has not perceived the links connecting the young woman abducted in the "old-world narrative" to the "modern" wife bound by—as well as to—her husband. This uncharacteristic, hence telling, failure to complete a logical chain is evident in his reply to the first question Mrs. Stapleton asks on being literally freed from her bondage:

"Is he safe? she asked. "Has he escaped?"
"He cannot escape us, madam."
"No, no, I do not mean my husband. Sir Henry? Is he safe?" (p. 158)

This double expostulation signals an impulse not only to correct but also to rebuke Holmes for mistaking the object of her solicitude. Holmes has solved the "supernatural" mystery of the hound, but is apparently clueless in understanding Beryl Stapleton once she is divested of her assumed "character of a free woman." We recall here that Holmes has linked Stapleton to the murdered Baskerville heir through a chain of physically abused and emotionally mistreated women, from the original victim of Sir Hugo's intemperate lusts to the female dupes of Stapleton's cunning—his wife, who masquerades as his unmarried sister (hence a "free woman"), and Laura Lyons, a minor character persecuted by her husband and hampered in her attempt to secure a divorce, whom Stapleton manipulates to advance his own murderous designs. The chain of evidence, as of victims, leads back to the primal scene of sexual and social origins: the exchange of women.

In his study *The Origin of the Family, Private Property and the State*, Engels recommended the Continental novel as the "best mirror" for observing bourgeois marriage in both its Catholic and Protestant "styles,"[23] but he might have a found an equally telling record in British tales of detection. Such fictions were more explicit in dramatizing the evil consequences of treating sexual relations as property relations.[24] In any estimation of the degree of social consciousness infiltrating such an ostensibly escapist form as the detective story, it is worth noting that Conan Doyle, who gives us a detective hero whose knowledge of politics is admittedly "feeble," was himself active in modernizing the marriage laws of England. When the Society for

Promoting Reforms in the Marriage and Divorce Laws of England (founded in 1903) and the Divorce Law Reform Association merged in the Divorce Law Reform Union in 1906, Conan Doyle was made president and went on to serve for ten years. Such efforts, as Samuel Hynes was among the first to stress, were "only a part of a larger, slower, and more complicated one—the vast change that took place in the relations between the sexes, and in the place of women in English society before the war."[25] Classic detective fiction, whose ascendancy as a popular and distinct genre coincided with these changes, was in league with the "New Realism" of the late 1890s and early modernist period in taking a more candid look at sexual mores, focusing especially on the marriage question and the protocols, both private and public, affecting the social fate of women.

We can gauge how sophisticated detective fiction became in its treatment of such volatile material by briefly comparing Holmes's first case, *A Study in Scarlet*, with Agatha Christie's first detective story, *The Mysterious Affair at Styles*, published at the beginning of the post–World War I decade, and Dorothy Sayers's *Strong Poison* (1930) at decade's end. *A Study in Scarlet* involves a murder whose origin, like those in *The Hound of the Baskervilles*, is traced to the abduction of a woman and her forced marriage. The "study" oddly combines a naturalistic avidity for realistic, incriminating detail (especially in the description of London's urban landscapes) with a romancer's fantastical sense of sexual ordeal (Holmes's investigation transports us to Utah, where a sensational story unfolds of demonic Mormons, polygamous marriage, and murdered heroines). Christie, with a strong sense of the comedy of human unions (indeed, of human behavior generally), concocts an ingenious story centered on fatal marriages and remarriages, threatened property rights, and conniving fortune hunters. Her mystery is amusingly told by a narrator invalided from the front, who, in the course of assisting Poirot in his investigation, proposes marriage to two women who promptly, understandably, refuse him.

Christie, who has been unfairly accused of ignoring the Great War, is busy remarking (and plotting) the social dislocations and emotional instabilities on the home front. Poirot, we should recall, enters literary history as a Belgian refugee, importing with him not only a singular talent for detection but also a pronounced set of values as indispensable to him as Holmes's unemotional science in solving mysteries. Paramount among them is the conviction that "the most serious of all things" is "a woman's happiness," even if happiness might demand, as it apparently does at a critical point in the story, leaving her husband. When an unhappy wife insinuates such a desire to be a "free woman," the narrator indulges in his lone flight of poetic fancy: "I seemed to see her for a moment as she was, a proud wild creature, as untamed by civilization as some shy bird of the hills."[26] Christie has paused midstride in her briskly paced narrative to dramatize the quandaries, both real and fanciful, posed by the increasingly uncertain status of women. In devising a solution to the mystery—and "novelistically" repairing the human bunglings, resentments, and wrongs it has brought to light—she resolutely sides with old-"style" marriage against the murderous liaisons of class interlopers (the murdered woman's young husband is in league with the cunning nurse attending his wife). Moreover, the woman who dreams of being free is revealed to be longing after all for the civilized embrace of her husband.[27]

By 1930 Sayers, who urged the novelistic potential of detective fiction as a criticism of life, could hazard a more radical (and less comical) appropriation of the "marriage plot" of the traditional novel. Lord Peter Wimsey is the detective who, in the best traditions of romance, resolves to "rescue" and eventually marry the beleaguered heroine, Harriet Vane, a woman on trial for her life. Sayers's cunning twist on this formula is in presenting us with a heroine whose alleged motive for murder is that she felt degraded by a man who *offered* rather than refused to marry her, since the offer was extended after she had agreed to live with him, in the most advanced modern style, without benefit of clergy![28]

In becoming increasingly candid, even scandalous, in representing the sex relation, detective fiction showed that it was not inhospitable to realism, perhaps not even to modernism. As my epigraph from Graham Greene so wryly epitomizes, to be a "realist" in the early modernist period meant—and to a certain extent continues to mean—that one knew women. It meant, for instance, that one was not blinded by dogma or blinkered by masculine conceit in describing female desire, but insisted on sexual candor. It meant that exploring the consciousness of the "New Woman," or that even more startling mutation the free woman, could provide the central, rather than contributory or patently satiric, interest of a novel. It meant that one had to address and provide imaginative answers to the "Marriage Question," the dominant feminist issue from the 1890s through the Edwardian era.[29] It meant that, like the naturalists, one considered the prostitute or the sexually menaced proletarian girl the modern subject par excellence: a victim of the deterministic social machinery, she illustrated the sexual destiny of women unprotected by money or class or the gallantry of myth. Still, I chose Greene precisely because, as his hard-boiled syntax verging on parody implies, anyone—whether a character, an author, or even a reader—asserting such unqualified knowledge of women is fooling himself, as indeed is the case with the character in *A Gun For Sale* who speaks these lines—speaks them, in fact, to himself. Who could presume to claim such knowledge when society endlessly debated the question of women, and when even the great unriddler of devious instinct confessed himself baffled by the primary riddle: What *is* woman and what does she want?

A Simple Tale of Murder

Of course, there are some things that do not stand much looking into. Such is the considered position of Winnie Verloc, the unlikely murderess of Conrad's *Secret Agent*, a novel provocatively liberal in using the plot formulas and stock types of sensationalist fiction, even going so far as to advertise itself, in shameless irony, as "a simple tale of the nineteenth century." It was Conrad, dour novelist of the high modernist persuasion, who mobilized the narrative techniques being perfected in the "low" genres to expose the revolutionary potential of the existentially as well as socially "free woman." Being Conrad, he did not embrace the free woman as a political ideal nor acclaim her as an emerging social reality. Instead, he contemplated her as a moral enigma, a mystery in the Dickensian, novelistic understanding of the word.

The Secret Agent may be said to be concerned with two outrages, one an abortive bomb attempt in Greenwich Park, the incident that activates the police thriller plot, and the "domestic tragedy" surrounding the murder of Verloc, the secret agent of the title, by his normally placid, incurious, and sexually accommodating wife. The derangement of mind dramatized in the murder proves more unsettling than the dogma advanced by the novel's demented terrorists and crazed reactionaries. This Conrad uneasily acknowledges in his preface, conceding that it is Winnie's story that converts his "simple tale" into a "gratuitous outrage on the feelings of mankind."[30]

Such an offense seems beyond expiation since it is directed against the most sacrosanct of the nineteenth-century idols—the Maternal Woman and her fierce protective passion.[31] Conrad finds it ironic, but hardly surprising, that the "specially choice incarnation of the feminine, wherein is recruited the tender, ingenuous, and fierce bodyguard of all sorts of men who talk under the influence of an emotion, true or fraudulent; for preachers, seers, prophets, or reformers" (p. 125), should take such a deadly form. As a novelist he seems to subscribe to Nietzsche's genealogy of morals, according to which all evil things were good things once. He is in fact unrelenting in working out the fatal symmetries of this reversal, not through any abstract reasoning but through the appalling details of Winnie's emotional life: Winnie renounces the man she loves, a poor butcher who cannot support both her and her beloved brother, Stevie, and marries the double agent Verloc, who is able to provide for them both, but who will later inadvertently butcher her brother, and with him her dream that they "might have been father and son" (p. 221). She was willing to fulfill the sexual terms of her marriage contract until the death of her brother, when the price of marriage became, as Conrad told us it would, "monstrously enormous, odious, oppressive, worrying, humiliating, extortionate, intolerable" (p. 82).

We can begin to gauge the originality of Conrad's sensational treatment of Winnie's story by comparing the novel to another work describing the private life of anarchists which also opens with the "mysterious affair" of a failed bombing outrage in a London park. *A Girl Among the Anarchists*, written by Helen and Olivia Rossetti, daughters of William Michael Rossetti, nieces of Christina and Dante Gabriel Rossetti, and cousins of Ford Madox Ford, appeared under the pseudonym Isabel Meredith. A thinly disguised fictional treatment of their years as adolescent editors of the *The Torch: A Revolutionary Journal of International Socialism*, the book is best read as a deliberately normalizing "insider's account" of anarchism. Its principal concern is both to explain and to challenge the anarchist indifference to questions of the personal life, and in this (but in this only) it resembles Henry James's novel *The Princess Casamassima* rather that Conrad's "low," lurid treatment of the personal life of anarchists. What is noteworthy about this account of a young, relatively affluent orphan's involvement with the anarchist cause is how law-abiding the narrator's attitude is toward narrative convention and how little passion is evidenced in either defense or repudiation of anarchist principles. Hers is a thoroughly pedestrian narrative, describing, without any modernist "tricks" or self-consciousness, her induction into anarchist circles (where, as a woman, she is greeted with suspicion), her experiences editing the propaganda organ *Tocsin*, her role in facilitating the escape of Italian anarchists, and her eventual withdrawal from the anarchist community. Her story concludes with the rather benign judgment that English anarchists should be regarded as cranks rather than dangerous insurrectionary beings. The heroine affects a kind of ideological composure in her final remarks, offering us a balanced assessment of the anarchist's principled dismissal of personal happiness: "I can understand and admire even as I deplore." The "memoir's" parting image is of her taking to the streets of London "a sadder if wiser woman."[32]

This same image of taking to the streets defines Conrad's conception of Winnie as a "free woman," but it is attended by no ideological composure. The first act Winnie performs after killing her husband is to put on her walking shoes, thus evoking the specter of licentiousness shadowing the figure of the free woman and completing Winnie's incarnation as a naturalist subject. The grotesquely comic bargain she strikes with the "robust" anarchist Ossipon, who has eyed her throughout the book—"I won't ask you to marry me, Tom" (p. 253)—confirms the social fears that love, too, might be free if women were left to revert to that lusus naturae, a free woman.

Winnie's freedom, of course, is not a social or spiritual good she can barter but the final phase of her release "from all earthly ties" once her brother dies (p. 226). It is also, however, the final term of her husband's increasing moral isolation, which Conrad ironically, if sympathetically, describes for the greater part of the book:

> She had her freedom. Her contract with existence, as represented by that man standing over there, was at an end. She was a free woman. Had this view become in some way perceptible to Mr Verloc he would have been extremely shocked. In his affairs of the heart Verloc had been always carelessly generous, yet always with no other idea than that of being loved for himself. Upon this matter, his ethical notions being in agreement with his vanity, he was completely incorrigible. (p. 226)

Verloc, upholder of the social system is incorrigible exactly in the way patriarchy remains incorrigible—in ministering to male vanity, the mother, according to Conrad's genealogy, "of all noble and vile illusions" (p. 82). In *Heart of Darkness* it is the distinctly womanish illusion of the "Intended" that is at once exposed and perpetuated as the mortal lie at the core of civilization's dream of life. Verloc seems selected out as a scapegoat who must pay the personal price for the collective vanity of men who flatter themselves that they are loved in themselves, or who, like the anarchist tribe of Ossipon, Michaelis, and Yundt, live off women, an arrangement conveniently divorced from whatever political system or dogma they espouse.

Indeed, Conrad takes some pains to identify both the hieratic and atavistic elements in Winnie's bearing as she moves in for the kill, creating the effect that what we are witnessing is not just a distressed woman's revenge but the retributive machinery of outraged Nature against the presumptions, and unnatural politics, of patriarchy: "Into that plunging blow . . . , Mrs Verloc had put all the inheritance of her immemorial and obscure descent, the simple ferocity of the age of caverns, and the unbalanced nervous fury of the age of bar-rooms" (p. 234). Winnie Verloc, murderess, is both a throwback to the age of caverns and a harbinger of the free woman degraded into a nerve-worn maenad of the barroom. Is it any wonder that she inspires horror?

What has brought her to this pass is not a conviction, nor even a thought, but an unsought yet irresistible and fatal moment of vision. Conrad, of course is the modernist who insisted that the intent of his fiction was "to make you see," even though such an imperative, however moral, is, as Conrad dramatized over and over again, potentially life-undermining. Making one see what does not stand looking into is one way of outraging the feelings of mankind, of demoralizing instinct, and Conrad knows it. Hence the insinuating courtesy that concludes *Heart of Darkness*, with Marlow's muffled assent to the Intended's view of the world, even though he suspects such illusions are "too beautiful altogether." Winnie Verloc's contention that life doesn't stand much looking into is not a motto to be sneered at, but comprises everything practical in Conradian wisdom.

Such a look, once taken, induces a life-transforming change in even the dimmest mind. Conrad renders the irresistibility of this moment through the uncanny image of Winnie's head straining to attention as she stares at "a whitewashed wall with no writing on it" (p. 219). There is something unseemly in Conrad's introducing this lofty biblical allusion into the naturalist detailing of Winnie's incapicitated mind struggling to take in the fact of her brother's death. Conrad apparently risks this indelicate irony in order to emphasize how Fate, which he had earlier described as having no discretion, has now moved beyond the tact of language as well. Conrad takes his novel to the brink of a total aphasia, where voice (Verloc's greatest asset as an anarchist agitator) fails utterly. The whitewashed wall is not a prophetic slate on which Winnie, reluctant seer, might read the "Mene, Mene, Tekel" of modern marriage, but a blank space for the projection of the grotesque images that flood her consciousness.

Hitchcock might have been subliminally exploiting this triumph of vision over language when, in adapting the novel to the screen, he turned the Verloc business from a seedy bookshop into a movie theater. Certainly the title of the film when it was first released in America, *The Woman Alone*, knowingly winks at the social anxiety gnawing at the heart of the respectable middle class—not that bombers walk the street, but that unescorted or unpoliced women might be left to do so. At any rate, his film retrospectively calls attention to Conrad's anticipation of *cinematic* techniques to tell Winnie Verloc's story of madness and despair, as the following description of her consciousness attests: "The exigencies of Mrs Verloc's temperament, which, when stripped of its philosophical reserve, was maternal and violent, forced her to roll a series of thoughts in her motionless head" (p. 219). In this moment of crisis, Winnie's head, like some primitive form of cinematic apparatus, unrolls her thoughts in a series of striking visual images. These images, following so close upon one another, flood her mind with "such plastic relief, such nearness of form, such a fidelity of suggestive detail," effects in which the celluloid arts excel (p. 221). Conrad here exposes a stark paradox of the modern age: that cinema, born out of new technologies of vision, is an atavistic art. Its pictorialism is non-Apollonian, overwhelming consciousness with its rush of images rather than permitting a distanced contemplation of visual forms. Its graphic, magnified, highly detailed and irresistible images appeal to the primordial rather than the meditative mind. Reacting precisely like the "dummy" her husband accuses her of being, Winnie, herself motionless, sees, as on the screen of the mind's eye, a gruesome montage of interlocking scenes that vividly recall the torments of her childhood, her courtship, and her marriage. The montage culminates in that virtuouso set piece of Dionysian cinema, the dismemberment of the human body:

> She remembered now what she had heard, and she remembered it pictorially. They had to gether him up with a shovel. Trembling all over with irrepressible shudders, she saw before her the very implement with its ghastly load scraped up from the ground. Mrs Verloc closed her eyes desperately, throwing upon that vision the night of her eyelids, where after a rainlike fall of mangled limbs the decapitated head of Stevie lingered suspended alone, and fading out slowly like the last star of a pyrotechnic display. Mrs Verloc opened her eyes. (p. 233)

In Winnie's vision the Dionysian myth of existence is emptied of its affective content—joy mixed with terror—and staged as a purely pyrotechnic display. Stevie's mutilation becomes a visual spectacle that literalizes the novel's political metaphor of life as a "cannibal feast," scatters the emotional energies that have held Winnie's fantasy family in place, and severs "her contract with existence," a contract based, like Conrad's art itself, on the ideal of fidelity.

To be released from this contract is to be freed not only from certain obligations but also from necessary illusions, that is, to experience freedom as a pure negativity. Such is the state attained by Mrs. Verloc, whose "perfection of freedom . . . left her nothing to desire and absolutely nothing to do" (p. 235). Winnie must now be considered a free woman in the absolute, Nietzschean sense (the Nietzschean free woman—impossible, fantastical and sensational creature!), who acts out the Professor's dictum, "No God and No Master." Confronted with a free woman *this* free, Conrad reaches an impasse. The conventions of detection have taken him to the point where the dark realities of the modern sex relation could be indignantly exposed and the hypocrisy of anarchist careers "sustained by the sentiment and trustfulness of many women" (p. 269) satirically, manfully denounced. But it could take him no farther in providing a "soothing" answer to the "impenetrable mystery" surrounding Winnie's act "of madness or despair" (p. 266). Although her death is circumstantially accounted for, the mystery attached to it lingers. Winnie, like the enigmatic individualities of Dickens's art, consigns her secret, as she does her life, to the deep. Conrad takes the detective figure of the murderess and the social enigma of the free woman and does the quintessentially novelistic thing—turns Winnie's secret into a haunting mystery.

Still, even this mystery is not beyond all conjecture, any more than the song the Sirens sang. Conrad obligingly plants a clue to help us attain the anarchist end of his simple tale. The novel's final scene is set in the Silenus beer hall, at whose door Ossipon first hears the Professor's urgent, savage advice: "Fasten yourself upon the woman for all she is worth" (p. 101). Although Winnie, the newly "free woman," will initially attract Ossipon with the money—and sex—she offers, her actual worth, as he will learn, must be reckoned differently. He will learn this under the symbolic tutelage of Silenus, the initiator and companion of Dionysius, a satyr born of the union of god and goat whom Socrates, according to Alcibiades in *The Symposium*, is said to resemble (as does the cabman, doleful progenitor of a Dickensian brood, who steers the "Cab of Death" that takes Winnie's mother to her final destination, and whose declaration of "paternity" strikes the impressionable Stevie with "its monstrous nature" [p. 167]). Silenus's notorious wisdom that the greatest good is not to be born at all, the second best to die young, epitomizes for Nietzsche the cruel but procreative mysteries of Dionysian existence.[33]

Ossipon, nicknamed the Doctor, derelict survivor of the Verloc tragedy, evinces all the symptoms of traumatic encounter with Dionysus. His "Apollo-like ambrosial head" begins to pulsate wrongfully to the "rhythm of an impenetrable mystery." He feels "menaced . . . in the very sources of his existence" by his "cursed knowledge" that behind a woman's "white mask of despair there was struggling against terror and despair a vigor of vitality" (pp. 266–67). He takes to drink, he takes to the street, but pointedly determines *not* to keep his appointment with a woman whom, like many others, he has exploited for emotional and financial gain. He, like the Professor, becomes a walking symbol of the limits of Apollonian science in solving the Dionysian mystery at once projected and concealed in the mask of Woman: vitality struggling against a primordial terror of Death.

Holmes never wrote the definitive *Book of Life*. Conrad, a true novelist, never dared. He would not affront Life by subjecting it to an Apollonian regime of systematic explanation to which the naturalistic novel, even more than the detective story, appealed for its authority over the Real. *The Secret Agent* pursues a different solution to the mystery of individual, and the secret of collective, existence. It advises that where novel and detective story meet, there Apollo and Dionysus, intellectual and primordial being, reencounter each other on modern ground. In their renewed antagonism a new realism is born, enlightened by modern methods of thought, yet riddled with a troubled knowledge of women.

Notes

1. Gertrude Stein, "Why I Like Detective Stories," in *Yale Getrude Stein*, ed Richard Kostelanetz (New Haven: Yale University Press, 1980), p. 146.

2. See Edmund Wilson's provocatively funny "Who Cares Who Killed Roger Ackroyd?," which originally appeared in the *New Yorker* of January 20, 1945, and is reprinted in *The Art of the Mystery Story*, ed. Howard Haycraft (New York: Carroll and Graf, 1983), pp. 390–97. After dutifully reading the authors recommended to him after he had questioned the merits of mystery writers, and refusing to be bullied by "convention and the portentously invoked examples of Woodrow Wilson and André Gide," Wilson decides, "Friends, we represent a minority, but Literature is on our side" (p. 397).

3. Edgar Allen Poe, "The Murders in the Rue Morgue," in *The Fall of the House of Usher and Other Writings* (New York: Penguin, 1986), p. 205.

4. Arthur Conan Doyle, "A Study in Scarlet," in *The Annotated Sherlock Holmes*, vol. 1 (New York: Clarkson Potter, 1967), p. 156. William Baring-Gould, the annotator, offers no comment on Holmes's nonexistent knowledge of literature, but does cite Clarke Olney's study "The Literacy of Sherlock Holmes," which argues that Holmes's knowledge of sensational literature includes familiarity with "the exploits and methods of the fictional detective M. Dupin of Poe and M. Lecoq of Gaboriau" (p. 157).

5. Ibid., p. 156.

6. Marjorie Nicolson, "The Professor and the Detective," in Haycraft, *The Art of the Mystery Story*, p. 114.

7. Charles Dickens, *A Tale of Two Cities* (New York: Penguin, 1985), p. 44.

8. Tzvetan Todorov, *The Poetics of Prose*, trans. Richard Howard (Ithaca, N.Y.: Cornell University Press, 1987), p. 43.

9. That is why Stein liked and admired detective stories, on the grounds that "it is much better to make an old thing alive than to invent a new one anybody can know that." Stein, "Detective Stories," p. 149.

10. Franco Moretti, "Clues," in *Signs Taken for Wonders* (New York: Verso, 1987), pp. 137 and passim.

11. For those who are irritated by unannotated puzzles, the figures, in order, are G. K. Chesterton, A. A. Milne, and Dorothy Sayers. Borges, an enthusiastic admirer of Chesterton's witty theological murder-mystery tales, was a major exponent of the uses of detection in propounding, if not unriddling, the most intriguing metaphysical mysteries.

12. These ideas are fully and urgently expounded in essays collected and translated in Alain Robbe-Grillet, *For a New Novel* (New York: Grove Press, 1965). See especially the opening essay, "A Future for the Novel" (1956).

13. Poe, "Murders in the Rue Morgue," p. 207.

14. The room is not hermetically sealed, as would be the ideal case. It was only a matter of time until this convention became codified. The time arrived in 1935, with the catalogue offered by John Dickson's Carr's Dr. Gideon Fell, who in "The Hollow Man or The Three Coffins" inventories all the possible variations. Carr allows for some tampering, but resolutely refuses to countenance the "outrage" of having a secret passageway.

15. Marie Bonaparte, *The Life and Works of Edgar Allan Poe* (London: Imago, 1949), p. 653.

16. Geraldine Pederson-Krag, "Detective Stories and the Primal Scene," in *The Poetics of Murder*, ed. Glenn Most and William Stowe (San Diego, Ca.: Harcourt, Brace, Jovanovich, 1983), p. 19.

17. The remark introduces Raymond Chandler's famous defense of detective fiction for its moral realism in *The Simple Art of Murder* (New York: Vintage, 1988), p. 10.

18. Gertrude Stein, *Blood on the Dining-Room Floor* (Berkeley: Creative Arts Books, 1982), p. 81.

19. G. K. Chesterton, "A Defense of Detective Stories," in Haycraft, *The Art of the Mystery Story*, p. 6.

20. Lionel Trilling makes just this argument in his influential essay "On the Teaching of Modern Literature," in *Beyond Culture* (New York: Oxford University Press, 1980), p. 3.

21. All quotations are from Arthur Conan Doyle, *The Hound of the Baskervilles* (New York: Ballantine, 1975), p. 150, hereafter cited in the text.

22. Ten years later Conrad's Dr. Ossipon will become "scientifically terrified" as he looks at Winnie Verloc's face and reads there all the "irrefutable" signs of a murderous criminality coded in the genes.

23. Frederick Engels, *The Origin of the Family, Private Property and the State*, in *Selected Works* (New York: International Publishers, 1977), p. 507.

24. It should also be noted that such consequences are by no means confined to the domestic sphere, but extend inevitably to the morality governing national and international conduct. Under the guise of a murder mystery, for example, Doyle can point out, almost incidentally, that the Baskerville line has been corrupted by the same lust for mastery as Britain's imperialist "investments" when he has Watson note how the Baskervilles' speculations in South African gold have financed the "modernizing" improvements to Baskerville Hall.

25. Samuel Hynes, *The Edwardian Turn of Mind* (Princeton, N.J.: Princeton University Press, 1968), pp. 192, 172.

26. Agatha Christie, *The Mysterious Affair at Styles* (New York: Bantam, 1983), p. 135.

27. David Grossvogel dismisses the solution in the following curt terms: "A spoilsport old lady has been eliminated, foreigners (or those who act like them) have either been justly punished or made to disappear. . . . The lovers are reunited, the upper-middle-class ritual is once again resumed. Law, order, and property are secure, and, in a universe that is forever threatening to escape from our rational grasp, a single little man with a maniacal penchant for neatness leaves us the gift of a tidy world, a closed book in which all questions have been answered." David I. Grossvogel, "Agatha Christie: Containment of the Unknown," in *The Poetics of Murder*, p. 265.

28. Although Sayers would assert of *Gaudy Night* (1936), her most novelistic detective tale, that however realistic the background, "the novelist's only native country is Cloud-Cuckooland, where they do but jest, poison in jest: no offense in the world," detective fictions were concocted out of real social dissatisfactions and anxieties. *Gaudy Night*, set in the turbulent thirties, actually summons a utopian fantasy of its heroine, in the company of university women, waging a holy war over the sex relation in changing times.

29. The relations between the "Woman Question," the "New Realism" of the 1890s, and modernism have been a subject of much fine research, including, most notably, Penny Boumelha's *Thomas Hardy and Women* (1982), Ann Ardis's *New Women, New Novels* (1990), Elaine Showalter's *Sexual Anarchy* (1990), and, most comprehensive of all, Jane Miller's *Rebel Women: Feminism, Modernism, and the Edwardian Novel* (1995).

30. Joseph Conrad, *The Secret Agent* (New York: Penguin, 1984), p. 41, hereafter cited in the text.

31. Conrad first approaches this theme by dramatizing the sacrifice Winnie's mother makes to secure the material future of her daughter and idiot son, Stevie, a poignant drama in its own right, one remarked and much admired by R. B. Cunninghame Graham, one of Conrad's more astute early readers. The poignancy derives from the Dickensian manner that characterizes the famous set piece of the novel—the family ride to the mother's final habitation in the "Cab of Death." But in telling Winnie's maternal passion for her brother to its anarchist end of madness and despair, Conrad is not only less traditional but also less seemly.

32. Isabel Meredith, *A Girl Among the Anarchists* (Lincoln: University of Nebraska Press, 1992), p. 320, hereafter cited in the text.

33. Nietzsche relates how Silenus, pursued by King Midas and pressed to divulge life's greatest good, finally breaks into a shrill laugh and reveals: "Ephemeral wretch, begotten by accident and toil, why do you force me to tell you what it would be your greatest boon not to hear? What would be best for you is quite beyond your reach: not to have been born, not to *be*, to be *nothing*. But the second best is to die soon." Friedrich Nietzsche, *The Birth of Tragedy* (New York: Doubleday, 1956), p. 29.

Cultural
Politics

Love, Politics, and Textual Corruption

Mrs. O'Shea's *Parnell*

◼   ◼   ◼

R. F. FOSTER

DR. YEATS: We had a good deal of trouble about Parnell when he married a woman who became thereby Mrs. Parnell.

AN CATHAOIRLEACH [The Speaker]: Do you not think we might leave the dead alone?

DR. YEATS: I am passing on. I would hate to leave the dead alone.

—Debate in the Irish Senate on the divorce bill, 1925

I

Yeats's preoccupation with Parnell developed quite late in life; and though the Chief was already a haunting presence in the poems of 1913, representing an Anglo-Irish integrity supposedly lost to modern Irish politics, Parnell's reception into the Yeatsian pantheon was given a more dramatic impetus the following year. For in May 1914 Parnell's widow, Katharine, once notorious as "Kitty O'Shea" in the 1890 divorce case that shattered Parnell's career, arrived back in the public eye with the publication of her memoir *Charles Stewart Parnell: His Love Story and Political Life*. Yeats, his father, and Lady Gregory all read the book avidly.[1] It affected the poet's view of the private Parnell, of English hypocrisy, of the conflict of passion and will; and it supplied him with images that recur in *The Trembling of the Veil* and *A Vision*.[2]

Nor were the Yeats circle alone in their preoccupation. "Everyone is reading the O'Shea revelations," noted Wilfrid Scawen Blunt.[3] Sales of the book were gratifyingly large, running into three printings and helped by prepublication serialization and widespread newspaper coverage. The story of Parnell's fall, and the political new world not so well lost for love, carried a particularly potent charge in 1914: the third Home Rule bill, having been passed by the Commons, was being stymied by Ulster's resistance and the Liberals' pusillanimity. For Irish nationalists, particularly his ex-colleagues, the publication of Parnell's letters revealing his cavalier attitude toward them and his "disgust" at the "hollowness" of the Land League, provided an additional traumatic shock. But beyond its immediate political relevance, the story of passion and betrayal revealed (often in an extraordinarily chatty and matter-of-fact way) a ten-year cohabitation between the Irish leader and his colleague's wife which not only defied convention but also at times defied belief. Belief, that is, in the central contention of the divorce court (unchallenged at the time because neither Parnell nor Mrs. O'Shea offered evidence): that Captain O'Shea had been a deceived husband, who had neither condoned nor connived at his wife's relationship with Parnell. Yet this unlikely assertion was also the central argument of Mrs. Parnell's book.

The internal contradictions of this picture, even as presented in Mrs. Parnell's own treatment, were obvious enough to raise some reviewers' eyebrows;[4] the reaction of Parnell's champion Henry Harrison, who had helped Mrs. Parnell in the weeks following her husband's death twenty-three years before and heard a very different story, was unequivocal. The book, he wrote, was "no less a forgery even though the weak fingers of the authoress may have held the pen which stronger fingers guided."[5] Yeats's father retailed a more lurid version to his old friend Rosa Butt (daughter of the man whom Parnell had supplanted in the leadership of the Irish Parliamentary Party): "Mrs Parnell did not write that book and never saw it or even heard of it, for she was in a Lunatic Asylum where she still is. Young O'Shea wanted money so he took all the letters and made a pecuniary arrangement with Costello, and they employed a skilful literary hack who wove these into a narrative."[6] The story of how the book came to be written deserves elucidation, and so does its composition. In the process the three figures of the divorce court triangle come into clearer focus, particularly the only one still alive in 1914. This was the very far from insane sixty-nine-year-old Katharine Parnell, previously O'Shea, née Wood, a strong-minded and well-bred Englishwoman, daughter of a clerical baronet and niece of a Liberal Lord Chancellor. She had never been to Ireland, never been called "Kitty," and (unlike nearly everybody else) pronounced her name O'Shee, not O'Shay.

II

In the case of *Charles Stewart Parnell*, gestation and composition are not completely interdependent processes. The immediate inspiration for the book was apparently an article in the *Cork Free Press* by Parnell's old colleague William O'Brien, which appeared on September 6, 1913; a mere eight months later Mrs. Parnell's two stout volumes were published, copiously glossed and illustrated. Initially advertised as a collection of letters, the book is in fact a detailed autobiography up to 1891; the quantity of material, and its sometimes haphazard arrangement, suggests that at least part of it was written over a far longer period. Chapters such as the one called "Captain O'Shea's Letters," as well as the highly tendentious introduction, represent the forensic element in the book, marshaled to attack the case presented by William O'Brien. But there is far more to it than this; and much of Mrs. Parnell's material is in implicit or explicit contradiction to the argument presented by the unnamed (though scarcely invisible) editors who doctored it in the O'Shea interest. Before separating out the two voices in the dialogue, we must ask what case the O'Sheas were trying to refute.

O'Brien's article, like Mrs. Parnell's book, was based on hitherto unknown letters from Parnell—particularly one dated January 14, 1890, after the divorce petition had been entered by Captain O'Shea, but well before the hearing: "If this case is ever fully gone into, a matter which is exceedingly doubtful, you may rest assured that it will be shown that the dishonour and the discredit have not been upon my side."[7] This letter, O'Brien added, proved that "it is now certain that if Parnell had been allowed to go into the witness box the public verdict would have been altogether revolutionised" and Parnell shown to have been "rather the victim than the destroyer of a happy home . . . and the divorce would never have taken place." O'Brien's implication was that the O'Sheas hunted Parnell down, and the subsequent liaison was facilitated by a "transaction" with the captain.

O'Shea himself had died in 1905, but his son Gerard promptly wrote to *The Times* denying this interpretation and quoting a letter sent to him by his mother, in which she wrote: "I quite agree with you as to the insult to myself, your father's memory, and above all to my late husband, Mr Parnell. I now propose, with your consent, to publish, as soon as possible, myself the letters of my late husband which, as you know, I had left directions should be published after my death."[8] Gerard (then aged forty-three) was an obstreperous and litigious character with an aggressive commitment to the rather forlorn cause of defending his father's character (at least, until the price was right). He had testified on his father's side and against his mother in the divorce case; now he apparently supervised the production of his mother's memoirs, and provided a preface. Bulletins started to appear in the newspapers, imaginatively recording threats to the author from "several Irish gentlemen" if their names were mentioned. Revelations were advertised about "Salisbury, Churchill, Labouchere, Davitt, . . . Constable, Landseer, Trollope, Manning, Meredith, Rhodes," most of whom merited a single allusion in the book when it appeared (and then simply as friends of Mrs. Parnell's mother, the popular novelist Lady Wood). More accurately, promises were also held out of "wire-pulling tactics in high political circles" and new material regarding the divorce proceedings.[9] From May 5, 1914, excerpts began to appear in the *Daily Sketch*, with all the accoutrements of a serial romance: the rosebud worn by Mrs. O'Shea at the lovers' first meeting, and kept by Parnell until his death, appeared as a motif at the head of each installment. Parnell's most sensational letters, larded with epithets like "Queenie" and "My Own Wife," appeared in heavy type; the serial was also embellished with photographs that did not appear in the book, including a recent one of Mrs. Parnell waving merrily from a bath chair on Brighton promenade. The linking narrative was similarly breezy ("notes such as the following . . . will give an idea of the shifts we were put to when Willie was down [at Eltham]"). The concluding excerpt was followed by an advertisement for "our next serial—'The Sacrifice of Love,' by Mr Paul Urquhart."

The general reaction by reviewers after the publication date (May 19, 1914) was correspondingly appalled. *The Times* denounced the "desecration" of "Mrs O'Shea's confessions."[10] "Lack of delicacy" was a charge often leveled, the *Bookman* remarking that "one shivers a little at the easygoing references to her unhappy husband as 'Willie.'"[11] The consensus was that she stood revealed as unworthy of Parnell: a frequent image invoked Delilah, proclaiming to the Philistines just how she had destroyed the hero.[12] A few voices, however, were raised in defense of such a "bravely written book": the *Pall Mall Gazette* thought its "power and sincerity" raised it "from the plane of scandal to that of drama,"[13] and the *Standard* called it "a most intensely interesting document . . . shameless in its proper sense, not connoting anything disgraceful. . . . [I]t talks of long years of intrigue with as little reserve as a professor describing the love affairs of a Roman Empress."[14] These are qualities that strike a modern reader too. But the most prescient reaction of all came from an Irish suffragette journal, which robustly pointed out that Parnell's fate was "the Nemesis of the anti-feminist . . . to fall victim to a woman of the highly-sexed, unintellectual type, developed by the restriction of women's activities to the sphere euphemistically styled 'the Home.'"[15]

Otherwise, the Irish reaction was an almost complete silence. This was due less to lofty disregard than to an effective boycott organized through the Dublin Vigilance Committee, a Catholic pro-censorship pressure group. The original *Cork Free Press* controversy had received much press attention, but there was very little coverage of what the *Leader* called "this vile traffic in a fallen woman's revelations": the *Freeman's Journal*, *Irish Times*, *Daily Express* (Dublin), and *Irish Book Lover* all ignored it. So did the *Cork Free Press* itself, despite its inspirational part in the book's genesis. Only the *Independent*, owned by Parnell's (and Yeats's) old enemy William Martin Murphy, gave any prominence to this "work of shocking character . . . giving the revolting details of a disedifying liaison . . . with an audacity and effrontery that must be repulsive to every decent man and woman."[16] After a monster meeting of the Vigilance Committee on June 14, English newspapers carrying notices of the book were boycoted, and country branches of the committee imposed undertakings on Catholic booksellers not to stock it—though advertisements continued to appear in some Dublin papers. By and large it was the most effective voluntary blackout of a scandal by the press until the abdication crisis. It was still read, however, even by respectable people. "Have you read the *Life*?," Lady Gregory was asked by the model of Irish rectitude and anti-Parnellism, John Dillon. "It is a wonderful love story. It would have been all right if it had not been made public. . . ."[17]

Thus the publication inevitably set old ghosts walking; and the one surviving principal suddenly advanced from the obscurity in which she had spent the years since Parnell's death. On May 18, 1914, many newspapers carried full accounts of an interview Mrs. Parnell gave to the Press Association.[18] Though ignored by both her biographers,[19] it is full of interest—apart from proving conclusively that the author was very far from entering a lunatic asylum. She had had, she said, no idea of publication until the O'Brien controversy. "But this thing is new, this bowdlerised, excusing, current version of his character and personality; and this I cannot bear." The book was therefore "in no sense an apology: I have never answered our critics before." She had not intended to include political matters, but could not avoid them; in any case, she read "newspapers of all shades of political opinion, because it is still an interest to me to deduct his views from the whole, and speculate what his probable action would be." To the inevitable question about the contemporary impasse in Ulster, she remarked that since Parnell's death "the Irish are beginning once more to look for favours from England instead of rights. . . . Sir Edward Carson's little army [the Ulster Volunteers] would have appealed strongly to him—only he would have tipped the Ulster rebellion into the Home Rule cauldron and directed the resulting explosion at England." She herself, however, was "no longer a whole-hearted Home Ruler" since the Home Rule bill had been "whittled down to a glorified local government bill, and even so forbidden in Ulster"; this was a punishment for "Ireland's blindness and England's hypocrisy." At the time of the Parnellite split, she confided, she had longed to expose the "hypocrisy" of English statesmen, but Parnell "would not lift a finger to retard or even make difficult for England that possible ultimate issue" (given Parnell's tactics in 1891, a very special piece of pleading indeed).

Most accounts of the interview emphasized her political speculations, but the *Daily Mail* recorded her statements about "Parnell the Lover": "[F]or a woman of my temperament he was the ideal lover." All interviewers described her charm, humor, and intellectual alertness; the *Cork Examiner* was struck by "an air of *distingué* about her, and an unmistakeable charm." Significantly, her son Gerard was by her side, though Mrs. Parnell confided that in the matter of answering O'Brien's allegations, "he considers two volumes less convincing than one fist."

III

The substance of those allegations concerned Captain O'Shea's knowledge of the affair, and this preoccupied many reviewers; but there was much else to chew upon, too. In Britain attention was concentrated on the revelation that Gladstone used the then Mrs. O'Shea as an intermediary to Parnell, in many letters and several interviews, beginning nearly ten years before the divorce case. This was a godsend to the Conservative press—given that he had withdrawn support from Parnell's leadership on the moral issue. Denunciation of the "Grand Old Humbug" was widespread and gleeful. In Ireland, the chief shock value of the book lay in Parnell's own letters, particularly from Kilmainham Jail in 1881–82, where he not only spoke dismissively of the "hollow" land movement that had brought him there, but also offered to give up politics and run away with his "own sweet wifie." The nostalgic relish with which she described their various feints and evasions to avoid public attention was also deprecated. But many reviewers assumed that such steps were being taken to deceive Captain O'Shea; and this was hardly the case. For a decade Parnell lived in Mrs. O'Shea's house, returned there after late-night sittings, stabled his horses there, had a cricket pitch constructed in the back garden and a study built on for his experiments (assaying minerals from his Wicklow estate and designing unsinkable ships). Meanwhile, "Willie" turned up occasionally on Sundays to take his children to Mass. As Mrs. Parnell had remarked to Henry Harrison in 1891, "How could he fail to know?"[20]

Yet one theme of her complex book dutifully insisted on his ignorance; and the theory of straightforward connivance from the beginning presents some problems. As told in *Charles Stewart Parnell*, Katharine O'Shea determined to meet Parnell in order to advance her husband's career. A recent and unfashionably Whiggish adherent to the Home Rule party, he showed no better hope of succeeding in politics than in previous disastrous involvements such as Spanish banking and Hertfordshire stud farming. They were living largely apart, he in London, she in a suburban villa at Eltham bought in her name by the rich aunt to whom she acted as companion. Well-connected, decisive, attractive, Mrs. O'Shea presented herself to Parnell at Palace Yard in July 1880 and commanded him to come to dinner. Love blossomed at once, and (from the evidence of letters) was apparently consummated by October. In January 1881 there was a quarrel with O'Shea over Parnell's presence at Eltham, after which, she reports, "Parnell and I were one without further scruple, without fear, and without remorse."[21]

This statement follows oddly on the previous assertion that O'Shea had been pacified by denials; she told Harrison in 1891 that a modus vivendi had been arrived at and "we were on a perfectly clear basis from that onward." In any case, it seems clear that this quarrel happened in July, not January (Parnell was in Ireland in January, and the dates of letters elsewhere indicate July). By 1882 the affair was already a staple of political gossip.[22] How long did Captain O'Shea remain in ignorance? It is tempting, and reflects better on the romantic hero and heroine, to accept Mrs. Parnell's line to Henry Harrison: "Of course he knew. . . . There was no bargain; there was no discussion; people do not talk of such things. But he knew, and he actually encouraged me in it at times."[23]

And yet there is Sophie Claude. This was the short-lived daughter born to Parnell and Katharine in February 1882, while Parnell was incarcerated in Kilmainham. She was conceived during a seaside holiday with Parnell in May 1881, and Katharine was therefore two months pregnant at the time of the quarrel in July. In *Charles Stewart Parnell* she states categorically that O'Shea thought the child was his. This is the scenario for the most extraordinary scene in the book. Parnell, on parole from jail, arrives at Eltham to work out the so-called Kilmainham Treaty whereby the Irish party would cooperate with the Liberal government in return for concessions on the Land Act and the release of prisoners. In one room husband and lover draft the historic terms; next door the wife/mistress keeps vigil by the dying infant whom each man believes to be his. "Willie wanted me to join them, but I would not leave my baby, and when the daylight came and they went to lie down for a few hours' rest before Parnell left for Ireland, my little one died as my love stole in to kiss us both and say good-bye."[24]

Unsurprisingly, this was a key scene in a recent television drama about Parnell; it mesmerized reviewers in 1914. It is rather spoiled by the fact that Parnell was still at Eltham two days after Sophie died;[25] and much of the effect would be ruined if O'Shea actually knew perfectly well that the child who carried his name was not his. This seems to have been the case with Parnell's other two daughters, Clare and Katie, born in 1883 and 1884. The London editor of the *Freeman's Journal* remembered Parnell and O'Shea visiting the office and Parnell, after showing a piece of paper to O'Shea and receiving his assent, handing it over casually for insertion in the paper. "It was an announcement in due and also rather curt form of the birth of a daughter to Mrs O'Shea."[26] Mrs. Parnell's book, faced with this awkwardness, opted for the simple expedient of never mentioning the existence of Clare and Katie at all, presumably because it would make the theory of O'Shea's consistent ignorance impossible to sustain.

The romantic Parnellite case would extend this to the birth of Sophie Claude, and assume that Mrs. Parnell's repeated statements that O'Shea believed he was the father were dictated by Gerard in 1914. A close reading of the key chapter adds some evidence. The language used is repetitive and clumsy; phrases such as "the deception I had to practise on Captain O'Shea" jar oddly, and one careless sentence deserves decoding: "Willie was very good; I told him my baby was dying and I must be left alone."[27] This hardly fits a situation where "my" baby was his, too. Other clumsy interpolations in this chapter—irrelevant letters to show the O'Shea family believed the child to be Willie's, and unsigned missives from Parnell, for which no facsimiles are given—suggest the hand of the pugilistic Gerard. In her own narrative Katharine remarks, "[S]ince my first meeting with Parnell, Willie knew *at least* that I frequently met him at the House."[28] The qualification is suggestive. And many of the formal "cover letters" from Parnell, instanced as evidence of the necessity to deceive O'Shea, relate to a period when the latter was out of the country.[29]

And yet for 1882 there remains an aura of doubt. All O'Shea's references to Sophie, in the divorce case and elsewhere suggest he thought she was his—as, of course, he had to. But he never mentioned Clare and Katie, letting the case go (so to speak) by default. How much did he want to know about the convenient friendship which during 1882 gave him the political role of inept Mercury, ferrying messages to the Liberal leaders? Recent biographers of Katharine have robustly accepted the possibility that she arranged a temporary resumption of marital relations with O'Shea in 1881, when she discovered her pregnancy, in order to cover herself—an assumption that Harrison found it impossible to make.[30] In 1891, and indeed in 1914, this made her look like a loose woman; by the 1970s it fit with the picture of a resourceful feminist heroine, trapped by divorce laws and settlements that discriminated against women, determined to keep her lover and assert a role for herself.

The interpolations on O'Shea's behalf continue unevenly throughout the book, but so does a less clumsy, more unforced strain of reference which probably reflects Katharine's own attitude toward O'Shea. By and large this is oddly, exasperatedly affectionate. "Willie" becomes a character, still recognizably the "gentlemanlike adventurer" epigrammatically described by Sir Alfred Robbins, "who makes the world his oyster and is disappointed at the size of the pearls."[31] Irritating as he was, a certain camaraderie with Katharine remained in the early 1880s, though as the decade wore on he became a cross to bear. Increasingly importunate and threatening, the subject of many of Katharine's letters to Gladstone as she sought a job for him, he was indirectly dependent (through Katharine) on handouts from "Aunt Ben," whose huge fortune and unaccountable longevity preserved the shaky triangular structure far longer than its constituents intended. Katharine's expectations from her aunt's will inspired resentment and litigation from the Woods even before the old lady finally died. Joyce Marlow believes that O'Shea was encouraged to his spectacularly belated divorce action in 1889 not by any shadowy political cabal but by Katharine's jealous family. Yet up to this the tone of her references to "Willie" remain quite friendly. After a coolness in 1882–84, when, possibly, an agreement was hammered out, their letters of the mid-1880s return to the affectionate nicknames of courtship days: "Boysie" and "Dick" alternate with "Wifie" and "King." It may not be heroic, but it carries a certain psychological conviction. Her grim efforts to find him a parliamentary seat in 1885–86, leading to the Galway election when coded public references were made to the affair by everyone from Lord Randolph Churchill to the *Pall Mall Gazette*, were urgently necessary for many reasons. O'Shea was hinting, obscurely and not so obscurely, at exposure. Her machinations to avoid this constitute one of the most riveting chapters in the book. It was the culmination of many years spent trying to "place" Willie.[32] Again, significantly, decoding Katharine's own narrative supplies a clue to the real state of affairs. She remarks that failure to land her husband a seat would endanger Home Rule by leading to action that would shatter "the silence of years."[33] "Silence," not "deception."

IV

If Willie sings baritone in this *verismo* opera, the tenor part belongs to Parnell; and the portrait of him in private life constitutes one of the chief values of the book. His existence outside politics has always been cloaked in obscurity, yet there is much evidence that it meant more to him than the public life he was constrained to lead.[34] "We will be so happy, Queenie; there are so many things happier than politics."[35] After a haphazard and loveless childhood (parents separated, mother mostly absent, himself packed off to English schools from the age of six), he had found the perfect partner, and her picture of their partnership is essential to any biographer. There are myriad small mistakes and confusions in the sequence of events as she describes them. Letters of Parnell's, for instance, are glossed "sent to Dublin to be posted" when in fact he can be shown to have been there;[36] and the story of his concealment for a fortnight in a room off her bedroom during 1880 (a delight to salacious-minded reviewers) simply does not fit with the record of Parnell's movements at this time. The context of his notorious letters from Kilmainham is ignored. Parnell's reassurances that he welcomed imprisonment, and was leading a life of ease and luxury there, must be seen in relation to the frantic letters from Katharine which can be reconstructed between the lines: she was pregnant, insecure, quarreling with Willie, deeply worried about Parnell's health, and strained to the breaking point. Her account of his movements at junctures such as the Phoenix Park murders, or the publication of the Pigott forgeries in *The Times*, does not always square with other sources. But often it is simply one recollection against another; and she was the person who was with him all the time.

Moreover, much of her evidence casts new light on Parnell—particularly on the psychology of a man deluded and solipsistic enough to believe that Mrs. O'Shea could safely visit him in prison, passed off as one of his sisters,[37] and whose whole attitude to the world was that it had no business to question his bizarre private life. (In the *Times* Special Commission hearings of 1888, investigating the Pigott forgeries, a little-noted correction is indicative of Parnell's attitude. Asked, "Did you go to see Captain O'Shea at Eltham" in April 1882, Parnell replied, *"He came to see me"* there.[38] Mrs. Parnell's book also threw light on Parnell's attitude to the divorce case, and the decision of the co-respondents not to follow up their countercharges against Willie as petitioner—though this whole issue had to be skirted carefully, as those very countercharges invalidated the central premise of the work. They listed connivance, unreasonable delay in instigating the suit, willful separation, cruelty, and the petitioner's own adultery. It is well established that the undefended story O'Shea told in the divorce court was a travesty; at least two jurors had severe doubts about it, and attempted to interrogate him on their own account. Although the English press accepted it with delight, American journalists—again as with the abdication—treated this version very differently. On December 29, 1891, for instance, the *New York Herald* ran a long piece under the unequivocal heading "UN MARI COMPLAISANT: Captain O'Shea At Last Objects To Mr. Parnell's Liaison With Mrs. O'Shea."[39] Then as now, English libel law forced the local press to be more circumspect; and in the Parnell case political bias also made the worst construction of events the most attractive.

More to the point, what of the contemporary belief (at least among Home Rulers) that Katharine refused to allow Parnell to contradict O'Shea's version of events in order to facilitate their marriage? In her book she gives exactly the opposite analysis: the insistence on letting the divorce go through was his. Either way, another vital issue could not be mentioned: the fact that they were hoping to pay O'Shea £20,000 to drop the suit, right up to the last moment.[40] And certainly her account of keeping their lawyers in doubt up to the very morning of the trial is borne out by completely independent, unpublished evidence—a memorandum in the James papers with an account by Sir Frank Lockwood (Katharine's counsel) describing his attempts to persuade them to prove Willie's connivance, Katharine's excuse of "neuralgia" for delaying a decision to the eleventh hour, and Parnell's violent quarrel with Lockwood (again at the last minute) on the grounds that he believed they had been promised custody of Clare and Katie in return for abstaining from pressing countercharges.[41]

Parnell's desire to be married to Katharine, at whatever cost, is undoubted. In this, and in the picture of a Parnell insulated from political reality, Katharine's account has been corroborated by recent analysis. And she provides a portrait of Parnell, the quixotic, single-minded, oddly shy man who "hated to be hated," which was a revelation.[42] Perhaps most striking of all was her account of his threat to leap off Brighton Pier with her in a storm:

> [A]s I turned to get a fresh hold on him, for I could not stand against the wind, and the motion of the sea sickened me, the blazing fires in his eyes leapt to mine, and, crushing me roughly to himself, he picked me up and held me clear over the sea, saying, "Oh, my wife, my wife, I believe I'll jump in with you, and we shall be free for ever." Had I shown any fear I think he would have done it, but I only held him tight and said "As you will, my only love, but the children?" He turned then, and carried me to the upper deck, hiding my eyes from the horrible roll and sucking of the sea beneath our feet.[43]

In scenes like this near-*Liebestod*, she added a new dimension to a Wagnerian hero more often seen as Siegfried than Tristan.

What of Isolde? Katharine's book is essentially an autobiography, and from early on she displays certain marked characteristics: an impatience with convention, a sense of humor, a feeling of frustration with her lot, a dogged persistence, and loyalty. There is also an asperity, a certain self-satisfaction, an air of the grande dame. She could write, on occasion, with astringency and facility (which makes the double stream of composition throughout the book all the more obvious) and possessed an individual and lively style, corroborated in her more recently released letters to Gladstone.[44] And for all her disclaimers ("I was never a 'political lady'"),[45] she reveled in her activity as intermediary. The Gladstone papers do not contradict her claims to an important role, despite attempts to discredit her account.[46] Gladstone certainly soothed his colleagues about her communications, claiming he could not control them but did not encourage them.[47] Equally certainly, he continued to approach Parnell though her as often as convenient, though not as often as she claimed, and frequently through the Chief Whip Lord Richard Grosvenor rather than directly. The Liberal leader's "hypocrisy" in later abandoning Parnell is a tricky question: Katharine's constant intercessions on behalf of jobs for Willie may have given him the impression that they were a devoted couple, and, rather like Willie himself, Gladstone may have known only as much as he wanted to know. He was certainly told of the liaison at least three times in 1882, but affected incredulity.[48]

Katharine's relationship with Parnell also had its political dimension. She advised him on speeches;[49] had more opportunity to discuss day-to-day strategy with him than anyone else; and authorized a number of important communications, signing them with the name of Parnell's secretary, Henry Campbell—as Parnell himself later admitted, with breathtaking insouciance.[50] Her personal influence is emphasized by all Parnell's modern biographers; her political influence receives less analysis, though she was an intelligent and astute woman from a Whig family who prized good conversation, and her mother and sister were well-known writers much in the social world. Here, as in many other ways, the background position Katharine occupied in Parnell's public life has led to an assumption that his political decisions, as well as his political appearances, were conducted independently of her, and this seems unlikely to say the least.[51] Between the lines, the Love Story certainly suggests otherwise. Generally, the only influence she is allowed lies in keeping him obdurate during the leadership negotiations after the split. She was explicitly linked by Vanity Fair to one of the most sexually threatening images of the 1890s, as "The Political Princess: O'Shea Who Must Be Obeyed."[52] But this seems unlikely on every level: Parnell's decision to fight against the majority of his followers and jeopardize Home Rule may have been unbalanced, but it was his own. It is not unnatural that his colleagues should have thought otherwise. Their attitude to Katharine was inimical, and so was hers to them. The Irish Parliamentary Party are often the butts of her malicious humor in Charles Stewart Parnell; ironically, they had been treated in a similar manner by her first husband. Parnell once came home to her with the diverting news that an Irish M.P. had threatened to kill Willie merely because he had smiled at his colleague's pronunciation of "Mr. Speaker, Sir." His leader remarked: "Willie's smile is a bit of a twister sometimes."[53] So was Katharine's, though her attitude was less grounded in otiose snobbery. She evidently enjoyed indicating over and over again how readily Parnell would have abandoned party commitments to be by her side. It was her revenge, not only for the myth of "Kitty O'Shea" created in 1891, but also for a decade of frustration in the political shadows.

When the crash came, cupidity rather than immorality might have been an accusation more relevantly leveled at the notorious couple. Katharine had kept her unconventional menage going for ten years, determined not to jeopardize a financial inheritance by divorcing O'Shea; and Parnell acquiesced in this. The dual stream of composition in her memoir replicates the duality preserved through that strange decade at Eltham and Brighton: uxorious with her lover, intermittently stormy with her husband, while soothing her imperious aunt across the park. But in 1914 she was much more responsible for her book than chivalrous Parnellite champions such as Henry Harrison allowed. Amid the obvious interpolations, the perfunctory tone of editorial "ghosting," the inescapable archness and coyness of the genre, an original voice comes through.

V

Katharine Parnell lived on for seven more years, dying in poverty in 1921. After litigation she had obtained less than half of her aunt's fortune; much had gone on legal costs, and more had been embezzled by a family solicitor. *Charles Stewart Parnell* had made her money, but that too ran out. She moved restlessly from watering place to watering place along the south coast of England, from Kent to Cornwall and back again. At the time of her death, she was living in a small terraced house in Littlehampton: "[T]he space and beauty of [the] home of my youth," she had written in 1914, "left me with a sad distaste for the little houses of many conveniences that it has been my lot to inhabit for the greater part of my life."[54] A letter from her daughter Norah to Henry Harrison delicately hinted at a taste for the bottle, and periods of nervous breakdown. In her last years she was described as "a sonsy, comfortable soul not unlike the best type of theatrical landlady."[55] This suggests an impression too much influenced by assumptions about the old age of scarlet women; but there are not many options for an Isolde or a Deirdre who survives, and perhaps Katharine became more like Rosie in Somerset Maugham's *Cakes and Ale*.

Still, the power of her story remained, and so did its potential for controversy. In 1936 there was another flurry when Elsie T. Schauffler's successful play *Parnell* was launched on Broadway, slightly based on Katharine's book, with a farrago of inaccurate embellishments. Gerard O'Shea was still active; that same year the husband of one of Parnell's daughters begged a historian not to quote him on his wife's paternity, "as Gerard O'Shea is somewhat rough at times, and I wish to live a little longer."[56] Gerard in fact drummed up a campaign to prevent Schauffler's play being produced in London, but eventually was bought off by a large fee and disappeared to America as "script consultant" on a projected film of the story—his father's son to the last.

The revived interest in the O'Shea–Parnell triangle inspired Henry Harrison, who had published his "vindication" of Parnell five years before, to write to Yeats asking him to "make it known in Dublin." Yeats had remained haunted by the story. In *A Vision*, written in 1922, he had recurred to the *Liebestod* on Brighton Pier, and placed Parnell in "Phase Ten" of his occult system of archetypes: the "Image-Breaker," his "Mask" conferring both "self-reliance" and "isolation"; "creates some code of personal conduct, which implies always 'divine right.'" Private desires in this phase conflict with public restrictions, which are undermined by "some woman's tragic love almost certainly."[57] Much of this was inspired by the *Love Story*, which also influenced some of Yeats's comments in the divorce bill controversy a few years later. So he was ready for Harrison in 1936. Reading *Parnell Vindicated* for the first time, and spending an afternoon with the author, induced high excitement; he was particularly delighted by Harrison's account of Parnell breaking up a tedious discussion with Willie by throwing Katharine over his shoulder and bearing her off to bed. The encounter with Harrison precipitated a relapse of ill health and a number of ballad poems.

> *The Bishops and the Party*
> *That tragic story made,*
> *A husband that had sold his wife,*
> *And after that betrayed . . .*

Meanwhile in Hollywood the film of Elsie T. Schauffler's play went ahead, directed by John M. Stahl for MGM, and was released in 1937.[58] To Gerard O'Shea's talents were added those of Clark Gable and Myrna Loy. One scene stays in the mind—an echo of Joyce's "Ivy Day in the Committee Room," a silver screen personification of the Yeatsian Phase Ten—or perhaps another, indirect manifestation of Katharine's revenge? Gable as Parnell, and Myrna Loy, arrive at a London hotel. Passing through the lobby, they glance into a room; it is inhabited by members of the Irish party, sitting around a table well supplied with bottles of stout. An expression of distaste crosses Gable's (unmustached) features. "*Those* fellows!" he remarks, with a twang of contempt, and masterfully steers Mrs. O'Shea away from them, up the stairs.

Notes

1. John Butler Yeats, *Letters to His Son W. B. Yeats and Others, 1869–1922*, ed. J. Hone (New York, 1946), pp. 184–85, 211.

2. See Michael Steinman, *Yeats's Heroic Figures: Wilde, Parnell, Swift, Casement* (London, 1983), pp. 82–83, 124.

3. W. S. Blunt, *My Diaries*, 2 vols. (London, 1919), 2:425–26.

4. See, for instance, the *Spectator*, May 30, 1914.

5. Henry Harrison, *Parnell Vindicated: The Lifting of the Veil* (London, 1931), p. 238. Harrison had been the youngest member of the Irish party, and a favourite of Parnell's in his last days.

6. J. B. Yeats to Rosa Butt, January 9, 1915, Yeats–Butt correspondence, letter 149, Bodleian Library. My thanks to W. M. Murphy for this transcription.

7. The letter is reprinted in William O'Brien, *Evening Memories* (London, 1920), p. 466.

8. *The Times*, September 10, 1913.

9. See *Irish Book Lover* (May 1914) for a roundup of reports, mostly occasioned by the

circulation of a publisher's prospectus in April. Most newspapers carried items on April 23, notably *The Times*, the *Standard*, and the *Daily News and Leader*.

10. *The Times*, May 19, 1914.

11. *Bookman* (June 1914).

12. *Truth*, May 20, 1914.

13. *Pall Mall Gazette*, May 19, 1914.

14. *Standard*, May 20, 1914.

15. *Irish Citizen*, June 6, 1914.

16. *Independent*, May 19, 1914.

17. Daniel J. Murphy, ed., *Lady Gregory's Journals*, vol. 1, bks. 1–29, 10 October 1916–24 February 1925 (Gerrard's Cross, 1978), April 15, 1922, p. 344.

18. This account is based on reports in the *Daily Express*, *Irish Independent*, *Morning Post*, *Standard*, *Daily Mail*, *Daily Telegraph*, and *The Times* for May 18, 1914, and the *Cork Examiner* for May 19.

19. Joyce Marlow, *The Uncrowned Queen of Ireland: The Life of "Kitty" O'Shea* (London, 1975); and Mary Rose Callaghan, *"Kitty O'Shea": A Life of Katharine Parnell* (London, 1989).

20. Harrison, *Parnell Vindicated*, p. 124.

21. Katharine O'Shea [Mrs. Parnell], *Charles Stewart Parnell: His Love Story and Political Life*, 2 vols. (London, 1914), 1:190; hereafter O'Shea.

22. See F. H. O'Donnell, *A History of the Irish Parliamentary Party*, 2 vols. (London, 1910), 2:52; Katharine Tynan, *Memories* (London, 1924), p. 15; Lewis Harcourt's diary for November 15, 1882, vol. 352, pp. 66–67, Bodleian Library; and newspaper hints in *Truth* (edited by a famous political gossip, Henry Labouchere), November 30, 1882.

23. Harrison, *Parnell Vindicated*, p. 123.

24. O'Shea, 1:247.

25. See a letter from him dated from Eltham on April 22, in O'Shea, 1:252, and a letter to him from O'Shea, April 24, 1882, O'Shea MSS, National Library of Ireland.

26. T. P. O'Connor, *Memories of an Old Parliamentarian*, 2 vols. (London, 1929), 1:228.

27. O'Shea, 1:204, 244.

28. O'Shea, 1:183; emphasis added.

29. See, e.g., O'Shea, 2:64–67, when Willie was in Ireland, and 2:69, when he was on the Continent.

30. See Callaghan, *"Kitty O'Shea,"* pp. 88–92; and Marlow, *Uncrowned Queen*, pp. 80–83.

31. Alfred Robbins, *Parnell: The Last Five Years* (London, 1926), p. 66.

32. For references to the affair at Galway, where Parnell imposed O'Shea's candidacy on a furious local party organization, see F. S. L. Lyons, *Charles Stewart Parnell* (London, 1977), chap. 10; there had been earlier public references from Philip Callan (ibid., pp. 306–7). Speeches like that of Churchill at Paddington on February 15, 1886, when he referred to O'Shea as "repugnant and loathsome" to the Galway people "politically and from every point of view," are indicators, as in Frank Hugh O'Donnell's letter to *The Times*, February 16, 1886, referring to "the accommodating Captain O'Shea." Against this background the famous paragraph in the *Pall Mall Gazette*, May 31, 1886, about "Mr Parnell's Suburban Retreat," identifying O'Shea as the owner of the Eltham house (actually it was Katharine's), appears as less of a bombshell.

33. O'Shea, 2:165.

34. See my *Charles Stewart Parnell: The Man and His Family* (Hassocks, 1976), passim.

35. O'Shea, 2:274.

36. O'Shea, 1:156–57.

37. O'Shea, 1:238.

38. *Proceedings of the Special Commission*, reprinted from *The Times*, 5 vols. (London, 1890), 2:716; emphasis added.

39. See Marlow, *Uncrowned Queen*, pp. 216–17, 238; and 235–36 for the jury's doubts.

40. Harrison, *Parnell Vindicated*, pp. 149–50; see also Sir Edward Clarke, *The Story of My Life* (London, 1918), p. 289.

41. Diary, M45/1864, in James Papers, Hereford Public Record Office. Lockwood told a similar story to T. M. Healy (Healy, *Letters and Leaders of My Day*, 2 vols. [London, 1928], 1:318), and to Alfred Pease (Pease, *Elections and Recollections* [London, 1932], p. 276).

42. Justin McCarthy, *Reminiscences* (London, 1899), 2:104.

43. O'Shea, 2:153–54.

44. Now available in BL Add. MSS 44, 269, with some additions in 44, 503. Her letters to Lord Richard Grosvenor about Willie's political difficulties are in BL Add. MSS 44, 315.

45. O'Shea, 1:xi (preface).

46. Herbert Gladstone, *After Thirty Years* (London, 1928), attempted to catch her out on small details. Three years earlier Peter Wright in *Portraits and Criticisms* (London, 1925) had used her book to claim that Gladstone not only knew of the liaison but also had a sexual interest in Katharine himself. Herbert Gladstone subsequently provoked a libel case, which Wright lost, and in which Mrs. O'Shea's political position was fully discussed; see *The Times*, January 28–February 24, 1927.

47. J. L. Hammond, *Gladstone and the Irish Nation* (London, 1938), p. 308; see Gladstone to Spencer, September 26, 1882. Hammond pointed out that Herbert Gladstone underestimated the number of letters his father wrote to Katharine in 1882–85 (twenty-two, not sixteen; neither Hammond nor Herbert knew about their later exchanges concerning O'Shea and the Wood family.

48. He was informed by his secretary, George Gower (see Blunt, *Diaries*, 2:281); by Harcourt at an informal meeting of cabinet members, May 17, 1882 (recorded in Dilke's diary, quoted by Henry Harrison, *Parnell, Joseph Garvin, and Mr. Chamberlain* [London, 1938], p. 29); and yet again by Granville on May 28 (Hammond, *Gladstone*, p. 669).

49. See a letter from Parnell in O'Shea, 2:53.

50. In June 1891 Henry Campbell was accused by the *Cork Herald* of "hiring houses for the immoral purposes of his master." He sued, saying that letters written over his name were forgeries. Parnell wrote a letter stating that Mrs. O'Shea had written the letters renting houses, signing them with Campbell's name, which Campbell had given Parnell permission to use. "I asked Mrs O'Shea to conduct the negotiation because I was shortly going to Ireland, and for the same reasons that I have frequently charged her with the conduct of vastly more important negotiations" (*Spectator*, June 27, 1891). In her book she mentions "wiring to a London agent of Parnell's (under such a name as he would know the message emanated from him)" during the 1885 election, instructing him to "beat up" the Irish vote for a certain candidate in Whitechapel—at Willie's request (O'Shea, 2:97).

51. Marlow, *Uncrowned Queen*, p. 73, asserts a countering case quite convincingly.

52. *Vanity Fair*, November 22, 1890. See also Robbins, *Parnell*, p. 153; Hammond, *Gladstone*, p. 655; Michael Davitt, *The Fall of Feudalism in Ireland* (London, 1904), p. 642; Maev Sullivan *No Man's Man* (Dublin, n.d.), p. 73; Healy, *Letters*, 1:373; Blunt, *Diaries*, 2:381.

53. O'Shea, 2:84.

54. O'Shea, 1:7.

55. Marlow, *Uncrowned Queen*, pp. 298–99, 309.

56. Bertram Maunsell to Denis Gwynn, September 22, 1936, Horgan MSS, National Library of Ireland.

57. W. B. Yeats, *A Vision: A Reissue with the Author's Final Revisions* (New York, 1938), p. 122.

58. It was a box office disaster. Curiously, it was plagued by sexual scandal: while shooting it in England, Gable was sued for paternity by the mother of a thirteen-year-old child.

The Demotic Lady Gregory

LUCY McDIARMID

When, in 1888, Wilfrid Blunt was imprisoned in Galway Gaol for speaking out against evictions of Irish tenants at a banned meeting in Woodford, County Galway, his former lover Lady Gregory wrote four poems inspired by that happy event. It was indeed a happy event for Blunt: he had sought it, challenging the police as they pulled him from the platform, "Are you all such damned cowards that not one of you dares arrest me?" His first night in detention, he proudly wrote, offered "the first recorded instance, in all the four hundred years of English oppression, of an Englishman having taken the Celtic Irish side in any conflict, or suffered even the shortest imprisonment for Ireland's sake."[1] For Lady Gregory, Blunt's imprisonment offered a literary opportunity: she got an imaginative charge from the combination of erotic memories and rebel politics.

Sir William and Lady Gregory were not at Coole Park at the time; they were wintering in Italy. But in the best of these poems (saved only by Blunt, and unknown till 1972), Gregory imagines herself outside the jail gate thinking of Blunt on the inside. Alternate stanzas focus on Gregory "[w]ithout the gate, without the gate," and Blunt "[w]ithin the gate, within the gate."

> Without the gate, without the gate
> The patient fishers antedate
> The dawn and watch with eager eyes
> The flashing sudden salmon rise
> Without the gate, without the gate.
>
> Within the gate, within the gate
> A prisoner wakes to poor estate
> The barren light of morning falls
> Upon the narrow whitened walls
> Within the gate, within the gate.
>
> . . . .

Within the gate, within the gate,
What dreams the captive's sleep await!
A couch of honor is his bed
A glory rests about his head
Within the gate, within the gate.

Without the gate, without the gate
I early come, I linger late,
I wait the blessed hour when he
Shall come and cross the bridge with me
Without the gate, without the gate.[2]

The last stanza is even more in the realm of fantasy than the others; if any woman had been waiting to cross the bridge with Blunt when he came out, it would have been his long-suffering wife, Lady Anne.

The situation Gregory imagines, the configuration of male prisoner inside and unimprisoned female outside, the woman through her literary effusions conferring "honor" and "glory" on the man, proved to be a lasting and important paradigm for her. For Lady Gregory literary powers are linked with intimacy with a rebel or felon—an intimacy that has a sexual or maternal feeling about it. At the moment when intimacy, though with a barrier, is acknowledged, a kind of intercourse manqué, there is an exchange, or release, of powers. He, the male felon, gets fame, visibility, publicity; she, the female nonfelon, gets literary powers. She is the bearer of his memory, the conduit of his name and sufferings. In other words, the felon is a kind of muse for Lady Gregory—a male muse, of course—and intimate contact with him, especially (but not exclusively) while he is imprisoned, leads to literary production of all kinds: drama, poetry, book reviews, essays, and letters to editors. The jail gate's presence precludes physical intimacy and ensures that the felon remains a muse and not a lover.

This is the trope that defines Gregory's literary vocation: it is a private ritual of affiliation through which she comes in contact with the source and grounding of her inspiration, an Ireland that is militant, bound, dependent, male. The culture from which Gregory's ritual emerged is mid–nineteenth-century Irish rebel culture, a cluster of symbols, tropes, genres, expressions, and practices entirely familiar to "Victorian" Ireland, though fairly recent in origin: their association as a cohesive "culture" dated only from the 1798 Rising. Irish literary nationalism began, as Mary Helen Thuente has argued, in the writings of the United Irishmen, in wake and drinking songs, ballads, and commemorative verses ("Emmet's Death," "The Memory of the Dead") in the invocations of Ierne, Erin, O'Rourke, and Paddy, and in the iconographic use of harps, liberty trees, shamrocks, chains, and gallows.[3] The Young Irelanders of the 1840s developed a more self-conscious and wider-ranging cultural nationalism, more rousing and vigorous in style and aggressively disseminated by Charles Gavan Duffy, Thomas Davis, and John Blake Dillon in *The Nation*, which had 10,000 subscribers and, it was said, 250,000 readers.[4] The anthology *The Spirit of the Nation* (1843) packaged in more permanent form many of the songs and ballads from the journal. Thus, although the Risings of 1848 and 1867 were military failures, the nationalist ideology that had inspired the thought of their leaders and the attendant cultural trappings survived and spread; and the newest martyrs immediately took their places in collective consciousness through the historical, political, and cultural traditions that had been developing since 1798.

This popular nationalism, given new focus by the founding of the Fenian Brotherhood in 1858, was consumed with enthusiasm by the young Augusta Persse (born in 1852), who spent her sixpences, earned by learning Bible passages, on the latest patriotic verses: "I look to Miss Augusta to buy all my Fenian books," said the old bookseller in Loughrea, who sold her "the paper covered collections of national ballads, *The Harp of Tara*, *The Irish Song Book*, and the like." She was given *The Spirit of the Nation* for a birthday present by a sister who took the precaution of inscribing in it Samuel Johnson's maxim, "Patriotism is the last refuge of a scoundrel." Lady Gregory and her sisters were forbidden to read the Waverley novels till they were eighteen, but she was grateful for this, because Scott "never won her heart and all her romantic sympathies were kept for Ireland."[5]

Central to the literary traditions of popular nationalism were genres originating in "galling chains" or "the hangman's rope" and "the gallows-tree," the "speech from the dock" spoken by the condemned rebel, and the prison memoirs of those imprisoned long enough to write them.[6] These genres were cherished by Lady Gregory, taken so passionately into her imagination that "prison" for her was virtually inseparable from literary exertions. When the Abbey Players, whom she took on tour in 1912, were briefly arrested in Philadelphia for putting on the "immoral" *Playboy of the Western World*, a reporter broached the subject of her own possible arrest to Lady Gregory. He must have been surprised by her enthusiasm: "Now, do you think so? I wouldn't mind going to prison. Bunyan wrote some magnificent stuff while in prison. So did Oscar Wilde. The prison cell is conducive to great literary effort."[7] Sixteen years later, reading the newest addition to the genre, Frank Gallagher's *Days of Fear*, Gregory rehearsed in her mind all the political prisoners she had known personally, taking down from the shelf Blunt's prison poems, *In Vinculis*, and moving in imagination to the "large photograph upstairs" of the Egyptian rebel Urabi.[8] Wilde's "Ballad of Reading Gaol" she often singled out for praise, claiming to Yeats that it "will outlive all Wilde's other work and a great deal of the work of his contemporaries."[9]

The conventions of literary history are such that Gregory and Wilde have rarely, if ever, been associated, though they are coevals (Gregory was born in 1852, Wilde in 1854), and each enjoyed a complicated colleagiality with Yeats and with Shaw. But their deeper connection lies in kinship through the poets of *The Nation*. "Miss Augusta" must surely have read the verses of "Speranza," Jane Francesca Elgee (later Lady Wilde); and "The Ballad of Reading Gaol" may have appealed to her because of its Young Ireland echoes. As A. J. Leventhal has demonstrated, its stanzaic structure was modeled on "A New Year's Song" by Denis Florence MacCarthy, a *Nation* poet and friend of Thomas Davis.[10] And in his review of Blunt's *In Vinculis*, Wilde sounds remarkably like Lady Gregory: "Prison has had an admirable effect on Mr Wilfred [sic] Blunt as a poet. . . . [I]t must be admitted that by sending Mr Blunt to gaol [Balfour] has converted a clever rhymer into an earnest and deep-thinking poet. . . . [A]n unjust imprisonment for a noble cause strengthens as well as deepens the nature."[11] But unlike Wilde, Blunt, Urabi, and the rest, Lady Gregory never did get to go to jail: her trope is historically grounded in the gendered customs of the nationalist movement.

Even her younger contemporaries who did serve time in prison, women such as Kathleen Clarke and Maud Gonne MacBride, had also served "without the gate" as cultural workers and publicists for imprisoned men. Their experiences show how threatening the freedom of the unimprisoned woman nationalist could be. When, early in her nationalist career, Maud Gonne was told that the National League did not admit "ladies," she took up the issue with Tim Harrington and his colleague Pat O'Brien. "But there used to be a Ladies' Land League and they did splendid work," Gonne argued.

> "Indeed they did, said Pat O'Brien; "they were great women and kept things lively while we were all in jail."
> "We disbanded the Ladies' Land League when we came out," said Harrington, I thought a little bitterly. "They did too good work, and some of us found they could not be controlled."[12]

When, as Clarke tells it, in 1917 de Valera "destroyed" her campaign for getting back the bodies of the Easter Rising martyrs by insisting that the demand be backed up by "force of arms," Clarke "tackled him the minute he came off the platform." She had hoped to succeed, she told him, "through the force of public opinion, which we women had been able to arouse when you men were in prison."[13]

Gregory's literary career, like the political careers of Anna Parnell and Kathleen Clarke, developed in a space made available by the imprisonment of men: she drew inspiration from the fact and the thought of jailed Fenians. Emerging directly from the symbols and practices of Fenian Ireland and the popular nationalism upon which it drew, Lady Gregory's trope situates her literary aspirations in the most accessible area of Irish culture: her work is pitched to an undifferentiated "people," those 250,000 who allegedly read *The Nation* in its heyday. Although Yeats aspired to be "counted one / With Davis, Mangan, Ferguson," he scorned the lesser lights: "I think it was a Young Ireland Society," he wrote in 1901,

> that set my mind running on "popular poetry." We . . . paid great honour to the Irish poets who wrote in English. . . . I knew in my heart that the most of them wrote badly, and yet such romance clung about them, such a desire for Irish poetry was in all our minds, that I kept on saying . . . that most of them wrote well, or all but well. . . . I thought one day . . . "If these poets, who have never ceased to fill the newspapers and the ballad-books with their verses, had a good tradition they would write beautifully and move everybody as they move me."[14]

Yet it was the poetry of those "newspapers" and "ballad-books" that first inspired Lady Gregory; and whereas Yeats wanted Irish poets to write about "something else . . . besides political opinions," those very opinions constituted the heart of the matter for Lady Gregory.

In "Poetry and Tradition" (1907) and elsewhere, Yeats defined, then praised, an Irish high culture centered on the Big House, European in its library, its statuary, its architecture, and the cultivated idiom of its denizens, and Irish in its close association with folk traditions. This composite culture, as Yeats imagined it, was created and sustained by "three types of people": "aristocracies," "countrymen," and "artists."[15] In "Coole Park and Ballylee, 1931," Yeats celebrated Lady Gregory as the "last inheritor" of this tradition and links her aesthetics with his. Both

> . . . chose for theme
> *Traditional sanctity and loveliness;*
> *Whatever's written in what poets name*
> *The book of the people . . .*[16]

In "The Municipal Gallery Revisited" he resituated that high culture in the museum. Lady Gregory, however, had paid her literary dues to the Big House early in her career, having edited her husband's autobiography and gathered the material for *Mr. Gregory's Letter-Box.*[17] And the country people she recorded and published in *Visions and Beliefs in the West of Ireland* and other volumes.[18] But her interest in popular nationalism embraced the "small shopkeepers" and "clerks" disparaged by Yeats for their "ignorance" and "superstitious piety" and therefore excluded from his "three types." In this context Gregory did not single out for praise or disparaise any social group: she was drawn to the jail gate, whatever the class of male prisoner on the other side.

Automatically, formulaically, Gregory is mentioned as one of an inevitable trio (Yeats, Synge, Gregory) of conservative purveyors of high culture, nostalgic, in the words of the *Field Day Anthology of Irish Writing*, for "a prelapsarian Ireland that knows nothing of the political and sectarian strife of the modern."[19] As another such unexamined comment puts it, "The sieve of their sensitivity retained only the purest gold of the Gaelic past."[20] The prominence of felons and prison literature in Gregory's writings for half a century, from her first published work in 1882 through some of the final entries in her journal before her death in 1932, shows indisputably that the "political . . . strife of the modern" was her chief subject, a militant and not a prelapsarian Ireland. For Lady Gregory the felon was muse and exemplary representative of Ireland.

The First Felons

With her first felons, Lady Gregory established the paradigm that lasted the rest of her life. Arbitrary, unconnected events linked with Wilfrid Blunt and with the rebel Egyptian nationalist Ahmed Urabi formed a configuration that Gregory re-created later, consciously or unconsciously, to affiliate her literary production with oppositional politics. Of course, neither of these first felons was Irish; but the aura of illicit romance and subversive activity that hung over Blunt was colorful and rebellious enough to suit Gregory's imagination, and in 1887–88 Blunt became an honorary Irishman in Galway Gaol. A handsome, wealthy, landed English Catholic gentleman, Blunt was hardly a "man of the people." He had married Byron's granddaughter Lady Anne Noel, and so had acquired by osmosis Byronic credentials: he became a notorious, flamboyant anti-imperialist (or "fighter for freedom," as Lady Gregory preferred to style him), and an equally notorious philanderer. His professional lineage also looked back to Blake and Shelley, with their exaltation of sexual and political "liberty," and forward to Roger Casement and T. E. Lawrence, whose anticolonial politics and sexual transgressions also occurred in exotic corners of empire.[21]

Lady Gregory's first publication, a three thousand–word piece in the London *Times* (1882) on Urabi, was composed under Blunt's auspices.[22] During the preceding year the Blunts and the Gregorys, wintering in Cairo, had become sympathetic to Colonel Urabi's efforts on behalf of the anti-European forces in Egyptian politics. Then, as Lady Gregory put it, "we tumbled into a revolution."[23] A native Egyptian officer, one of many such from "humble social backgrounds, sons of conservative, traditional provincial families," Urabi became minister of war, and for a while, in the shifting alliances among Egyptian, Turkish, British, and French supporters, was perceived as the leader of a popular nationalist movement. But early in the summer of 1882, when the Blunts and the Gregorys had returned home, Urabi and the army forces loyal to him were attacked and defeated by British forces in Alexandria. Urabi surrendered and became a prisoner of the British. Sentiment in England was for turning him over to the Turks to be executed; and back home, in the autumn of that year, Sir William lost interest in the cause. Blunt, however, stirred up public opinion on Urabi's behalf in *The Times*, started a defense fund, and paid for lawyers to go to Egypt to defend Urabi, who was ultimately sent into exile in Ceylon.[24]

Lady Gregory's continuing support for Urabi and the Egyptian nationalist cause became inextricable from her attraction to Blunt. As he recorded, her loyalty

> naturally drew us more closely than ever together, and at the climax of the tragedy by a spontaneous impulse we found comfort in each other's arms. It was a consummation neither of us, I think, foresaw, and was a quite new experience in her quiet life. It harmonised not ill with mine in its new phase of political idealism and did not in any way disturb or displace it. On the contrary to both of us the passionate element in our intercourse at this time proved a source of inspiration and strength.[25]

This "passionate element" lurks behind the piece "Arabi and His Household": there was an aura of Blunt around Arabi, and Lady Gregory's engagé rebel politics hid sexual excitement—hid it well, because there is nothing sexy about the article. It tells the story of two visits to his house: the title is "Arabi and His Household," and much emphasis is put on his mother, his wife, and his children; Urabi's place in a family unit is never forgotten. The family appears to be the Egyptian version of an English family, except that its members are Muslim: "Why should the Christian Powers want to harm my husband?" his wife keeps asking Lady Gregory. Gregory wisely does not tell all she knows, that (as she mentions in her autobiography) this is Urabi's third wife, nor, in her emphasis on the simplicity of the rooms, does she mention a photograph of Urabi framed in diamonds. The narrative trappings of folk tale shape the situation: after his imprisonment, "Arabi's wife has had to find refuge with a high minded princess," his mother is "hidden in a poor quarter of the town," and the family—"simple, honest, hospitable"—is now "poor, hunted, in danger." Lady Gregory publishes her recollections not, of course, to save a felon's life, but "hoping to interest Englishmen in this family."[26]

In positioning herself between the imprisoned rebel and the rest of the world,

Lady Gregory here establishes for the first time the trope in which the felon inspires her literary activity. Her opening sentence—"Report me and my cause aright to the unsatisfied"—invokes the dying Hamlet's request to Horatio and suggests that an enemy of the state may be heroic. Gregory herself was reporting "aright" on the anti-imperialist Urabi, urging nationalist or at least humanitarian sympathies on the Victorian *Times*-reading public. Her gender, she coyly claims, enables her to plead the case. Englishmen have confided to her, "Arabi is a good man, and his aims are honest. I know it and you know it, but we dare not say it. . . . A lady may say what she likes, but a man is called unpatriotic who ventures to say a word that is good of the man England is determined to crush. . . ." Colonial turf wars belong to men; but in the literary arena women are free to "speak what [they] know to be the truth." With these separate spheres established, Gregory can utter a "truth" consisting primarily of homely anecdotes about family meals, women's confidences, and children's cute remarks. The cloying domesticity of the article should not, however, obscure its daring oppositional stance—so daring that Sir William Gregory changed his mind several times before permitting his wife to publish the piece.[27]

Like Urabi, Blunt was not a Fenian, but there was romance enough around him already, the frisson of the adulterous lover; and when he got himself locked up in Galway Gaol, he was in Fenian territory, in a building long associated in Lady Gregory's imagination with the mystery and excitement of Irish rebels.[28] The most important of the poems she wrote, "Without the gate," dramatizes the inspiration of the whole lot: Lady Gregory ardently positioned at the jail gate, longing for the moment of Blunt's release, but in the meantime using the opportunity of his imprisonment to talk about their relative situations, he "within," she "without." The "glory" and "honor" that Gregory imagined around Blunt were also what he was imagining himself: of his transfer to Kilmainham Gaol in Dublin he wrote, "The halo of martyrdom, which in Galway gaol had seemed to surround me, had faded away. . . ."[29] As poet, Lady Gregory served as the conduit of her felon's glory; she announced and disseminated it to the world, moving outwards (in one of the other poems in the group) to include his family and the Irish people:

> Let her who bears your name rejoice
> That it is grown of triple worth
> And let your child lift up her voice
> And thank you for her honoured birth.
>
> Let sons of Erin cry your fame
> And call for blessings on your days
> And in their cities set your name
> And sing your memory in their lays.[30]

The poem did not disseminate that glory very far until its first publication in 1994, but for its author it was good practice in contributing to Fenian cultural nationalism, validating Blunt's place in that tradition in the same grandiose language that Blunt himself would use ("the first recorded instance, in all the four hundred years of English oppression . . .").

The space of Blunt's suffering "within the gate" represented more than a literary

Wilfrid Blunt in prison clothes, 1888.
Courtesy of Fitzwilliam Museum, Cambridge.

trope to Lady Gregory: she fetishized it altogether. After Blunt had been released and the Gregorys were back at Coole, she had herself admitted to the cells he had occupied, sketched them, and sent the sketches to Blunt, who hung them in his bedroom. Happily acquiescing in her fetishism, he sent her a photograph of himself in prison garb and a piece of the oakum he had worked on, which she used as a bookmark in his prison poems and kept all her life. And Blunt left her his prison Bible in his will.[31] Both of them were aware that his jail time made him sexier: she noted in her diary that he was "looking none the worse for his imprisonment."[32] And he wrote: "As to my women friends, my prison adventures, I soon found, had done me no real discredit with them. . . . [T]he episode was a title to romantic interest. . . . Their kindness did me full amends and for the next few years strewed my path with flowers. . . ."[33]

For Blunt the game of playing Fenian offered a distinctive thrill, and fortunately for him the British Empire offered many places around the globe for an anti-imperialist to stage his civil disobedience. Blunt hardly needed Lady Gregory (who, after all, did not publish her poems) to trumpet his fame: the *London Illustrated News* sported a dashing picture of him on its front page of November 5, 1887. But for Lady Gregory the jail gate provided a trope as powerful as any Petrarchan convention for turning sexual feeling and nationalist sympathies into literature. When her muses became genuine Irish felons, nationalist politics were separated from sexual infatuation and moved from Fenian erotics to Fenian piety; but the sense of excitement lingered over them in hidden ways, and all her later felons would be permutations of Blunt.

"Felons of Our Land"

The joy of the writer who has at last found her subject sounds through Lady Gregory's 1900 essay "The Felons of Our Land," which is virtually a manifesto for a demotic cultural nationalism.[34] So demotic is the essay in its articulation of national collective memory, so steeped in nineteenth-century rebel culture, that its closest kin is the national monument erected in the center of Cork, at the end of the Grand Parade. A piece of Victorian Gothic monumental architecture with ecclesiastical niches, unveiled on St. Patrick's Day 1906, the Cork memorial reads:

ERECTED
through the efforts
of the
Cork Young Ireland Society
To Perpetuate the Memory of
The Gallant Men of
1798 1803 48 and 67
Who Fought and Died
In the wars of Ireland
To Recover Her
Sovreign Independence
And to Inspire the Youth of
Our Country to Follow in Their
Patriotic Footsteps and
Imitate Their Heroic Example
And Righteous Men Will Make Our Land
A Nation Once Again.

(The same inscription is carved in Irish on the stone in the adjacent niche.) An architectural martyrology, the monument on different sides lists the years of the failed risings and the names of men who fought in each. In the center a pensive free-standing Hibernia, leaning on a Celtic cross, is flanked by statues of Wolfe Tone and Thomas Davis (born in Mallow, County Cork, and hence a local hero), O'Neill Crowley (a Cork Fenian who died in '67), and the United Irishman Michael Dwyer. Linking 1798, 1803, 1848, and 1867, the monument, only ten years before the Easter Rising, embodied and kept alive a popular nationalist ideology.

Like the monument, Gregory's essay systematizes and consolidates the traditions of rebel culture, with particular emphasis on the names of the "felons," or political prisoners. "Irish history," she argues, "having been forbidden in the national schools," has "lifted up its voice in the streets"; forbidden by the state, it has found its way into folklore, the oppositional tradition of rebel poems and ballads.[35] Deliberately choosing popular verses with only slight apology, Gregory quotes at length because "in spite of the stilted words of one who has learned a style from newspapers and from mob oratory, there is something touching in the conscientious attention to detail where it concerns those whose names might be slipping out of memory." The poem so justified is a rhyming version of the 1803 panel of the Cork monument:

> September, eighteen-three,
> Closed this cruel history,
> When Emmet's blood the scaffold flowed upon—
> Oh, had their spirits been wise,
> They might then realise
> Their freedom—but we drink to Mitchel that is gone, boys, gone,
> Here's the memory of the friends that are gone![36]

Another poem frames its history as a mnemonic exercise in rebel genealogy:

> Now to begin to name them, I'll continue in a direct line,
> There's John Mitchel, Thomas Francis Maher, and also William Smith O'Brien,
> John Martin and O'Donoghue, Erin sorely feels their loss,
> For to complete their number I will include O'Donovan Ross.[37]

"There is a redeeming intensity and continuity of purpose through even such doggerel verses as these," writes Lady Gregory; "they are not without dignity if looked on as roughly hammered links in an unequally wrought chain."[38] As unofficial publicist for the Fenian tradition, Gregory articulates a demotic aesthetic. The "chain" is a leveling metaphor common in popular political movements, like the linked arms of protesters singing "We Shall Overcome." Transferring terms of praise from political activism to poetry, Gregory voices approbation of "intensity," "continuity of purpose," and "dignity": what makes a good Fenian makes a good poem. All those lists of proper names constitute links in the chain, embodying each poet's and each rebel's consciousness of a collective identity. (Gregory so loved these lists of names that when "Easter 1916," another historical-mnemonic verse ["MacDonagh and MacBride, / And Connolly and Pearse"] was published, Blunt thought that Lady Gregory had written it and allowed Yeats to publish it under his name.)

Yeats "knew in his heart that the most of them wrote badly." Like Auden in 1939 writing that Time pardons Yeats "for writing well," in spite of political opinions Auden didn't share, Yeats uneasily pits "aesthetic" qualities against "political opinions" and yet pardons the Young Irelanders because "such a desire for Irish poetry was in all our minds." Neither Shelley nor Spenser, Yeats confesses, "ever moved me as did these poets."[39] But Gregory looks at the songs and poems she cites from a different angle: she might have used the phrase "resistance literature" had it existed in 1900. The verses are, quite simply, the way Irish history "lift[s] up its voice"; this "doggerel" is the voice of the people. The chain may indeed be "unequally wrought," some links "roughly hammered," but it is a tradition of resistance, not a luxury item. Distinctions of class and mode such as Yeats repeatedly made do not obtain in demotic writing, which Lady Gregory's essay turns into a kind of folklore. Her valorization of Fenian writings and customs emphasizes that they constitute an indigenous popular culture as worthy of preservation and study as the rural "folk" culture admired and anthologized by Yeats. Gregory's justification of both cultures is the same, namely, that they record what has been denied official status, "forbidden in the schools," as she says in "The Felons of Our Land," or "shut out of the schools," as she writes in the *Kiltartan History Book*.[40] The best folklorist of the revivalists, Gregory was not a snob about printed, "middle-class" sources; for her the verses of the "newspapers and ballad books" form another kind of "Book of the People."

In "The Felons of Our Land" Gregory mixes together all sorts and degrees of writing: John Keegan Casey's ballad "Rising of the Moon," Thomas Davis's "Lament for Owen Roe," Yeats's early poem on Parnell, and the doggerel quoted earlier. Felons, like patriotic poems, come in all classes too, and Gregory notes the difference between the more educated and sophisticated United Irishmen (Lord Edward Fitzgerald, Wolfe Tone, Robert Emmet) and the Manchester Martyrs: "They were all men of good character, working for their bread. O'Brien was the son of an evicted farmer; Larkin, the grandson of a farmer flogged and transported in '98; Allen, for whose fate most pity was felt, had been brought up a carpenter, was only 19, and was soon to have been married." Gregory points out approvingly their significance for Fenian culture: "Their fate gave the touch of pathos that had been wanting to the Fenian movement."[41] In the enthusiastic spirit of the thousands who attended the mock funerals all over Ireland for the Manchester Martyrs, Gregory lists the many songs written in their honor, inspired by their famous, simultaneous cry from the dock, "God save Ireland!"

Because "The Felons of Our Land" was published in the English *Cornhill Magazine*, it could be understood as a repeat of "Arabi and His Household": virtually "without the gate" of all the felons in Irish tradition, Gregory wrote sympathetically about them to the English audience against whose government they were rebelling. In fact here Lady Gregory has grafted the middle-class Egyptian Urabi and the upper-class English Blunt to the popular traditions of nineteenth-century Irish nationalist culture. Blunt lurks here as usual, and his secret presence suggests one reason, at least, for Gregory's joy and excitement at the thought of felons. Blunt is hidden in a quotation: asserting that the ballads "written by the felons themselves . . . stand outside criticism," she writes,

As some old lines say;—

> And he was also in the war,
>   He who this rhyme did write;
> Till evening fought he with the sword,
>   And sang the song at night.[42]

But the lines were not old at all, or anonymous; they had recently been inscribed by Blunt in her copy of his subversive anticolonial poem *The Wind and the Whirlwind*.[43] Who but Blunt, with his anti-imperialist theatricality, would have described himself as fighting "with the sword"?

That sly secret allusion to Blunt marks the final touch of eroticism in Lady Gregory's felons, otherwise in "The Felons of Our Land" so notably unsexual. Her Irish felons are all de-eroticized: two of her early plays trace the process of the felon's separation from erotic ties, as a keening woman presides over his passage from the family unit to collective memory. Seen from this point of view, *Kathleen ni Houlihan* (written in autumn 1901) dramatizes the man's choice to become a "felon," loosely defined. Kathleen—here taking the woman's role in Gregory's trope—gets her poetry from dead felons:

> *I will go cry with the woman,*
> *For yellow-haired Donough is dead,*
> *With a hempen rope for a neckcloth,*
> *And a white cloth on his head . . .*[44]

As others have noted, the source of these lines is "Fair-haired Donagh," a sister's keen for her brother, "hanged in Galway" for an unspecified political crime.[45] Elsewhere, "Donncha bán" is identified with Mayo, but the Galway connection in the version Gregory collected links him with Blunt.[46]

Entranced by such songs and by Kathleen's mysterious power, the elder son of the house, Michael Gillane, forgets his fiancée and his parents and follows Kathleen to fight in the 1798 Rising. The choice is an explicit rejection of the erotic. Kathleen has made her position clear: "With all the lovers that brought me their love I never set out the bed for any." But through her songs he is assured, like yellow-haired Donagh, a place in popular memory:

> *They shall be remembered for ever,*
> *They shall be alive for ever,*
> *They shall be speaking for ever,*
> *The people shall hear them for ever.*[47]

A conduit for men's names, like all the women who sing of patriots "without the gate," Kathleen has renewed her poetry, if not her four green fields, and will soon add Michael Gillane's to her store of names.

In *Gaol Gate*—first performed in 1906, the same year the Cork monument was unveiled—the keening woman discovers her opportunity to make and determine popular memory. The play can be seen as a reconfiguration of *Kathleen ni Houlihan*, but with the women dominant. Gregory's shaping of the plot is significant; the felon's offstage action determines the outcome of the play, but he has no role in it. He has been hanged before the story starts, and all the action takes place "outside the gate of Galway Gaol." The hints of Blunt remain—the play is a dramatized version of her 1882 poem "Without the gate"—but in entirely de-eroticized form. Two women, both named Mary, have come to the jail where their son and husband, Denis Cahel, has been imprisoned: they have received a letter about him, but they cannot read it. Before the gatekeeper talks to them, they believe the rumor they have heard: that Denis informed on his friends involved in "moonlighting," or nocturnal agrarian violence. Much drama focuses on the *gate*. The mother says, "I'm in dread of it being opened," and when it is, they hear "the rattling of keys." The gatekeeper reads the letter and says, "You poor unfortunate women, don't you know Denis Cahel is dead? . . . Dead since the dawn of yesterday, and another man now in his cell."[48]

At this point, still believing in Denis's betrayal of his friends, the women consider Denis a failure as family man and as nationalist. When the gatekeeper goes off to get Denis's clothes, the mother breaks into a distraught keen: "But my boy that was best in the world . . . to have died with his name under blemish. . . . Better for him have killed the whole world than to give any witness at all!" Soon the wife, Mary Cushin, begins a keen of her own:

> *What way will I be going back through Gort and through Kilbecanty?*
> *The people will not be coming out keening you, they will say*
> *no prayer for the rest of your soul! . . .*
> *I would not begrudge you, Denis, and you leaving praises after you.*
> *The neighbours keening along with me would be better to me*
> *than an estate.*
> *But my grief your name to be blackened in the time of the*
> *blackening of the rushes!*[49]

When, however, they learn from the gatekeeper that Denis did not die of natural causes in his cell, but that he was hanged and was not an informer, they are overjoyed. It is to the *mother* that Lady Gregory gives the joyful utterances that end the play:

> *Are there any people in the streets at all till I call on them*
> *to come hither? Did they ever hear in Galway such a thing to*
> *be done, a man to die for his neighbour?*
> *Tell it out in the streets for the people to hear, Denis Cahel from*
> *Slieve Echtge is dead. It was not a little thing for him to*
> *die, and he protecting his neighbour! . . .*
> *I will go through Gort and Kilbecanty and Druimdarod and Daroda; I*
> *will call to the people and the singers at the fairs to make a*
> *great praise for Denis!*[50]

Denis's political death is his mother's artistic opportunity. After the gatekeeper says, "The judge got no evidence and the law set them free," according to the words of the stage direction, "He goes in and shuts gate after him." Then, standing once more at the shut gate ("without the gate"), Mary Cahel bursts into a full page of praise for her son, rejoicing that "[t]he child he left in the house that is shook, it is great will be his boast in his father!" This moment is reminiscent of the lines from Gregory's 1882 poem for Blunt: "Let her who bears your name rejoice / That it is grown of triple worth / And let your child lift up her voice / And thank you for her honoured birth." In fact, the mother here takes the place of the (absent) adulterous lover, Lady Gregory, in the original *Gaol Gate* configuration, because it is she who bursts into song and asserts the value of his name, just as Gregory had spoken for Urabi on behalf of his wife and mother. Mary Cushin, the wife, has no more role to play, because it is the mother who will assure Denis's place in the people's memory; like Michael Gillane's, his passage is marked by an old woman's keen. Lady Gregory's trope releases erotic feeling that will never be fulfilled erotically, feeling that is displaced and transmuted at once into literary or artistic effusions. In *Gaol Gate*, connubial intimacy concedes pride of place to the maternal, and maternal intimacy to popular memory: "I will call to the people and the singers at the fairs to make great praise for Denis!"

The Rising of the Moon, written in 1904, shows what happens when the felon is not locked up. This play has only male characters, and the felon escapes, so there is no impassable jail gate, and no opportunity for keening. The relative weakness of women in a world where felons get out of jail is shown by the one song among many through which the rebel persuades the police sergeant to let him escape. It is an *aisling*, or vision poem, about Granuaile, the poetic name of the pirate Grace O'Malley, another female personification of Ireland. The male bonding occurs over the image of the enchained woman.

> Her head was bare, her hands and feet with iron bands were bound,
> Her pensive strain and plaintive wail mingles with the evening gale,
> And the song she sang with mournful air, I am old Granuaile.[51]

For there is a whole other tradition of *women* bound, of the passive, weak, sad female Irelands whom male poets traditionally invoke. The rebel tries out many patriotic songs, but it is the one about the *bound woman* that gets him his freedom.

Soft Fenianism

"After all, what is wanted but a hag and a voice?" So Lady Gregory, in 1919, wrote herself into the title role of her most famous play, performing as Kathleen ni Houlihan in the Abbey on Saint Patrick's Day.[52] But to be a hag at that time in Ireland was not necessarily a negligible role. The Rising, the Great War, and the Irish War of Independence (1919–21)—and later the Civil War (1922–23)—left many women to mourn dead men: the death of Major Robert Gregory in Italy in January 1918 made Lady Gregory the mourning mother of contemporary iconography. The ubiquitous Pietà, with its configuration of mother and son, was, as Belinda Loftus sees it, a transformation of Kathleen ni Houlihan and her dead Volunteer: "[I]n its commemorative images Ireland was the Virgin mourning her dead or a female variation on the risen, Transfigured or ascending Christ. . . . Such religious poses were familiar from illustrations to Irish Catholic devotional booklets. . . . They were images appropriate for a sacrificial rebellion which took place at Easter." Loftus judges them suited to "the anti-feminist mood of the period," and Gregory, by most accounts, should have had a bad time of it then: she was Protestant, female, and old.[53] Edna Longley has written about the "marginalisation" of Protestant writers after the treaty, and about the opposed sectarian ideologies determining official memory of the Rising and of the First World War.[54] Quoting Pearse's poem "The Mother," Elizabeth Cullingford argues that in Republican ideology "women are venerated only to be marginalised as producers of sons for slaughter."[55] Most notorious of all, Yeats, in a 1924 essay on his visit to Sweden to receive the Nobel Prize, referred to Lady Gregory, still extraordinarily active, able, and fit, as "an old woman sinking into the infirmities of age." As she indignantly wrote in her journal, "Not even fighting against them!"[56]

Contrary to all these assumptions, Lady Gregory enjoyed Ireland in the 1920s—the Free State was, after all, being run by former felons. As she cheerfully wrote in her journal in 1929, "I like official Dublin, everyone in office seems to have gone through fights or imprisonments for country's sake."[57] Her felon trope proved easily adaptable; it already offered a role for old ladies in mourning, for a hag and a voice. In "The Mother" Pearse had "appropriated the maternal voice": Cullingford imagines that a "real" mother might not happily sacrifice her son "in bloody protest for a glorious thing" but might say, with Bridget Gillane of *Kathleen ni Houlihan*, "Tell him not to go."[58] Lady Gregory's literary Fenianism, however, draws on the same traditions and ideology as Pearse's did, and in the 1920s she had the opportunity Pearse never had to grow sentimental and reminiscent. No longer transgressive or oppositional, the trope of the felon softens into an uncritical reverence for dead male heroes. In the trope's final manifestation, Lady Gregory identifies with the woman whose songs have created for the hero his place in popular memory and made him "remembered forever."

In "The Old Woman Remembers" (1923) and *The Story Brought by Brigit* (1924), the male heroes derive importance from the storytelling woman's narrative: the increase in her age has only made her control over popular memory stronger. "The Old Woman Remembers" is *Kathleen ni Houlihan* without any expressions of ambivalence about martyrdom, *Gaol Gate* without the sharp, passionate, changeable emotion of Mary Cahel. It is Young Ireland poetry written by Old Ireland. Gregory herself called it "doggerel," though one might give her the benefit of the doubt, according to her own demotic aesthetic, and call it "touching" for its "conscientious attention to detail." A more pious Gaelic piece of 1923 doggerel would be hard to imagine: "This is our rosary of praise / For some whose names are sung or said / Through seven hundred years of days / The silver beads upon the thread. . . ." According to its stage direction, "An old woman is sitting in an almost dark room. She has placed seven candlesticks on the table. At the end of the first verse she lights a candle and puts it in a candlestick. . . ."[59] The martyrology, the iteration of phrases like "my grief," and candles and rosaries create the demotic flavor of the poem; it is entirely topical, extending the roll call of martyrs from 1185 to the present moment. Yoking together, at the end, the names of Michael Collins (d. August 1922) and Cathal Brugha (d. June 1922), who fought on pro- and anti-Treaty sides in the Civil War, praying that "bitter battle-angers cease," the Old Woman shows herself of a mind with the official state iconographers who placed paintings of Collins and Brugha in the lobby of the Dáil.

Lady Gregory had another personal reason to think about the end of biological motherhood, because in early June 1923 she was operated on for breast cancer and had a single mastectomy. Within three weeks, on June 22, she wrote in her journal, "My mind is turning again towards a Passion Play"; by July 16 she was writing "a rough dialogue scenario," and by August 27 she was typing *The Story Brought By Brigit*.[60] The very formulation of the title shows the versatility of Gregory's trope; this is, in fact, a "passion play," and its subject is the Crucifixion; but the frame story is Brigit's presence at that site. To one of the chorus of women she announces at the start, "It was in a dream or a vision of the night I saw a Young Man having wounds on him. And I knew him to be One I had helped and had fostered, and he a Child in his mother's arms." Christ, of course, has become an Irish felon, his followers "rebels," and his transgressions political: "Raising riots he is! Pulling down the country!" Had Padraic Pearse lived to 1923, might he not have written this drama of a Gaelicized Crucifixion? Not quite, because its emphasis throughout falls as much on literary production as on religious salvation. Christ immediately becomes an inspiration for Brigit's narrative activity: "If I see him you are speaking of, and that he is the same I fostered, it is a great story I will have to bring back to the West."[61] Lady Gregory drew on many Irish traditions about Brigit, ones she had collected and published in A Book of Saints and Wonders (1906). Saint Brigit was said to have been Mary's midwife and the foster mother of Christ; and she is associated with butter, milk, beer, feeding, and poetry. A statue in Brittany represents Brigit breast-feeding; and the first keen was said to have been sung by Mary over Christ. Irish legend and oral tradition link Brigit with Mary in many ways, calling her "the Mary of the Gael."

Gregory extended the tradition that imputed literary powers to Saint Brigit. As she wrote in notes for the first production of the play at the Abbey, "[I]t is not going very far from tradition to suppose she may have been present at the end of His life as at the beginning, and have told the story in her own way, as she had seen it in the body or in vision." Pearse is unlikely to have seen the Crucifixion as a literary opportunity for Brigit. "Without the gate," she can assure the dead but redemptive felon of his place in the people's memory. Mourning her son and recovering from her mastectomy, Gregory has split herself between Mary with her attendant keening women and Brigit with her exhilaration at the power of narrative, her "great story." One of the women sings the traditional song, "The first great joy that Mary had, it was the joy of one, / To see her own son Jesus to suck at her breastbone," and others keen in lines that must have been meant for Robert: "Her darling to be taken from her that is comely without and within. And he young, that I thought his keeners would not yet be born." But Brigit, like Kathleen ni Houlihan, goes beyond the keen to the social power of the one who tells the story: "[A] great story and a great praise I will bring with me."[62] Stationed at the Crucifixion, the site of the felon's suffering, Brigit, like the Old Woman of the 1923 poem, transforms a dead son into literature.

When a felon's not engaged in his employment but has become part of "official Dublin," what is there for the hag to do? She can always market his prison memoirs. In the last few of her active years, Lady Gregory "adopted" two former felons, Seamus Murphy and Frank Gallagher, who were about the right age to be her sons. Through them she reenacted aspects of her affair with Blunt, though of course in a chaste maternal mode. Not maternally intimate but solicitous for their manuscripts, Gregory hovered like a literary agent over their memoirs. Seamus Murphy, one of the Dublin city commissioners, supported Gregory's efforts to retrieve for Ireland her nephew Hugh Lane's collection of Impressionist paintings, left in an ambiguous will to the National Galleries of both London and Dublin. Once after a meeting Murphy began telling stories of 1916, and Lady Gregory recorded an episode:

> The first gaol was very bad, not even bedding given them—he had to roll up his coat for a pillow. No books. Later he was moved to a better one. He had been in Galway in the later fighting—had been in Claregalway one day when a military lorry suddenly came down the road and he and his comrades had just time to scramble over a high wall and hide among some trees. A little girl had come by after a while and they had ventured to speak to her and ask where they were. And a little later she came back with a basket of food.[63]

When Lady Gregory "urged him to write down his memories," he said he was too busy. The next day, Gregory writes, "I tried to find a pleasant looking blank book to send to Commissioner Murphy, but could but get a plain black one, so took some gold paint and smudged on the cover 'A Claregalway Wall,' gilded stones showing the light through, put it up, and have sent it to him hoping he may continue or begin to write his memories."[64] Murphy's stories had all her favorite elements: jail experiences, a Galway episode, a wall, a helpful little girl. The wall she painted on the notebook re-created the situation of "within" and "without."

But the journalist Frank Gallagher became the final permutation of Blunt.[65] At one point during the late 1920s he was de Valera's aide, and Gregory met him during her appointments with Dev about the Lane paintings. In their first conversation, in May 1928, he told her he was going to publish a book with John Murray. Gregory was amused, she says, because Murray had published her book on Hugh Lane, and she had had to censor some of the more nationalist passages in deference to his feelings. Murray had said of her, "I'm afraid Lady Gregory is a rebel." And, she wrote of Murray, "now he is ready to publish a *real rebel's* book!"[66] That schoolgirlish phrase places Gallagher in the romantic Fenian tradition that Augusta Persse had spent her childish pennies on. When *Days of Fear*, Gallagher's diary of his 1920 hunger strike in Mountjoy Prison, came out in the summer of 1928, Lady Gregory clipped every review to send him and seems constantly to have been sending copies of the book to other people and then copies of their letters about the book to Gallagher.

Moved as usual to literary action by intimacy with a felon, Lady Gregory herself wrote *two* reviews of the book, and in *both* of them she reenacts the structure of her main prison poem about Blunt. She looked up in her journals her own record of response to the very hunger strike his book describes, and in both reviews flips back and forth between "inside the gaol" (his book) and "outside the gaol" (her journals). She alludes to Byron in the opening of the *Athenaeum* review, another sure sign of Blunt's presence; and in the *New Republic* she quotes at the end her own play *Gaol Gate*: "I think of my old woman in 'The Gaol Gate'—'It is not a little thing for a man to die, and he protecting his neighbor!'" [67] In her journal she wrote that it "will be one of the great books of the world. Sometimes I think this an exaggerated estimate but when I read a page or two . . . I believe it again."[68]

Gregory reread *Days of Fear* regularly and added it to her private anthology of prison literature. On one occasion in 1929 a rereading prompted her to take down from her shelf Blunt's prison poems, *In Vinculis*, still with his letter thanking her for reading the proofs, and with the "wisp of oakum" stuck in. "I have known other prisoners," she wrote in her journal, and quotes the inscription of her photograph of Urabi: "This is my portrait in the days of my imprisonment and my distress and on it I have written with my own hand—I offer it to the gentle and noble Lady Gregory to remind her of what has befallen me."[69]

When Gregory revised Yeats's antidemotic aesthetics in "The Felons of Our Land," she was staking a claim for the "popular," even when contaminated by printer's ink, as a form of folklore rather than a vulgarization of it. The spuriousness of Yeats's position is nowhere more evident than in the very essay where he attempts to distinguish "folk" from "popular" writing ("What Is 'Popular Poetry'?"). Disparaging the quality of most Young Ireland poetry, he then cites as an example of the superior "poetry of the people" not a "poem of the people" but Lady Gregory's own English *translation* of an Irish song, "The Grief of a Girl's Heart." Under such circumstances distinctions of authenticity lose their force; Lady Gregory's emphasis on the suppressed native histories in Irish culture, on the "unofficial" stories omitted in schools and government records, accommodates both the folk and the demotic, tales told in cottages and doggerel printed in newspapers, the voice of the rural poor and that of the urban middle class—and even, in one special instance, the voice of a rich English "freedom-fighter."

A revisionist in other arenas besides the aesthetic, Lady Gregory was an active worker in a resistance culture whose traditions she quietly—perhaps too quietly—revised. Seemingly as respectful of Fenian customs as she was of landlords, Gregory created a trope that resisted the patriarchal customs of the resistance movement as well as the political system of its enemy. Her trope remained a private ritual with a private code of significance; she was never so provocative nor so mischievous as Wilde, reviewing Blunt's prison sonnets and suggesting that "literature" is "indebted" to the colonial oppressors for improving the quality of the prisoner's writing.[70] But Gregory's felon trope constitutes a protofeminist revision of literary Fenianism, reveling in the man's imprisonment for the professional opportunity it offers the woman.

In resisting so much so subtly, Gregory may be vulnerable to attacks by many contemporary critics: post-Nationalists will disapprove her apparently uncritical acceptance of Fenian ideology, and feminists may dislike her enthusiasm for catalogues of male heroes and her strictly gendered assignment of political roles. Antirevisionists will no doubt insist that she was only a "Big House" Fenian. But out of her adolescent "romantic sympathies" for rebels and ballads, out of the adulterous attractions and anti-imperialist involvements of her youth, out of her bereavements, her cancer, and all her literary and nationalist work emerged a more comprehensive and compassionate vision of Irish culture than most of her contemporaries were able to imagine.

Notes

I would like to thank Adrian Frazier for his generous help with revisions of this essay; Nicholas Grene for inviting me to give a lecture at the Synge Summer School, Wicklow, in 1994, from which the present essay developed; and Angela Bourke, John Buckley, Elizabeth Butler Cullingford, Grace Neville, and Patrick Sheeran for odd bits of demotic information.

1. Elizabeth Longford, *A Pilgrimage of Passion: The Life of Wilfrid Scawen Blunt* (London: Weidenfeld and Nicholson, 1979), pp. 251–52. That "first recorded instance" occurred the night of October 23, 1887, when Blunt was detained in Loughrea. Blunt's imprisonment in Galway Gaol began January 8, 1888; he was moved to Kilmainham on February 8 and released March 6. For more details, see James Mitchell, "The Imprisonment of Wilfrid Scawen Blunt in Galway: Cause and Consequence," *Journal of the Galway Archaeological and Historical Society* 46 (1994): 65–110.

2. Mitchell, "Imprisonment of Wilfrid Scawen Blunt," pp. 91–92. All the surviving poems written by Lady Gregory to Blunt during his imprisonment are printed in Mitchell's arti-

cle. They were found among Blunt's papers at the Fitzwilliam Museum, Cambridge, in 1972, when the papers were opened. According to Mitchell, above the title of the poem "Without and Within" Blunt wrote: "written to me while in prison by Lady Gregory 1888" (p. 91).

3. Mary Helen Thuente, The Harp Re-strung: The United Irishmen and the Rise of Irish Literary Nationalism (Syracuse, N.Y.: Syracuse University Press, 1994), pp. 228–29, 237–46.

4. D. J. Hickey and J. E. Doherty, A Dictionary of Irish History, 1800–1980 (Dublin: Gill and Macmillan, 1987), p. 383.

5. Lady Gregory, Seventy Years (New York: Macmillan, 1976), pp. 13–15.

6. Thuente, The Harp Re-strung, pp. 243–45.

7. Philadelphia Public Ledger, January 18, 1912.

8. Lady Gregory, The Journals, vol. 2, bks. 30–44 (New York: Oxford University Press, 1987), pp. 361–63; see also pp. 531–32.

9. Ibid., 2:327.

10. J. Leventhal, "Denis Florence MacCarthy," Thomas Davis and Young Ireland, M. J. MacManus, ed. (Dublin: Stationery Office, 1945), 106.

11. Oscar Wilde, "Poetry and Prison: Mr Wilfrid Blunt's 'In Vinculis,'" Pall Mall Gazette, January 3, 1889, p. 3.

12. Maud Gonne MacBride, A Servant of the Queen (Woodbridge, Suffolk: Boydell Press, 1983), p. 96.

13. Kathleen Clarke, Revolutionary Woman (Dublin: O'Brien Press, 1991), pp. 145–46.

14. W. B. Yeats, "What Is 'Popular Poetry'?," in Essays and Introductions (New York: Macmillan, 1961), p. 3.

15. W. B. Yeats, "Poetry and Tradition," in Essays and Introductions, p. 251.

16. W. B. Yeats, The Variorum Edition of the Poems, ed. Peter Allt and Russell K. Alspach (New York: Macmillan, 1957), pp. 491–92.

17. Lady Gregory, ed., Sir William Gregory, An Autobiography (London: John Murray, 1894), and Mr. Gregory's Letter-Box: 1813–1835 (London: Smith Elder & Co., 1898).

18. Lady Gregory's books of folklore include Poets and Dreams (1903), A Book of Saints and Wonders (1906), The Kiltartan History Book (1909), The Kiltartan Poetry Book (1919), and Visions and Beliefs in the West of Ireland (1920).

19. Terence Brown, "Cultural Nationalism, 1880–1930," in The Field Day Anthology of Irish Writing, vol. 2, ed. Seamus Deane et al. (Derry: Field Day Publications, 1991), p. 518.

20. Maurice Goldring, Pleasant the Scholar's Life (London: Serif, 1993), p. 66.

21. The lineage Byron–Blunt–Casement–T. E. Lawrence was deliberately cultivated by the three later men. Both Casement and Lawrence visited Blunt, and Lawrence at one point considered writing a biography of Casement. One of Casement's last messages from Pentonville Prison before his execution was to Blunt. See Longford, A Pilgrimage of Passion, pp. 399, 418, for the visits to Blunt; and Janet Dunbar, Mrs. G.B.S.: A Portrait (New York: Harper and Row, 1963), p. 257, for Lawrence's interest in Casement. The ultimate ancestor of this particular lineage is Milton's Satan, whose influence is acknowledged in Blunt's poem "Satan Absolved." Evan Radcliffe kindly discussed this point with me.

22. Lady Gregory, "Arabi and His Household," The Times, October 23, 1882, p. 4. Blunt, Lady Gregory, and most English people at the time spelled the name Arabi. It is currently being spelled Urabi. See, for instance, Juan R. I. Cole, Colonialism and Revolution in the Middle East: Social and Cultural Origins of Egypt's Urabi Movement (Princeton, N.J.: Princeton University Press, 1993).

23. Lady Gregory, Seventy Years, p. 34.

24. P. J. Vatikiotis, The History of Egypt, 3rd. ed. (Baltimore: John Hopkins University Press, 1985), p. 158. For Blunt and Urabi see Longford, A Pilgrimage of Passion, pp. 167ff.

25. Ibid., p. 191.

26. Lady Gregory, "Arabi and His Household."

27. Ibid. Lady Gregory began writing the piece on Urabi in July 1882. Sir William Gregory first saw no objection to publication; then, once Urabi had surrendered to British forces, would not allow publication; and finally, when the danger of execution seemed imminent, allowed Lady Gregory to publish the article. I am grateful to Maureen Lees for letting me see her transcriptions of the holograph letters from Lady Gregory to Blunt during this period. The letters are in the Berg Collection.

28. See Lady Gregory's comments on her play *The Gaol Gate*, in *Collected Plays: The Tragedies and Tragic Comedies*, ed. Ann Saddlemyer (Gerrards Cross: Colin Smythe, 1971), pp. 281–82, and *Collected Plays: The Comedies*, ed. Ann Saddlemyer (Gerrards Cross: Colin Smythe, 1971), pp. 261–62.

29. W. S. Blunt, *The Land War in Ireland* (1912), cited in Mitchell, "Imprisonment of Blunt," p. 104.

30. Mitchell, "Imprisonment of Blunt," p. 92.

31. For Blunt's gift of the Bible, see Mitchell, "Imprisonment of Blunt," p. 102, and for the sketches of the cell see p. 98. For her use of the oakum as a bookmark, see Gregory, *The Journals*, 2:362.

32. Mary Lou Kohfeldt, *Lady Gregory: The Woman Behind the Irish Renaissance* (New York: Atheneum, 1985), p. 83.

33. Mitchell, "Imprisonment of Blunt," p. 100.

34. Lady Gregory, "The Felons of Our Land," *Cornhill Magazine* (May 1900): 622–34.

35. Ibid., p. 624.

36. Ibid., p. 626.

37. Ibid., p. 631.

38. Ibid.

39. Yeats, "What Is 'Popular Poetry'?," p. 3.

40. Lady Gregory, *The Kiltartan Books, Comprising the Kiltartan Poetry History and Wonder Books* (Gerrards Cross: Colin Smythe, 1971), p. 149.

41. Lady Gregory, "The Felons of Our Land," p. 630.

42. Ibid., p. 632.

43. This discovery was made by James Pethica; see his "Dialogue of Self and Service: Lady Gregory's Emergence as an Irish Writer and Partnership with W. B. Yeats" (Ph.D. diss., Oxford University, 1987), p. 106.

44. Lady Gregory, *Selected Writings*, ed. Lucy McDiarmid and Maureen Waters (Harmondsworth: Penguin, 1995), p. 306.

45. Richard Finneran, *Editing Yeats's Poems* (New York: St. Martins' Press, 1983), p. 130. For the connection between the manuscript of the play and the translation of the lament, see James Pethica, "'Our Kathleen': Yeats's Collaboration with Lady Gregory in the Writing of *Cathleen ni Houlihan*," *Yeats Annual*, vol. 6, ed. Warwick Gould (London: Macmillan, 1988), p. 13.

46. For the association with Mayo, see Seán Ó Tuama and Thomas Kinsella, *An Duanaire, 1600–1900: Poems of the Dispossessed* (Portlaoise: 1981), p. 337.

47. Lady Gregory, *Selected Writings*, p. 309.

48. Lady Gregory, *Gaol Gate*, p. 8.

49. Ibid., pp. 8–9.

50. Ibid., p. 10.

51. Lady Gregory, *The Rising of the Moon*, in *Selected Plays: The Comedies*, p. 64.

52. Lady Gregory, *The Journals*, 1:54–59.

53. Belinda Loftus, *Mirrors: William III and Mother Ireland* (Dundrum: Picture Press, 1990), p. 64.

54. Edna Longley, *The Living Stream* (Newcastle upon Tyne: Bloodaxe Books, 1994), pp. 69–85, 130.

55. Elizabeth Butler Cullingford, *Gender and History in Yeats's Love Poetry* (Cambridge: Cambridge University Press, 1993), p. 69.

56. Lady Gregory, *The Journals*, 1:514.

57. Ibid., 2:438.

58. Cullingford *Gender and History*, p. 69.

59. Lady Gregory, "The Old Woman Remembers," in Saddlemyer, ed., *Collected Plays: Tragedies and Tragic Comedies*, p. 357.

60. Lady Gregory, *The Journals*, 1:467, 469, 473.

61. Lady Gregory, *The Story Brought by Brigit*, in Saddlemyer, ed., *Collected Plays: Wonder and Supernatural Plays*, pp. 306, 327.

62. Ibid., pp.

63. Lady Gregory, *The Journals*, 2:403.

64. Ibid., 2:405.

65. Frank Gallagher later became the first editor of the *Irish Press*.

66. Lady Gregory, *The Journals*, 2:260–61.

67. Reviews of *Days of Fear*, by Frank Gallagher, *The Nation & Athenaeum*, December 15, 1928, pp. 422, 424; also *New Republic*, March 20, 1929, pp. 141–43. See Appendix for text of the earlier review.

68. Lady Gregory, *The Journals*,

69. Ibid., 2:362–63.

70. See note 11 above.

Appendix
Lady Gregory's Review of *Days of Fear*

The Nation and Athenaeum, December 15, 1928,
pp. 422 and 424

Days of Fear, by Frank Gallagher

When I was told by whom this journal was being published, I said, "Murray!—John Murray—Sir John—Why, he suspects even me. . . ." But then remembering that his having been the house that sponsored Byron, who died in the fight for a nation's freedom, I felt it fitting it should make known this record of brave men, who went for the same cause into the very Valley of the Shadow of Death. A beautiful, heart-rending book.

The publisher's note on the cover says—"It is a record of spiritual strength, of reckless suffering, and of frank cowardice. The honest, candid, and truthful sensations of a mind under the sustained physical suffering of a Hunger Strike in Mountjoy Jail, Dublin, in 1920. The prisoners had pledged themselves 'to the honour of Ireland and the lives of our comrades not to eat food nor drink anything except water until all have been given prisoner-of-war treatment or are released.'" And Field-Marshal Lord French, Lord Lieutenant of Ireland, had pledged himself to no concessions.

Frank Gallagher gives the diary day after day: Easter Monday, April 5th, to Thursday, April 15th.

On that first day:—

"[T]here is a queer happiness in me. If it were not so quiet in the cell and in the whole jail I would sing and call out in sheer gaiety of spirit. The fight is on, the fight that can have but one ending—triumph and freedom, something done for liberty and the rights of all men. The porridge tasted sweet this morning. Perhaps it knew its mission, that it will have to keep me alive until we have won. 'This is the last time you will be washed by me,' I said to the enamel plate, though dear knows there was not much need to wash it at all. 'This is the last time,' I said to the bare, translucent spoon, as I licked the last flick of creaminess from it. And later. 'We trooped back to our cells joking, jubilant, and each to himself—a little uneasy.'"

But on the next day:—

"[T]o-night my head aches. The hardest thing of all to bear is that there are no meal hours. Jail life hinges on the three meals, and now there is no division of the day, no beginning and no end—the head aches, the body is damp and weak, even sleep has gone."

Then on the Wednesday:—

"Not many in the exercise ring this morning—late last night young Mitchell fainted in his cell. They raced Mitchell over to the hospital and called three doctors. We walked silently for a little while. I was thinking of young Mitchell as he fainted."

Then a new Monday:—

"I am not ready to die for earth or for a people. Ireland is something else—when the essential things are clear, death has nothing but a beautiful meaning. But—I would prefer to die in the daytime. It is no harm to have a preference. It would be so horrible at night."

"Tuesday 13th. —I am not mad, they are trying to make me mad. They are watching me, they have red eyes like coals. They are waiting till I sleep so that they can steal in and take my mug of water away. Beautiful water with a thousand tastes!—I must fight these mad thoughts when they come."

"This is the darkest night yet. Death alone could find his way in here now. —Yes— he is there again to-night—I feel him coming towards me, not walking but as it were, floating.

'Well, Death, how goes it?' 'Better with me than with you.' 'You are judging by men's bodies, Death. It is by their souls these men are living.' 'But I am concerned only with the body.' 'In that struggle you always win?' 'I always win, for that struggle always kills. Death is the robbing from man of his great desire.' 'But if a man's great desire be unity with God, what then?' 'Then he does not struggle. His senses are extinguished one by one, and I cannot rob him of his great desire. That which he yearns for is given him in death.'"

"The Doctors told the Government that to-night some of us would be dead."

And outside the jail?

It happened that on Tuesday morning, the 13th, arriving from London, I wrote:—

"At Kingstown I bought the papers and the news of the Hunger Strike turned me sick. A General Strike on behalf of the prisoners ordered. The Gresham staff are to leave at 10 a.m. and the hotel is to be shut. Excitement in the streets and everywhere. 'Stop-Press' editions, giving news of the prisoners on hunger strike and the ordered strike outside. I expected to be turned out, but the Gresham will still keep me. I say I think the one-day strike may make the Government give in, but the housemaid is doubtful, says 'The military are very cruel.'"

"14th.—The streets crowded, all shops shut, the people without any look of enjoyment.

"This morning the housemaid says, 'No deaths, but all are sinking.' It is terrible. I had prayed so hard last night for them and awoke to find myself praying to *America*."

Later,

"I saw on the posters 'Prisoners dying." A constant, quiet tramping of feet on the pavement, all going towards Mountjoy. No voices except the newsboys now and again 'Stop-Press,' and the buzzing of the aeroplanes."

"But now 'Stop-Press' says the Lord-Mayor has been asked to go to the Viceregal Lodge! Then, later, the Hotel Manager, delighted, told me the prisoners had been released. Such a mercy! I met Douglas Hyde and his daughter bicycling back from Mountjoy where they had been with the watching crowd. A man had called out to them in Irish that the Government had given in. Then Susan Mitchell, radiant, and we rejoiced together. It has been a terrible strain all day."

And now in reading this book it is almost as great a relief to come to its last pages: "Midnight, April 14th:—"

"The taxi driver would not take his fare. He said he would be proud all his life that he had driven one of us. . . ."

And then:—

"As long as I do not open my eyes I can have my dream—it must be real—I hear the birds again—yes—thrush. I will look now—just now, give me a minute more and I'll look—a square window, green trees, a blue, blue sky and such sweet birds. It is true—I want to sing too."

A. Gregory

Broadcasting News from Nowhere

R. B. Cunninghame Graham and the Geography of Politics in the 1890s

▩　　▩　　▩

CHRIS GoGWILT

> When Dante walked about the streets . . . the people used to point him out as the man who had seen Hell. You may, perchance yet live, and living, may see . . . me pointed out as the man who [has] seen Socialism.

> —R. B. Cunninghame Graham,
> "Life in Tangiers"

Karl Marx, in one of his less famous writings arguing against a utopian project of emigration to America, concluded: "I cry out to the communists in every country: Brothers, stay at the battlefront of Europe. Work and struggle here, because only Europe has all the elements to set up communal wealth. This type of community will be established here, or nowhere."[1] This imperative against utopia marks the general cultural predicament producing that problem of the geography of politics in the 1890s which I explore in this essay: the theoretical and practical limit, implied in Marx's rhetorical appeal, to realizing a new globalism of social and political relations. In order to reflect on how the "battlefronts" of revolutionary struggle were drawn in the 1890s, I consider, in counterpoint to that imperative "here, or nowhere," the oddly representative example of R. B. Cunninghame Graham and the distinctive form of his own geography of politics as revealed in his sketch artistry.

Scottish aristocrat, socialist agitator, close friend of Joseph Conrad, and voluminous correspondent with many famous people (and many more forgotten) of the turn of the century, Cunninghame Graham is a figure who crops up in the margins of many different histories.[2] The eccentric images of the wild barricade socialist and wild colonial adventurer which constitute the legend of "Don Roberto," as he was and still is popularly known, have in fact worked to obscure the link his writing makes between two particular histories—that of the labor movement in its struggle for parliamentary representation, and the modernist movement in its experimenta-

Figure 1, R. B. Cunninghame Graham (1893), Sir
John Lavery (1856–1941). *Courtesy of Glasgow
Museums: Art Gallery & Museum, Kelvingrove.*

tion with "impressionist" representation. G. K. Chesterton wrote of Cunninghame
Graham: "No Cabinet Minister would ever admire his Parliamentary style; though
he had a much better style than any Cabinet Minister. Nothing could prevent Balfour being Prime Minister or MacDonald being Prime Minister; but Cunninghame
Graham achieved the adventure of being Cunninghame Graham."[3] That "style"
which Chesterton praises precisely because it disqualifies him from a prime place in
political history applies also to evaluation of his place in literary history: he lived,
so the legend reads, the adventure that others sought to realize in artistic form or
practical politics.

Figure 2, Scottish Labour Party ticket with Keir Hardie and R. B. Cunninghame Graham.
Courtesy of Glasgow Museums: The People's Palace.

The persistence of his legend may be illustrated by a set of images of R. B. Cunninghame Graham from the 1890s which I offer in place of a biographical sketch. The first is the full-length portrait of Graham by Sir John Lavery (Figure 1), painted in 1893 "in the manner of Velasquez, full-length and life size, a harmony in brown."[4] Lavery renders Graham with a Whistler-like aristocratic aestheticism. Along with the characteristic traits of Don Roberto's pose as gaucho horseman of the South American pampas, the portrait registers the influence of Graham's adventurous aura on a range of turn-of-the-century artists and writers.[5] Until recently this Lavery portrait illustrated the front cover of the Penguin edition of Joseph Conrad's *Nostromo*, all at once framing the South American setting and indicating Conrad's debt to his close friend Cunninghame Graham (suggesting the argument that Charles Gould is a literary portrait of Don Roberto). The second image is that of "Cunninghame Graham, M.P." side by side with Keir Hardie, two prominent founders of the Scottish Labour party and thus figureheads on the first party ticket, which has since been reproduced as a tea towel by the People's Palace in Glasgow to commemorate the party's founding in 1888 (Figure 2). It is an image that places Graham in suggestive, if eccentric, relation to that icon of labor history, Keir Hardie, the first member of Parliament to be elected as representative of a labor party.

These afterimages of the Don Roberto legend, each characteristically eccentric, situate Cunninghame Graham at key turning points in the histories of early mod-

Figure 3, Portrait of Sir John Lavery. *Courtesy of Museo Nacional de Bellas Artes,*
Buenos Aires, Argentina.

ernism and democratic socialism. Indeed, what makes that legend representative is
the intersection of those histories, a conjuncture of literary and political representation best grasped in the form of the literary sketch which Graham developed in the
1890s. Emphasizing the role of Graham's own sketch artistry in the fashioning of
these images is a third image, an earlier portrait by John Lavery of Graham and a
horse, about which Lavery wrote: "Graham had purchased from the tramway company a wild Argentine pony that refused to go into harness. He named him Pampa,
and insisted on my painting a picture of himself in complete cowboy outfit on the
pacing steed" (Figure 3).[6] It was this portrait which Graham himself chose to illustrate *The Ipané,* the early volume of sketches which marks Graham's transformation
from political journalist to literary stylist and perhaps most fully articulates the geography of politics in Graham's sketch artistry. John Lavery echoed G. K. Chesterton's
assessment of "the adventure of being Cunninghame Graham" when he wrote, "I
think I did something to help Graham in the creation of his own masterpiece—him-

self."[7] The publication of *The Ipané* in 1899 reflects on Cunninghame Graham's self-conscious manipulation of that "masterpiece" throughout the 1890s. In all these images, in the combined anomalies of an aristocratic Scottish M.P. representing labor and dressed up in gaucho drag, there emerges that problem Graham's writing explores in seeking to imagine a geography of politics beyond the imperative of Marx's "here, or nowhere."

His first three full-length books would seem to suggest that Cunninghame Graham's socialist utopia is most likely to be found, if anywhere, in the past. Vanishing precapitalist forms of life seem increasingly his preoccupation in *Notes on the District of Menteith, for Tourists and Others* (1895), his parodic genealogy of his own ancestors and their lands; in *Mogreb-el-Acksa: A Journey in Morocco* (1898), an account of his notorious failure to reach the forbidden holy city of Tarudant; and in *A Vanished Arcadia: Being Some Account of the Jesuits in Paraguay, 1607 to 1767* (1901), the first of his many histories of the Spanish in America. These vanished arcadias—antiquated Scottish customs, the Moroccan empire of Islam's "far west," and the maligned history of Jesuit missions in South America—seem very far removed from the socialist futures imagined by utopian narratives of the 1890s. To understand what links the progressive socialist figure of Cunninghame Graham, M.P., and the image of "Don Roberto" acting out the romance of a vanished arcadia, we should turn to the style of storytelling Graham forged into a unique form of sketch artistry, from the political journalism of the late 1880s and early 1890s to the "impressionism" of the late 1890s. It is really the sketch that defines the genre of all Graham's works, and his sketch artistry is the medium through which "the adventure of being Cunninghame Graham" links the battlefronts of socialist struggle and colonial politics.

The Ipané (1899), his first volume of sketches,[8] illustrates the idiosyncrasy of Graham's sketch artistry in its political and geographical range. The book consists of previously published sketches, their organization emphasizing the sometimes bewildering juxtaposition of divergent concerns that is a hallmark of Graham's writing. The first of many such volumes to come, it is also revealing in emerging from the period of Graham's most intense correspondence, friendship, and collaboration with Joseph Conrad and Edward Garnett. If the volume marks Graham's transformation from political journalist to literary stylist, it also shows how Graham's style of political newswriting informed the artistic ambitions shared with the more famous figures of early modernist experimentation, Garnett and Conrad. A characteristic of the Graham sketch is its combination of realistic reportage and stylistic impressionism: the political column is broken up by the storyteller's yarn; and the crafted tale can become at any moment the stage for direct political commentary.

"Sursum Corda," although it was one of the sketches Garnett had Graham exclude from *The Ipané* (it was collected in *Success* in 1901), is a revealing example. It is of particular interest for its reminiscence of Graham's six-week prison experience, which makes the sketch a reflection on an event that helped secure his prestige—and notoriety—as socialist leader. In November 1887 Graham, together with his fellow labor activist John Burns, was arrested, beaten, tried, and convicted for his part in the violently suppressed demonstrations of "Bloody Sunday." Ten years after the demonstrations called to affirm the principle of free speech, Graham's "Sursum

Corda" takes up the topic of speech in an extended editorial comment which almost only incidentally achieves something of the effect of a carefully crafted modern short story. As "Sursum Corda" tightens the wide latitude of its editorial meditations on speech and silence, political editorial turns into the form of a tale crafted around an almost epiphanic moment: the sense of the title, "lift up your hearts," referring to the prelude to consecration of the host in the holy Mass, unfolds in Graham's reminiscence of hymn-singing among fellow prisoners; and it is through this that the sketch figures the bond of humanity—through speech—denied to the prisoner but reconstituted through the uplifting message of the hymn. In characteristically turning that message against the Christian moralizing of the enforced Sunday exercise, the epiphany of "Sursum Corda" affirms a consciousness of human bonds different from either the bondage within prison or the hypocrisies of church singers outside prison, creating an aesthetic effect around the question of class consciousness:

> So in a side street when the frequent loafer sidles up, and says mysteriously "Gawd bless yer, chuck us arf a pint; I was in with you in that crooil plaice," I do so, not that I think he speaks the truth nor yet imagine that the prison, large though it was, contained two million prisoners, but to relieve his thirst and for the sake of those condemned to silence, there "inside," and for the recollection of the "bloomin' 'ymn."[9]

The story's "sursum corda," turning a religious into a political incitement to courage and fervor, makes the sketch an unregenerate account of what Graham learned from "Bloody Sunday." In crafting the lesson of his prison experience into a lesson in class consciousness, he thus confirms and sustains one of the central questions of the Trafalgar Square demonstrations—the relation between class consciousness and labor leadership.

"Bloody Sunday" as the watershed moment in raising class consciousness and beginning the revolution: this is how the events of 1887 are portrayed in William Morris's *News from Nowhere*, where the "'Battle' of Trafalgar Square" provided a lesson in how working-class consciousness could lead to the "overturn" of capitalist society, the Great Change that would transform England into a communist utopia. "Bloody Sunday" was not the watershed moment of history Morris makes it, but, as the British labor historian Chushichi Tsuzuki explains, it did provide the occasion for a realignment of affiliations following the split in the Social Democratic Federation of the mid-1880s.[10] Tsuzuki emphasizes the lesson in political leadership drawn from "Bloody Sunday" by the labor activist John Burns, one of Graham's close allies in working-class politics, and with whom he was arrested on "Bloody Sunday." Burns, in his speech at their trial, emphasized the role of the unemployed: "These men, the unemployed . . . taught the politicians the very element of government: how to organize society during the transitional period from the present competitive system where the policeman is absolutely necessary, to the co-operative system where the teacher will take his place." This was a lesson that became central for the activist work of both John Burns and Tom Mann, impressed by Burns's speech, in their role in helping organize the London dockers' strike of 1889, whose success Tsuzuki characterizes in terms of a "new awakening of the working class as a class."[11]

The shifting political alignments around "Bloody Sunday" presented lessons of leadership that reflect a more general shift of alignments within international social-ism. Ernesto Laclau and Chantal Mouffe have argued that the crisis of Marxism over the turn of the century may be traced to the presumed unity of interests of the work-ing class—the proletariat—laid down by the laws of the economic base, or "histor-ical necessity," that "cornerstone" of Second International Marxism.[12] In some ways the events of "Bloody Sunday," and Cunninghame Graham's participation in them, reproduce in miniature the theoretical lessons Laclau and Mouffe draw from the cri-sis in Second International Marxism. They show the heterogeneous elements at work in the set of political demonstrations and strikes from the 1880s into the early 1890s which gave impetus to the formation of new social democratic political parties—the Scottish Labour party and the Independent Labour party—as well as to the so-called New Unionism of the 1890s. Cunninghame Graham was no Marxist theoretician, but his practice of political activism during a peculiarly important moment in the history of the British labor movement situates the eccentric myth of "Don Roberto" in suggestive relation to the underlying theoretical question of the class unity of the labor movement.

To the extent that "Sursum Corda" reflects the lessons of "Bloody Sunday" ten years later, however, it is in a sketch artistry whose stray lines follow a different, if related, problem of class unity and consciousness. One such stray line occurs in the penultimate paragraph, appearing to deflect the coherence of the epiphany: "'Does you good, No. 8, the bloomin' 'ymn,' an old lag says, but for the moment dazed by the ceasing of the noise, as Bernal Diaz says he was when the long tumult ended and Mex-ico was won, I do not answer . . ." (p. 98). The reference to the conquest of Mexico would be a defect in a pure short story—for precisely the reason Graham, I think, insists on it: one would want to find a more self-consistent image to secure the point that the Anglican hymn grafts an exalted sense of worship onto a fundamentally dif-ferent sense of human community. Yet the image is not simply drawn uneconomically from Cunninghame Graham's store of adventurous interests. It echoes an earlier dis-cordant image deliberately placed to mark the stray lines of the sketch: "Think on a silent world, a world in which men walked about in all respects equipped with every organ, every sense, but without speech. They might converse by signs as Indians do upon the trail, but I maintain no city of tremendous night could be more awful than the horror of a speechless world" (p. 88). These stray lines are part of the geography of politics characteristic of Graham's style. E. J. Hobsbawm, reflecting on the optimism with which Second International Marxism made class the lever of its vision of world history, writes: "[W]hat, from one point of view, looked like a concentration of men and women in a single 'working class' could be seen from another as a gigantic scat-tering of the fragments of societies, a diaspora of the old and new communities."[13] Gra-ham's sketches, straying now to the rhetoric of class struggle and now to the contem-plation of vanishing forms of social life, are shot through with this double vision.

The art and political strategy of Graham's sketches emerge from a mixture of the "low" literary form of his early political reporting and the "high" art form perfected in collaboration with Garnett and Conrad. Yet if this places the sketches in eccen-tric relation to most accounts of literary history, his sketch artistry foregrounds an important change in the nature of narrative form at the turn of the century. The Gra-

ham sketch springs from the widening split between "low" and "high" literary production at a time—the moment of early modernism—when narrative form is tilted
from the axis of time and history to an axis of space and geography.

Selection and organization of the tales in *The Ipané* is revealing, in this respect,
not only because it took place against the backdrop of Graham's friendship and correspondence with Edward Garnett and Joseph Conrad. Garnett had chosen *The Ipané*
for the first volume of a new series,[14] which he had been pressing his employer Unwin
to launch since 1897.[15] Garnett's aims are revealed in the prospectus and call for sub-
missions which appeared on the flyleaf of *The Ipané*. He begins:

> Where are the "Ends of the Empire"? and which are the Over-Seas? At "the
> Ends" of one may arise the beginnings of other Empires to come. It is noto-
> rious that wherever an English-speaking community settles and opens up
> new lands, it speedily speaks for itself as a Centre; and so rapid is the growth
> of the great Colonies, that Ministers to-day writing despatches to Depen-
> dencies over-seas, receive their answers from nations to-morrow.

In looking toward the "Ends of the Empire," Garnett's idea, otherwise entirely in
keeping with the mass industry of publishing colonial and imperial tales, takes on a
critical edge closer to Garnett's personal views on the cant of imperialism. *The Ipané*
was perfect for piloting such an idea. It was perfect not only in approaching Garnett's
high artistic ambitions, but also for the popularity to which the sketches and their
author might appeal—as is suggested by Garnett's humorous comments on Graham's
deliberations on a picture for the frontispiece: "[W]ho knows but that your portrait
may spread an "overseas" movement which the colonial Tories may never check."[16]
The portrait Graham finally chose was Lavery's "Don Roberto" on his horse Pampa;
and Garnett was delighted.[17]

The Over-Seas Library was, then, a more or less conscious attempt to articulate
an anti-imperialist artistic movement, and the coordinates for Garnett's aim are suggested by a letter to Graham in July 1898: "Ah the South! But you are North &
South both in your writings. You double the parts & leave us to be onesided. By the
way Conrad to my mind is born on the dividing line between East and West."[18] Garnett's abstractions—North–South, East–West—reduce, of course, the specific cultural and political experiences of Cunninghame Graham's sketches and Joseph Conrad's tales. Yet around 1898 it is possible to discern in all three writers an adoption
of just this kind of reductive generalization.[19] This simplification is a studied response
to the rhetoric of the "New Imperialism," whose high tide mark was 1897, the year
of Queen Victoria's Golden Jubilee celebrations. What these writers were up to in
consciously appealing to the charm of the New Imperialism is indicated by their discussions of Kipling. Complex though Kipling's own political vision was—and it was,
moreover, undergoing a crucial change in reaction against the popular enthusiasm of
the 1897 Jubilee celebrations—nonetheless Kipling was still the Bard of Empire.
Indeed, Garnett's geographical abstractions might justly be described as Kiplingesque.
As Orwell would note in the 1930s, Kipling was "the only English writer of our time
who has added phrases to the language,"[20] and it is notable (although Orwell does not
note it) that almost all the examples he gives are catchphrases whose simplifications

Where are the "Ends of the Empire"? and which are the Over-Seas? At "the Ends" of one may arise the beginnings of other Empires to come. It is notorious that wherever an English-speaking community settles and opens up new lands, it speedily speaks for itself as a Centre; and so rapid is the growth of the great Colonies, that Ministers to-day writing dispatches to Dependencies over-seas, receive their answers from nations to-morrow.

But great as is the growth of the Empire and the enterprise of its peoples, the new native-born literatures take years to germinate and generations to arrive. Thence comes it that often we do not understand the atmospheres of the new English-speaking peoples, and often misunderstand the problems, the attitudes, befitting them as new races. And while the British Empire grows richer daily in patriotic fervours, in speeches, in splendour, in cant, and in the oracular assurances of Statesmen, the English people seeks to understand its cousins by the interchange of cablegrams, by debates, and by all the ambiguities of official memoranda.

It is, however, the artist's work to bring the people of his nation and their atmosphere before the eyes of another. It is the artist alone, great or small, who, by revealing and interpreting the life around him, makes it living to the rest of the world. And the artist is generally absent! In the case of the English in India, ten years ago, while the literature of information was plentiful, the artist was absent; Mr. Kipling arrived and discovered modern India to the English imagination. And

to-day, in the midst of a general movement for Empire expansion, with talk of Federation, Jingoism, and with the doing of real work, the artists in literature are generally absent, the artists who should reveal the tendencies, the hidden strength and weakness, the capacities of the new communities.

The aim of "The Over-Seas Library" is purely experimental. It proposes to print literature from any quarter that deals with the actual life of the English outside England, whether of Colonial life or the life of English emigrants, travellers, traders, officers, over-seas, among foreign and native races, black or white. Pictures of life in the American States will not necessarily be excluded.

"The Over-Seas Library" makes no pretence at Imperial drum-beating, or putting English before Colonial opinion. It aims, instead, at getting the atmosphere and outlook of the new peoples recorded, if such is possible. It aims at being an Interchange between all parts of the Empire without favour, an Interchange of records of the life of the English-speaking peoples, and of the Englishmen beyond seas, however imperfect, fragmentary and modest such records or accounts may be.

The Editor will be glad to receive any MSS. addressed to him, c/o the Publisher.

E. G.

11, Paternoster Buildings,
    London.

articulate a new sense of global political proportion: "East is East and West is West"; "What do they know of England who only England know"; "Somewheres East of Suez"; "the White Man's burden."

It is revealing that in their first exchange of letters, Graham and Conrad are attempting to evaluate Kipling's art. Garnett, writing to Graham in January 1899 after two years of intense literary collaboration among the three men, comments:

> As for Kipling, as I think I've reiterated to you Kipling is the enemy. But he did cre-ate India to the Saxon world that world of dulness that said it owned it! He is a cre-ator; & he is the genius of all we detest. (Some day I hope to analyze his genius, & I shall write with keen joy, for how joyous it is to hate perfectly.) I hate his essence.[21]

Garnett never produced his critical analysis, but the prospectus for the Over-Seas Library shows how he had been waging his war by other means:

> It is the artist alone, great or small, who, by revealing and interpreting the life around him, makes it living to the rest of the world. And the artist is generally absent! In the case of the English in India, ten years ago, while the literature of infor-mation was plentiful, the artist was absent; Mr. Kipling arrived and discovered mod-ern India to the English imagination. And to-day, in the midst of a general move-ment for Empire expansion, with talk of Federation, Jingoism, and with the doing of real work, the artists in literature are generally absent, the artists who should reveal the tendencies, the capacities of the new communities.

Garnett's work in helping Graham select, arrange, and edit his sketches forms a significant part of the story of Graham's transition from political journalist to liter-ary artist, as suggested by Garnett's comment in a letter from June 23, 1898: "I sue for the artist in you, the artist you concealed so long under the man of action, the artist that is most important." At the same time, the politics of Graham's style challenged Garnett's sense of the artist's role. Garnett's first response to Graham's sketches was to exclude the "social & political papers" (as he put it to Graham in May 1898), to conform to his evolving Over-Seas idea: "[T]he character of the volume of sketches I had projected was necessarily *exclusive of Social, Political & Historical Sketches. I thought of a volume to be made of sketches of a local character & atmosphere*—out-side England." But Garnett soon came to recognize that Graham's method of sketch artistry depended on juxtaposing reminiscence and political essay, and this collabo-ration over the shape of *The Ipané* illuminates how Graham's imaginative geography of politics informed Garnett's Over-Seas idea.

Deliberation over Graham's most polemical attack on British imperialism, "Bloody Niggers," reveals Garnett's evolving insight into the artistry of Graham's style. The biting satirical sketch, originally published in *The Social-Democrat* in April 1897, creates, as Cedric Watts and Laurence Davies summarize it, "a tapestry-like pic-ture of the world, its inhabitants, and its history, while announcing, ironically of course, that all these riches were designed by their Creator for British use."[22] In June, Garnett praised the piece—"The *quintessence* is there of your attitude, your insight"—but resisted its political rhetoric as inappropriate for the volume: "But the core of it, the blasphemy against the stupidities might damage all the other sketches with those who do not understand—i.e. with Everybody. . . . It is too good to leave out, but it would be a sheer luxury to tempt every ordinary creature to make himself more ordinary over it."[23]

The lever of Graham's polemic is his use of the racist term "nigger" to concentrate the "stupidities" of British attitudes towards "foreign and native races" (to use Garnett's formulation from the Over-Seas prospectus). In the coda to the sketch, he returns to the title: "What is a 'nigger'? Now this needs some words in order to explain his just position. Hindus, as Brahmins, Bengalis, dwellers in Bombay, the Cingalese, Sikhs and Pathans, Rajpoots, Parsis, Afghans, Kashmiris, Beluchis, Burmese, with all the dwellers from the Caspian Sea to Timur Laut, are thus described. Arabs are 'niggers.'" Pausing for a new paragraph, the sketch launches into another list of peoples obliterated by the term; and in a further paragraph dwells on how "'niggers' of Africa occupy first place."[24] The polemic necessarily provokes extreme unease about the ingrained racism permeating all shades of imperialist and colonial ideology. It is worth noting that a prominent supporter of the Zulus, Harriette Emily Colenso, writing to Graham about Olive Schreiner's political attitudes toward race and racism, expressed concern about Graham's title: "I am rather inclined to think that 'we' ought to exclude the word 'nigger' from general conversation, & literature. It is not required, & only expresses contempt."[25]

The sketch illustrates something of the limits to Garnett's Over-Seas idea not so much because of Garnett's concerns for his ignorant readers, but rather because it strikes at the very "range" of the series. No editor can manage all the news coming out of the colonies, and Garnett's project, however anti-imperialist in its inspiration, assumes a sort of hegemonic control over the artistic talent he hopes might reimagine the relation between center and periphery. Scanning the list of proposed books for the series, and those ultimately published by Unwin, one finds it perhaps too easy to recognize how Garnett's Over-Seas idea would only follow in the "general movement for Empire expansion" rather than redirect it politically. The limitations of the series's ability to imagine the "new communities" forming at "the Ends of the Empire" are visible already in Garnett's proposal to address "the actual life of the English outside England, whether of Colonial life or the life of English emigrants, travellers, traders, officers, over-seas, among foreign and native races, black or white." One of the series's books, Sir Hugh Clifford's *In Court and Kampong*, in some respects a worthy example of Garnett's artistic aims, illustrates how the Over-Seas Library could provide the platform for a new stage of colonial hegemony over the "new communities," since its sketches of Malay life, though written by a colonial administrator increasingly uneasy with the system of colonial governance in the Malay Federated States, still provided the ethnographic detail and ideological rationale that would make the "benevolent" governor system of British Malaysia a model for sustaining British colonialism both in British Malaysia and in Africa.

These limitations in imagining an anti-imperialist geography of politics go to the heart of Garnett's perceptive insights into Graham's style of sketch artistry. Garnett recognized, from the start, the strength of Graham's juxtaposition of widely different cultural settings.[26] The substance of most of Garnett's advice to Graham for editing, amending, and arranging *The Ipané* concerns the relation between that diversity and the personal point of view that Graham brings to that diversity:

[A] volume of such sketches give [sic] through its diversity, (& through the writer's strong central point of view) a really connected harmonious picture of life—the sketches fall into harmony, & form an artistic whole. The wider the range the more powerful artistically does the volume become—with each fresh atmosphere the reader yields more and more to the eyes that saw, to the spirit that interpreted.[27]

In light of this characteristic emphasis on Graham's personal experience (recalling Chesterton's "adventure of being Cunninghame Graham"), it is striking now to turn to the argument Garnett makes for including "Bloody Niggers" after all:

I sat down & read Niggers when it came & was so ravished that the folly of criticism passed leagues away . . . now you sting us & glide away like a beautiful snake. Formerly, you remained on the spot after an outburst, defying the Anglo-Saxon world, with your best card played. But now you have struck & vanished! The booted perspiring Britain gazes round, with the heavens grinning at him.[28]

It is, like most of Garnett's remarks, an astute appreciation which shows his growing recognition of Graham's art of political rhetoric, even as it also testifies to the value of Garnett's advice, since Graham had revised the essay slightly to produce an argument that, according to Watts and Davies, "is clearer, because more controlled."[29] What is remarkable, however, is Garnett's stress on Graham's strategy of striking and vanishing, since this is the one element of Graham's method of shifting narrative perspective which, in other sketches, Garnett sought to control by stressing "the eyes that saw, . . . the spirit that interpreted."

Garnett's clearest exposition of this sense of Graham's method is in a letter from 1901, when, having praised the sketch "The Gualichu Tree," he wrote: "But analysing your work, & demanding the finest forms for your fineness, I think that where your work succeeds is where *everything* converges to a centre [here Garnett sketches a circle of arrows aimed at a central spot] & where your work sometimes is unsatisfactory in form is where you have turned & shot arrows at many targets."[30] Yet this fault defines the very success of Graham's sketch artistry, and above all its geography of politics. One thinks of the stray references to Indians and to the conquest of Mexico in "Sursum Corda." If the unpredictable juxtaposition of widely different cultural contexts seems to deflect from the coherence of "the eyes that saw, the spirit that interpreted," that is part of the success with which Graham's sketch artistry probes a perceived new geography of experience in the 1890s.

This, it seems to me, is the greatness of another tale from *The Ipané*, "Heather Jock," one of the finest examples of Graham's craft of unsettling the tale through the insertion of personal reminiscence. It unfolds with all the unpredictability of Graham's characteristic obsessions, weaving the character sketch of an eccentric mad peddler from the West of Scotland into a personal reminiscence from the Argentinian pampas, where the narrator learned the news of the man's death, itself the occasion to relate another death, the violent killing, by Indians, of one of the men who brought Graham the news. The juxtaposition of place—the Argentinian pampas, the frontier of violence between Indian and gaucho, and the West Highlands of Scotland—coordinates a strange and disturbing miscellany of memories, culminating in the funeral song for the dead gaucho rider, in which the narrator "seemed to hear the jangling of the dead fool's bells, and listen to the minstrelsy, such as it was, of the hegemonist of Bridge of Weir." It is likely that Conrad drew something from Graham's method of relating the news of "Heather Jock's" death in developing the art of having Marlow relate his news from the nowhere of Patusan, in *Lord Jim*, or the Inner Station of *Heart of Darkness*. Yet in the authors' collaborative efforts to devise ways of bringing the horrors of imperialist exploitation home to their readers, Graham's sketch artistry remains distinctive in its insistence on the "nowhere" of news-telling itself.[31]

In what seems like a stale political side thrust at the established press in the beginning of "Heather Jock," Graham offers an editorial comment that will introduce the figure of the mad Scottish weaver-turned-traveling-merchant of the story's title: "The wandering semi-madman was a feature in Scotch life. In ancient times he filled, to some degree, the function of a newspaper, retailing news distorted to the taste of those he catered for, after the fashion of the modern editor" (p. 112). Given the story's emphasis on the imponderable cost of bearing the news, this apparent throwaway provides a guiding parable for the story's contemplation of the geography and politics of storytelling.[32]

The effect of piling up stories in "Heather Jock" goes beyond the self-reflexive strategy for commenting on the function of news reporting set within the frame of a storyteller retailing experiences of past memories, as Graham reflects on his Argentinian adventures of the 1870s and early 1880s. It is crucially determined by the "immediate" place of the narrator as reporter, inviting the reader's search for the present location of the special correspondent. But that search is constantly deflected by the style of Graham's rendering of personal experience, as we see in the description of the character of Heather Jock: "What he had seen during his wandering life he treasured up, relating it, on invitation, to his hearers in the same way an Arab or a Spaniard quotes a proverb as if it were a personal experience of his own" (p. 111).

This deflection of personal experience through multiplying geographical contexts defines the political practice, as well as the limits, of his anti-imperialist sketch artistry. The style of impressionism is designed for readers eager to see the world of Empire reflected in an actuality of experience. This is perhaps illustrated best through the appreciation of a rare audience. Writing to Graham in 1898, Conrad described his enthusiasm upon reading Graham's *Mogreb-el-Acsa* with "a man," who was possibly Ford Madox Hueffer:

> A man staying here has been reading over my shoulder; for we share our best with the stranger within the tent. No thirsty men drank water as we have been drinking in, swallowing, tasting, blessing, enjoying gurgling, choking over, absorbing, your thought, your phrases, your irony, the spirit of your vision of Your expression. . . . You are magnificently generous. You seem to be plunging your hand into an inexhaustible bag of treasure and fling precious things at every paragraph. We have been shouting slapping our legs, leaping up, stamping about. There was such an enthusiasm in this solitude as will meet no other book. I do not know really how to express the kind of intellectual exultation your book has awakened in me. . . .[33]

Here is evidence of the manner in which Graham became "a writer's writer," the treasure of his experiences generously scattered for the great masters of style to set into works of art. Conrad's enthusiasm suggests not only that Graham's adventures themselves could provide a model for Conrad's rather different art of narrative; in Conrad's metaphors one may also read the shared interest in displaying the loot and plunder of experiences culled from distant places.

The "intellectual exultation" provoked in Conrad by Graham's style—both here and throughout the letters collected by Cedric Watts—provides an invaluable record of the archive of literary modernism in its formative stages. In the almost sensual excitement of what might be done with the treasure trove of Graham's news from nowhere, we may recognize the changing shape of "narrative as a socially symbolic act."[34] The image of Graham's readers "shouting slapping our legs, leaping up, stamping about" recalls the situation of Marlow retailing his story to his auditors, whose grunts and interjections are the echo of that howling and dancing Marlow heard from the natives as he maneuvered his steamboat upriver to "the back of nowhere."

The controlled narrative structure of Conrad's *Heart of Darkness* most fully illustrates the reorientation of the utopian narrative structure of a Bellamy, a Morris, and most particularly Wells's *Time Machine*, from whose narrative frame Conrad may well have drawn for his own tale. Conrad's achievement, moreover, though it owes some debt to the "intellectual exultation" over Graham's sketch artistry, is I think clearly more powerful in conveying the horrors of imperialist exploitation. In "Heather Jock," one of Graham's characteristic stray sentences catches at an economic point about that "gigantic scattering of the fragments of societies" Hobsbawm sets in perspectival relation to the increasing "concentration of men and women in a single 'working-class.'" Describing the gaucho rider who brings the news of "Heather Jock's" death, along with the news of his own brother's death, Graham pauses on the detail of the messenger's handkerchief, "a handkerchief which had been white when it left Manchester some years ago" (p. 181). This detail might be compared to one of the most powerful moments in *Heart of Darkness*, when Marlow encounters, cast aside with the crowd of slave laborers because they are too weak to be useful, a dying worker with a piece of white thread tied around his neck: "He had tied a bit of white worsted round his neck—Why? Where did he get it? Was it a badge—an ornament—a charm—a propitiatory act? Was there any idea at all connected with it? It looked startling round his black neck, this bit of white thread from beyond the seas."[35]

In moments like these it seems that Conrad's skepticism was able to transform Cunninghame Graham's rough sketch artistry into a powerful rendition of the political logic of violence separating first and third worlds. And there is some truth to the idea that, while Graham sought to realize an impossible geography of political connection between the proletarian battlefield of Europe and the frontiers of colonialism, of the two, only Conrad could break the spell of Second International Marxism: "The Internationale will be the human race."[36] Both writers sought a form of storytelling that might push the reality of lived experience a little beyond experience, to paraphrase Conrad reflecting on *Heart of Darkness*, in order to "bring home to the readers" the horror of imperialist exploitation.[37] In Conrad's controlled narrative structures the axis of the utopian tale is most fully reoriented from its attempt to bear news of the communist future to the problem of bearing the news from overseas.

Indeed, Conrad goes further, enacting a direct reversal of at least Wells's *Time Machine*, when Marlow's journey up the Congo River is projected as a journey back in time. Here we might note how Conrad's controlled narrative structure departs from the principles of Cunninghame Graham's sketch artistry, insofar as the symbolic logic of Marlow's journey into the time of "pre-historic man" defines the geography of imperialist horror as, precisely, "nowhere": "this nowhere"; "some ghastly Nowhere, where he [Kurtz] intended to accomplish great things."[38]

The "nowhere" of Graham's sketches is defined differently, in its hybrid of political commentary, personal reminiscence, and the stray lines juxtaposing quite different geographical locations. In "Heather Jock" the news is neither from "nowhere" nor addressed to "nowhere." Rather, the weight—and narrative effect—of the news is constituted by the diverse spaces across which it is borne. Contemplating the "unpleasant news" of the gaucho's brother's death at the hand of an "infidel," Graham as narrator describes with uncanny leisure his receipt of "home news" before the discovery of the announcement of "Heather Jock's" death in "a scrap of newspaper":

> Whilst he [the gaucho] caught a horse—a lengthy operation when the horses have to be driven first to a corral and then caught with the lazo—I took the bag, with the feeling, firstly, that it had cost a man his life, and then with the instinctive dread which, when in distant lands, always attends home news, that some one would be dead or married, or that at least the trusted family solicitor had made off with the money entrusted to him for investment. (p. 111)

In certain respects the effect is one of simple macabre humor, but through Graham's narrative art it lends the story a pace and suspense that calls attention to the stray details of discrepant geographical and cultural contexts. In its most powerful effects, this deflection from personal experience points to the present "nowhere" of shifting geographical and political identifications.

The shifting lines of geographical and cultural alignments in Graham's sketches help explain the irony of his success as a writer remembered not as a writer but as "a man of action"; or, when invoked as a writer, consistently described as underrated. The success of the "Don Roberto" legend—and here both Lavery portraits are telling—owes much to the global political realignments marked by the Spanish–American War of 1898. The United States' defeat of the vestiges of Spain's empire in Cuba, the Philippines, and elsewhere marked a decisive new stage in the policies and practices of imperialist nations, articulating virtually overnight the terms of the United States' emergence as a world power. It stood as a striking example of Garnett's point, from the Over-Seas prospectus, that at the ends of one empire may be found the beginnings of another. Graham's response to the war found fullest literary expression in "Victory," a sketch whose bitterly ironic title is given affirmatively to a Spanish nobleman. "Success," a slimmer reflection on the war, is another ironic title, more resignedly bitter, which became the title of his third collection of stories, published in 1902. In a sense the combination of bitterness and irony in this title reflects how bitterly Graham's own literary success was won.

More significant, perhaps, Graham's response to the war was decisive in the Graham–Garnett–Conrad collaboration, determining the political geography of Graham's contribution to this formative moment of modernism. "Victory," a sketch that Watts and Davies select as exemplary for Graham's impressionism, became the occasion for a disagreement over method between Garnett and Graham which led to a certain victory, so to speak, in Graham's articulation of his artistic style. Set in Paris, the story unravels the effect of the news of an American victory over the Spanish in the war. Garnett insisted that the Spanish nobleman, whose response to that news produces what Watts and Davies interpret as the "moral victory," ought to be introduced *first* in order to make sense of the narrator's digressive reminiscences of reminiscences. Graham stood his ground, insisting, "I am not a story teller, but an impressionist," terms he had already used in defending "Heather Jock." In response Garnett wrote: "I admire, I admire fully & deeply. Your method is so much your own nobody will ever come after you—& You will remain *alone*." Watts and Davies illuminate the significance of this exchange when, having quoted from "Victory" the complex digression of Graham's memory of being in Cadiz remembering the scent of the mimosa of the pampas, they pose the question: "Beyond establishing . . . that Graham knows the Hispanic world, what on earth has this to do with either Paris or the War of 1898?" Their answer explains the way the sketch works, and is a fine demonstration of Graham's impressionistic technique; yet it strangely reduplicates Garnett's concession: the center of the story, they claim, is not the Spanish noble but "Graham himself," a conclusion that locks up the experience of the story into Chesterton's "adventure of being Cunninghame Graham."[39]

There is, I believe, another answer to the question Watts and Davies pose. For Graham's digression (the story uses the Scots word "dwawm") momentarily offers a glimpse of that space of news-telling in "Heather Jock," where the intertwined stories linking Indians, gauchos, and Scottish semi-madmen constitute an open-ended geography of political affiliations governing the reporting of news. The center of the story, then, is neither the Spanish nobleman nor "Graham himself," but the way in which, as Watts and Davies brilliantly show, "we have to re-align our perception of the way the sketch works" in shifting from the one to the other. In a sense Garnett knew too well where Graham's political sympathies lay, and at first wanted those sympathies clarified by making the Spanish nobleman the story's center. In his later response he recognized, and admired, the central place of Graham's personal impressions: the story's problem is not so much the conflict between the Latin and Anglo-Saxon worlds, but rather a reflection on the vanishing place of Graham's memories within the convergence of responses to the news of the war.

Garnett's recognition of Graham's success is, in effect, double-edged, and when he claims, "You remain *alone*," there is the suggestion that Graham's world has been eclipsed by the events of the Spanish–American War. The passion of Graham's identification with the old Spanish Empire against the industrialized power of North America had an immense symbolic appeal for Conrad, as suggested by Conrad's letters to Graham on the subject, and confirmed most notably in the striking achievement of *Nostromo*. Conrad's novel reconstitutes the imaginative appeal of Graham's Spanish and Spanish-American sympathies as an identification with the old, eclipsed New World *against* the new world order of "Pax Americana." The result is a powerful and complex articulation of the new North–South axis of imperialist struggle across the emerging global formations of an industrialized "first" world and an economically dependent "third" world.

Yet Conrad's ability to transform the politics of Graham's response to the war into the "nowhere" of *Nostromo*'s fictional Latin America crucially obscures the geography of politics in Graham's sketch artistry. Graham's South America includes a sense of space outside the imagined political logic of *Nostromo*. Indeed, the gaucho costume of Lavery's portrait of Don Roberto draws attention to that sense of space—the pampas of the gaucho rider, whose local color does not, after all, well illustrate Conrad's novel. If the scene of gaucho riding is quintessential Cunninghame Graham "adventure," it is neither as local color nor as setting—nor as ethnographic detail—that the pampas provide a key sense of the "nowhere" of Graham's sketches. In "A Vanishing Race" we read "Pampa, in the quichua tongue, signifies 'Space.'"[40] The detail calls attention to the many vanishing moments of Graham's sketches, particularly those that allude to the decimation of Native Americans, either explicitly in "A Hegira" or in drawing toward the vanishing trail of Indians, for instance, in "Heather Jock": "Just at the crossing of the Guaviyu, close to a clump of "Espinillo de Olor" [mimosa], we found the body, cut and hacked about so as to be almost unrecognizable, but holding in the hand a tuft of long black hair, coarse as a horse's tail, showing the dead man had behaved himself up to the last like a true Christian" (p. 186). The "Space" of the Pampa captures Graham's sense of "nowhere" by being triply removed through Indian (Quichua), Spanish (gaucho), and English (Scottish) tongues.

The geography of politics in Graham's sketch artistry is not explained, however, by a Quichua concept of space, by the gaucho life-style, or through Graham's nostalgia for the pampa of his youth (signaled by the naming of his horse and stylized through the Lavery portrait). If Graham shared a nostalgic, utopian view of the South American pampa with his friend W. H. Hudson, the "nowhere" of Graham's Spanish and Spanish-American world cannot be characterized, as Fredric Jameson characterizes Hudson's work, as a "return to some earlier precapitalist form" with "an appeal to a generalized and global nostalgia."[41] Even to the extent that the Spanish and Spanish-American world of Graham's sketches is projected as a "vanished arcadia" not unlike the world of Hudson's pampa in *Far Away and Long Ago: A History of My Early Life*, it is important to specify the negative dialectic by which the aura of the "Don Roberto" myth registers a resistance to the global political realignments following the Spanish–American War—a resistance to a whole range of Anglo-Saxon imaginings, most notably Rudyard Kipling's address to Americans to "take up the white man's burden." Yet the Hispanic aura of "Don Roberto's" Spanish America is rarely an exotic utopia, as indicated by the title "The Ipané." Far from an exotic evocation of the name of a place or of a people, it is the name of the old steamer whose explosion yields the macabre climax to the title story of the volume, with its gruesome depiction of the scattered bodies of its passengers, some of that "nondescript society" of life in Paraguay, which includes "all the waifs and strays of cosmopolitan humanity who, 'outside our flag,' pursue their useless lives, under the sixfold international code of law so neatly codified by Colonel Colt."[42] As a name, of course, it is not unimportant, lending a local color entirely in keeping with Graham's geography of politics: primarily a place name from the Guarani, it translates into the Spanish *laguna hedionda*—as one might say, "fateful waters"; or, alternatively, "stinking hole."[43]

The realignment of geography and politics in Graham's sketches provides a counterweight to the paradigms of geopolitics emerging in the 1890s. Still more important, their stray lines present open-ended possibilities of political affiliation across disparate cultural experiences. The myth of "Don Roberto" does not simply register a global nostalgia for a lost Spanish–American world. Nor can the glamor of "R. B. Cunninghame Graham, M.P." as socialist activist appeal in terms simply of a lost art of political struggle. These eccentric afterimages of Cunninghame Graham register, rather, an imagined geography of politics articulated against the emergent dominance of twentieth-century discourses of geopolitics. To the extent that such a "utopian" perspective may be ascribed to Cunninghame Graham, it is because his sketches link the battlefront of socialist struggle with the frontier of colonial violence to transform that utopian imperative of the 1890s—Marx's "here, or nowhere"— into the problematic lesson of the "here" as "nowhere."

Notes

This essay draws on research begun during the summer of 1990 with the support of a Fordham faculty research grant. For permission to consult and cite from manuscript collections concerning Cunninghame Graham, I thank Lady Polwarth and the National Library of Scotland.

1. Cited in Louis Marin, *Utopics: Spatial Play*, trans. Robert A. Vollrath (London: Macmillan, 1984), p. 278.

2. In *Cunninghame Graham: A Critical Biography* (Cambridge: Cambridge University Press, 1979), Cedric Watts and Laurence Davies offer the best account of Cunninghame Graham in historical context.

3. G. K. Chesterton, *Autobiography* (London: Hutchinson, 1936), p. 269.

4. The dating of the portrait is from Walter Shaw-Sparrow, *John Lavery and His Work* (London: Kegan Paul, 1912), p. 98. The quotation is from Lavery's autobiography, *The Life of a Painter* (London: Cassell, 1940), p. 89. The comparison to Whistler is discussed by Kenneth McConkey in *Sir John Lavery, R. A., 1856–1941*, the catalogue for an exhibition organized by the Ulster Museum, Belfast, and the Fine Arts Society (1984–85), pp. 43–44.

5. Graham was much sought after as an artistic "model"—by Lavery, Will Rothenstein, Jacob Epstein, and William Strang (who used Don Roberto as a model for his etchings of Don Quixote); and also, notably, by G. B. Shaw, whose Captain Brassbound is the dramatic portrait (one of a number) most explicitly modeled on Cunninghame Graham.

6. John Lavery, *The Life of a Painter* (London: Cassell, 1940), p. 89.

7. Ibid., p. 92.

8. After *Father Archangel of Scotland and Other Essays* (1895), a volume of tales and essays by himself and Gabriela Cunninghame Graham, his wife.

9. R. B. Cunninghame Graham, "Sursum Corda," in *Success* (London: Duckworth, 1902), p. 99; hereafter cited in text.

10. Chushuchi Tsuzuki, *Tom Mann, 1856–1941: The Challenges of Labour* (Oxford: Clarendon Press, 1991), p. 23.

11. Ibid., pp. 24, 70.

12. Ernesto Laclau and Chantal Mouffe, *Hegemony and Socialist Strategy* (London: Verso, 1985).

13. E. J. Hobsbawm, *The Age of Empire, 1875–1914* (New York: Vintage, 1989), p. 119.

14. A choice whose importance is underscored by the fact that, together with the prospectus, it was designed to broadcast the news of the series throughout the world: "Of course the *First Vol* should be scattered very widely & sent to all parts of the Colonies on sale." Edward Garnett to T. Fisher Unwin, n.d., Berg Collection, New York Public Library.

15. For discussion of the series, see C. T. Watts, *Joseph Conrad's Letters to R. B. Cunninghame Graham* (Cambridge: Cambridge University Press, 1969); and Watts and Davies, *Cunninghame Graham*, pp. 169ff. Further information on the *Over-Seas Library* is from Garnett's correspondence with T. Fisher Unwin, housed at the Berg Collection of the New York Public Library.

16. Garnett to Graham, January 2, 1898, National Library of Scotland (hereafter NLS), Deposit 205.

17. "The Lavery delights me. I gaze at it with affection. . . . It is a thing of art and as the democracy will not understand it, that makes all the difference. I think the aloof air goes with the atmosphere of the Sketches. Now the photograph was too personal—it was a thing on which to found paragraphs about 'that brilliant personality CG etc etc'" (February 17, 1899, NLS).

18. July 31, 1898, NLS.

19. The implications of this adjustment for Conrad's literary work I examine at length in *The Invention of the West: Joseph Conrad and the Double-Mapping of Europe and Empire* (Stanford: Stanford University Press, 1995).

20. George Orwell, *Dickens, Dali, and Others* (New York: Harcourt Brace Jovanovich, 1946), p. 153.

21. January 26, 1899, NLS.

22. Watts and Davies, *Cunninghame Graham*, p. 162; see also pp. 161–64.

23. June 23, 1898, NLS.

24. R. B. Cunninghame Graham, *Selected Writings of Cunninghame Graham*, ed. Cedric Watts (Rutherford, N.J.: Fairleigh Dickinson University Press, 1981), p. 66.

25. April 6, 1897, NLS. For details about Harriette Colenso, see Shula Marks, "Harriette Colenso and the Zulus, 1874–1913," *Journal of African History* 4, no. 3 (1963): 403–11.

26. Upon receiving the sketches, he praised them for their variety in portraying "everyday, commonplace, exceptional, or vanishing human figures, the Gaucho on the plains, Mistress Campbell in Gart-na-Cloich, Heather Jock, or the Bristol Steamer, all remote from each other, all part of the great ridiculous common Human Family." May 22, 1898, NLS.

27. May 22, 1898, NLS.

28. August 9, 1898, NLS.

29. Watts and Davies, *Cunninghame Graham*, p. 162.

30. May 16, 1901, NLS.

31. R. B. Cunninghame Graham, "Heather Jock," *Saturday Review*, January 30, 1897, p. 112, hereafter cited in text. "Heather Jock" bears an interesting relation to Conrad's "Karain: A Memory," published later that year, and a forerunner of the Marlow tales. See also Aniela Kowalska, *Conrad 1896–1900: Strategia Wrazen i Refleksji w Narracjach Marlowa* [The Strategy of Impressions and Reflections in the Narrations of Marlow] (Lodz: Lodskie Towarzystwo Nankowe, 1973), listed in John Walker, "R. B. Cunninghame Graham: An Annotated Bibliography of Writings About Him," *English Literature in Transition* 22, no. 2 (1979): 78–156, 115.

32. The force of the parable remains, even though Graham discarded this line from the version that appears in *The Ipané*.

33. Watts, *Conrad's Letters to Cunninghame Graham*, p. 109.

34. This is the subtitle of Fredric Jameson's book *The Political Unconscious*.

35. Joseph Conrad, *Youth, a Narrative; and Two Other Stories* (London: Dent, 1902), p. 157.

36. Hobsbawm, *Age of Empire*, p. 117.

37. In the "Author's Note" to *Youth, a Narrative; and Two Other Tales*, Conrad writes: "'Heart of Darkness' is experience, too; but it is experience pushed a little (and only very little) beyond the actual facts of the case for the perfectly legitimate, I believe, purpose of bringing it home to the minds and bosoms of the readers" (p. xi).

38. Conrad, *Youth*, pp. 189, 238.

39. See Watts and Davies, *Cunninghame Graham*, pp. 173, 174, 175–76.

40. R. B. Cunninghame Graham, "A Vanishing Race," in *Father Archangel of Scotland and Other Essays* (London: Adam and Charles Black, 1896), p. 68.

41. Fredric Jameson, "Of Islands and Trenches: Neutralization and the Production of Utopian Discourse," in *The Ideologies of Theory: Essays, 1971–1986*, vol. 2, Syntax of History, (Minneapolis: University of Minnesota Press, 1988), p. 82.

42. R. B. Cunninghame Graham, "The Ipané," in *The Ipané* (London: Unwin, 1899), p. 24.

43. See *Diccionario Guaraní-Español y Español-Guaraní*, ed. A. Jover Peralta and T. Osuna (Buenos Aires: Editore Litocolor, 1984).

Contributors

DAVID BROMWICH, Housum Professor of English at Yale University, is the author of *Hazlitt: The Mind of a Critic*, *A Choice of Inheritance*, and *Politics by Other Means*.

JAY DICKSON teaches at Princeton University. He is currently revising his dissertation, "*Modernism Post-Mortem: Narrative and Sentimental Bereavement after Victoria.*"

MARIA DiBATTISTA teaches literature and film at Princeton University. She is the author of *The Fables of Anon: The Major Novels of Virginia Woolf* and *First Love: The Affections of Modern Fiction*.

R. F. FOSTER is Carroll Professor of Irish History at the University of Oxford; previously he was professor of modern British history at Birbeck College, University of London, and has held visiting appointments at St. Antony's College, Oxford, and the Institute for Advanced Study, Princeton University. His books include *Charles Stewart Parnell: The Man and His Family*, *Lord Randolph Churchill: A Political Life*, *Modern Ireland, 1600–1972*, *The Oxford Illustrated History of Ireland*, *The Sub-Prefect Should Have Held His Tongue: Selected Essays by Hubert Butler*, *Paddy and Mr. Punch: Connections in Irish and English History*, and numerous introductions, essays, and articles. The first volume of his authorized biography of W. B. Yeats, *The Apprentice Mage*, is to be published by Oxford University Press.

CHRIS GoGWILT is an associate professor of English at Fordham University. He has published articles on turn-of-the-century literature and culture and is the author of *The Invention of the West: Joseph Conrad and the Double-Mapping of Europe and Empire*.

NICHOLAS GRENE is an associate professor of English and head of the department at Trinity College, Dublin. His books include *Synge: A Critical Study of the Plays*,

Bernard Shaw: A Critical View, and *Shakespeare's Tragic Imagination*. With Dan H. Laurence he has edited *Shaw, Lady Gregory and the Abbey: A Correspondence and a Record*.

A. WALTON LITZ is Holmes Professor of Literature (emeritus) at Princeton University. He is the author of numerous articles and books on modern literature, most recently having edited Ezra Pound's *Personae* and *The Collected Poems of William Carlos Williams*.

EDNA LONGLEY is a professor of English at Queen's University, Belfast. She has edited the poetry and prose of Edward Thomas. Her most recent book is *The Living Stream: Literature and Revisionism in Ireland*. She is an editor of the *Irish Review* and has coedited *Yeats Annual*, no. 12, "That Accusing Eye," which focuses on the reception of Yeats in Ireland.

LUCY McDIARMID is a professor of English at Villanova University. She will serve as president of the American Conference for Irish Studies in 1997–99. Her books include *Saving Civilization: Yeats, Eliot, and Auden Between the Wars, Auden's Apologies for Poetry*, and *Selected Writings of Lady Gregory*, of which she is coeditor.

LOUIS MENAND is professor of English at the Graduate Center of the City University of New York.

EDWARD MENDELSON is professor of English and comparative literature at Columbia University. His book *Early Auden* will be followed by *Later Auden*. He has edited books by and about Thomas Pynchon, Thomas Hardy, and George Meredith.

HARVEY TERES is associate professor of English at Syracuse University. His book, from which this essay is adapted, is entitled *Renewing the Left: Politics, Imagination, and the New York Intellectuals*.

Index